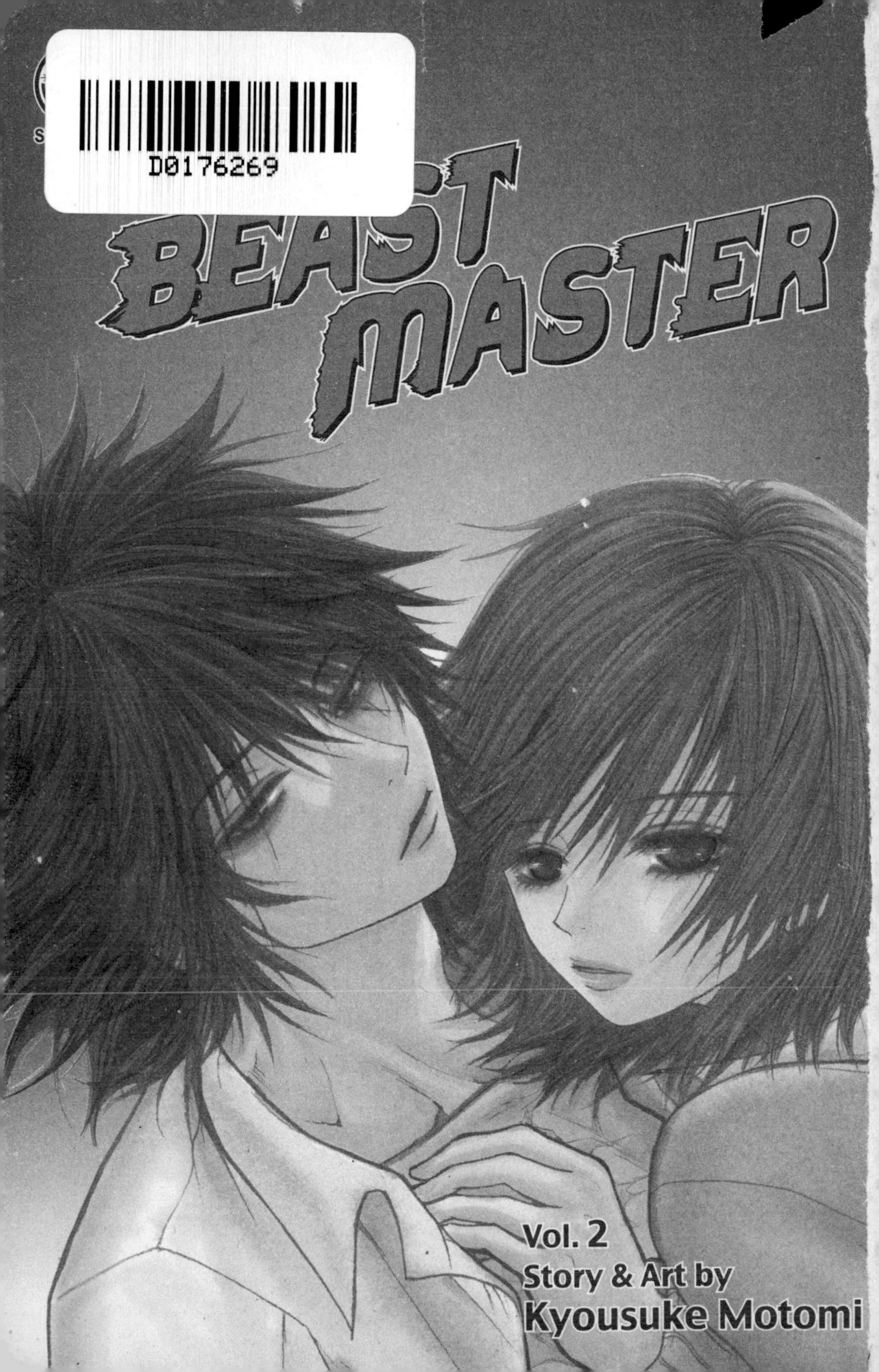
BEAST MASTER
Vol. 2
Story & Art by
Kyousuke Motomi

BEAST MASTER

Volume 2
CONTENTS

Characters

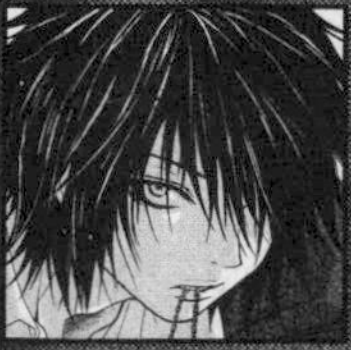

Leo Aoi

A transfer student who joins Yuiko's class. When he feels threatened by danger, he becomes savage and beastlike.

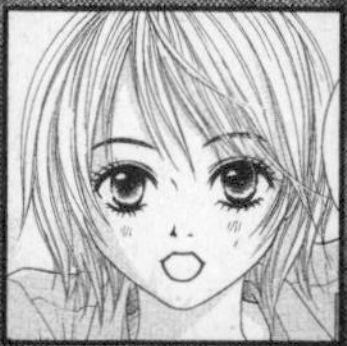

Yuiko Kubozuka

She loves animals, but they don't like her. Then she meets a wild boy named Leo, and her whole life suddenly changes.

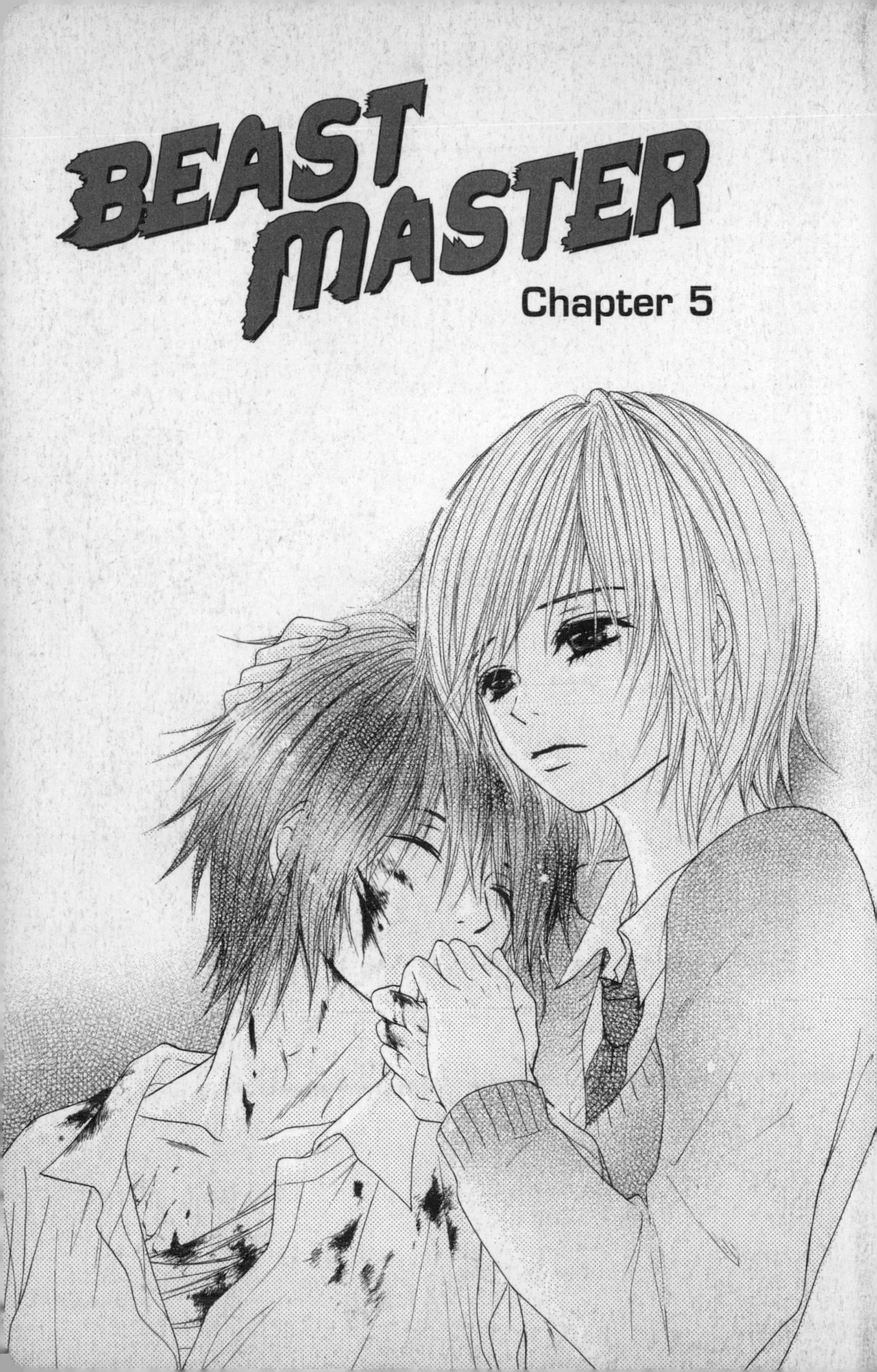
BEAST MASTER
Chapter 5

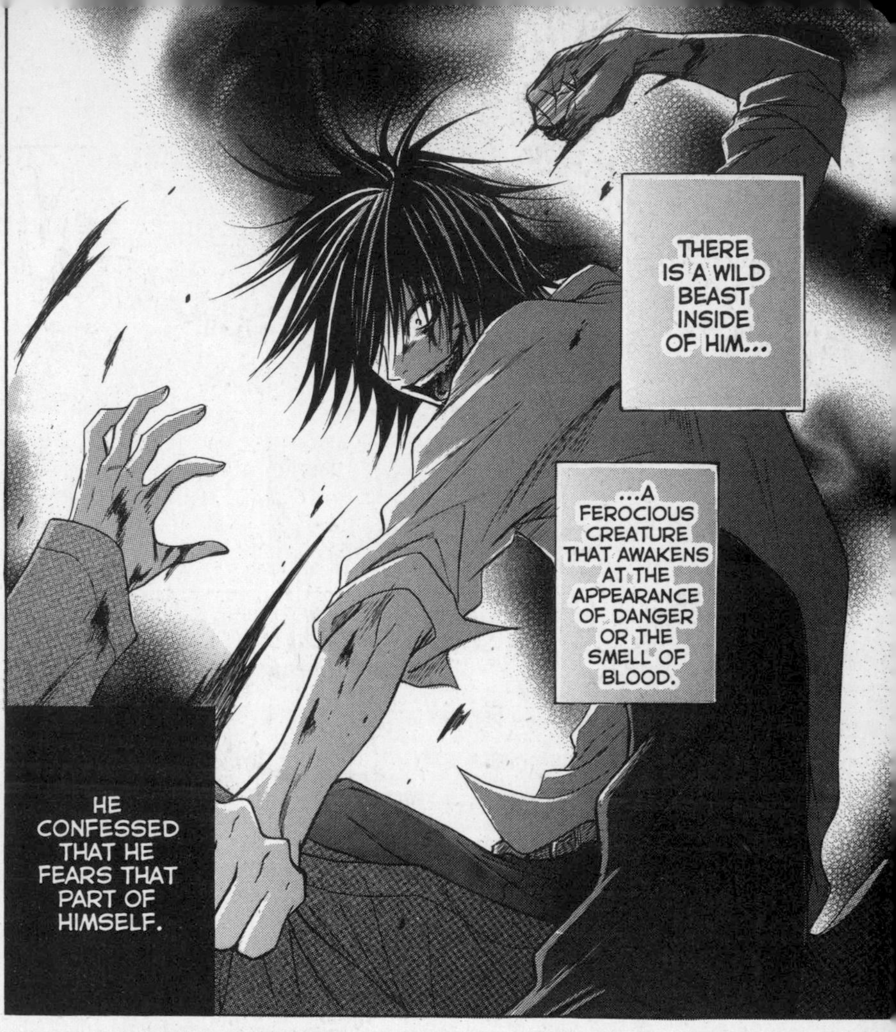
THERE IS A WILD BEAST INSIDE OF HIM...
...A FEROCIOUS CREATURE THAT AWAKENS AT THE APPEARANCE OF DANGER OR THE SMELL OF BLOOD.
HE CONFESSED THAT HE FEARS THAT PART OF HIMSELF.

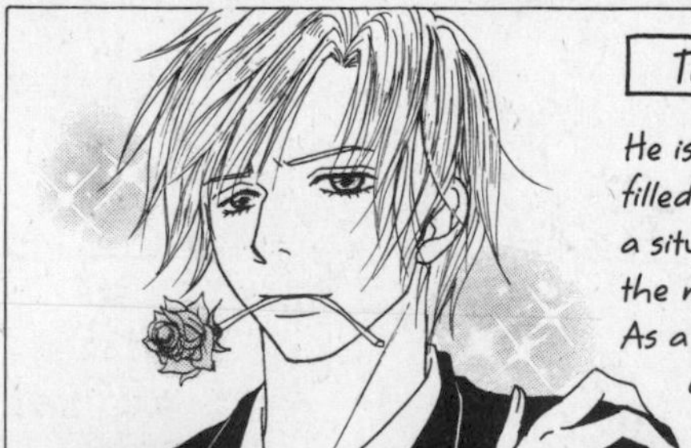

Toki

He is the King of Fools in this manga filled with fools. No matter how tense a situation is, his presence can lighten the mood. And he's a former mercenary! As a writer, I'm extremely fond of this character.

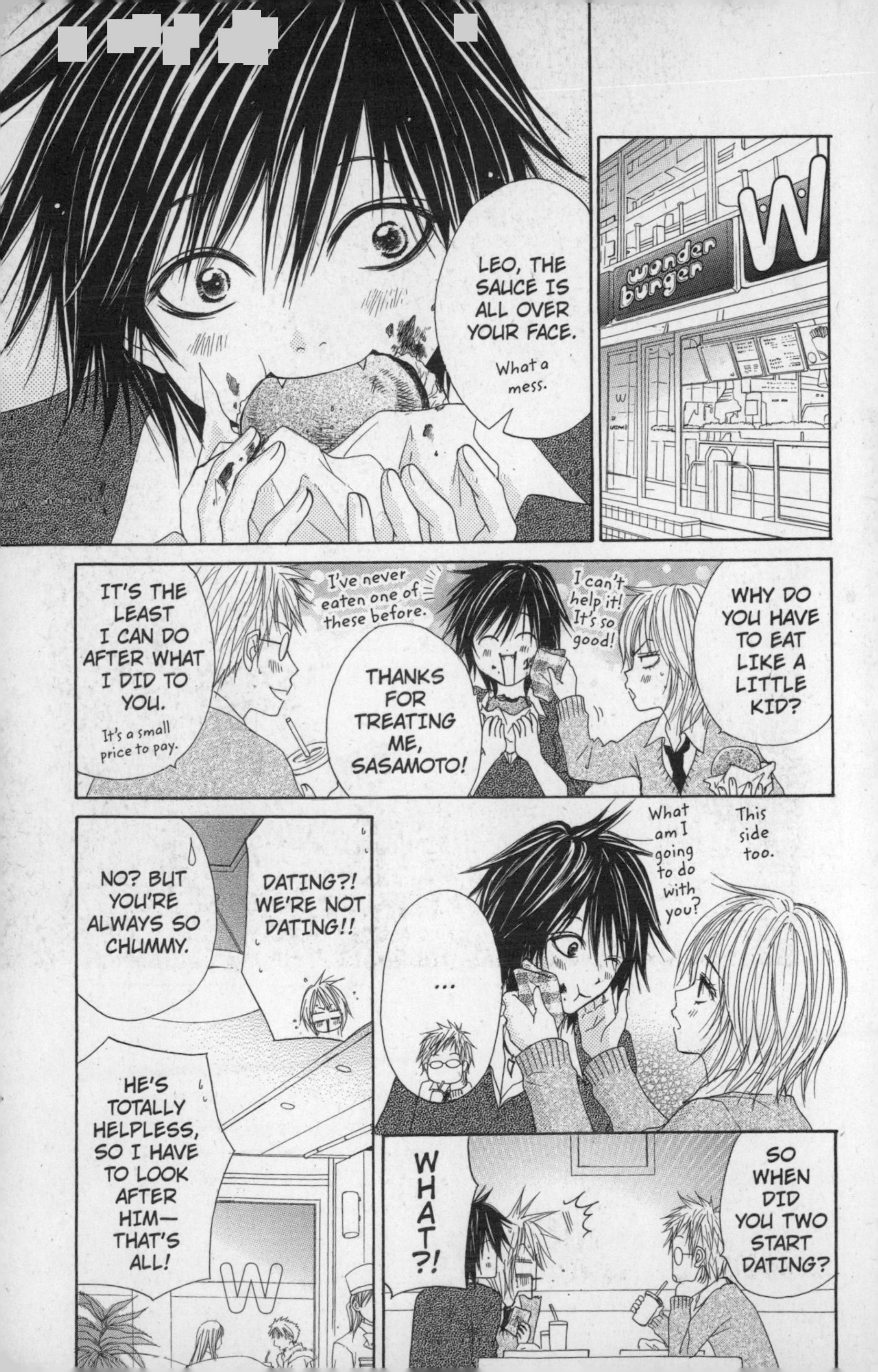
wonder burger
W
LEO, THE SAUCE IS ALL OVER YOUR FACE.
What a mess.
WHY DO YOU HAVE TO EAT LIKE A LITTLE KID?
I can't help it! It's so good!
I've never eaten one of these before.
THANKS FOR TREATING ME, SASAMOTO!
IT'S THE LEAST I CAN DO AFTER WHAT I DID TO YOU.
It's a small price to pay.
This side too.
What am I going to do with you?
...
SO WHEN DID YOU TWO START DATING?
WHAT?!
DATING?! WE'RE NOT DATING!!
NO? BUT YOU'RE ALWAYS SO CHUMMY.
HE'S TOTALLY HELPLESS, SO I HAVE TO LOOK AFTER HIM—THAT'S ALL!
W

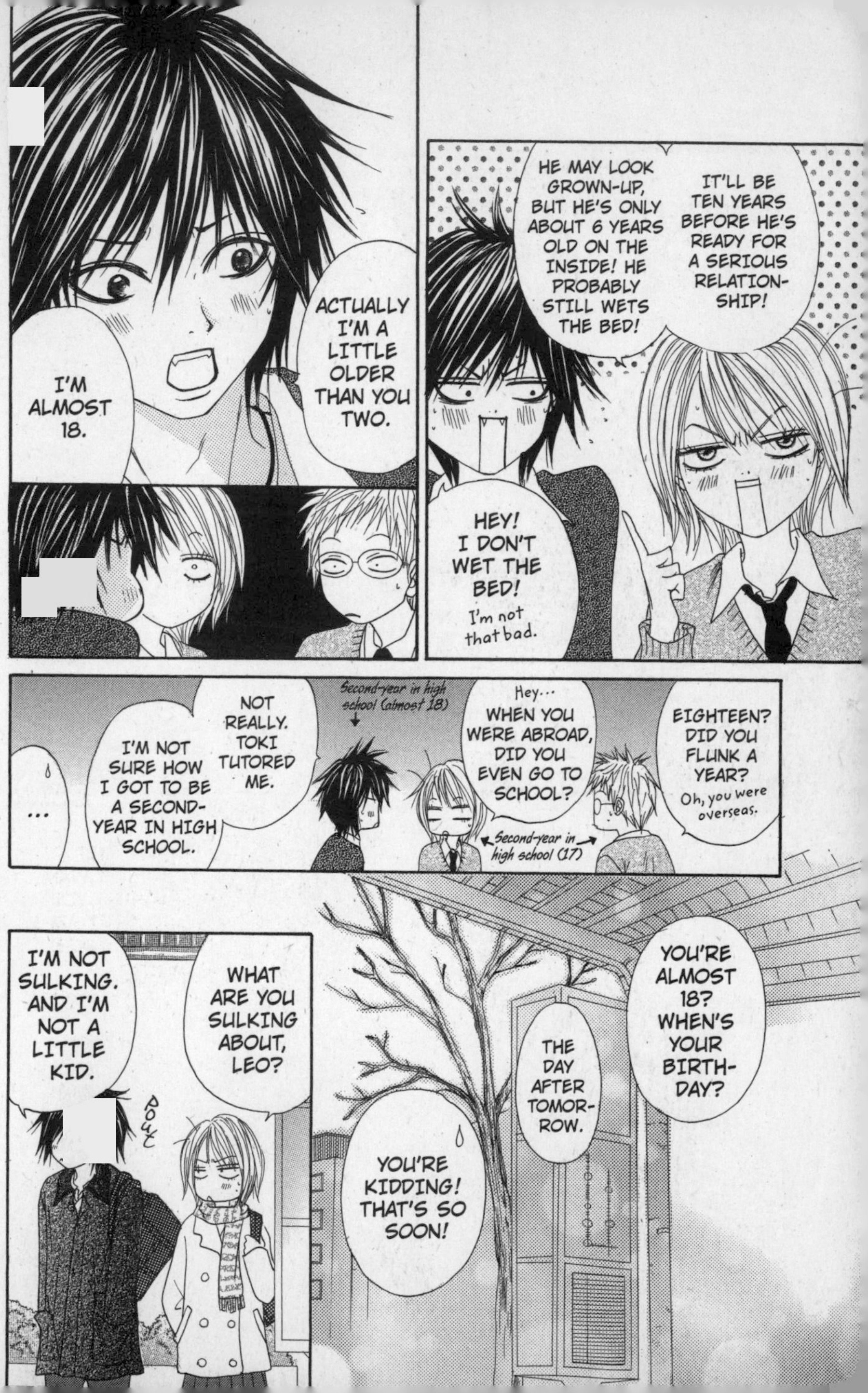
HE MAY LOOK GROWN-UP, BUT HE'S ONLY ABOUT 6 YEARS OLD ON THE INSIDE! HE PROBABLY STILL WETS THE BED!
IT'LL BE TEN YEARS BEFORE HE'S READY FOR A SERIOUS RELATION-SHIP!
HEY! I DON'T WET THE BED!
I'm not that bad.
ACTUALLY I'M A LITTLE OLDER THAN YOU TWO.
I'M ALMOST 18.
EIGHTEEN? DID YOU FLUNK A YEAR?
Oh, you were overseas.
Hey... WHEN YOU WERE ABROAD, DID YOU EVEN GO TO SCHOOL?
Second-year in high school (17)
Second-year in high school (almost 18)
NOT REALLY. TOKI TUTORED ME.
I'M NOT SURE HOW I GOT TO BE A SECOND-YEAR IN HIGH SCHOOL.
...
YOU'RE ALMOST 18? WHEN'S YOUR BIRTH-DAY?
THE DAY AFTER TOMOR-ROW.
YOU'RE KIDDING! THAT'S SO SOON!
WHAT ARE YOU SULKING ABOUT, LEO?
I'M NOT SULKING. AND I'M NOT A LITTLE KID.
POUT

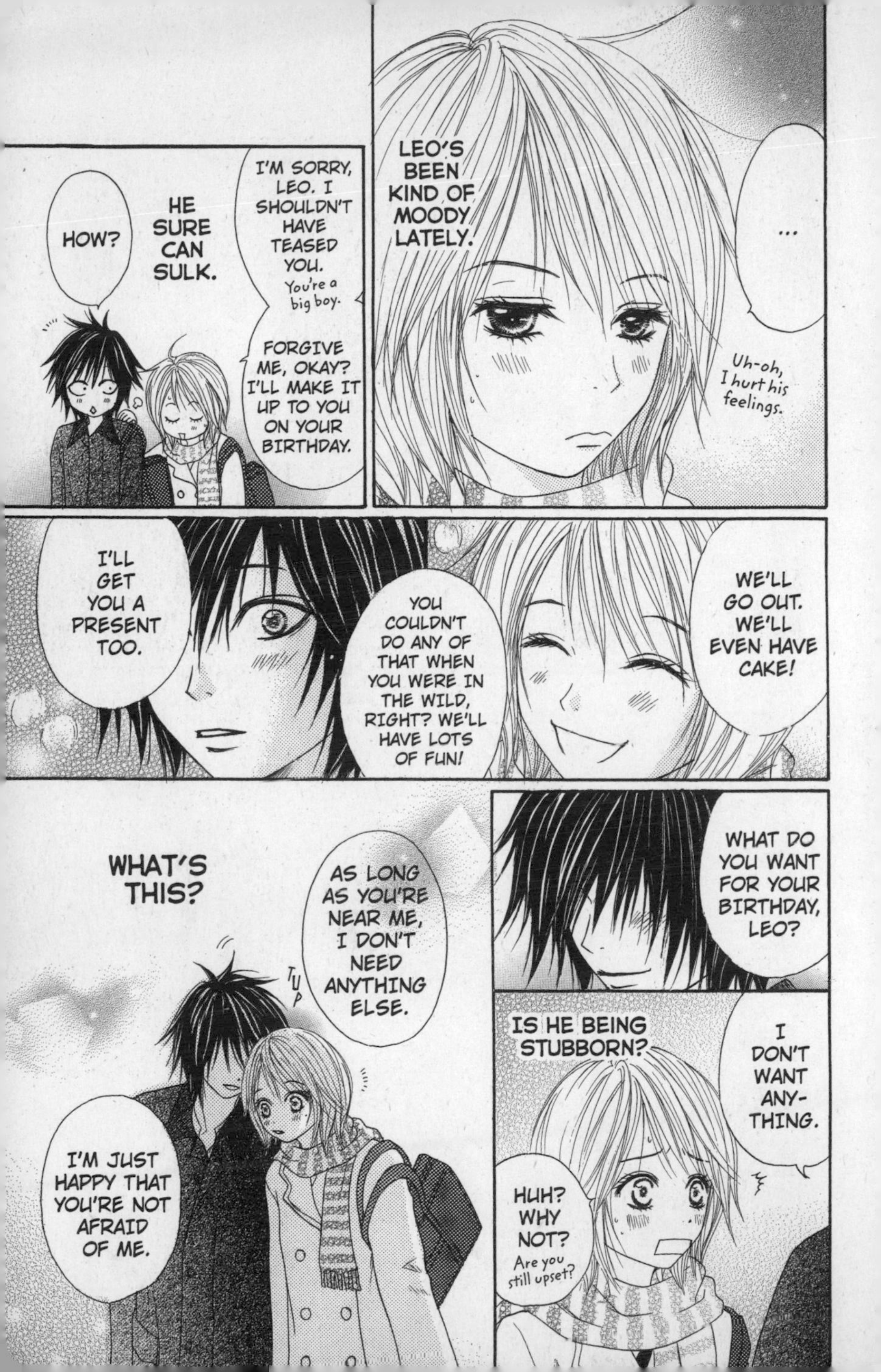
...
Uh-oh, I hurt his feelings.
LEO'S BEEN KIND OF MOODY LATELY.
I'M SORRY, LEO. I SHOULDN'T HAVE TEASED YOU.
You're a big boy.
FORGIVE ME, OKAY? I'LL MAKE IT UP TO YOU ON YOUR BIRTHDAY.
HE SURE CAN SULK.
HOW?
WE'LL GO OUT. WE'LL EVEN HAVE CAKE!
YOU COULDN'T DO ANY OF THAT WHEN YOU WERE IN THE WILD, RIGHT? WE'LL HAVE LOTS OF FUN!
I'LL GET YOU A PRESENT TOO.
WHAT DO YOU WANT FOR YOUR BIRTHDAY, LEO?
I DON'T WANT ANY-THING.
IS HE BEING STUBBORN?
HUH? WHY NOT?
Are you still upset?
AS LONG AS YOU'RE NEAR ME, I DON'T NEED ANYTHING ELSE.
TUP
WHAT'S THIS?
I'M JUST HAPPY THAT YOU'RE NOT AFRAID OF ME.

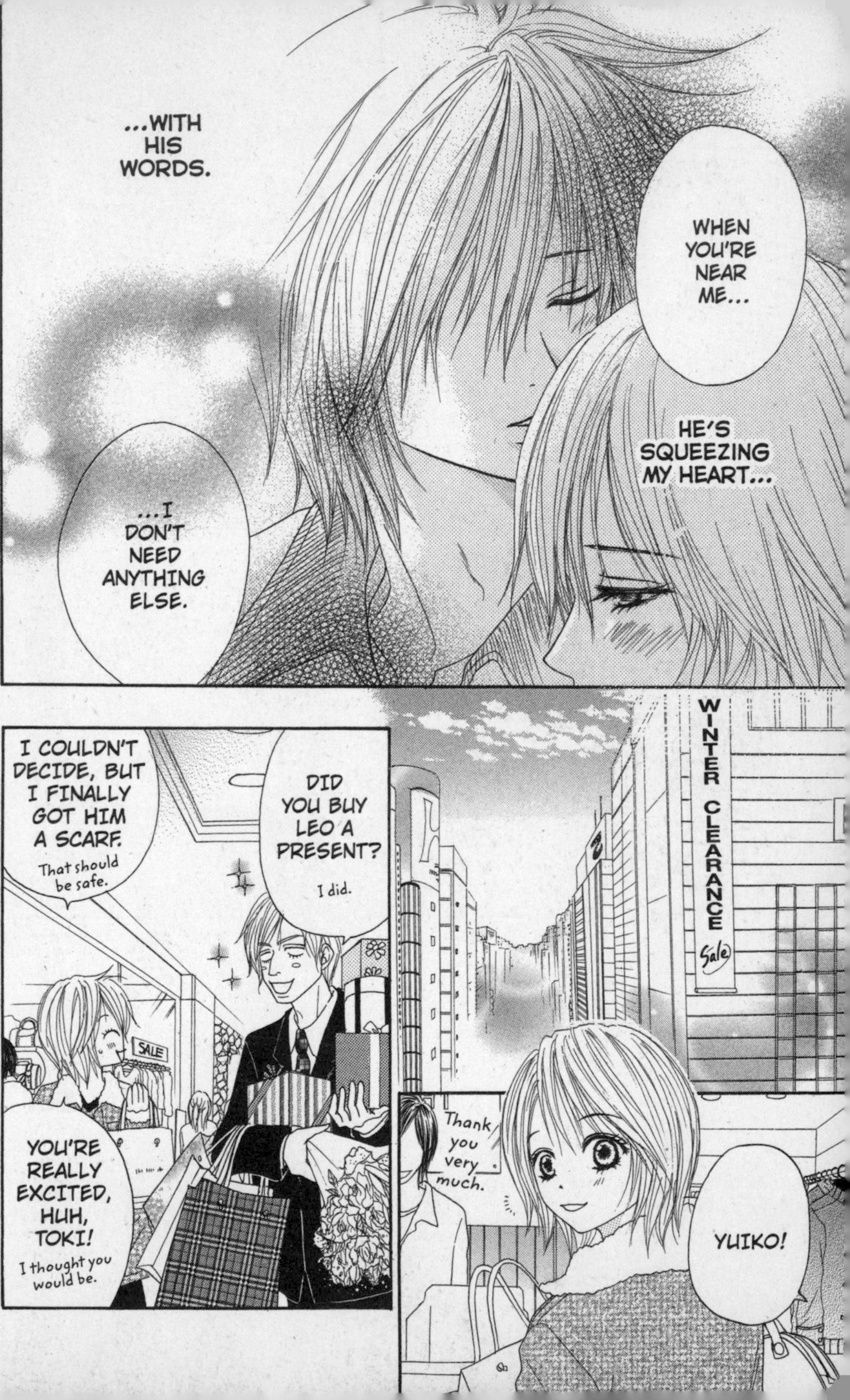
WHEN YOU'RE NEAR ME...
HE'S SQUEEZING MY HEART...
...WITH HIS WORDS.
...I DON'T NEED ANYTHING ELSE.
WINTER CLEARANCE
Sale
Thank you very much.
YUIKO!
DID YOU BUY LEO A PRESENT?
I did.
I COULDN'T DECIDE, BUT I FINALLY GOT HIM A SCARF.
That should be safe.
SALE
YOU'RE REALLY EXCITED, HUH, TOKI!
I thought you would be.

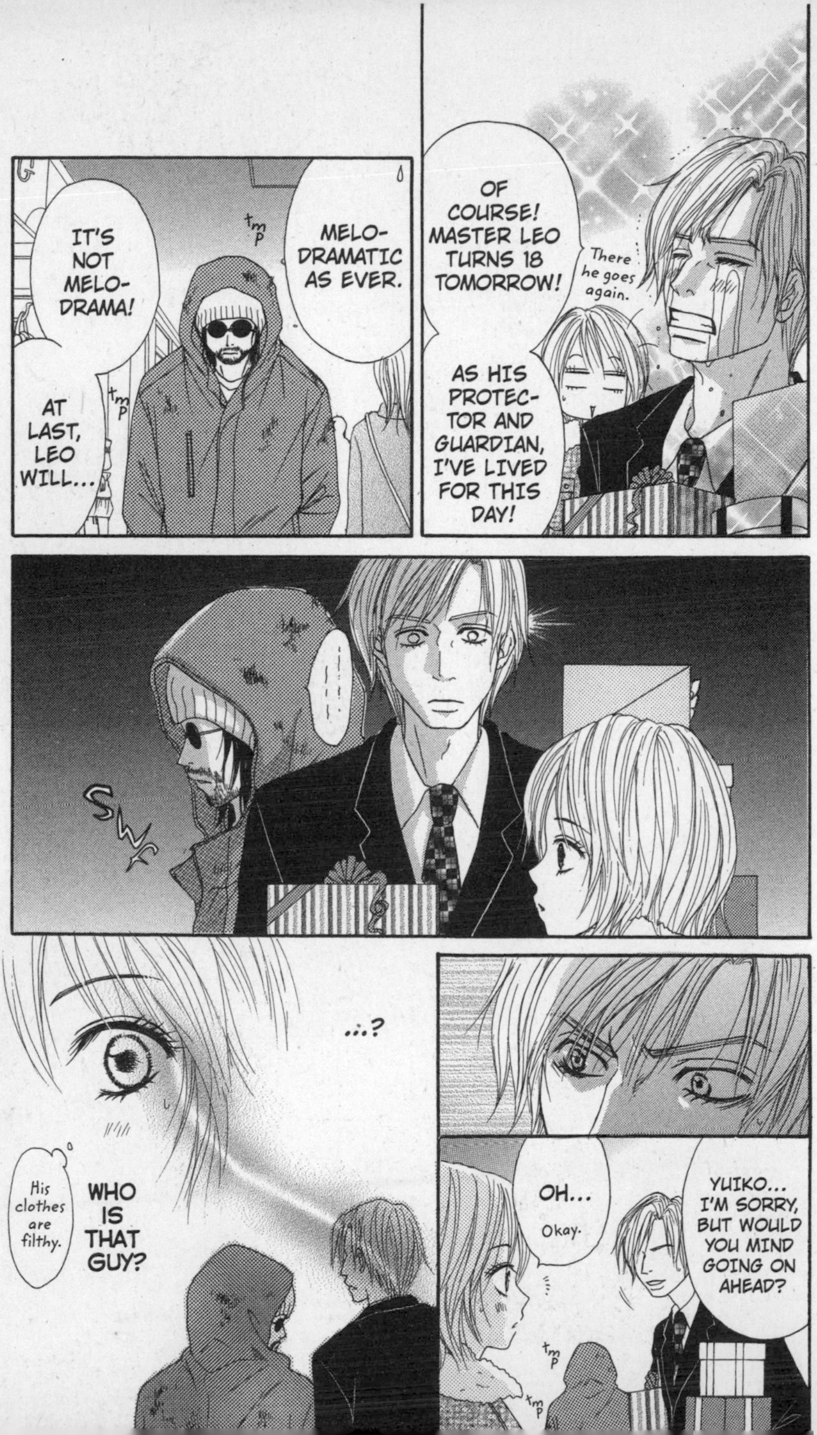
OF COURSE! MASTER LEO TURNS 18 TOMORROW!
There he goes again.
AS HIS PROTECTOR AND GUARDIAN, I'VE LIVED FOR THIS DAY!
MELO-DRAMATIC AS EVER.
tmp
IT'S NOT MELO-DRAMA!
tmp
AT LAST, LEO WILL...
...
SWF
YUIKO... I'M SORRY, BUT WOULD YOU MIND GOING ON AHEAD?
OH...
Okay.
tmp
tmp
...?
WHO IS THAT GUY?
His clothes are filthy.

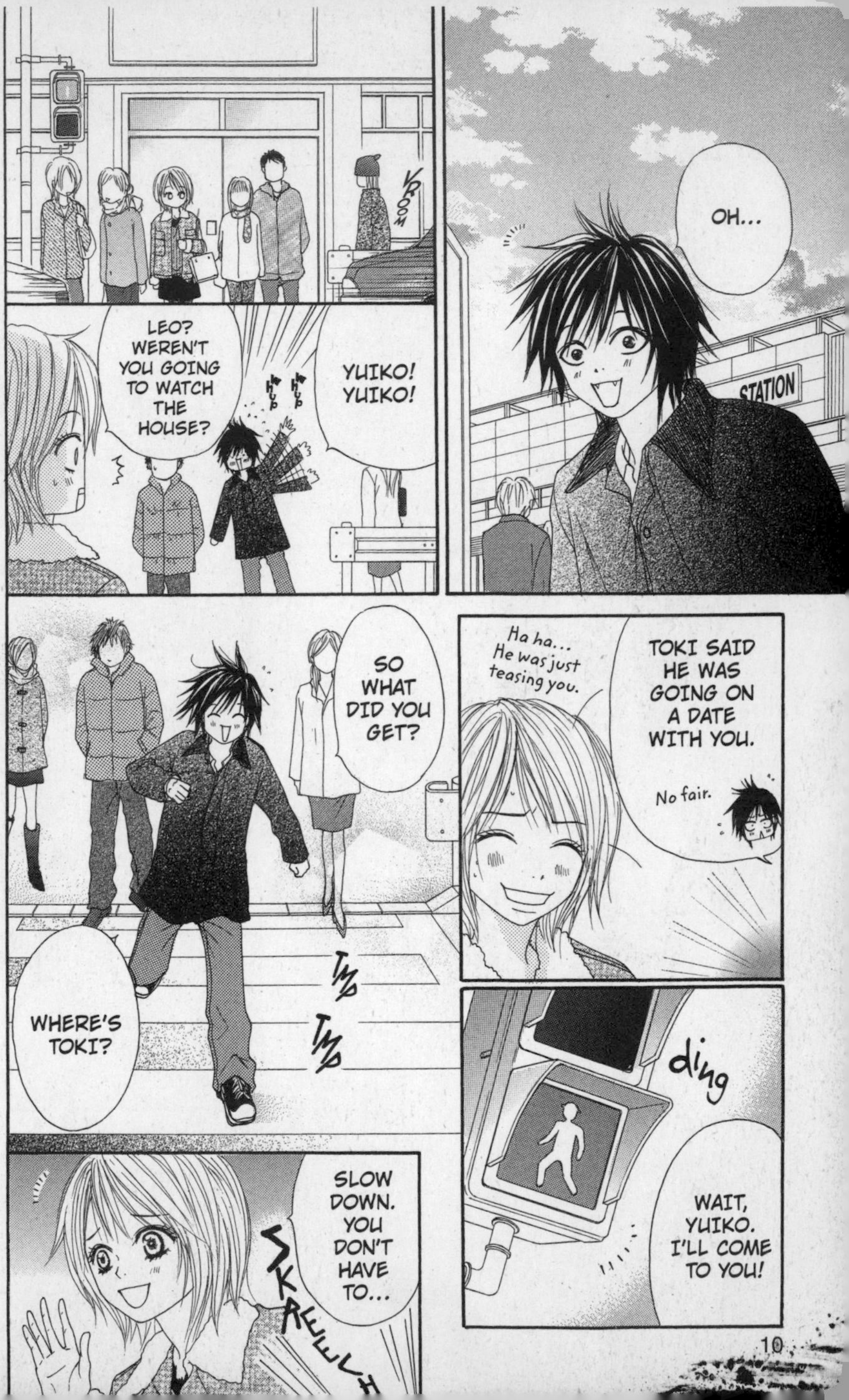
OH...
STATION
VROOM
YUIKO! YUIKO!
HUP HUP
LEO? WEREN'T YOU GOING TO WATCH THE HOUSE?
TOKI SAID HE WAS GOING ON A DATE WITH YOU.
Ha ha... He was just teasing you.
No fair.
ding
WAIT, YUIKO. I'LL COME TO YOU!
SO WHAT DID YOU GET?
TMP TMP
WHERE'S TOKI?
SLOW DOWN. YOU DON'T HAVE TO...
SKREEELH

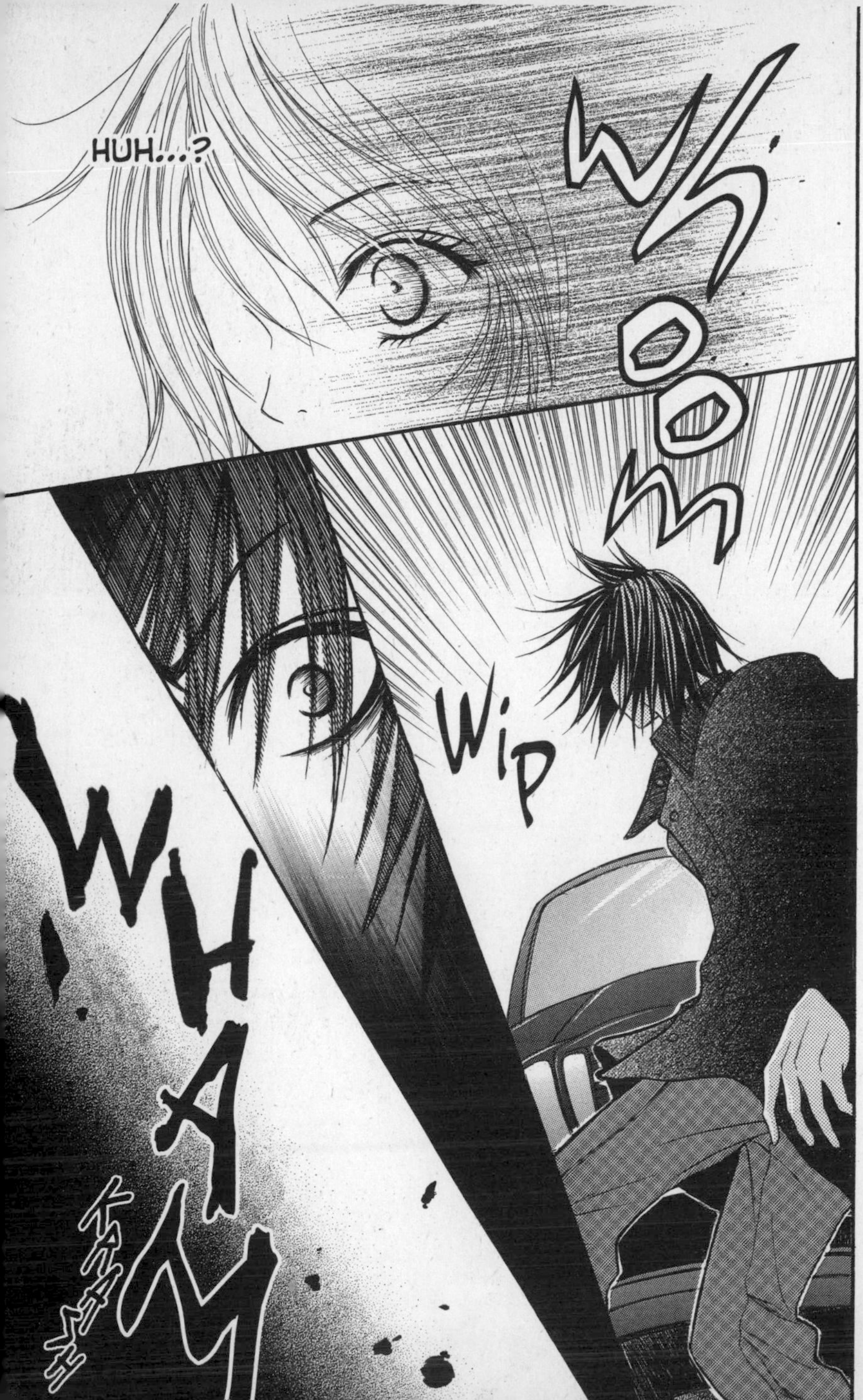
WHOOSH
HUH...?
Wip
WHAM

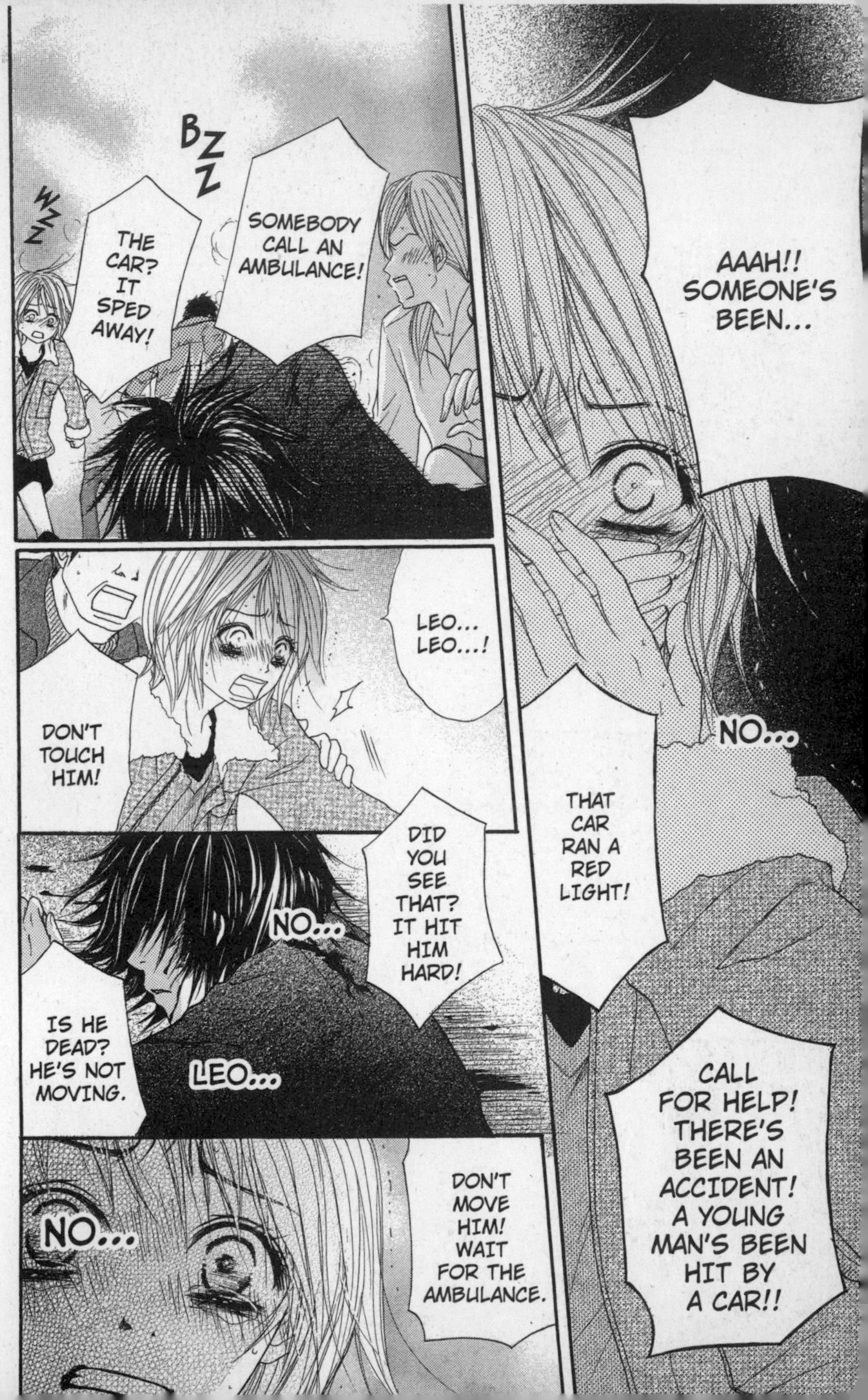
AAAH!! SOMEONE'S BEEN...
NO...
THAT CAR RAN A RED LIGHT!
CALL FOR HELP! THERE'S BEEN AN ACCIDENT! A YOUNG MAN'S BEEN HIT BY A CAR!!
BZZ
SOMEBODY CALL AN AMBULANCE!
THE CAR? IT SPED AWAY!
LEO... LEO...!
DON'T TOUCH HIM!
DID YOU SEE THAT? IT HIT HIM HARD!
NO...
LEO...
IS HE DEAD? HE'S NOT MOVING.
DON'T MOVE HIM! WAIT FOR THE AMBULANCE.
NO...

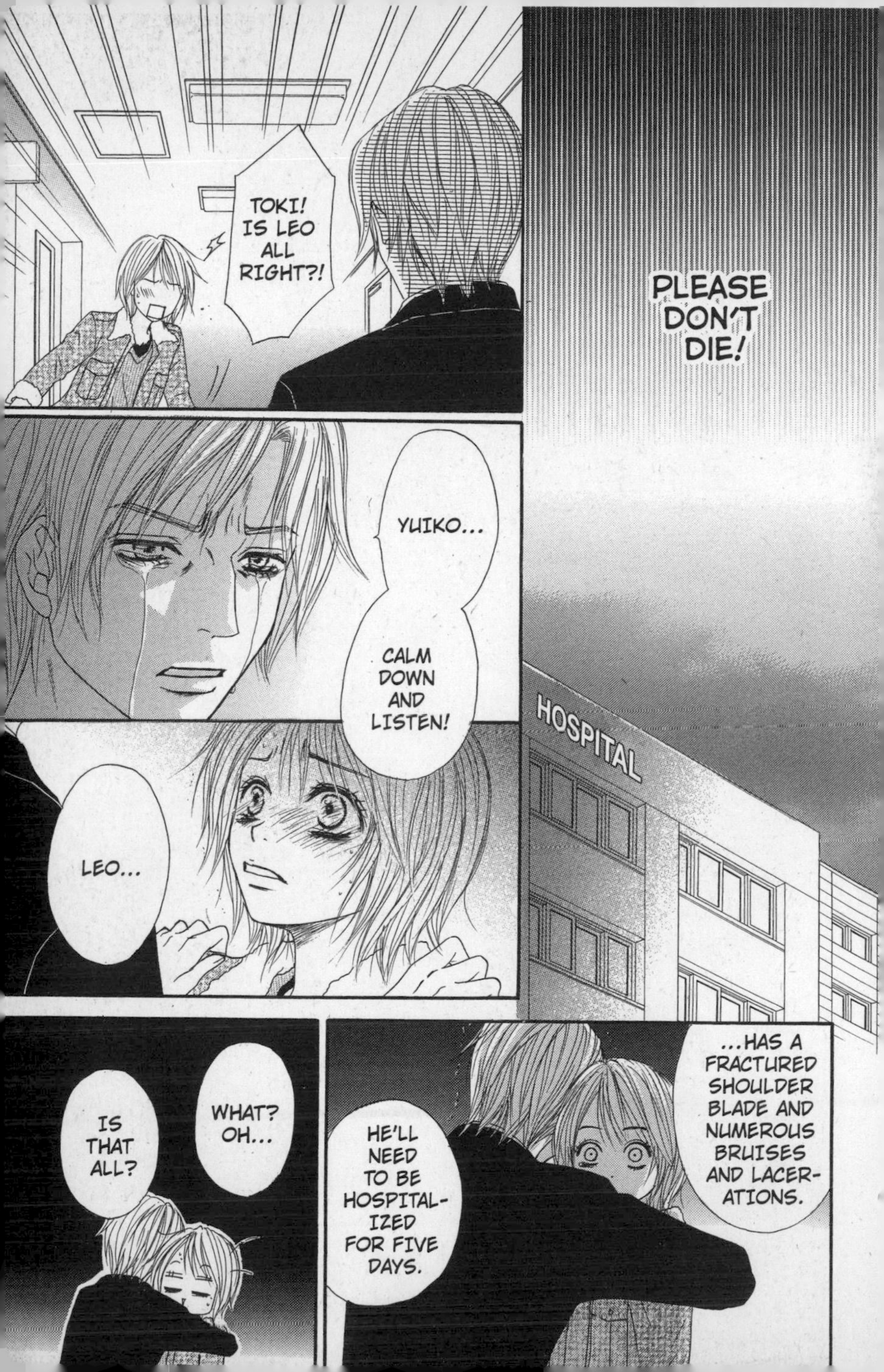

PLEASE DON'T DIE!
HOSPITAL
TOKI! IS LEO ALL RIGHT?!
YUIKO...
CALM DOWN AND LISTEN!
LEO...
...HAS A FRACTURED SHOULDER BLADE AND NUMEROUS BRUISES AND LACER-ATIONS.
HE'LL NEED TO BE HOSPITAL-IZED FOR FIVE DAYS.
WHAT? OH...
IS THAT ALL?

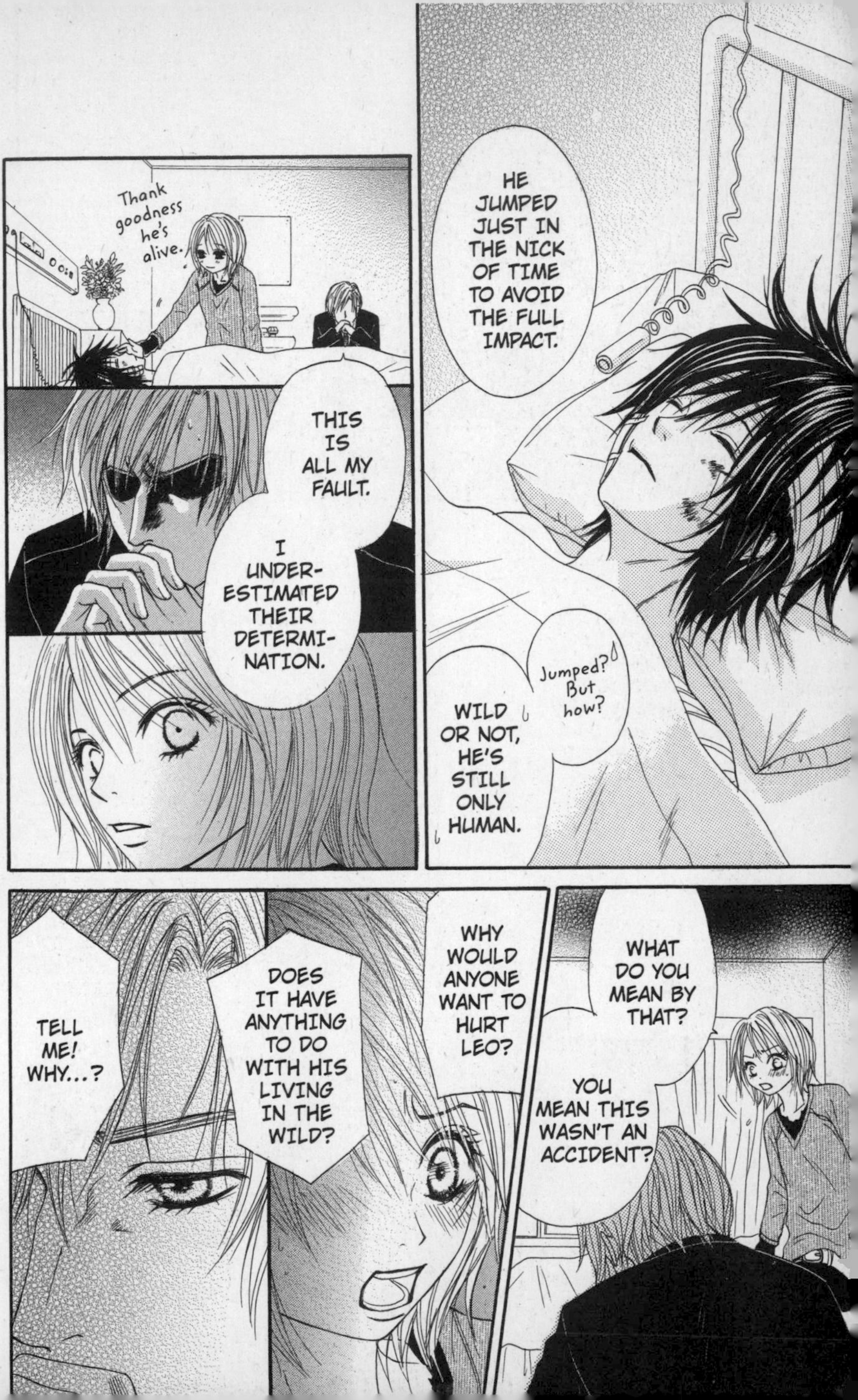
HE JUMPED JUST IN THE NICK OF TIME TO AVOID THE FULL IMPACT.
Jumped? But how?
WILD OR NOT, HE'S STILL ONLY HUMAN.
Thank goodness he's alive.
THIS IS ALL MY FAULT.
I UNDER-ESTIMATED THEIR DETERMI-NATION.
WHAT DO YOU MEAN BY THAT?
YOU MEAN THIS WASN'T AN ACCIDENT?
WHY WOULD ANYONE WANT TO HURT LEO?
DOES IT HAVE ANYTHING TO DO WITH HIS LIVING IN THE WILD?
TELL ME! WHY...?

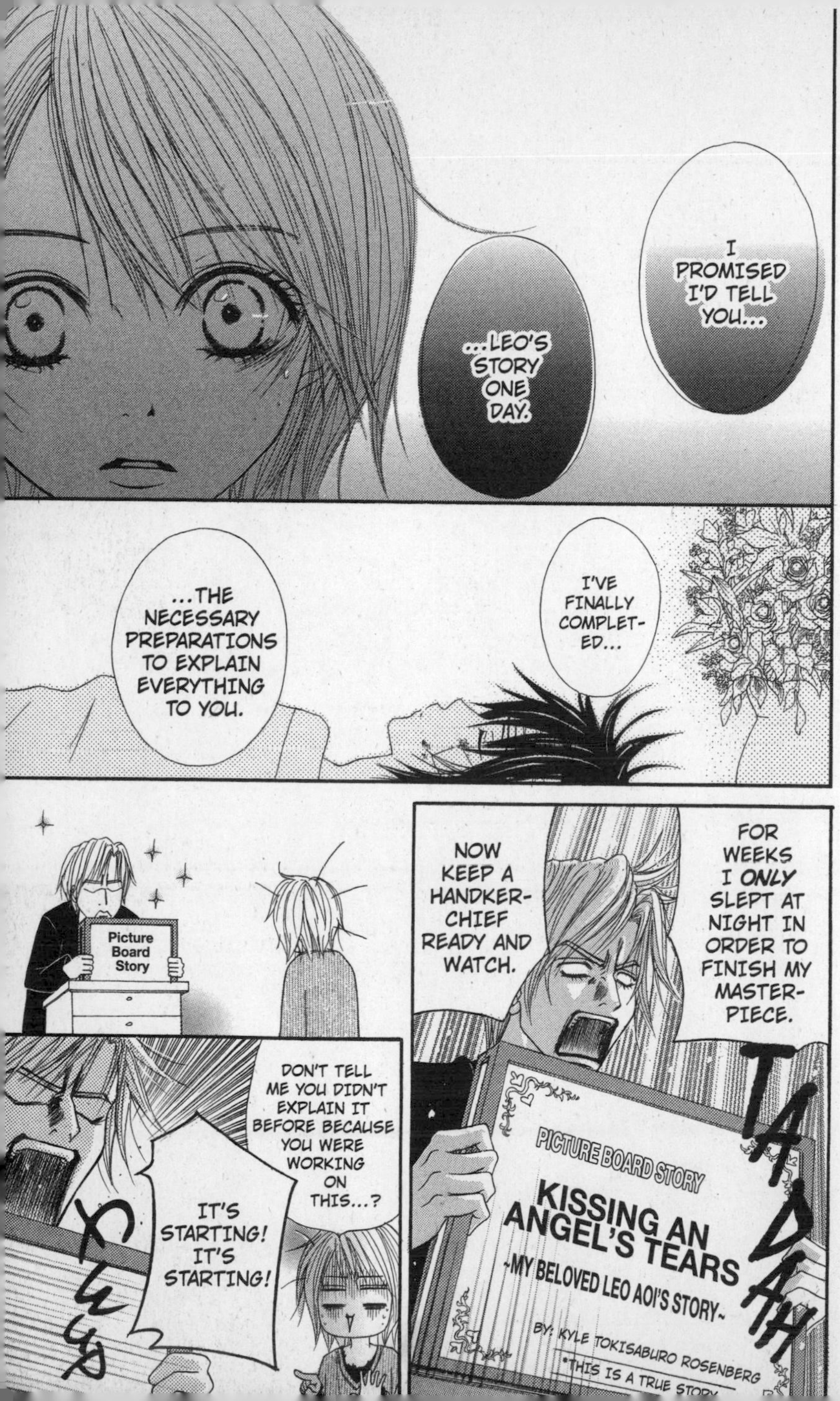
I PROMISED I'D TELL YOU...
...LEO'S STORY ONE DAY.
I'VE FINALLY COMPLETED...
...THE NECESSARY PREPARATIONS TO EXPLAIN EVERYTHING TO YOU.
FOR WEEKS I *ONLY* SLEPT AT NIGHT IN ORDER TO FINISH MY MASTERPIECE.
NOW KEEP A HANDKERCHIEF READY AND WATCH.
TA DAH
PICTURE BOARD STORY
KISSING AN ANGEL'S TEARS
~MY BELOVED LEO AOI'S STORY~
BY: KYLE TOKISABURO ROSENBERG
*THIS IS A TRUE STORY
Picture Board Story
DON'T TELL ME YOU DIDN'T EXPLAIN IT BEFORE BECAUSE YOU WERE WORKING ON THIS...?
IT'S STARTING! IT'S STARTING!
CLAP

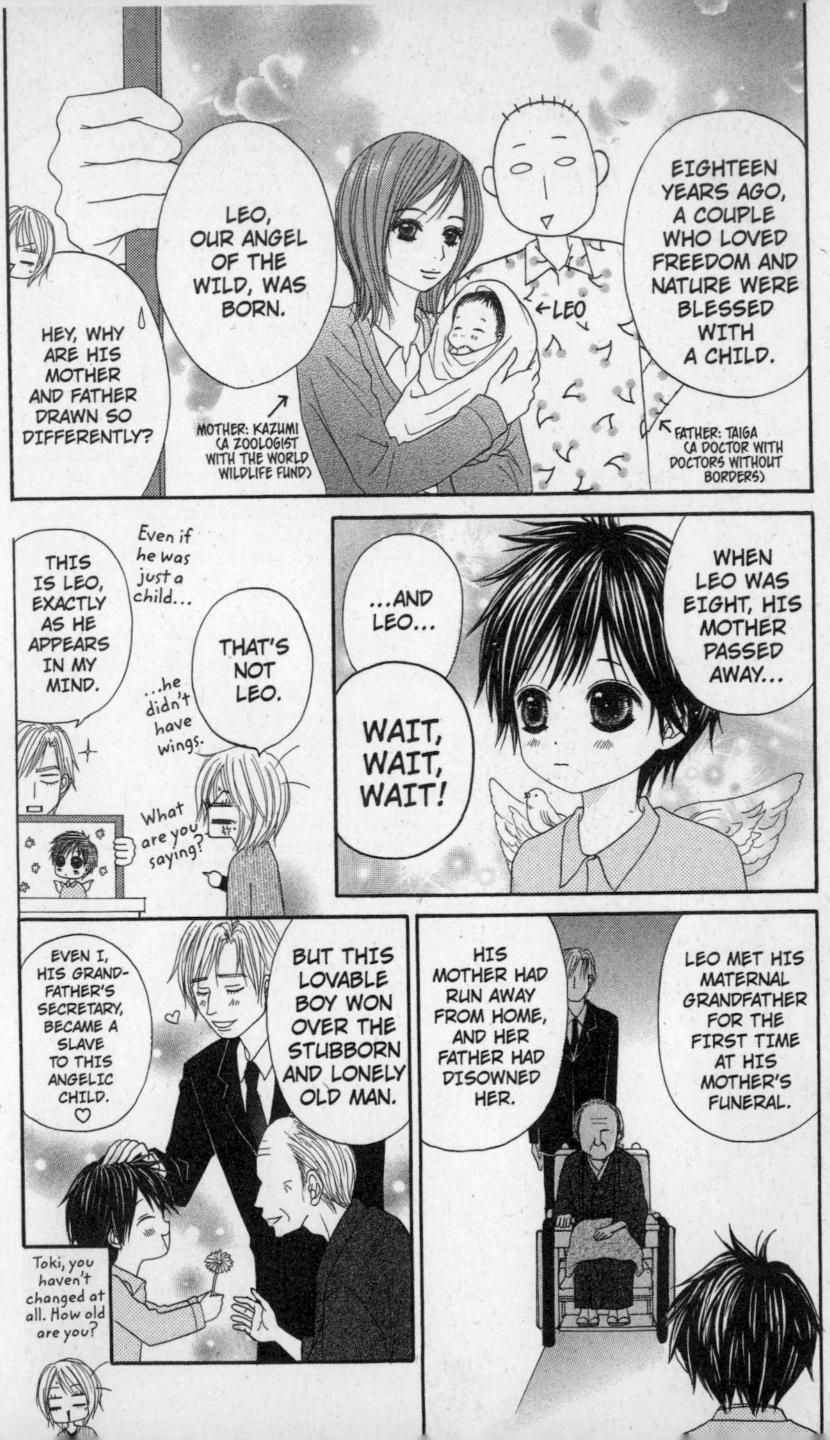
EIGHTEEN YEARS AGO, A COUPLE WHO LOVED FREEDOM AND NATURE WERE BLESSED WITH A CHILD.
←LEO
FATHER: TAIGA (A DOCTOR WITH DOCTORS WITHOUT BORDERS)
LEO, OUR ANGEL OF THE WILD, WAS BORN.
MOTHER: KAZUMI (A ZOOLOGIST WITH THE WORLD WILDLIFE FUND)
HEY, WHY ARE HIS MOTHER AND FATHER DRAWN SO DIFFERENTLY?
WHEN LEO WAS EIGHT, HIS MOTHER PASSED AWAY...
...AND LEO...
WAIT, WAIT, WAIT!
Even if he was just a child...
THAT'S NOT LEO.
THIS IS LEO, EXACTLY AS HE APPEARS IN MY MIND.
...he didn't have wings.
What are you saying?
LEO MET HIS MATERNAL GRANDFATHER FOR THE FIRST TIME AT HIS MOTHER'S FUNERAL.
HIS MOTHER HAD RUN AWAY FROM HOME, AND HER FATHER HAD DISOWNED HER.
BUT THIS LOVABLE BOY WON OVER THE STUBBORN AND LONELY OLD MAN.
EVEN I, HIS GRANDFATHER'S SECRETARY, BECAME A SLAVE TO THIS ANGELIC CHILD. ♡
Toki, you haven't changed at all. How old are you?

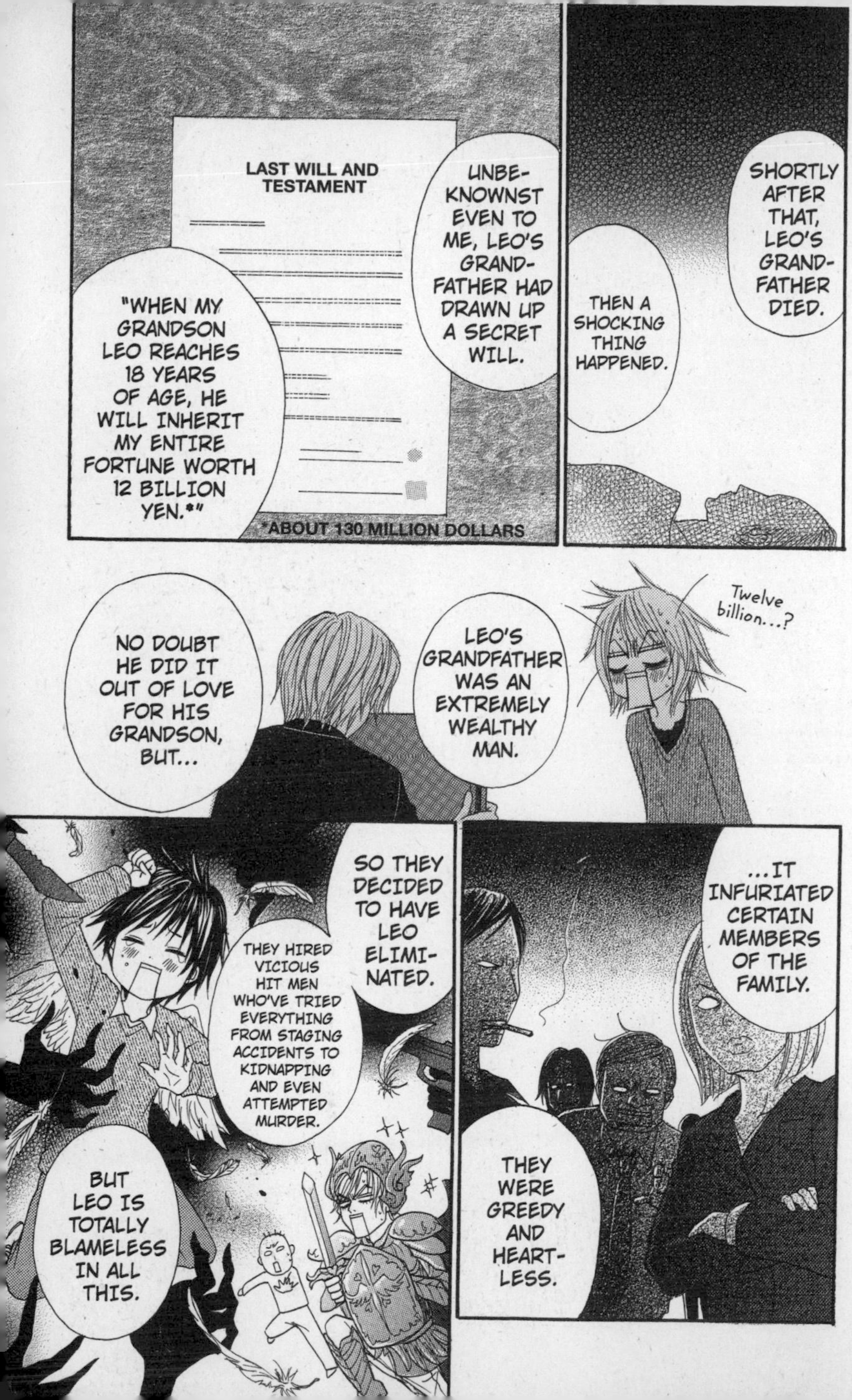
SHORTLY AFTER THAT, LEO'S GRANDFATHER DIED.
THEN A SHOCKING THING HAPPENED.
UNBEKNOWNST EVEN TO ME, LEO'S GRANDFATHER HAD DRAWN UP A SECRET WILL.
LAST WILL AND TESTAMENT
"WHEN MY GRANDSON LEO REACHES 18 YEARS OF AGE, HE WILL INHERIT MY ENTIRE FORTUNE WORTH 12 BILLION YEN.*"
*ABOUT 130 MILLION DOLLARS
Twelve billion...?
LEO'S GRANDFATHER WAS AN EXTREMELY WEALTHY MAN.
NO DOUBT HE DID IT OUT OF LOVE FOR HIS GRANDSON, BUT...
...IT INFURIATED CERTAIN MEMBERS OF THE FAMILY.
THEY WERE GREEDY AND HEARTLESS.
SO THEY DECIDED TO HAVE LEO ELIMINATED.
THEY HIRED VICIOUS HIT MEN WHO'VE TRIED EVERYTHING FROM STAGING ACCIDENTS TO KIDNAPPING AND EVEN ATTEMPTED MURDER.
BUT LEO IS TOTALLY BLAMELESS IN ALL THIS.

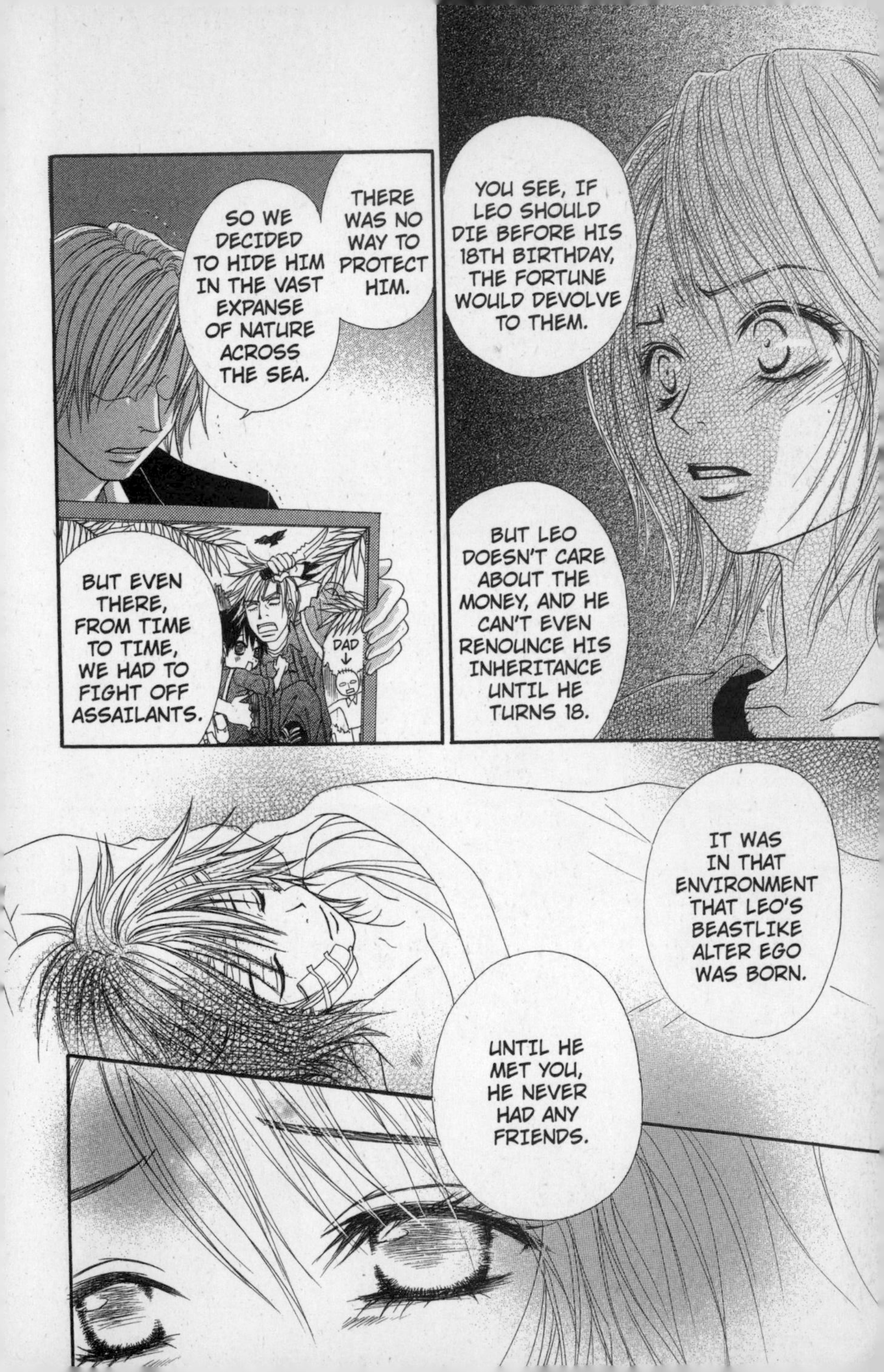
YOU SEE, IF LEO SHOULD DIE BEFORE HIS 18TH BIRTHDAY, THE FORTUNE WOULD DEVOLVE TO THEM.
BUT LEO DOESN'T CARE ABOUT THE MONEY, AND HE CAN'T EVEN RENOUNCE HIS INHERITANCE UNTIL HE TURNS 18.
THERE WAS NO WAY TO PROTECT HIM.
SO WE DECIDED TO HIDE HIM IN THE VAST EXPANSE OF NATURE ACROSS THE SEA.
BUT EVEN THERE, FROM TIME TO TIME, WE HAD TO FIGHT OFF ASSAILANTS.
DAD
IT WAS IN THAT ENVIRONMENT THAT LEO'S BEASTLIKE ALTER EGO WAS BORN.
UNTIL HE MET YOU, HE NEVER HAD ANY FRIENDS.

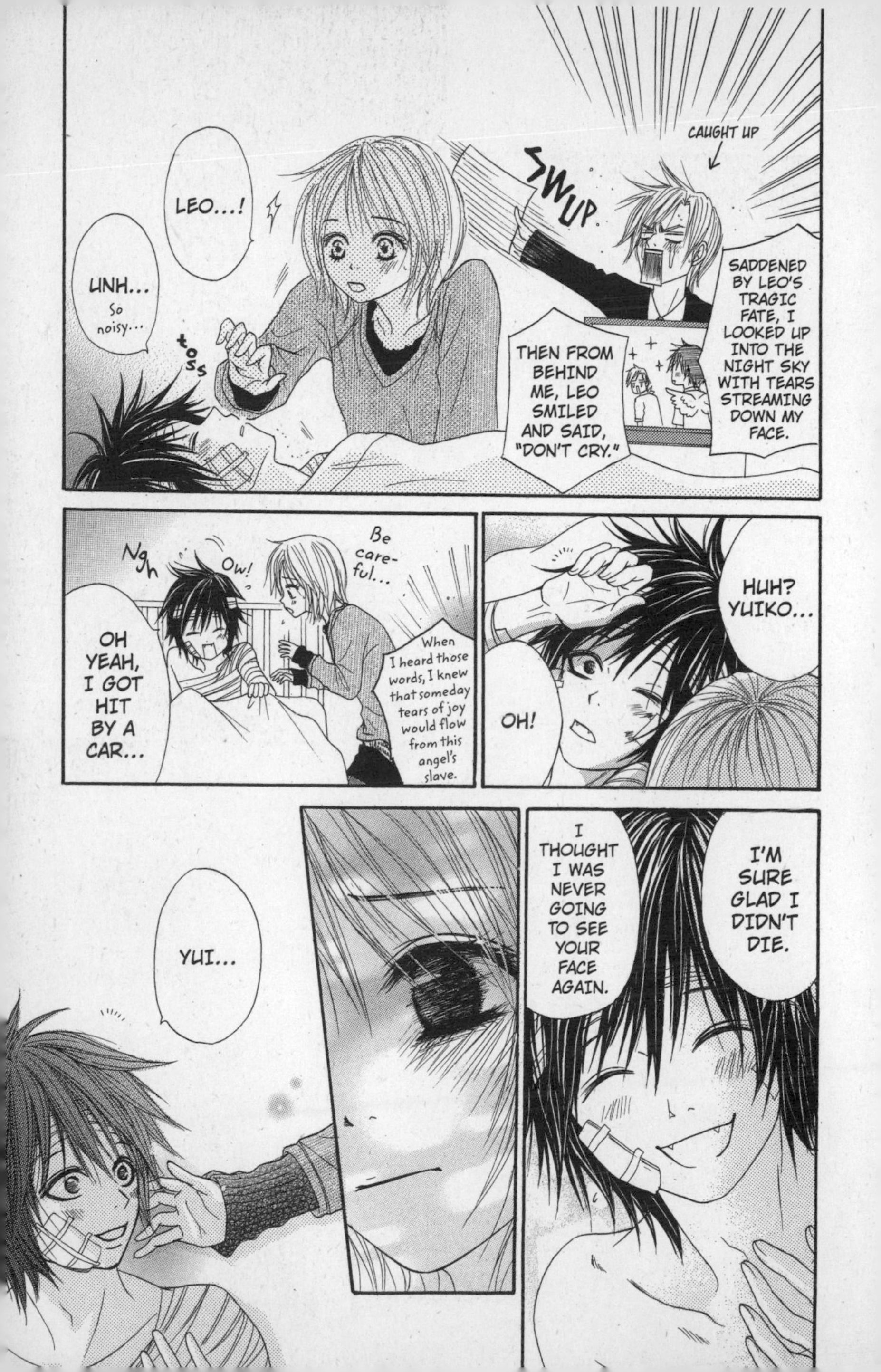
CAUGHT UP
SWUP
SADDENED BY LEO'S TRAGIC FATE, I LOOKED UP INTO THE NIGHT SKY WITH TEARS STREAMING DOWN MY FACE.
THEN FROM BEHIND ME, LEO SMILED AND SAID, "DON'T CRY."
LEO...!
UNH... So noisy...
toss
HUH? YUIKO...
OH!
Be careful...
Ow!
Ngh
When I heard those words, I knew that someday tears of joy would flow from this angel's slave.
OH YEAH, I GOT HIT BY A CAR...
I'M SURE GLAD I DIDN'T DIE.
I THOUGHT I WAS NEVER GOING TO SEE YOUR FACE AGAIN.
YUI...

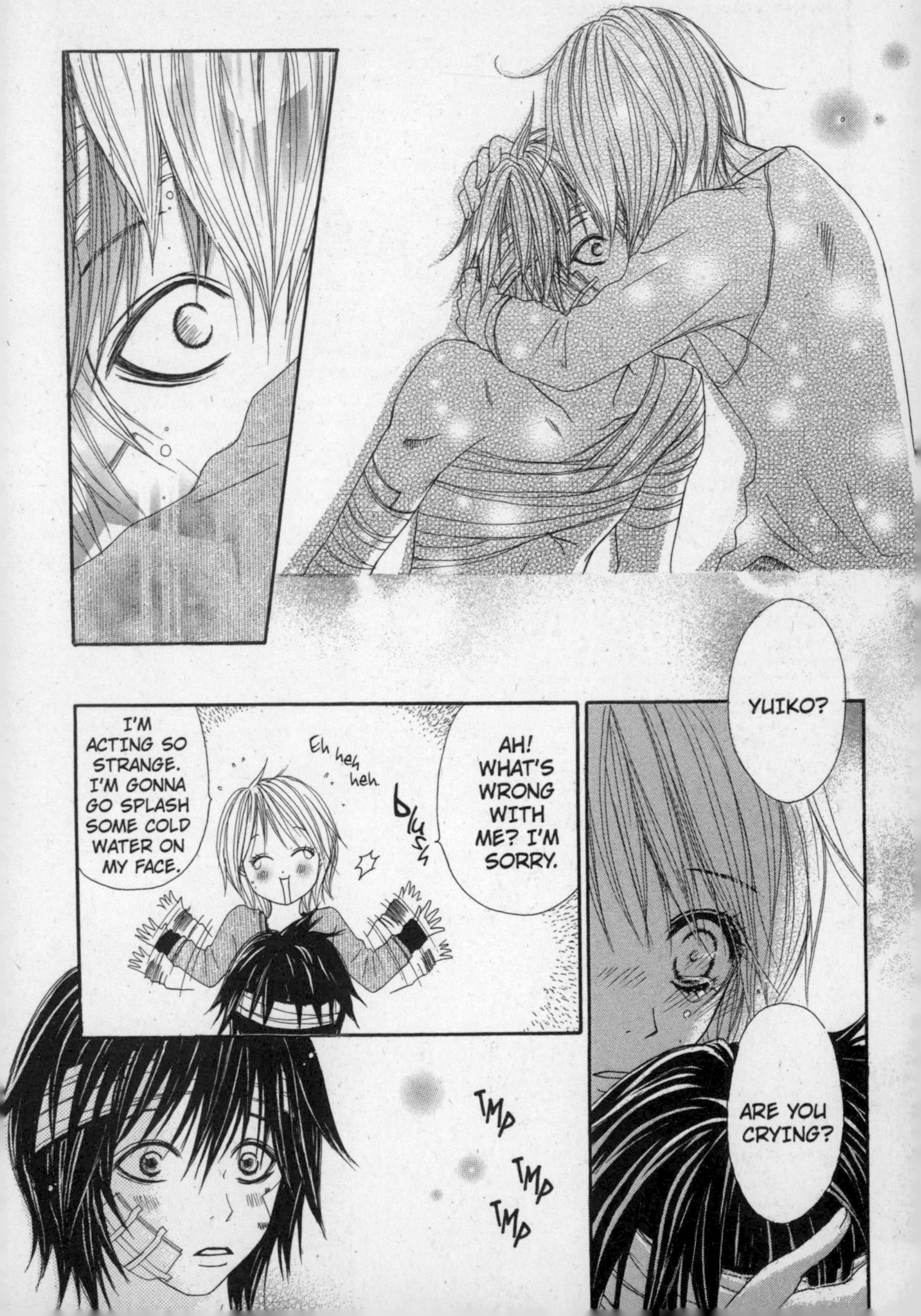
YUIKO?
ARE YOU CRYING?
AH! WHAT'S WRONG WITH ME? I'M SORRY.
blush
Eh heh heh.
I'M ACTING SO STRANGE. I'M GONNA GO SPLASH SOME COLD WATER ON MY FACE.
TMP
TMP
TMP

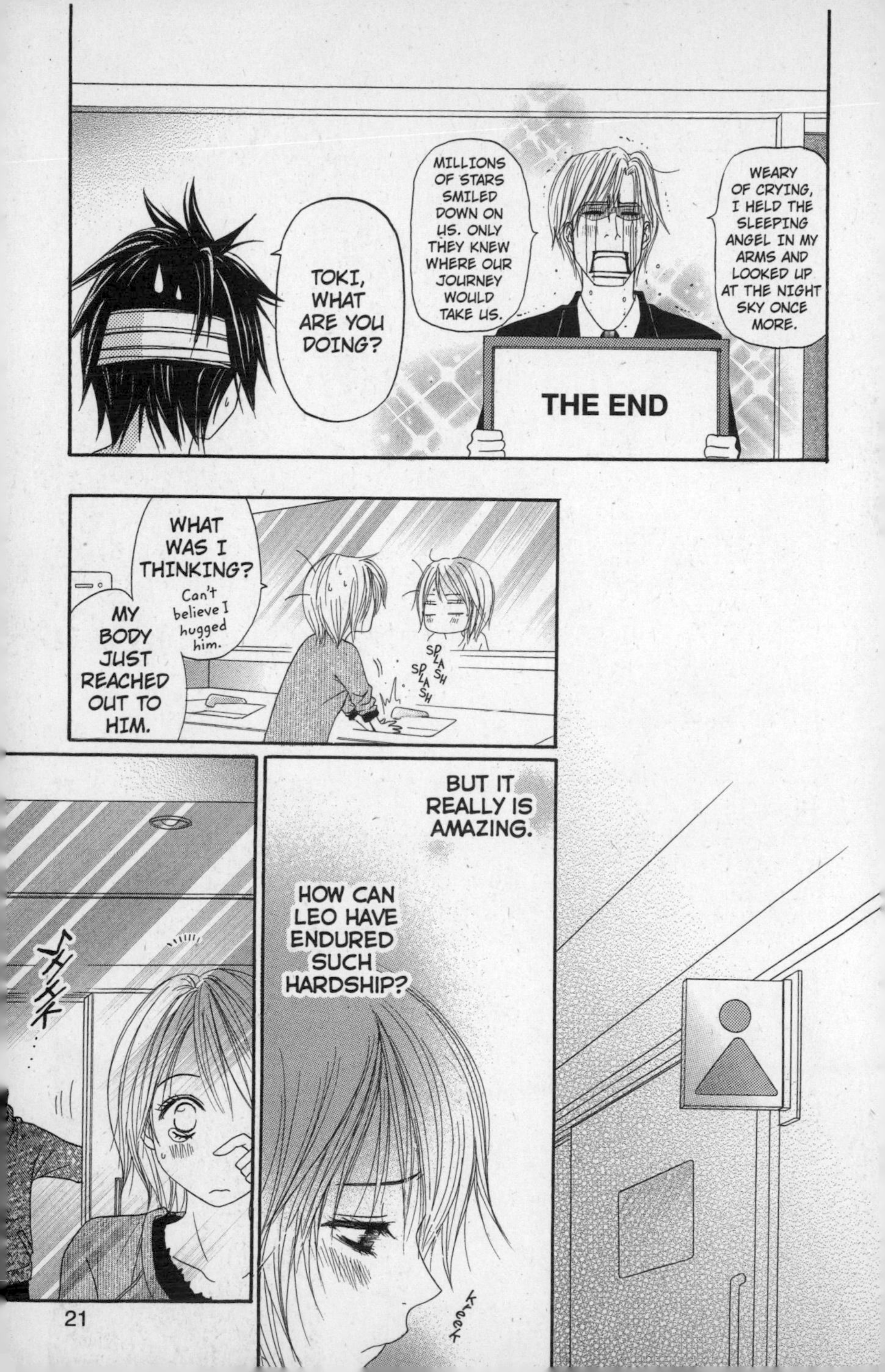
WEARY OF CRYING, I HELD THE SLEEPING ANGEL IN MY ARMS AND LOOKED UP AT THE NIGHT SKY ONCE MORE.
MILLIONS OF STARS SMILED DOWN ON US. ONLY THEY KNEW WHERE OUR JOURNEY WOULD TAKE US.
THE END
TOKI, WHAT ARE YOU DOING?
WHAT WAS I THINKING?
Can't believe I hugged him.
MY BODY JUST REACHED OUT TO HIM.
SPLASH
SPLASH
BUT IT REALLY IS AMAZING.
HOW CAN LEO HAVE ENDURED SUCH HARDSHIP?
KREEK
SHHK

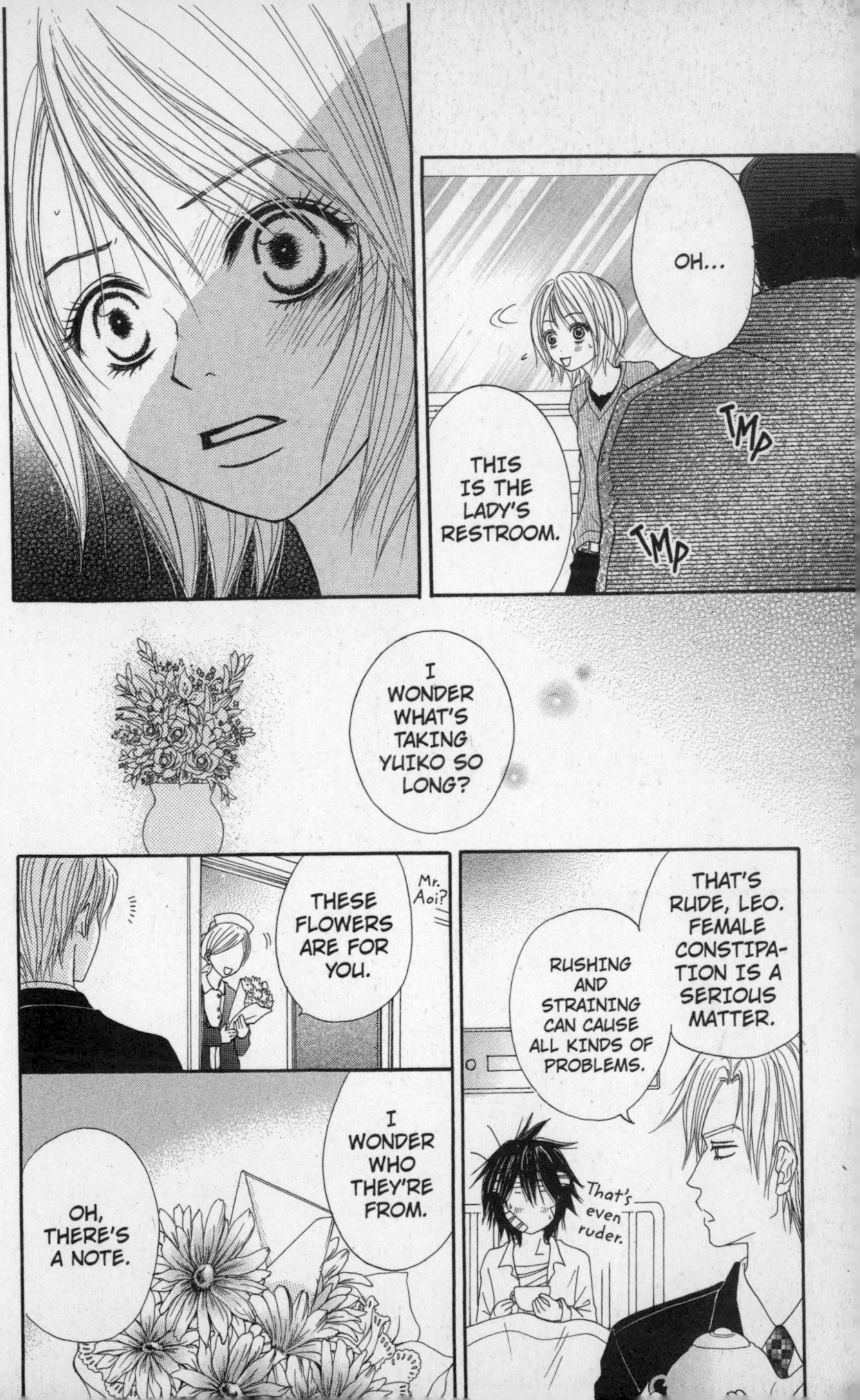
OH...
THIS IS THE LADY'S RESTROOM.
TMP
TMP
I WONDER WHAT'S TAKING YUIKO SO LONG?
THAT'S RUDE, LEO. FEMALE CONSTIPATION IS A SERIOUS MATTER.
RUSHING AND STRAINING CAN CAUSE ALL KINDS OF PROBLEMS.
That's even ruder.
Mr. Aoi?
THESE FLOWERS ARE FOR YOU.
I WONDER WHO THEY'RE FROM.
OH, THERE'S A NOTE.

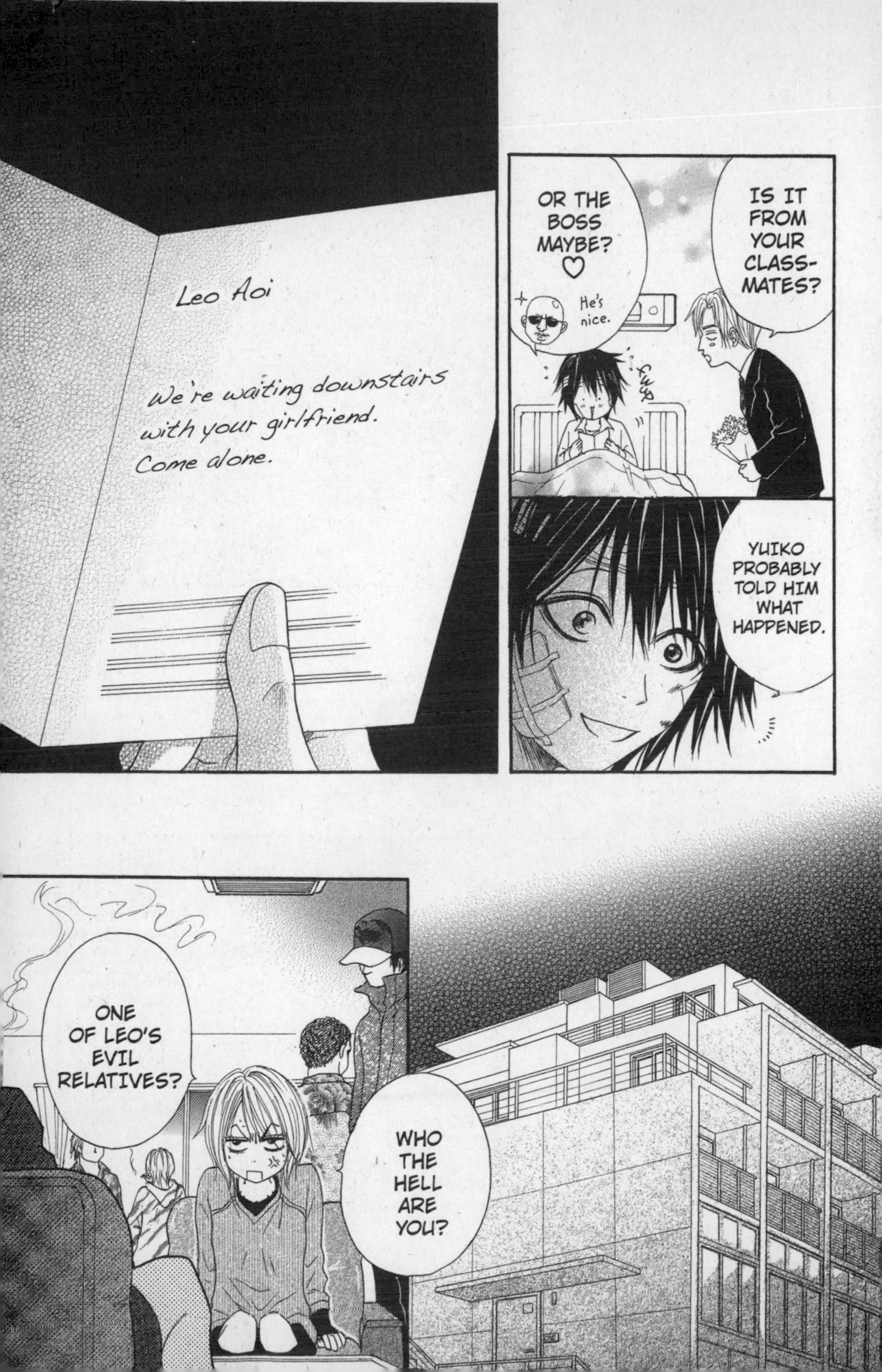
IS IT FROM YOUR CLASSMATES?
OR THE BOSS MAYBE? ♡
He's nice.
YUIKO PROBABLY TOLD HIM WHAT HAPPENED.
Leo Aoi
We're waiting downstairs with your girlfriend. Come alone.
WHO THE HELL ARE YOU?
ONE OF LEO'S EVIL RELATIVES?

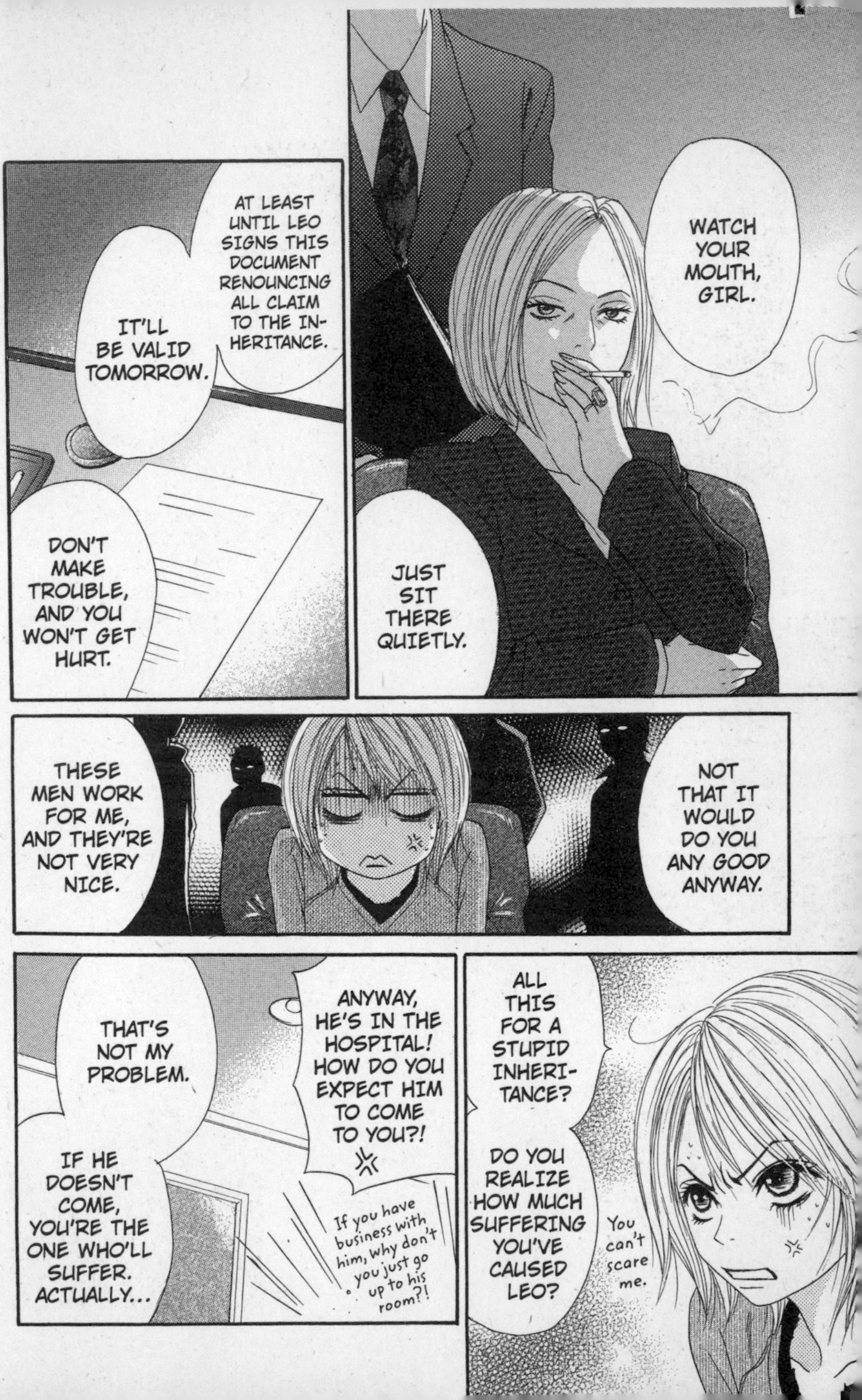
WATCH YOUR MOUTH, GIRL.
JUST SIT THERE QUIETLY.
AT LEAST UNTIL LEO SIGNS THIS DOCUMENT RENOUNCING ALL CLAIM TO THE INHERITANCE.
IT'LL BE VALID TOMORROW.
DON'T MAKE TROUBLE, AND YOU WON'T GET HURT.
NOT THAT IT WOULD DO YOU ANY GOOD ANYWAY.
THESE MEN WORK FOR ME, AND THEY'RE NOT VERY NICE.
ALL THIS FOR A STUPID INHERITANCE?
DO YOU REALIZE HOW MUCH SUFFERING YOU'VE CAUSED LEO?
You can't scare me.
ANYWAY, HE'S IN THE HOSPITAL! HOW DO YOU EXPECT HIM TO COME TO YOU?!
If you have business with him, why don't you just go up to his room?!
THAT'S NOT MY PROBLEM.
IF HE DOESN'T COME, YOU'RE THE ONE WHO'LL SUFFER. ACTUALLY...

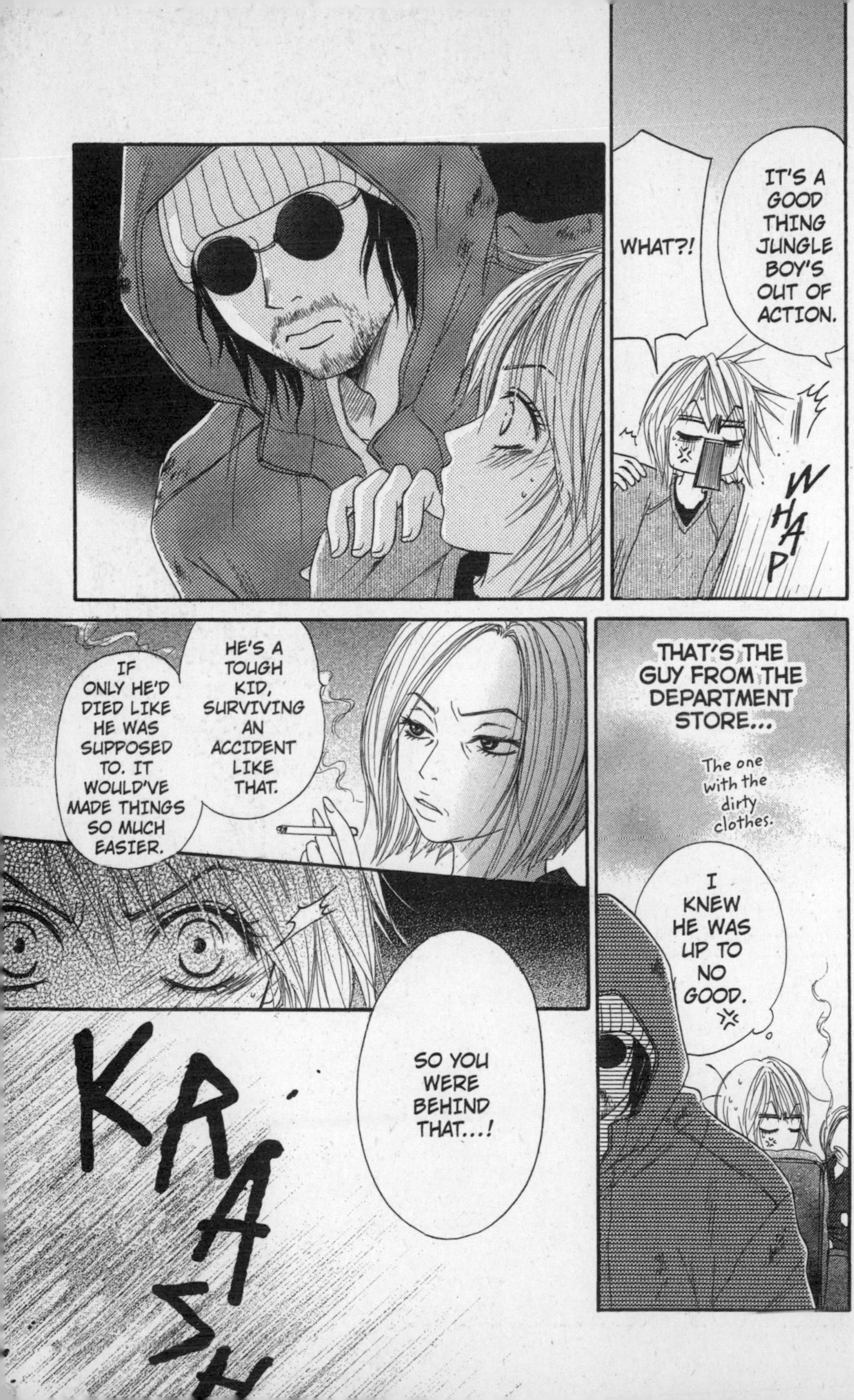
IT'S A GOOD THING JUNGLE BOY'S OUT OF ACTION.
WHAT?!
WHAP
THAT'S THE GUY FROM THE DEPARTMENT STORE...
The one with the dirty clothes.
I KNEW HE WAS UP TO NO GOOD.
HE'S A TOUGH KID, SURVIVING AN ACCIDENT LIKE THAT.
IF ONLY HE'D DIED LIKE HE WAS SUPPOSED TO. IT WOULD'VE MADE THINGS SO MUCH EASIER.
SO YOU WERE BEHIND THAT...!
KRASH

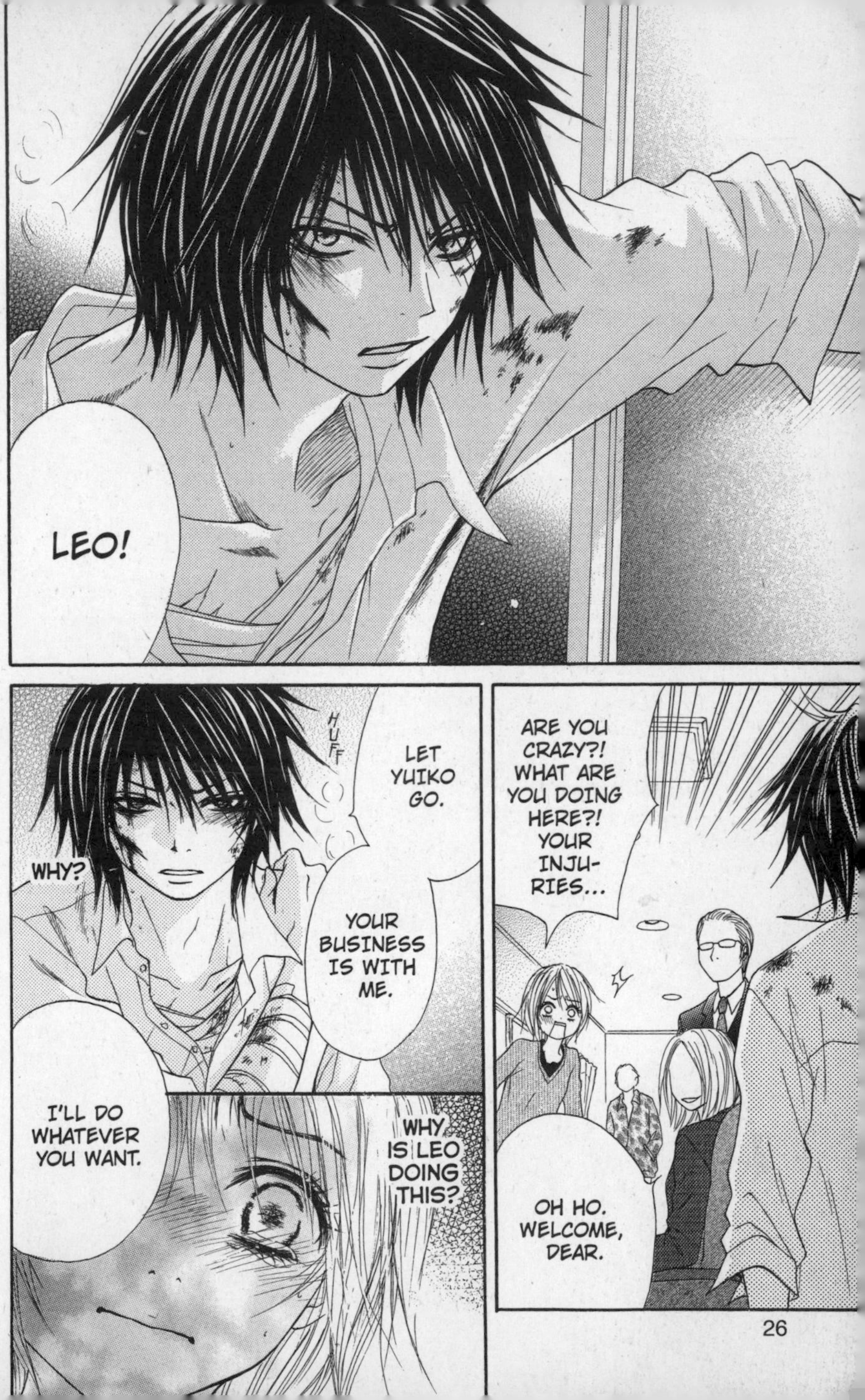
LEO!
ARE YOU CRAZY?! WHAT ARE YOU DOING HERE?! YOUR INJU-RIES...
OH HO. WELCOME, DEAR.
HUFF
LET YUIKO GO.
YOUR BUSINESS IS WITH ME.
WHY?
WHY IS LEO DOING THIS?
I'LL DO WHATEVER YOU WANT.

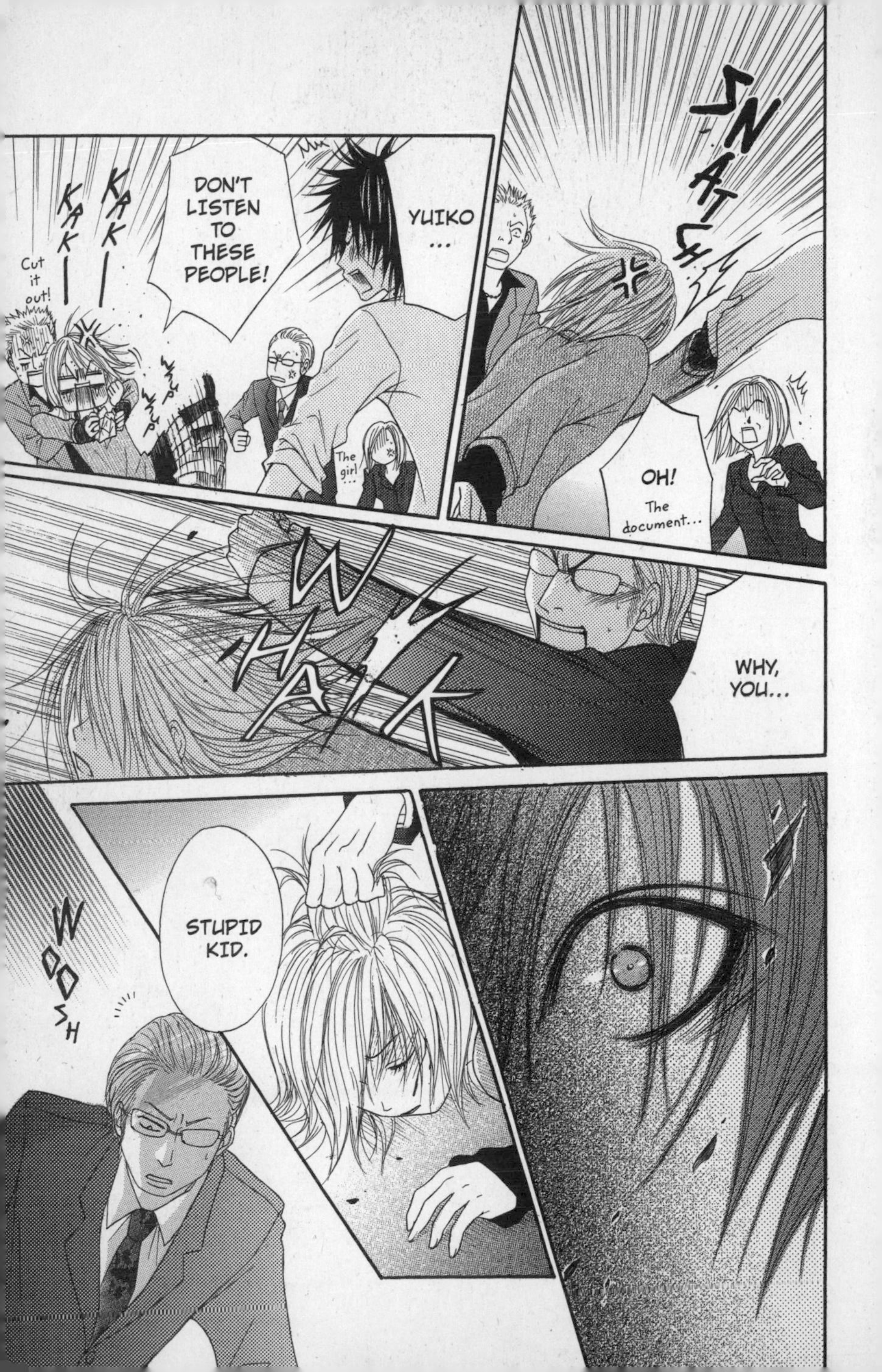
SNATCH
OH!
The document...
YUIKO ...
DON'T LISTEN TO THESE PEOPLE!
KRAKI
KRAKI
Cut it out!
The girl ...
WHY, YOU...
WHAK
STUPID KID.
WOOSH

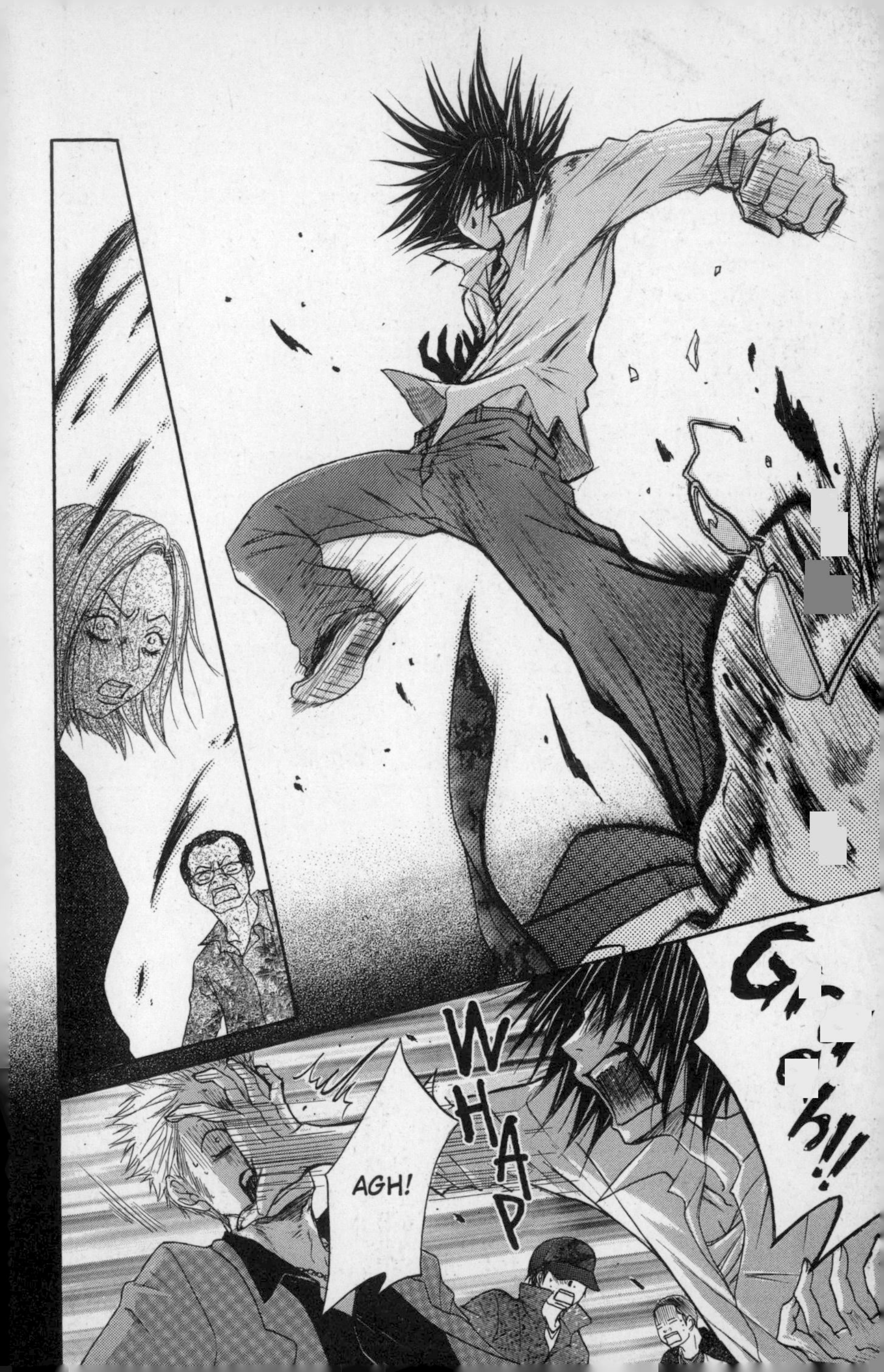
WHAP
AGH!

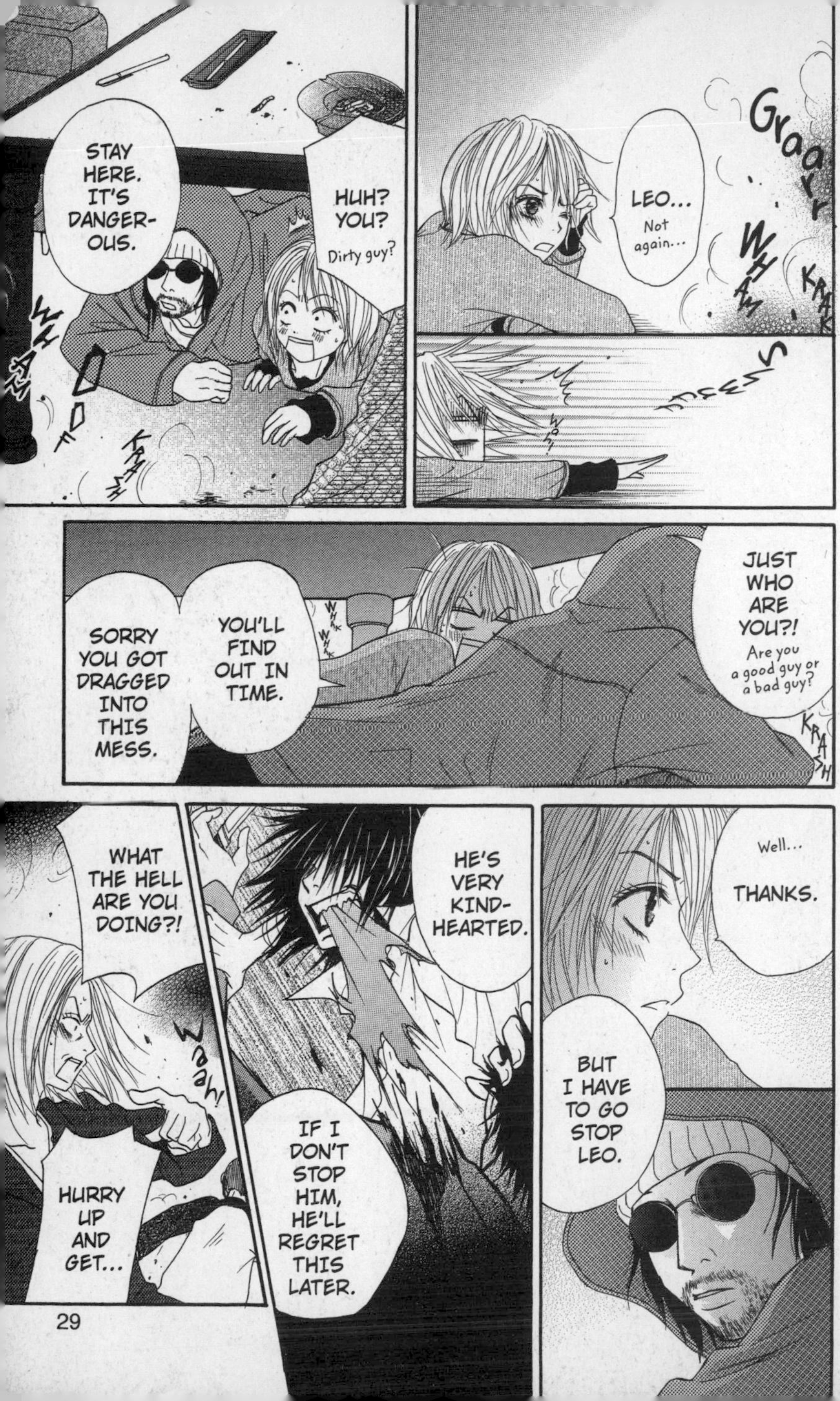
Graar
LEO... Not again...
WHAM
KRAK
HUH? YOU? Dirty guy?
STAY HERE. IT'S DANGER-OUS.
KRASH
JUST WHO ARE YOU?! Are you a good guy or a bad guy?
KRASH
YOU'LL FIND OUT IN TIME.
SORRY YOU GOT DRAGGED INTO THIS MESS.
Well... THANKS.
BUT I HAVE TO GO STOP LEO.
HE'S VERY KIND-HEARTED.
IF I DON'T STOP HIM, HE'LL REGRET THIS LATER.
WHAT THE HELL ARE YOU DOING?!
Waah!
HURRY UP AND GET...

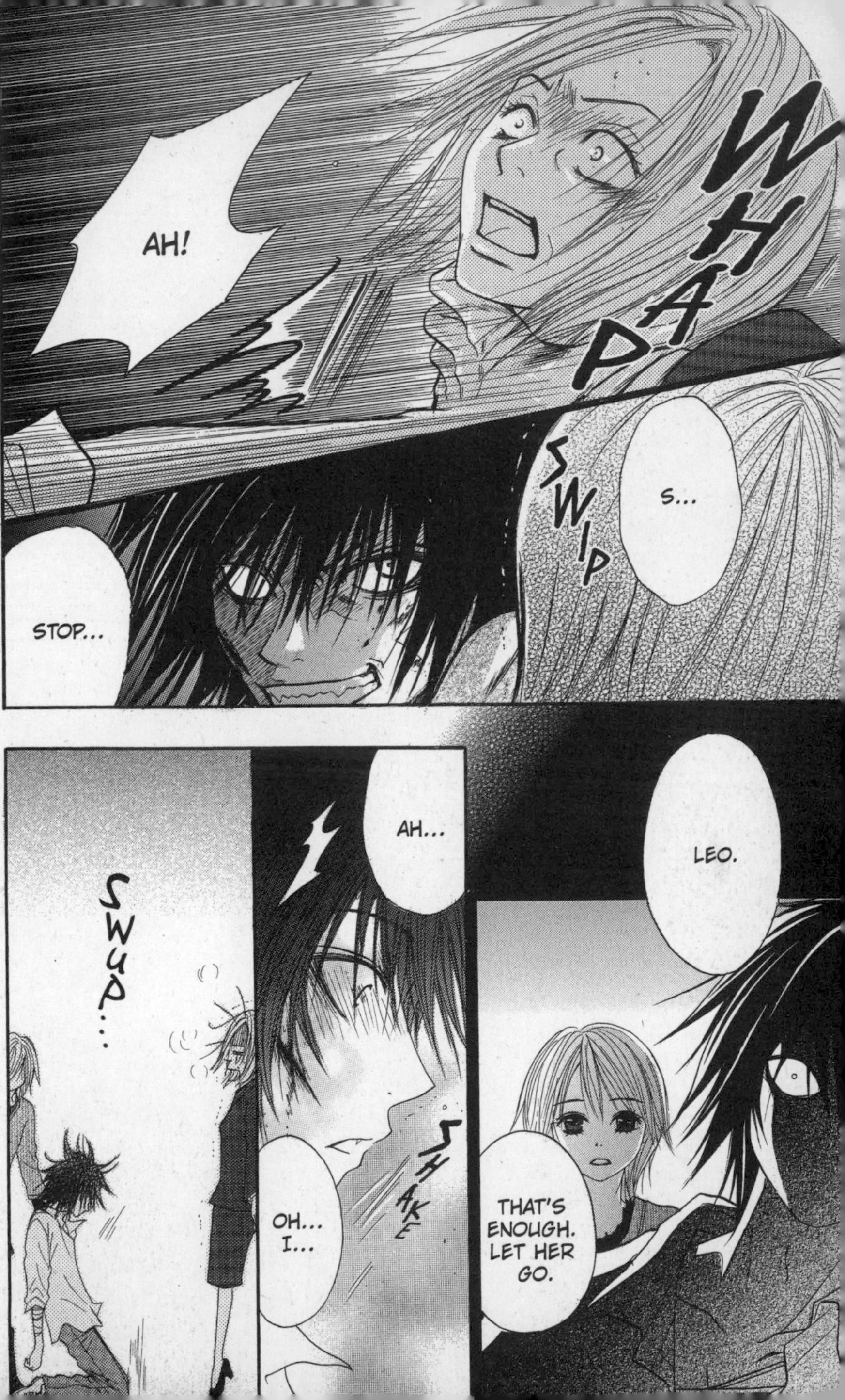
WHAP
AH!
SWIP
S...
STOP...
LEO.
THAT'S ENOUGH. LET HER GO.
AH...
SHAKE
OH... I...
SWUP...

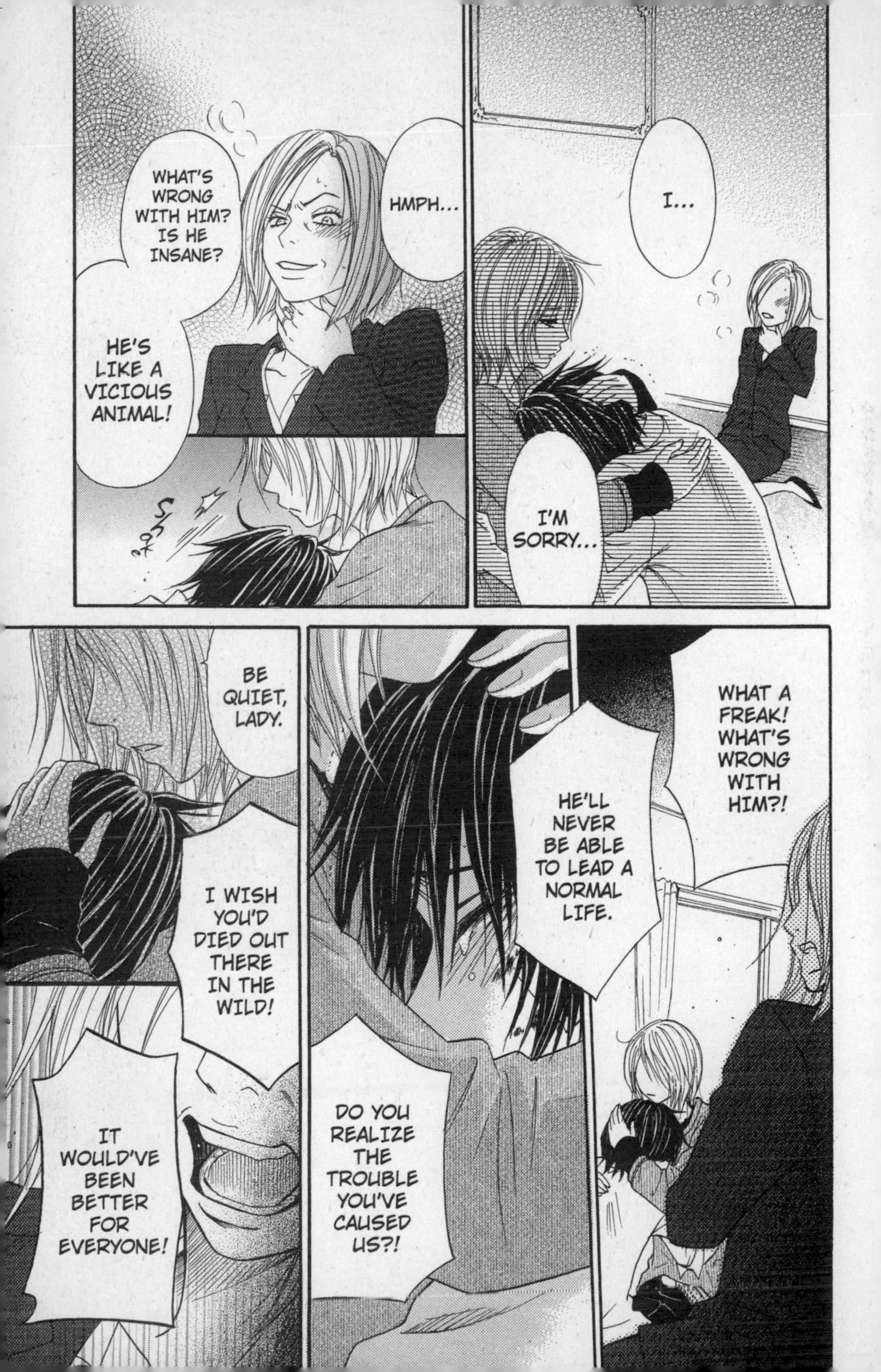
I...
I'M SORRY...
HMPH...
WHAT'S WRONG WITH HIM? IS HE INSANE?
HE'S LIKE A VICIOUS ANIMAL!
WHAT A FREAK! WHAT'S WRONG WITH HIM?!
HE'LL NEVER BE ABLE TO LEAD A NORMAL LIFE.
DO YOU REALIZE THE TROUBLE YOU'VE CAUSED US?!
BE QUIET, LADY.
I WISH YOU'D DIED OUT THERE IN THE WILD!
IT WOULD'VE BEEN BETTER FOR EVERYONE!

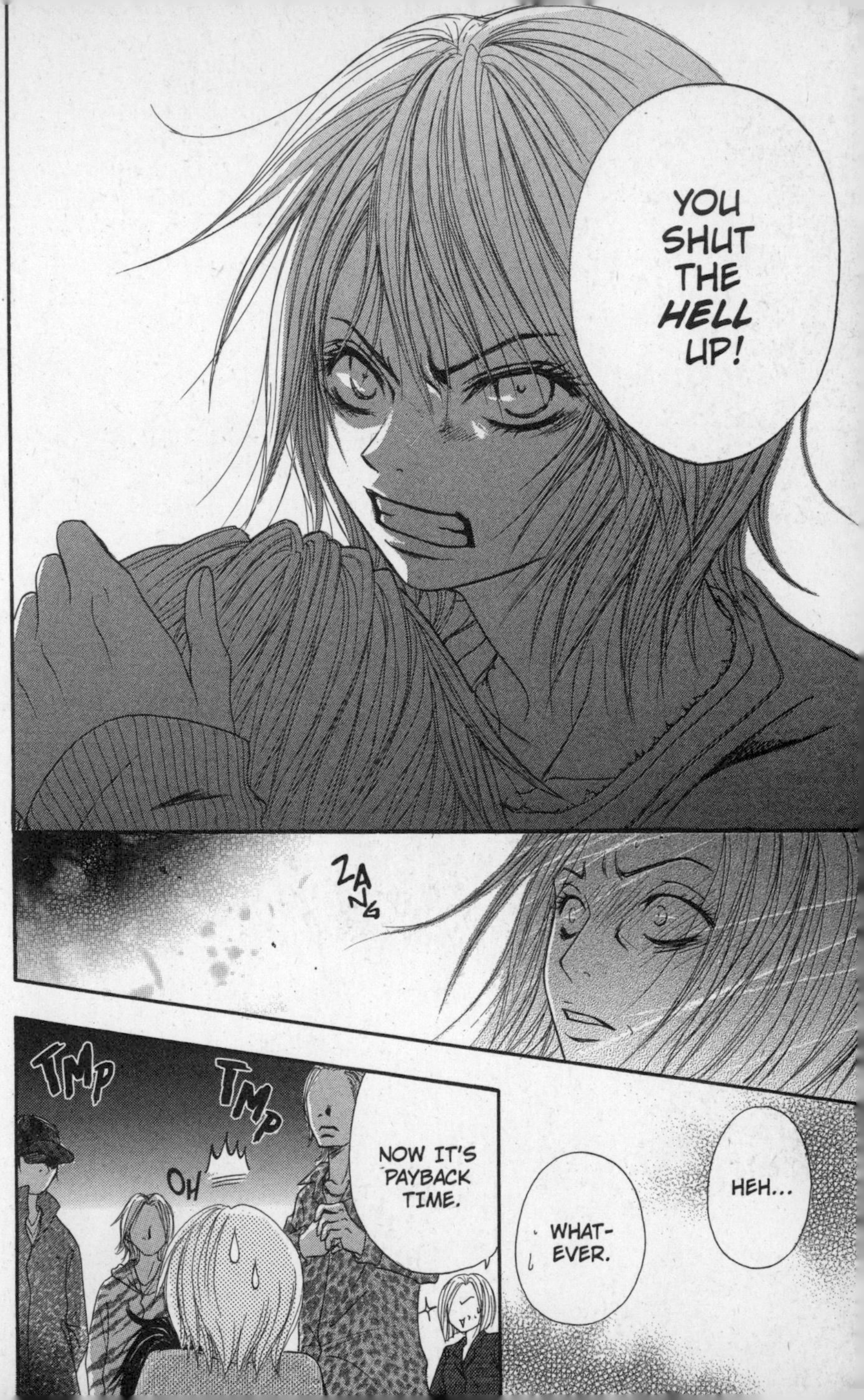
YOU SHUT THE HELL UP!
ZANG
HEH...
WHAT-EVER.
NOW IT'S PAYBACK TIME.
TMP
TMP
OH

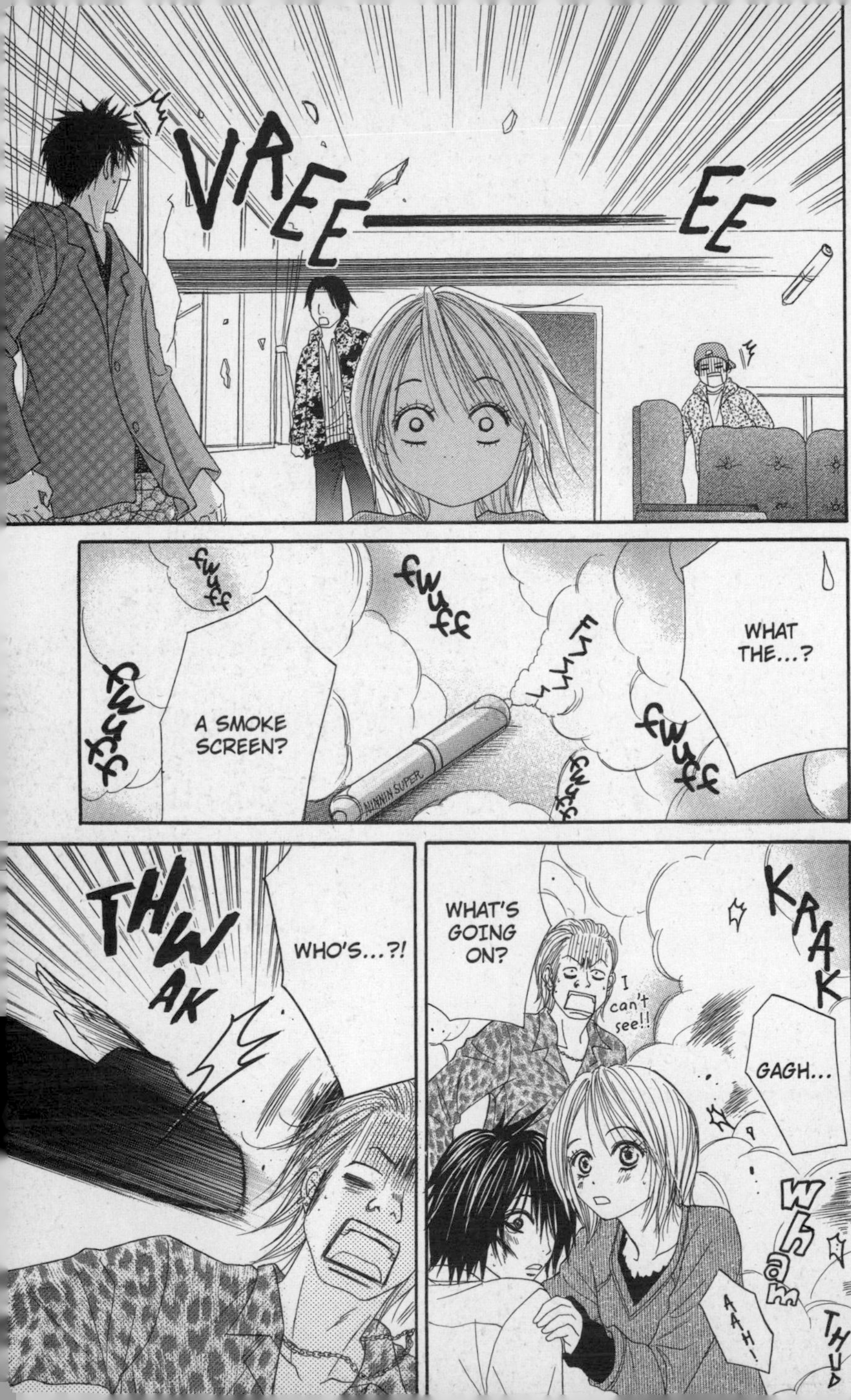

VREE——EE
WHAT THE...?
fwuff
fwuff
fwuff
fwuff
fwuff
A SMOKE SCREEN?
KRAK
WHAT'S GOING ON?
I can't see!!
GAGH...
Wham
THUD
AAH!
THWAK
WHO'S...?!

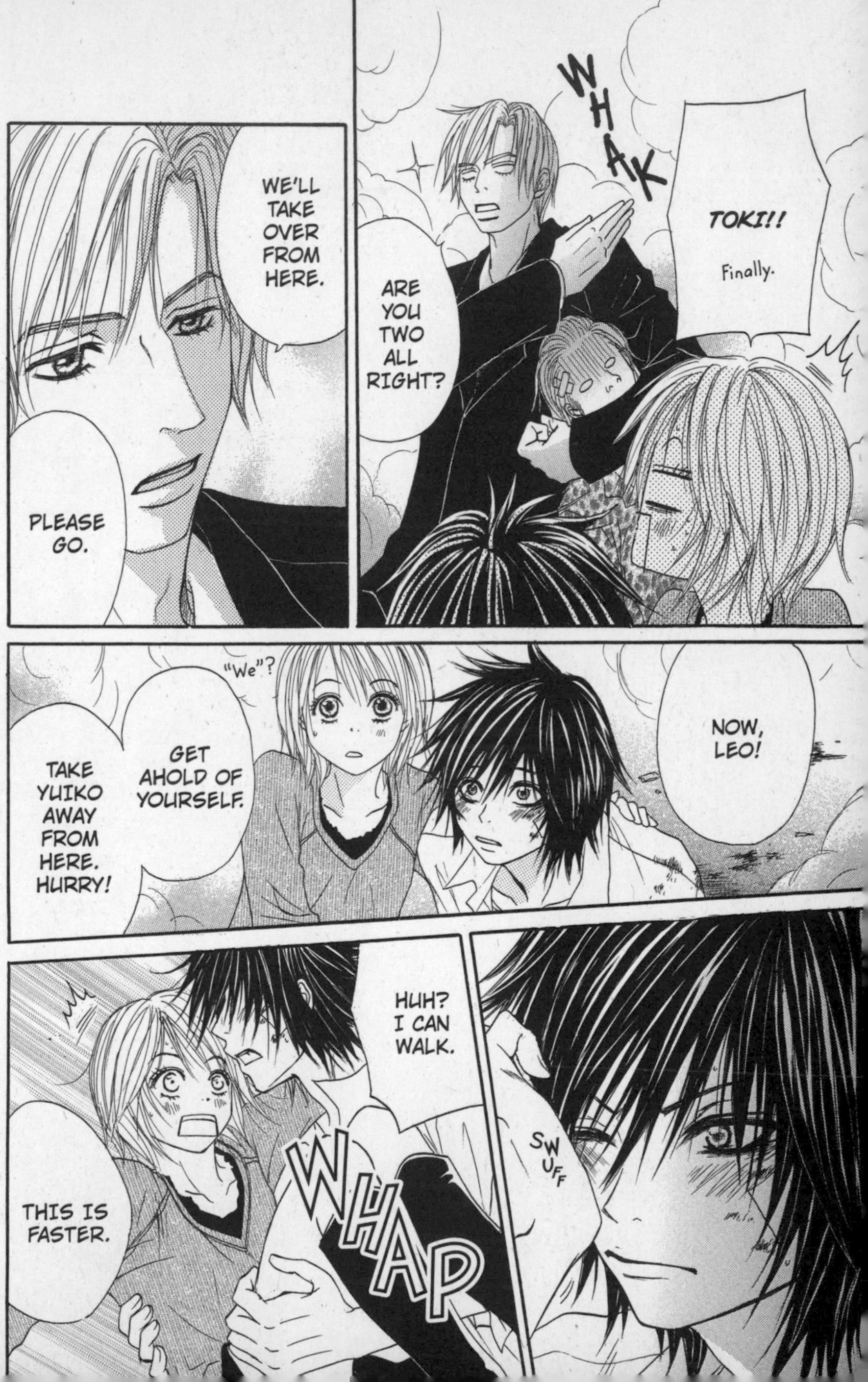
WHAK
TOKI!!
Finally.
ARE YOU TWO ALL RIGHT?
WE'LL TAKE OVER FROM HERE.
PLEASE GO.
NOW, LEO!
"We"?
GET AHOLD OF YOURSELF.
TAKE YUIKO AWAY FROM HERE. HURRY!
SWUFF
HUH? I CAN WALK.
WHAP
THIS IS FASTER.

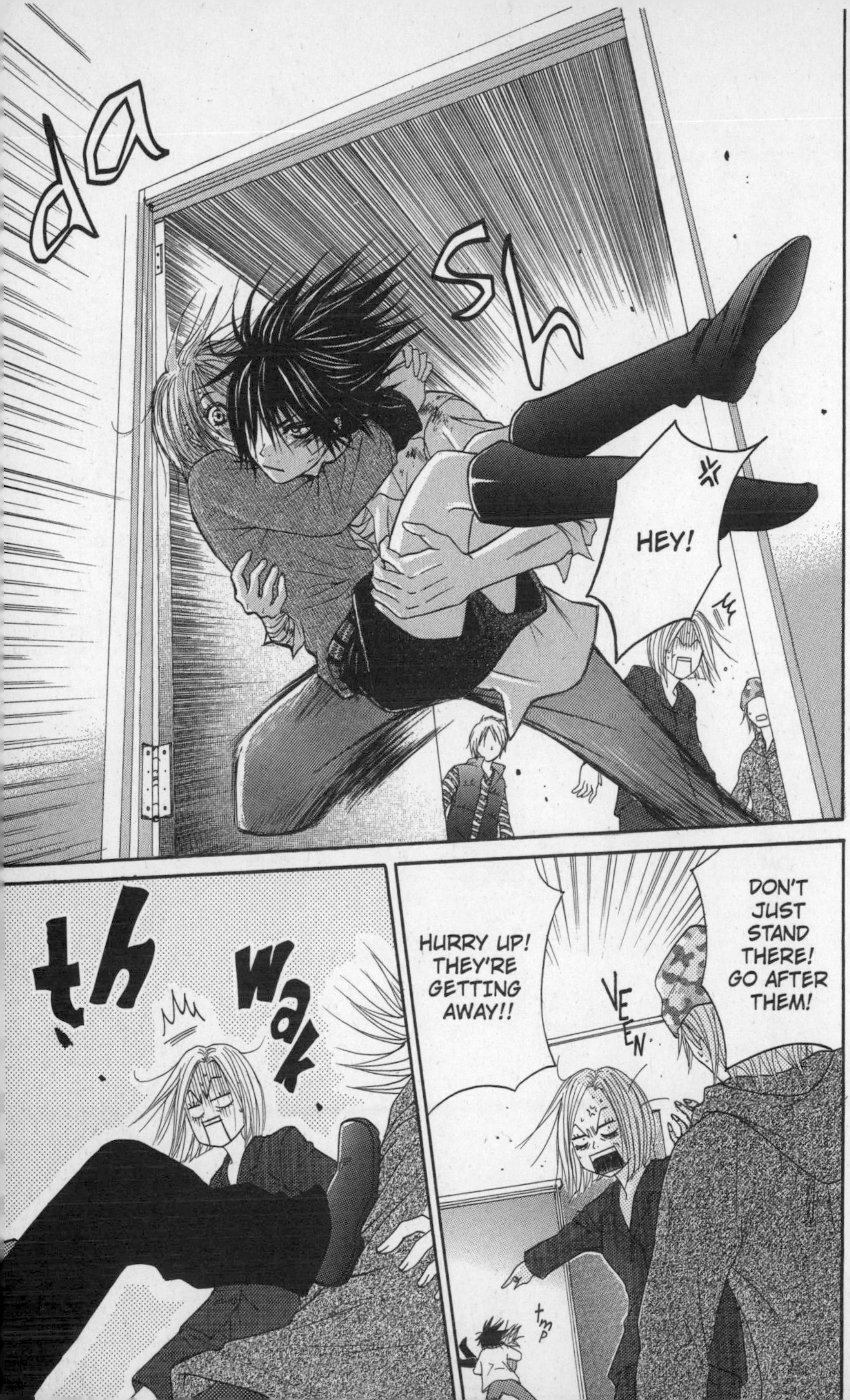
HEY!
dash
DON'T JUST STAND THERE! GO AFTER THEM!
HURRY UP! THEY'RE GETTING AWAY!!
VEEEN
tmp
thwak

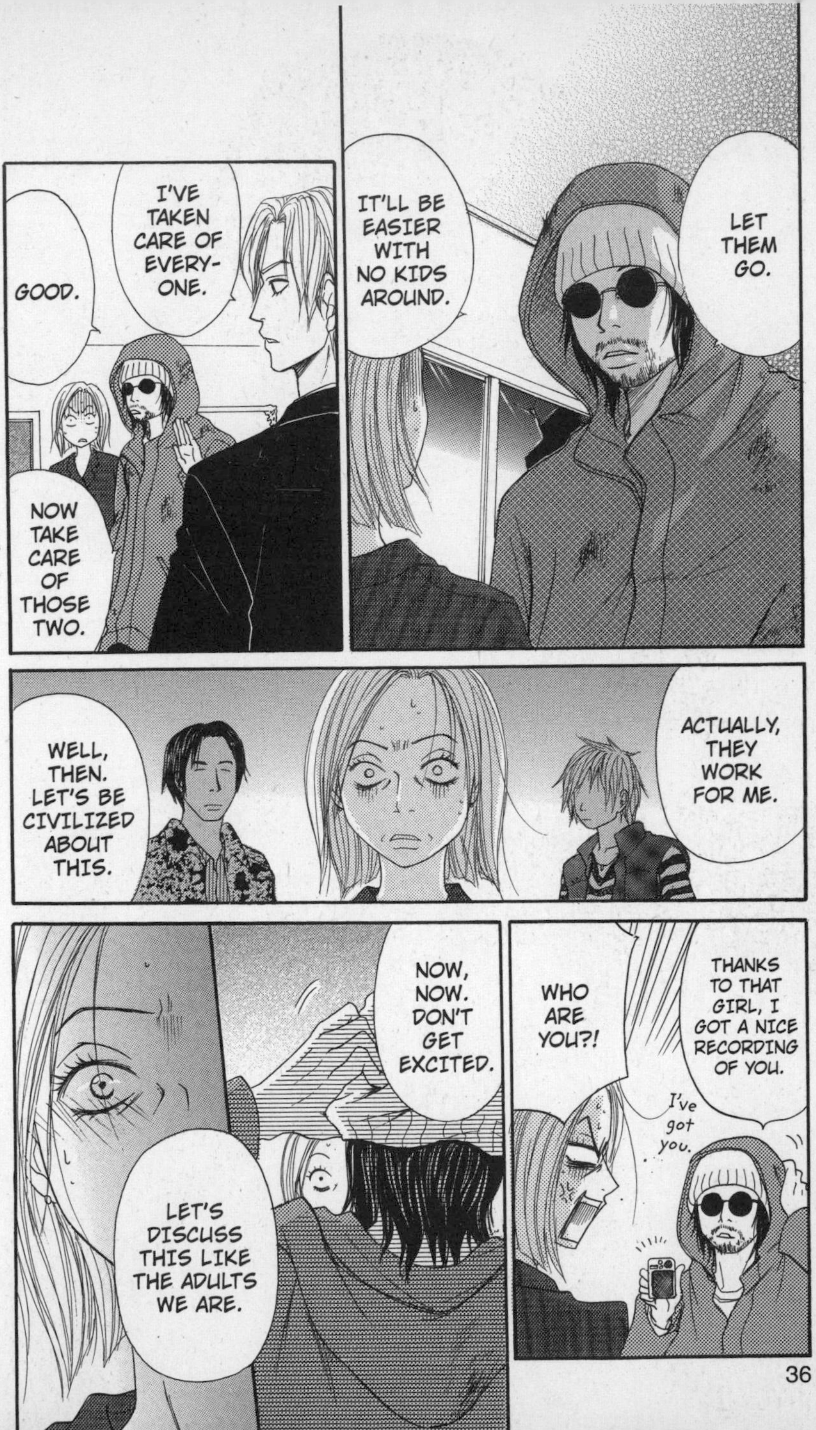
LET THEM GO.
IT'LL BE EASIER WITH NO KIDS AROUND.
I'VE TAKEN CARE OF EVERY-ONE.
GOOD.
NOW TAKE CARE OF THOSE TWO.
ACTUALLY, THEY WORK FOR ME.
WELL, THEN. LET'S BE CIVILIZED ABOUT THIS.
THANKS TO THAT GIRL, I GOT A NICE RECORDING OF YOU.
WHO ARE YOU?!
I've got you.
NOW, NOW. DON'T GET EXCITED.
LET'S DISCUSS THIS LIKE THE ADULTS WE ARE.

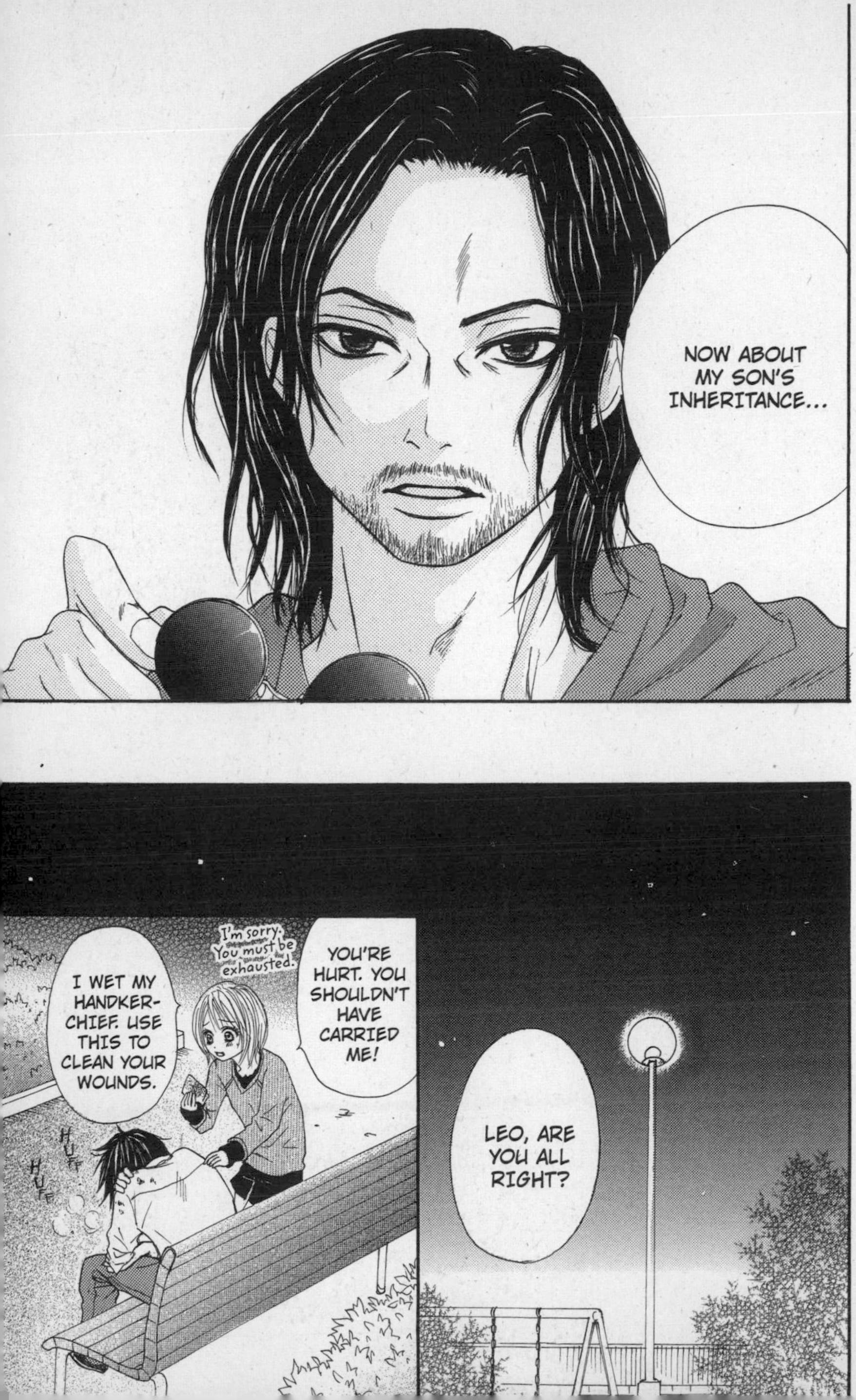
NOW ABOUT MY SON'S INHERITANCE...
LEO, ARE YOU ALL RIGHT?
YOU'RE HURT. YOU SHOULDN'T HAVE CARRIED ME!
I'm sorry. You must be exhausted.
I WET MY HANDKER-CHIEF. USE THIS TO CLEAN YOUR WOUNDS.
HUFF HUFF

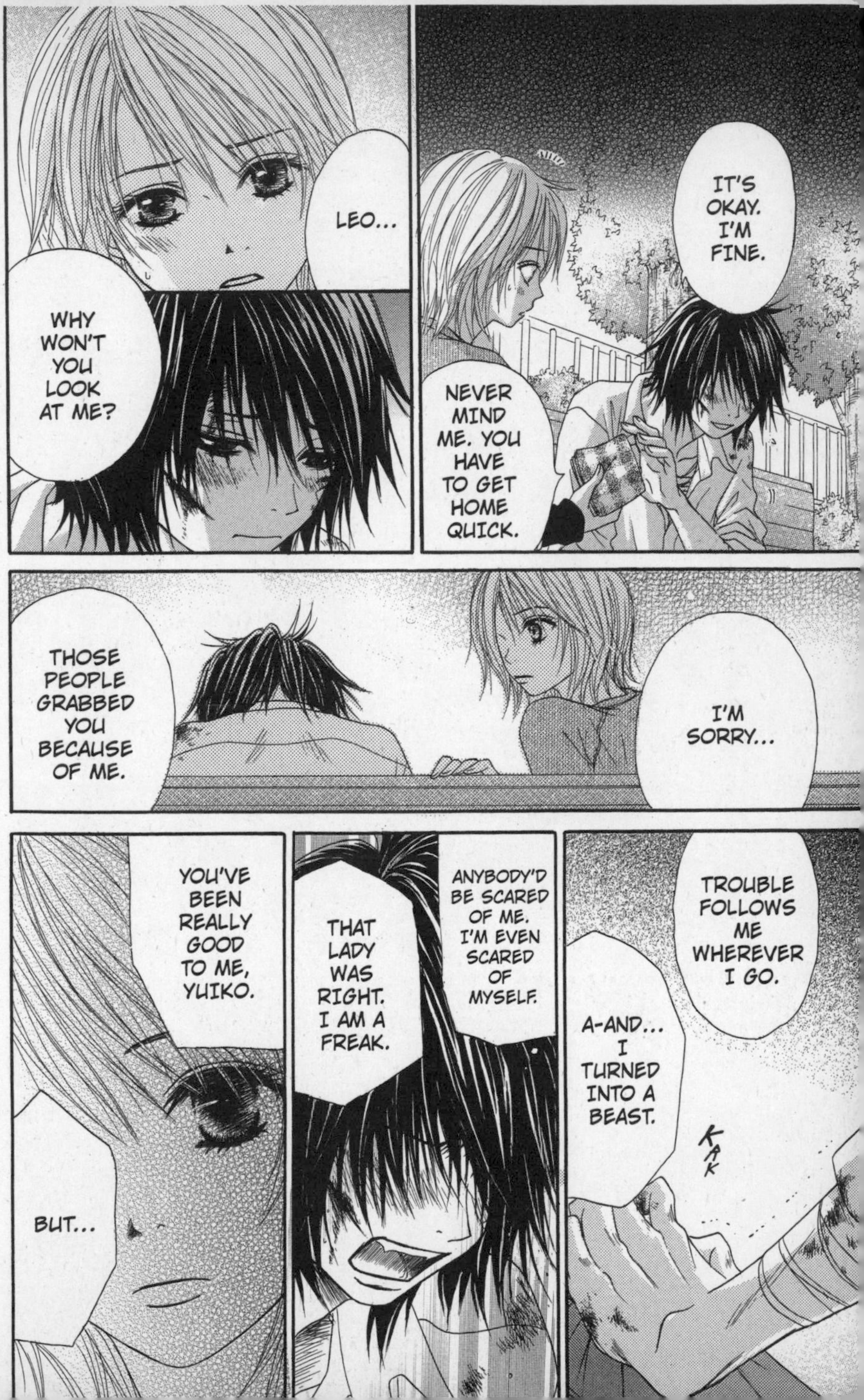
IT'S OKAY. I'M FINE.
NEVER MIND ME. YOU HAVE TO GET HOME QUICK.
LEO...
WHY WON'T YOU LOOK AT ME?
I'M SORRY...
THOSE PEOPLE GRABBED YOU BECAUSE OF ME.
TROUBLE FOLLOWS ME WHEREVER I GO.
A-AND... I TURNED INTO A BEAST.
KAK
ANYBODY'D BE SCARED OF ME. I'M EVEN SCARED OF MYSELF.
THAT LADY WAS RIGHT. I AM A FREAK.
YOU'VE BEEN REALLY GOOD TO ME, YUIKO.
BUT...

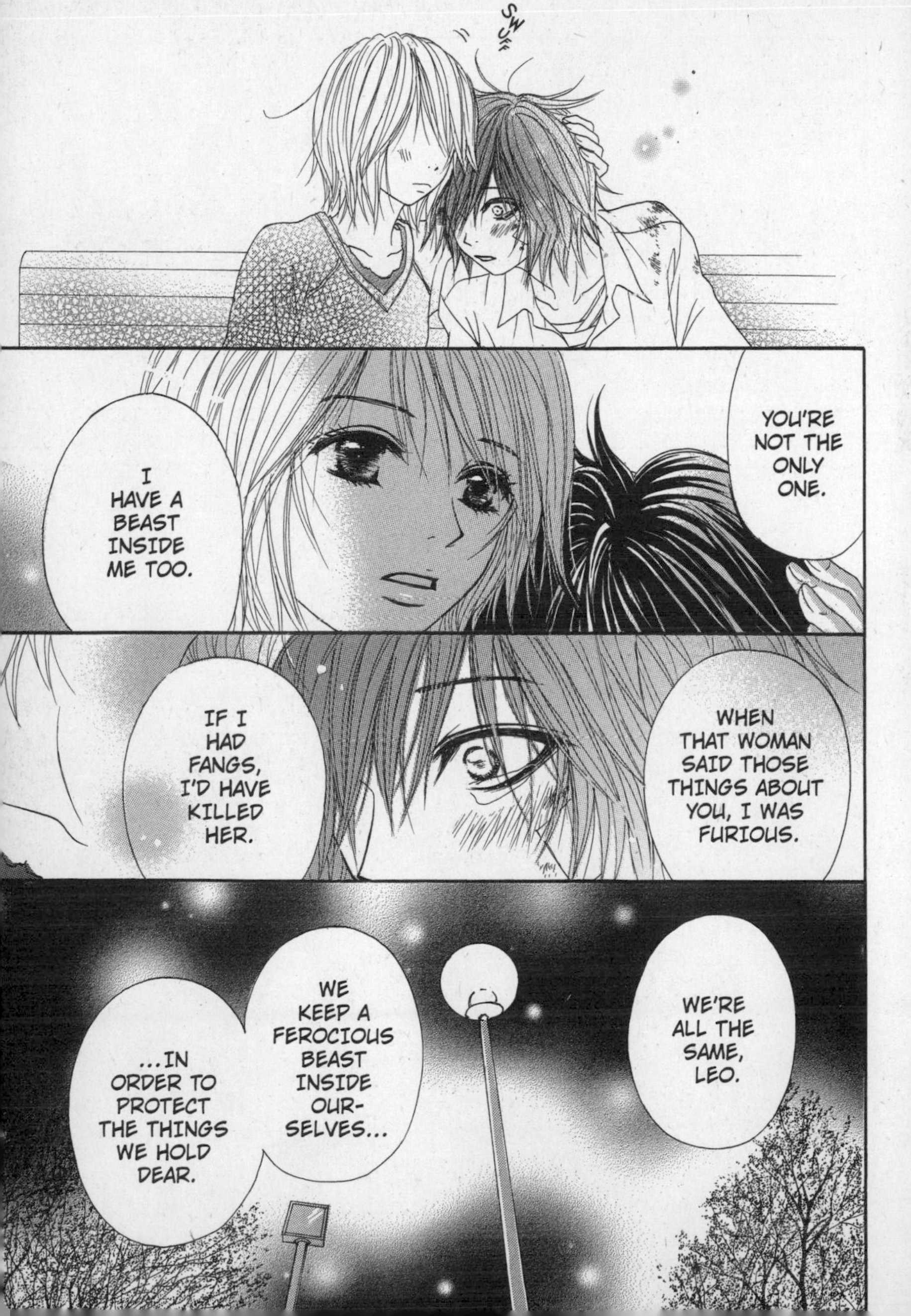
SWUFF
YOU'RE NOT THE ONLY ONE.
I HAVE A BEAST INSIDE ME TOO.
WHEN THAT WOMAN SAID THOSE THINGS ABOUT YOU, I WAS FURIOUS.
IF I HAD FANGS, I'D HAVE KILLED HER.
WE'RE ALL THE SAME, LEO.
WE KEEP A FEROCIOUS BEAST INSIDE OUR-SELVES...
...IN ORDER TO PROTECT THE THINGS WE HOLD DEAR.

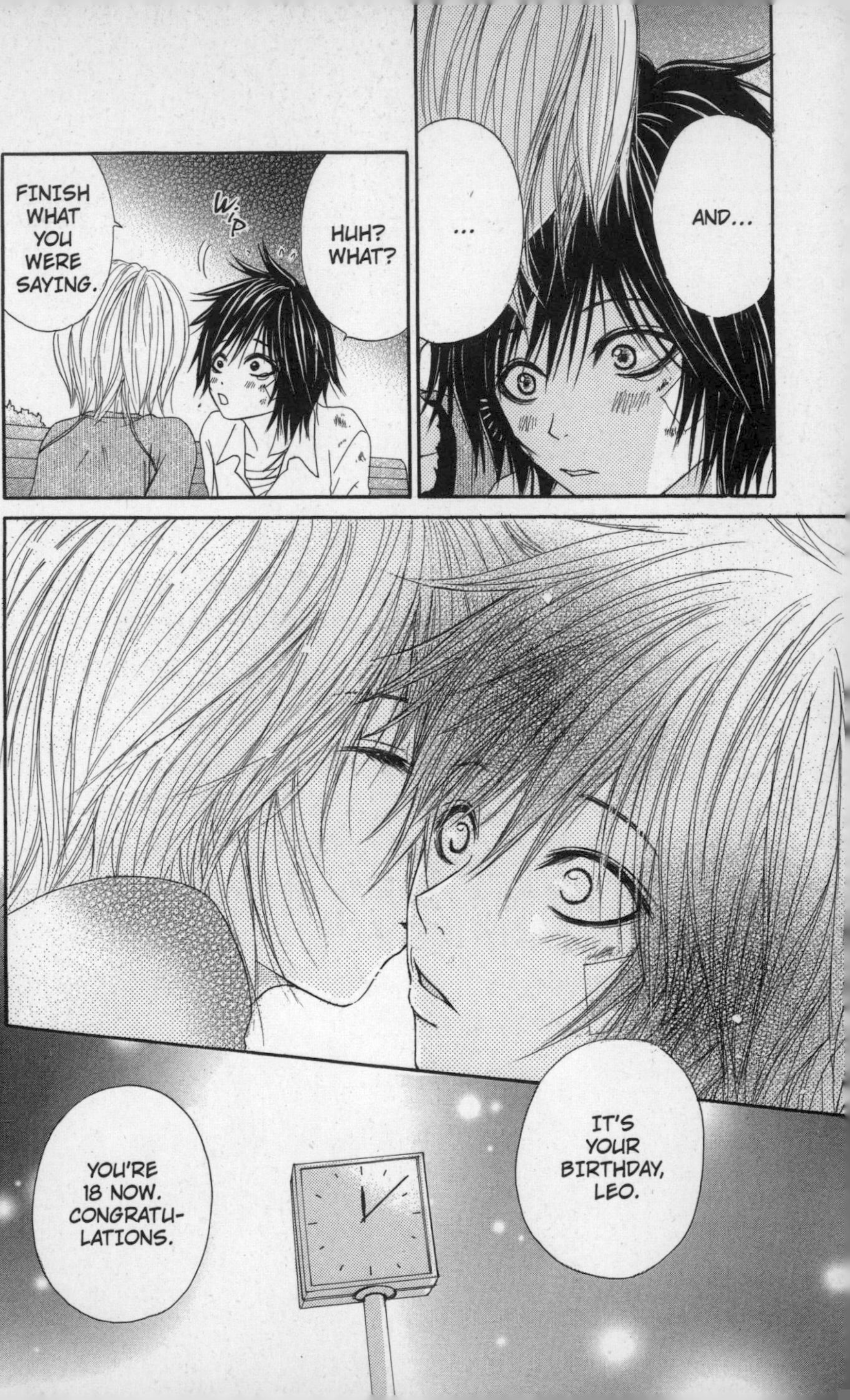
AND...
...
HUH? WHAT?
WIP
FINISH WHAT YOU WERE SAYING.
IT'S YOUR BIRTHDAY, LEO.
YOU'RE 18 NOW. CONGRATU-LATIONS.

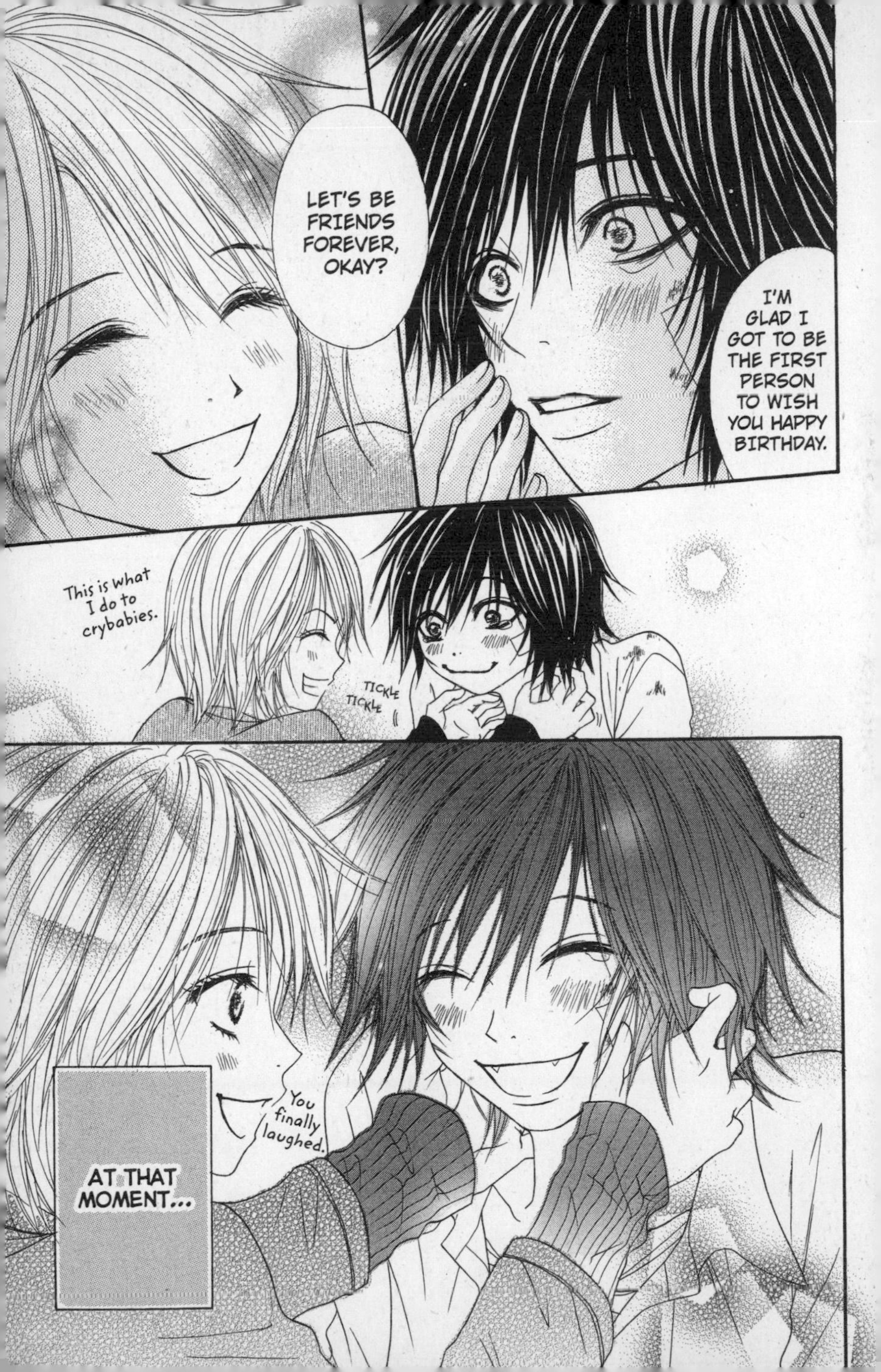
I'M GLAD I GOT TO BE THE FIRST PERSON TO WISH YOU HAPPY BIRTHDAY.
LET'S BE FRIENDS FOREVER, OKAY?
This is what I do to crybabies.
TICKLE TICKLE
You finally laughed.
AT THAT MOMENT...

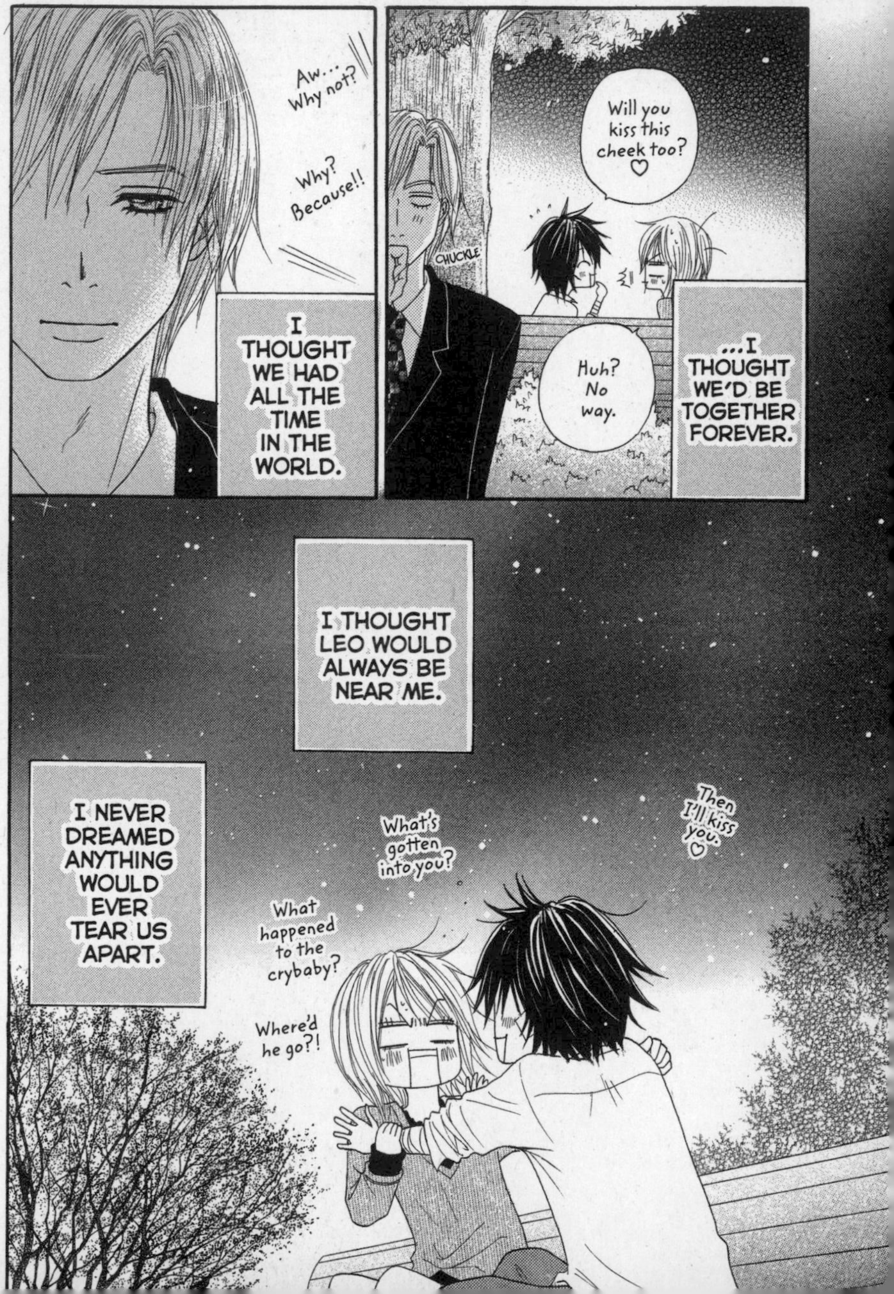
Will you kiss this cheek too? ♡
CHUCKLE
...I THOUGHT WE'D BE TOGETHER FOREVER.
Huh? No way.
Aw... Why not?
Why? Because!!
I THOUGHT WE HAD ALL THE TIME IN THE WORLD.
I THOUGHT LEO WOULD ALWAYS BE NEAR ME.
Then I'll kiss you. ♡
What's gotten into you?
What happened to the crybaby?
Where'd he go?!
I NEVER DREAMED ANYTHING WOULD EVER TEAR US APART.

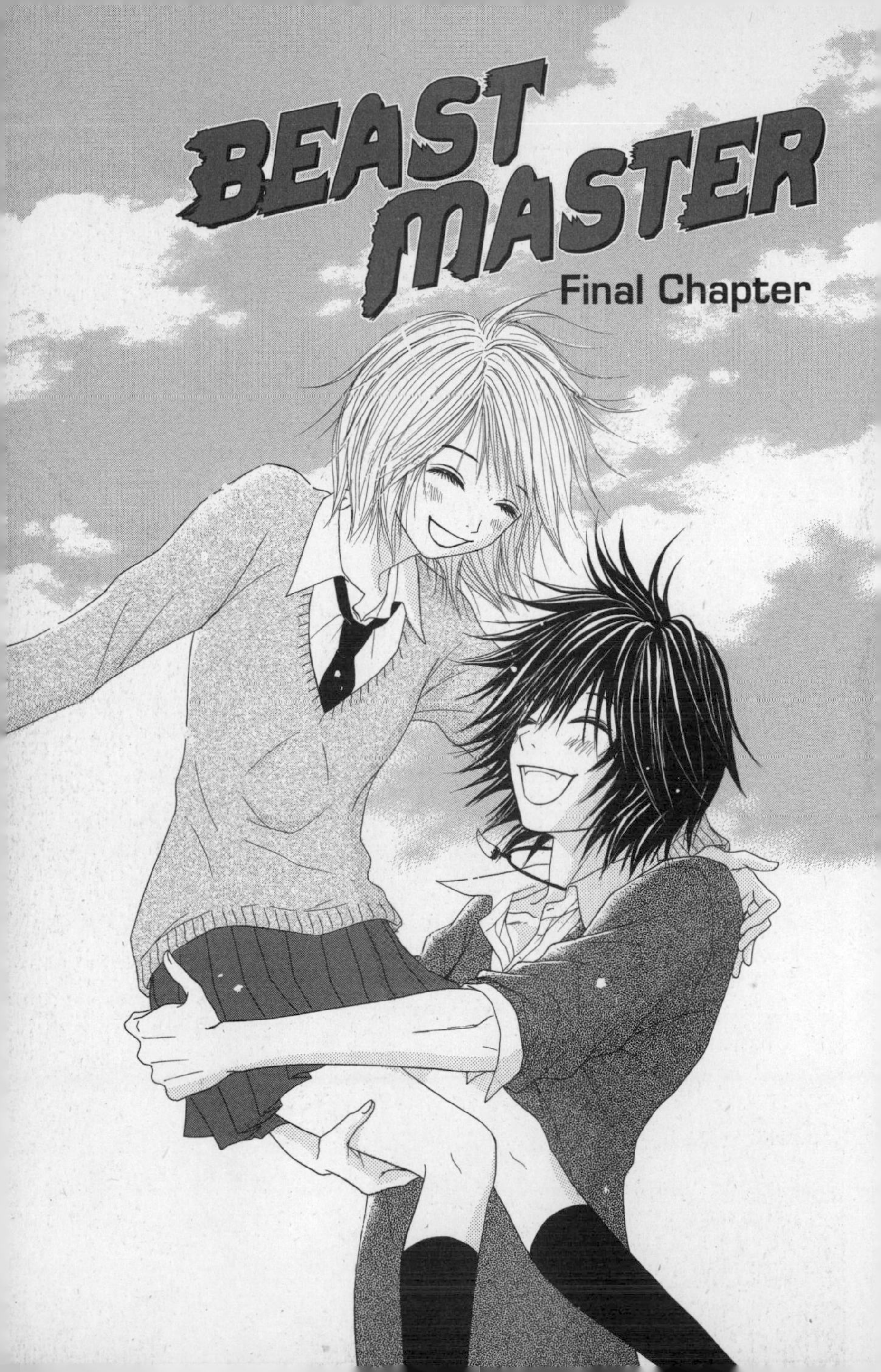
BEAST MASTER
Final Chapter

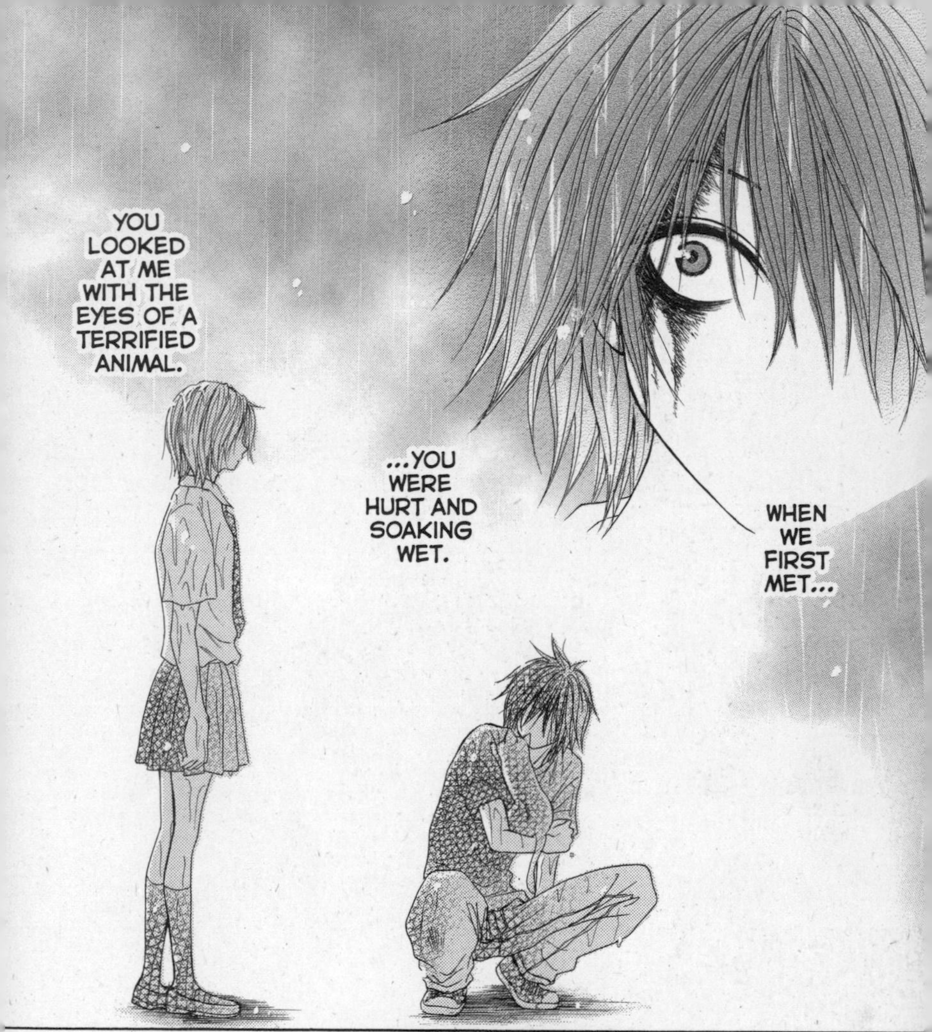
WHEN WE FIRST MET...
...YOU WERE HURT AND SOAKING WET.
YOU LOOKED AT ME WITH THE EYES OF A TERRIFIED ANIMAL.

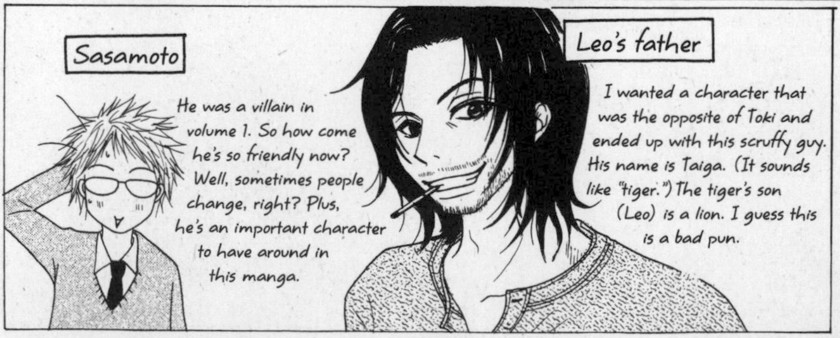
Leo's father
I wanted a character that was the opposite of Toki and ended up with this scruffy guy. His name is Taiga. (It sounds like "tiger.") The tiger's son (Leo) is a lion. I guess this is a bad pun.
Sasamoto
He was a villain in volume 1. So how come he's so friendly now? Well, sometimes people change, right? Plus, he's an important character to have around in this manga.

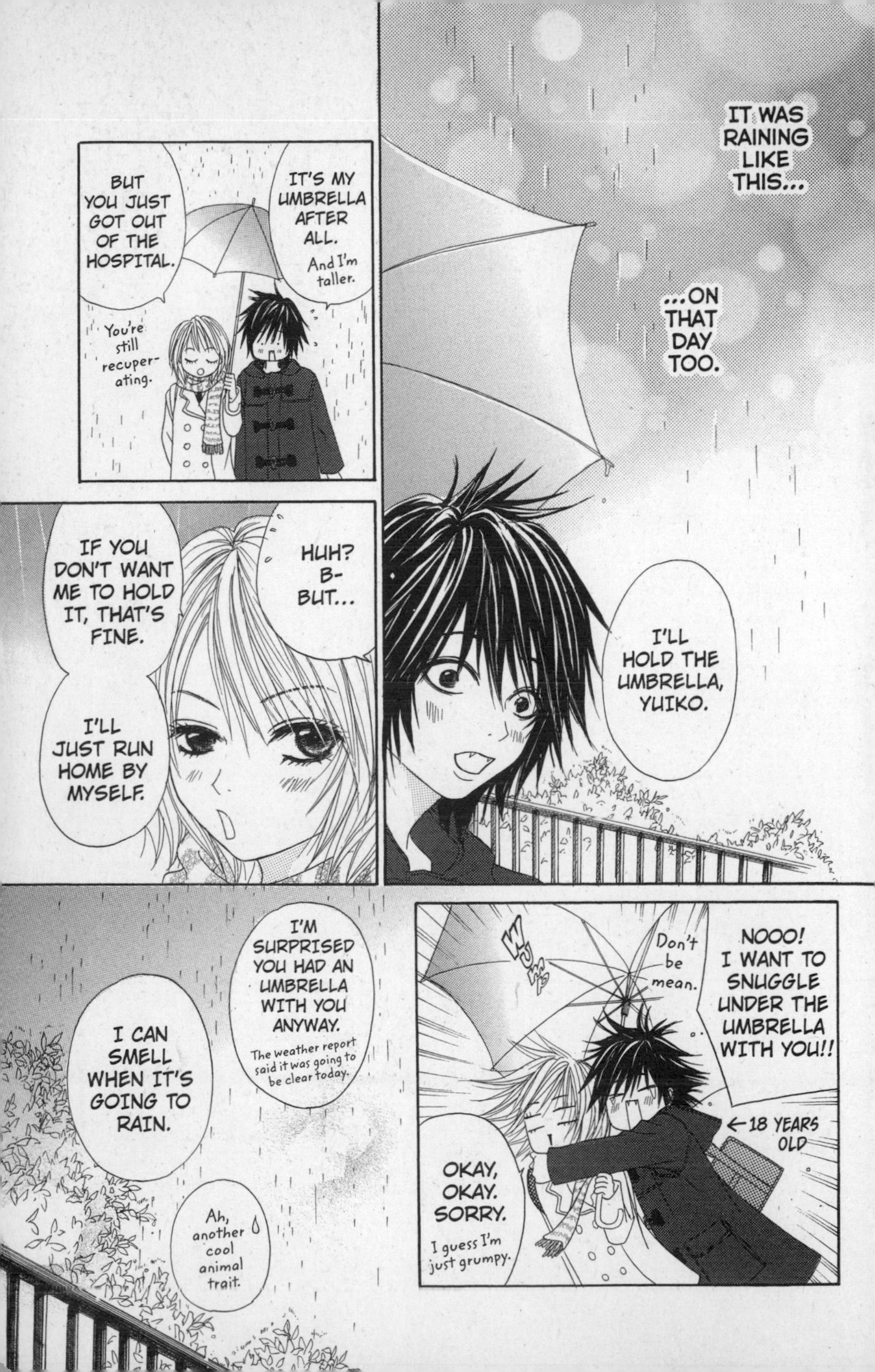
IT WAS RAINING LIKE THIS...
...ON THAT DAY TOO.
I'LL HOLD THE UMBRELLA, YUIKO.
IT'S MY UMBRELLA AFTER ALL.
And I'm taller.
BUT YOU JUST GOT OUT OF THE HOSPITAL.
You're still recuperating.
HUH? B-BUT...
IF YOU DON'T WANT ME TO HOLD IT, THAT'S FINE.
I'LL JUST RUN HOME BY MYSELF.
NOOO! I WANT TO SNUGGLE UNDER THE UMBRELLA WITH YOU!!
Don't be mean.
←18 YEARS OLD
OKAY, OKAY. SORRY.
I guess I'm just grumpy.
I'M SURPRISED YOU HAD AN UMBRELLA WITH YOU ANYWAY.
The weather report said it was going to be clear today.
I CAN SMELL WHEN IT'S GOING TO RAIN.
Ah, another cool animal trait.

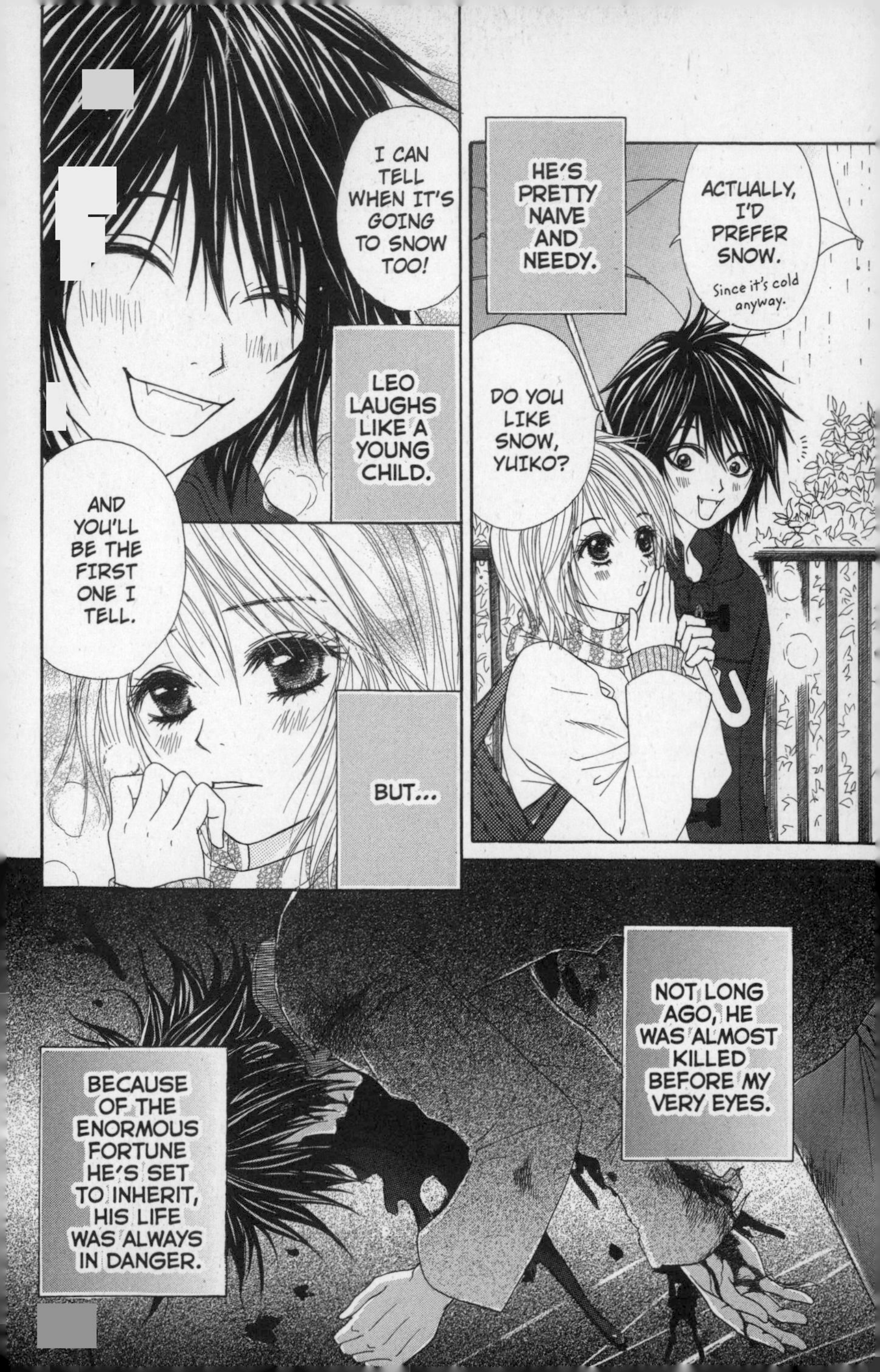
ACTUALLY, I'D PREFER SNOW.
Since it's cold anyway.
HE'S PRETTY NAIVE AND NEEDY.
DO YOU LIKE SNOW, YUIKO?
I CAN TELL WHEN IT'S GOING TO SNOW TOO!
LEO LAUGHS LIKE A YOUNG CHILD.
AND YOU'LL BE THE FIRST ONE I TELL.
BUT...
NOT LONG AGO, HE WAS ALMOST KILLED BEFORE MY VERY EYES.
BECAUSE OF THE ENORMOUS FORTUNE HE'S SET TO INHERIT, HIS LIFE WAS ALWAYS IN DANGER.

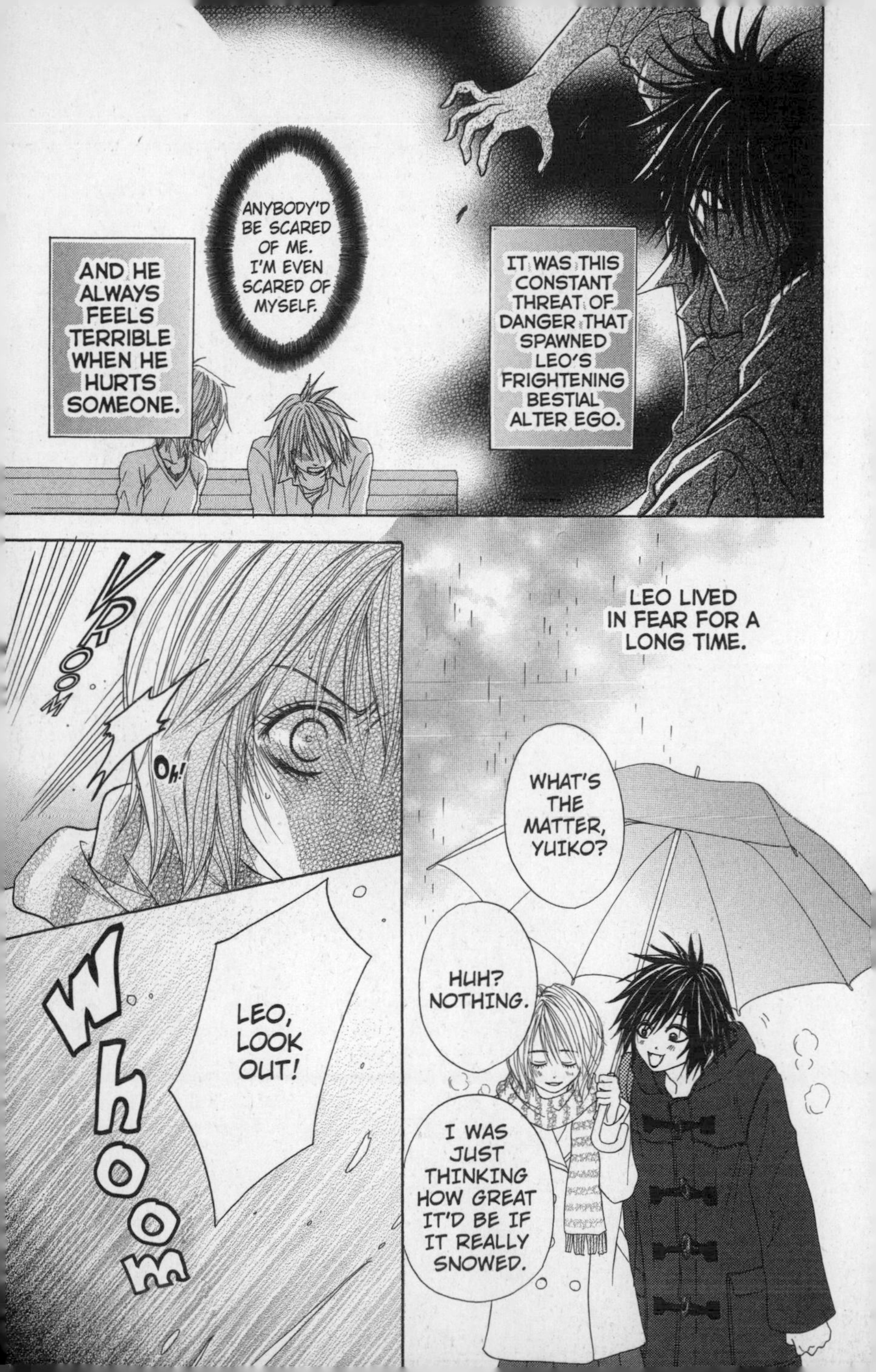
IT WAS THIS CONSTANT THREAT OF DANGER THAT SPAWNED LEO'S FRIGHTENING BESTIAL ALTER EGO.
ANYBODY'D BE SCARED OF ME. I'M EVEN SCARED OF MYSELF.
AND HE ALWAYS FEELS TERRIBLE WHEN HE HURTS SOMEONE.
LEO LIVED IN FEAR FOR A LONG TIME.
WHAT'S THE MATTER, YUIKO?
HUH? NOTHING.
I WAS JUST THINKING HOW GREAT IT'D BE IF IT REALLY SNOWED.
VROOOM
OH!
LEO, LOOK OUT!
WHOOM

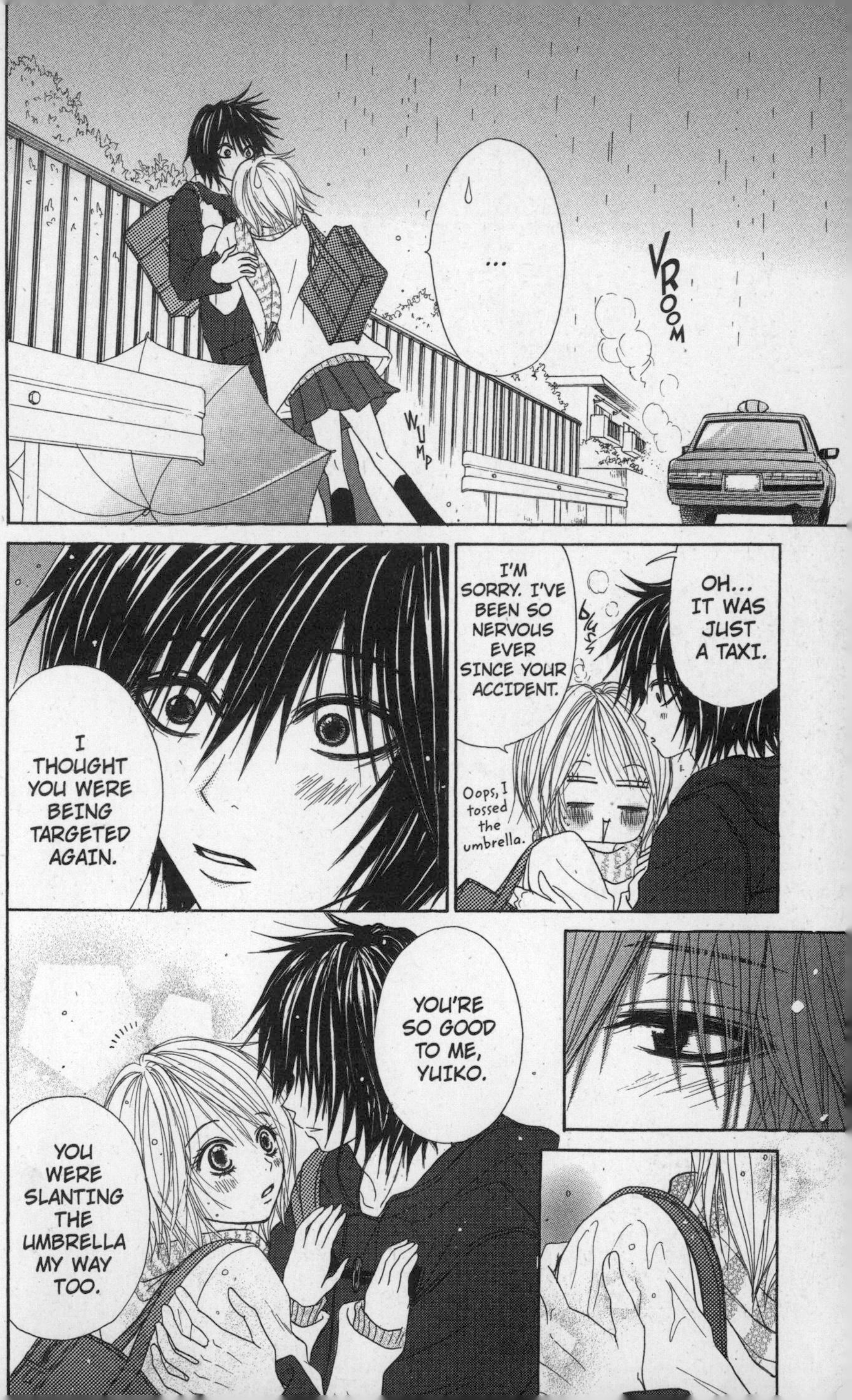
...
VROOM
WUMP
OH... IT WAS JUST A TAXI.
I'M SORRY. I'VE BEEN SO NERVOUS EVER SINCE YOUR ACCIDENT.
blush
Oops, I tossed the umbrella.
I THOUGHT YOU WERE BEING TARGETED AGAIN.
YOU'RE SO GOOD TO ME, YUIKO.
YOU WERE SLANTING THE UMBRELLA MY WAY TOO.

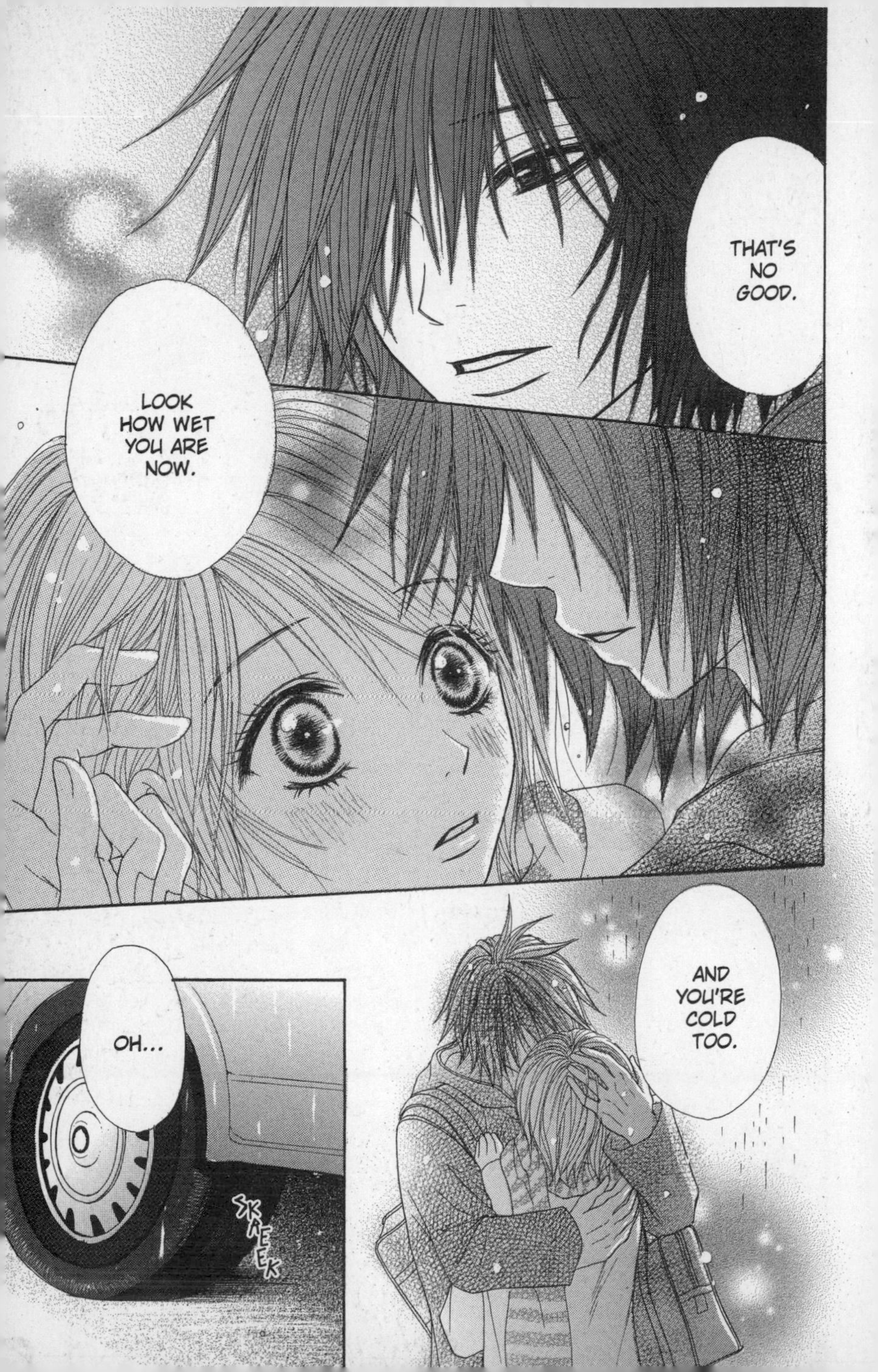
THAT'S NO GOOD.
LOOK HOW WET YOU ARE NOW.
AND YOU'RE COLD TOO.
OH...
SKREEK

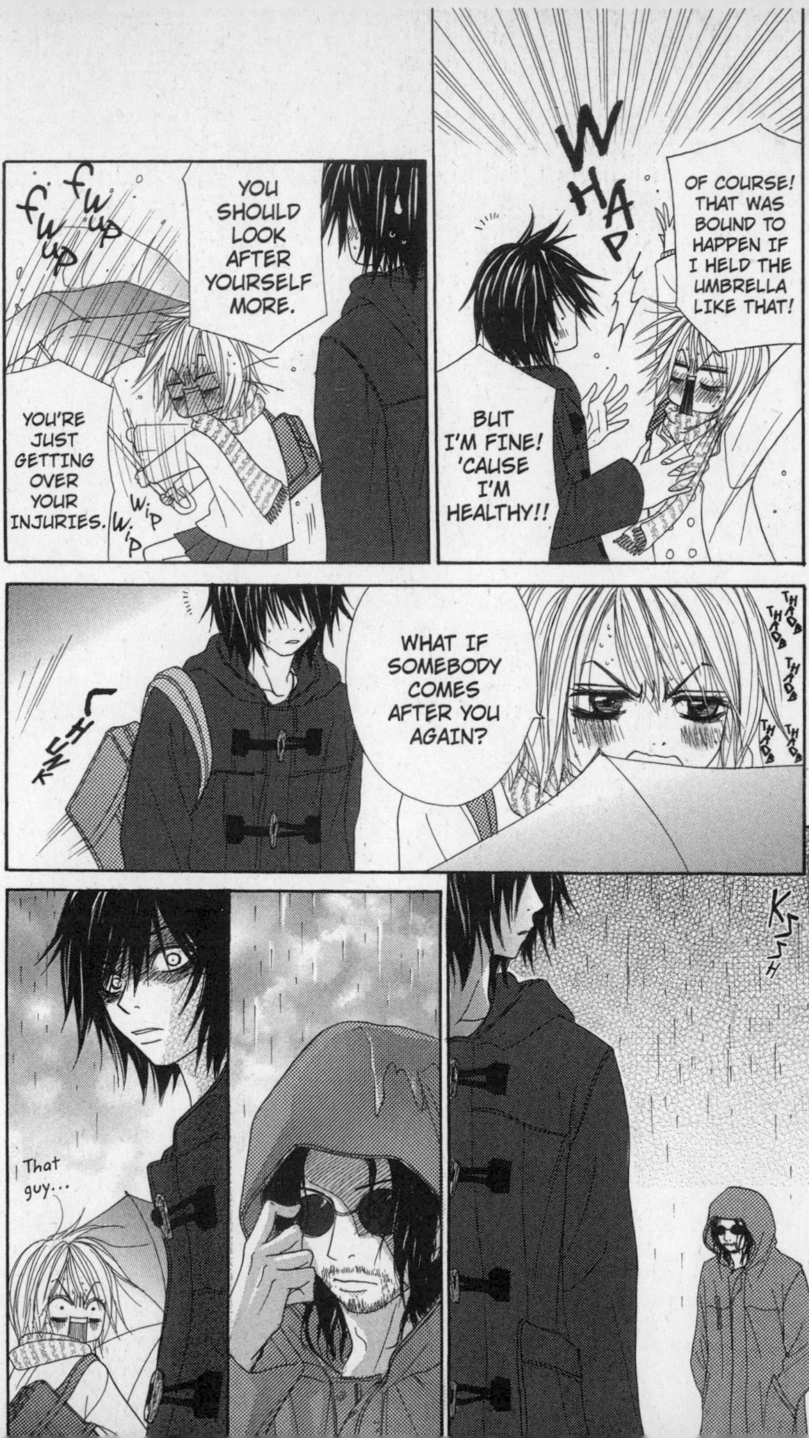
OF COURSE! THAT WAS BOUND TO HAPPEN IF I HELD THE UMBRELLA LIKE THAT!
WHAP
BUT I'M FINE! 'CAUSE I'M HEALTHY!!
YOU SHOULD LOOK AFTER YOURSELF MORE.
fwup fwup
YOU'RE JUST GETTING OVER YOUR INJURIES.
Wip Wip
THROB THROB THROB THROB THROB
WHAT IF SOMEBODY COMES AFTER YOU AGAIN?
CHUNK
KSSH
RRMM
That guy...

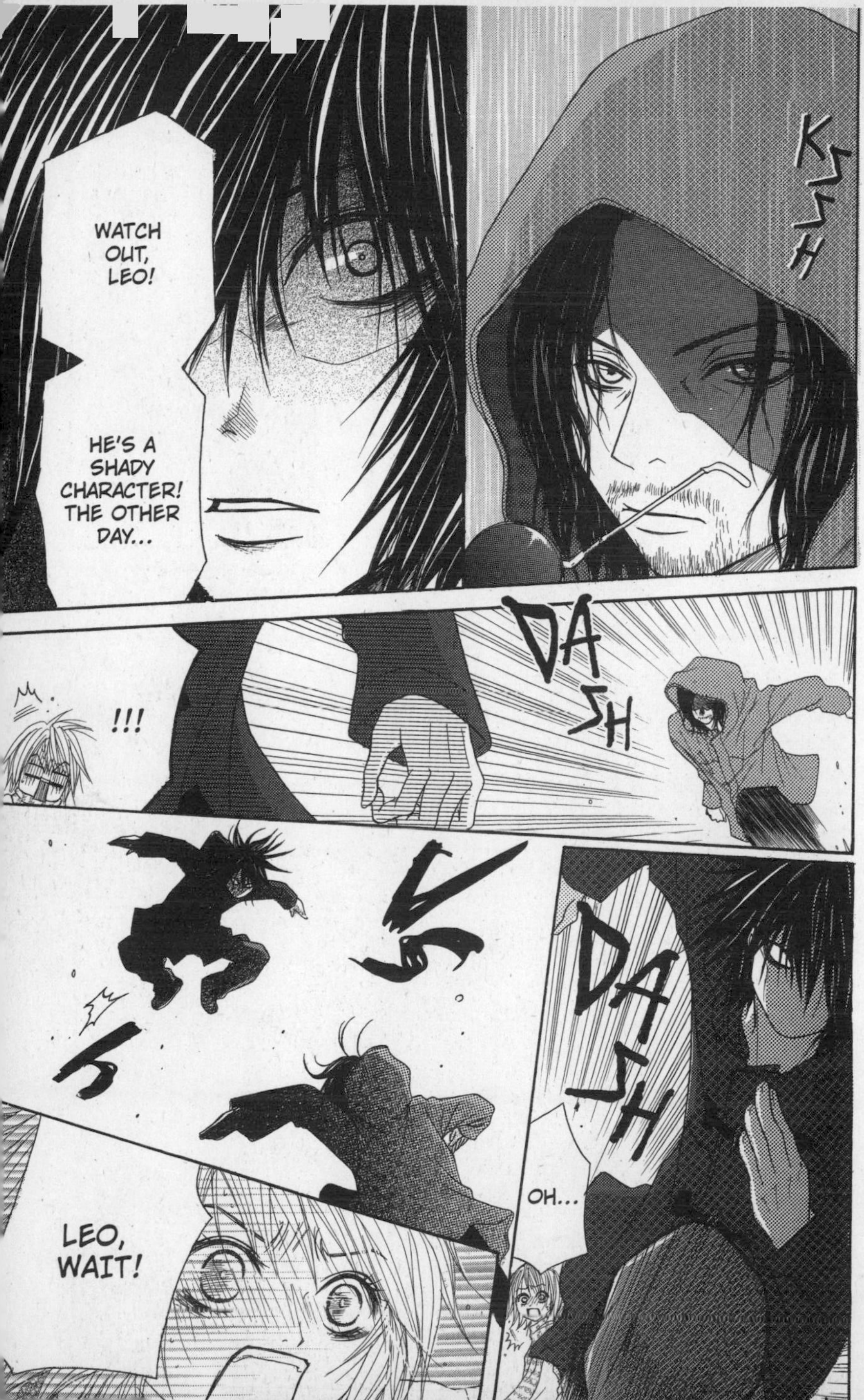
KSSH
WATCH OUT, LEO!
HE'S A SHADY CHARACTER! THE OTHER DAY...
DASH
!!!
DASH
OH...
LEO, WAIT!

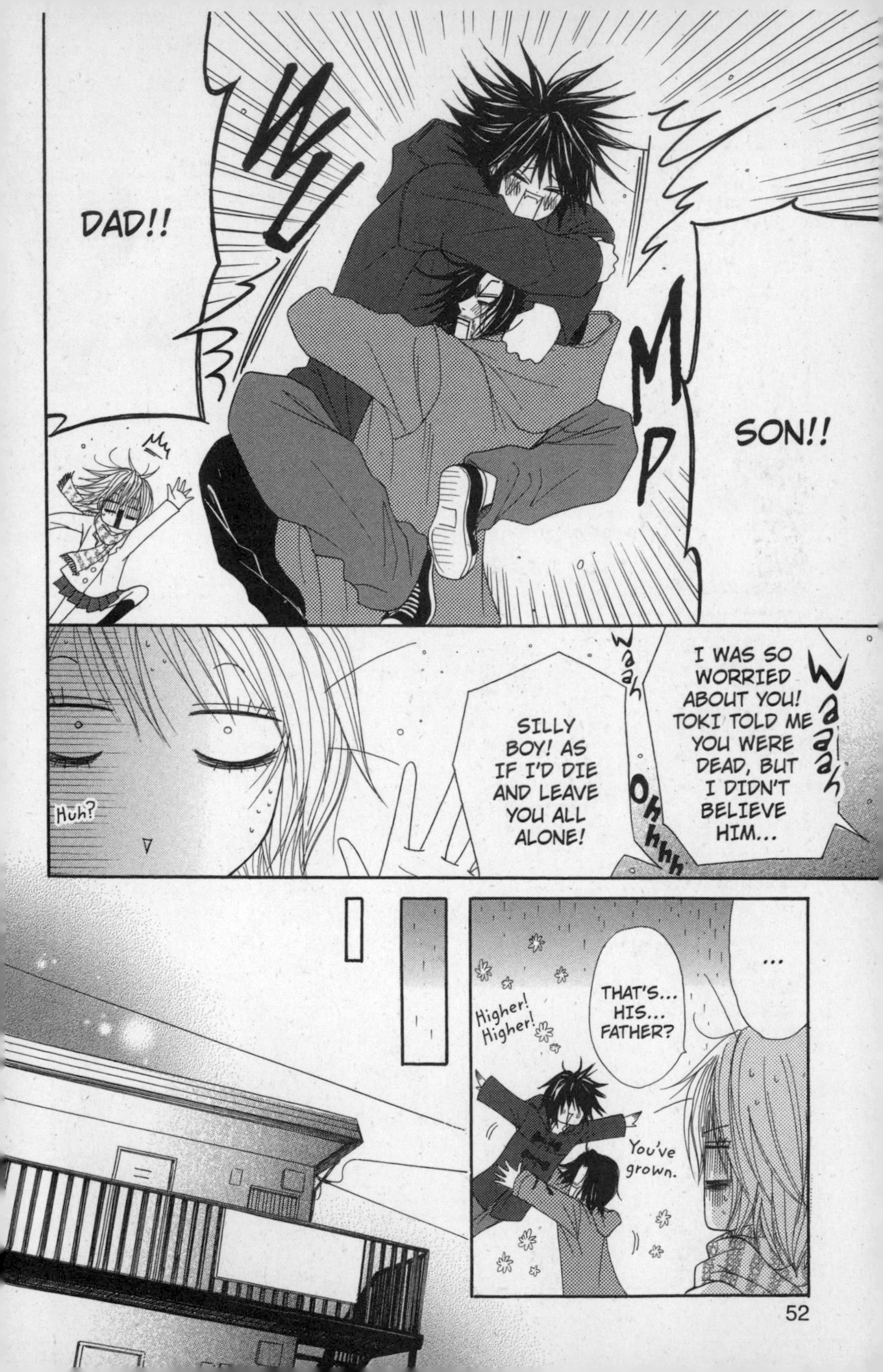
WUMP
DAD!!
SON!!
I WAS SO WORRIED ABOUT YOU! TOKI TOLD ME YOU WERE DEAD, BUT I DIDN'T BELIEVE HIM...
Waaah
Waaah
Ohhhh
SILLY BOY! AS IF I'D DIE AND LEAVE YOU ALL ALONE!
Huh?
...
THAT'S... HIS... FATHER?
You've grown.
Higher! Higher!

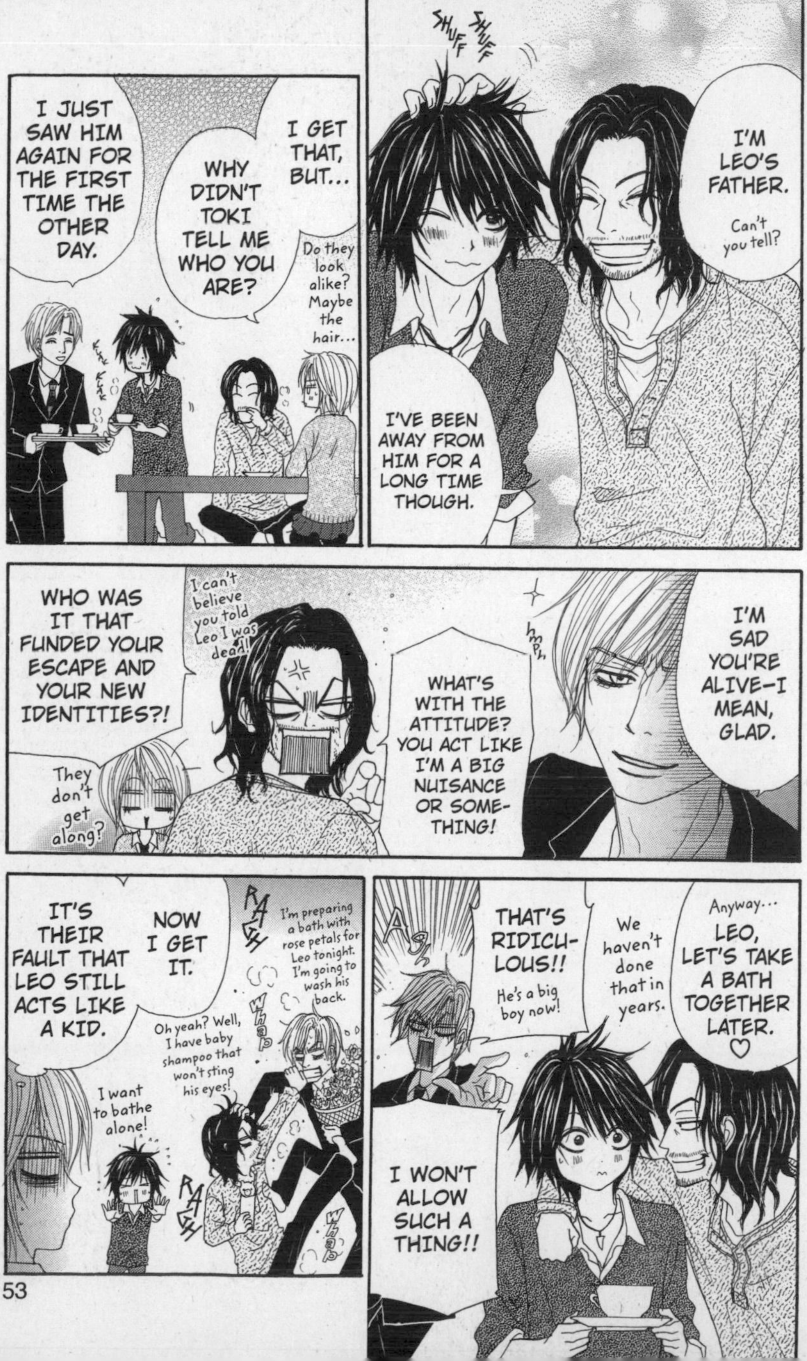
SHUFF SHUFF
I'M LEO'S FATHER.
Can't you tell?
I'VE BEEN AWAY FROM HIM FOR A LONG TIME THOUGH.
I GET THAT, BUT...
WHY DIDN'T TOKI TELL ME WHO YOU ARE?
Do they look alike? Maybe the hair...
I JUST SAW HIM AGAIN FOR THE FIRST TIME THE OTHER DAY.
KLAK KLAK
I'M SAD YOU'RE ALIVE—I MEAN, GLAD.
hmph
WHAT'S WITH THE ATTITUDE? YOU ACT LIKE I'M A BIG NUISANCE OR SOME-THING!
I can't believe you told Leo I was dead!
WHO WAS IT THAT FUNDED YOUR ESCAPE AND YOUR NEW IDENTITIES?!
They don't get along?
Anyway... LEO, LET'S TAKE A BATH TOGETHER LATER. ♡
We haven't done that in years.
THAT'S RIDICULOUS!!
He's a big boy now!
Agh
I WON'T ALLOW SUCH A THING!!
RAGH
I'm preparing a bath with rose petals for Leo tonight. I'm going to wash his back.
NOW I GET IT.
IT'S THEIR FAULT THAT LEO STILL ACTS LIKE A KID.
Oh yeah? Well, I have baby shampoo that won't sting his eyes!
whap
I want to bathe alone!
RAGH
whap

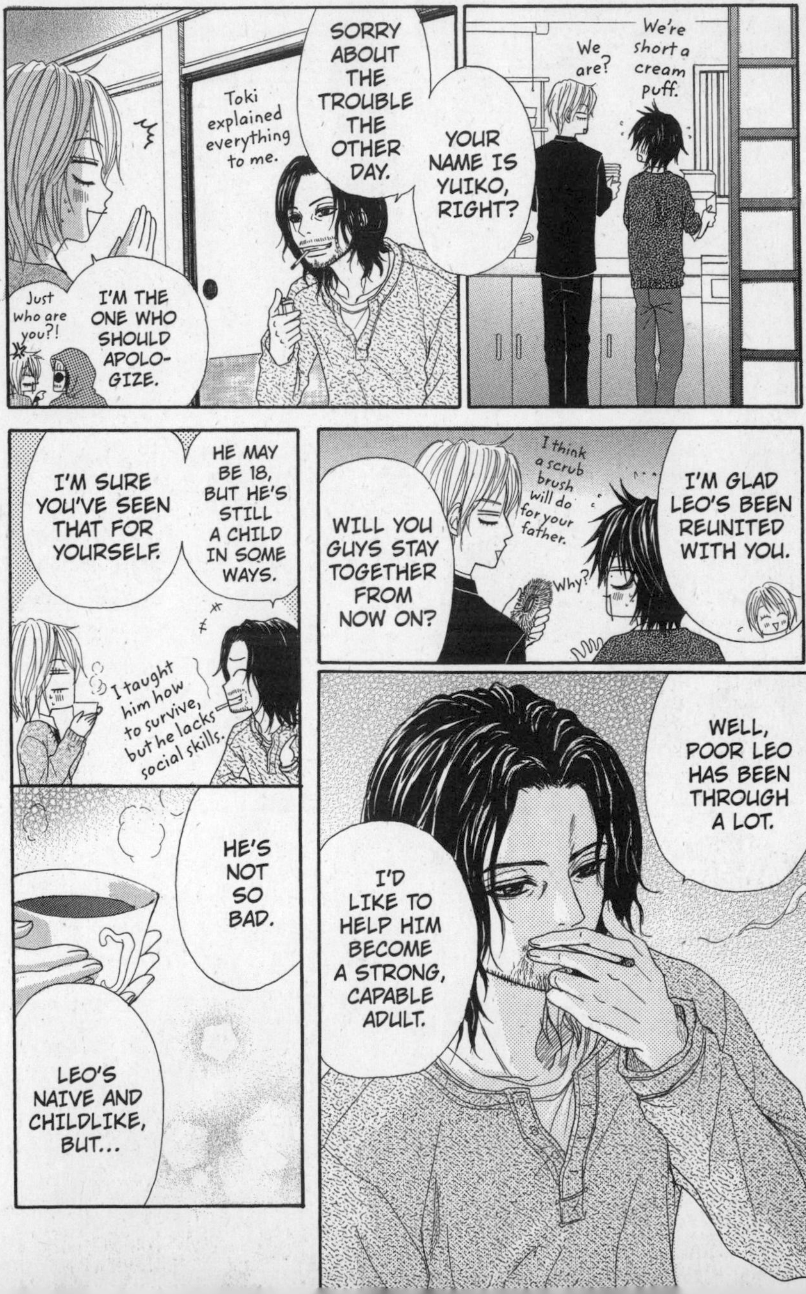
We're short a cream puff.
We are?
SORRY ABOUT THE TROUBLE THE OTHER DAY.
YOUR NAME IS YUIKO, RIGHT?
Toki explained everything to me.
I'M THE ONE WHO SHOULD APOLO-GIZE.
Just who are you?!
I'M GLAD LEO'S BEEN REUNITED WITH YOU.
I think a scrub brush will do for your father.
Why?
WILL YOU GUYS STAY TOGETHER FROM NOW ON?
HE MAY BE 18, BUT HE'S STILL A CHILD IN SOME WAYS.
I'M SURE YOU'VE SEEN THAT FOR YOURSELF.
I taught him how to survive, but he lacks social skills.
WELL, POOR LEO HAS BEEN THROUGH A LOT.
I'D LIKE TO HELP HIM BECOME A STRONG, CAPABLE ADULT.
HE'S NOT SO BAD.
LEO'S NAIVE AND CHILDLIKE, BUT...

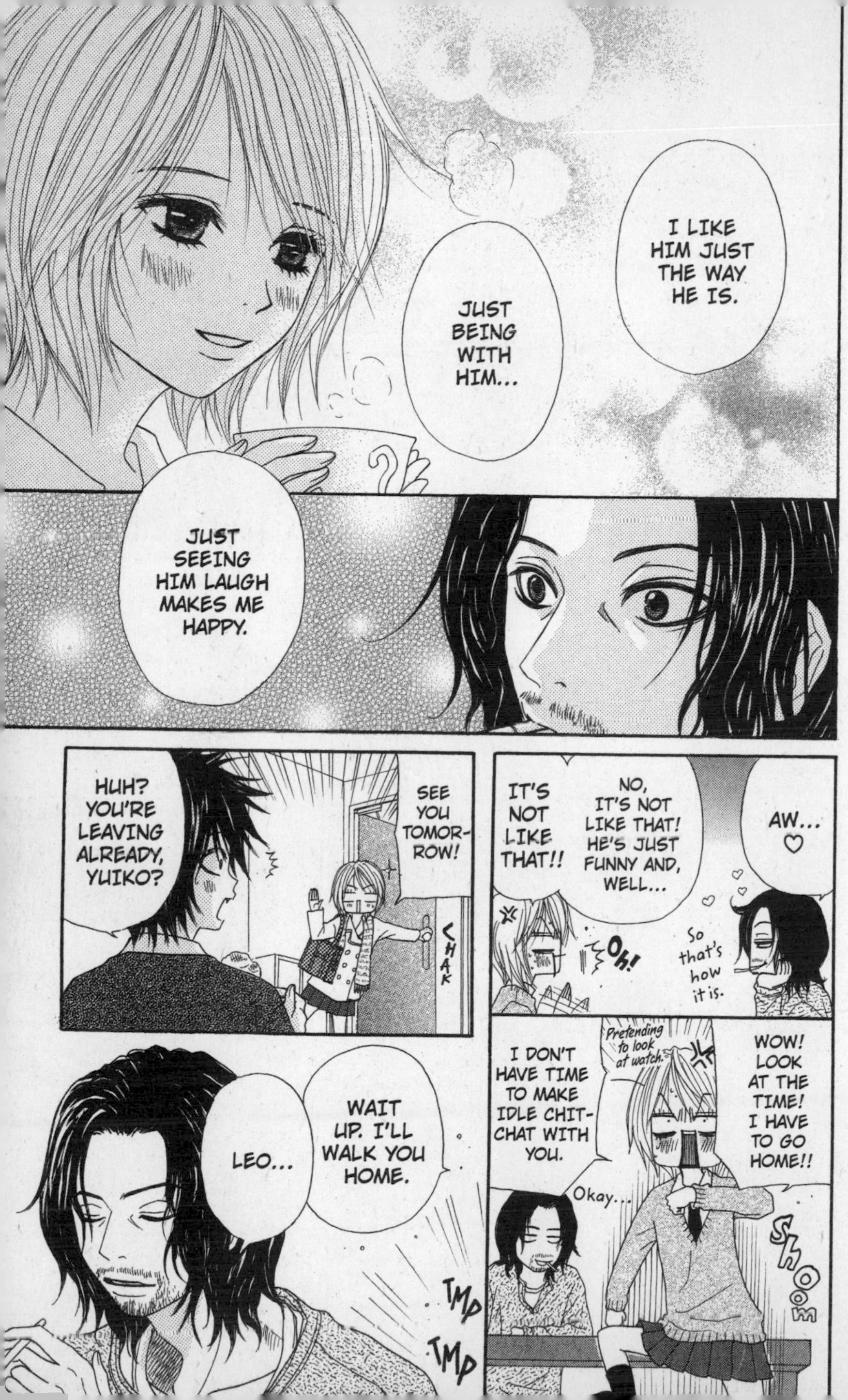
I LIKE HIM JUST THE WAY HE IS.
JUST BEING WITH HIM...
JUST SEEING HIM LAUGH MAKES ME HAPPY.
AW... ♡
NO, IT'S NOT LIKE THAT! HE'S JUST FUNNY AND, WELL...
IT'S NOT LIKE THAT!!
Oh!
So that's how it is.
WOW! LOOK AT THE TIME! I HAVE TO GO HOME!!
Pretending to look at watch.
I DON'T HAVE TIME TO MAKE IDLE CHIT-CHAT WITH YOU.
Okay...
SHOOM
SEE YOU TOMOR-ROW!
HUH? YOU'RE LEAVING ALREADY, YUIKO?
CHAK
WAIT UP. I'LL WALK YOU HOME.
LEO...
TMP
TMP

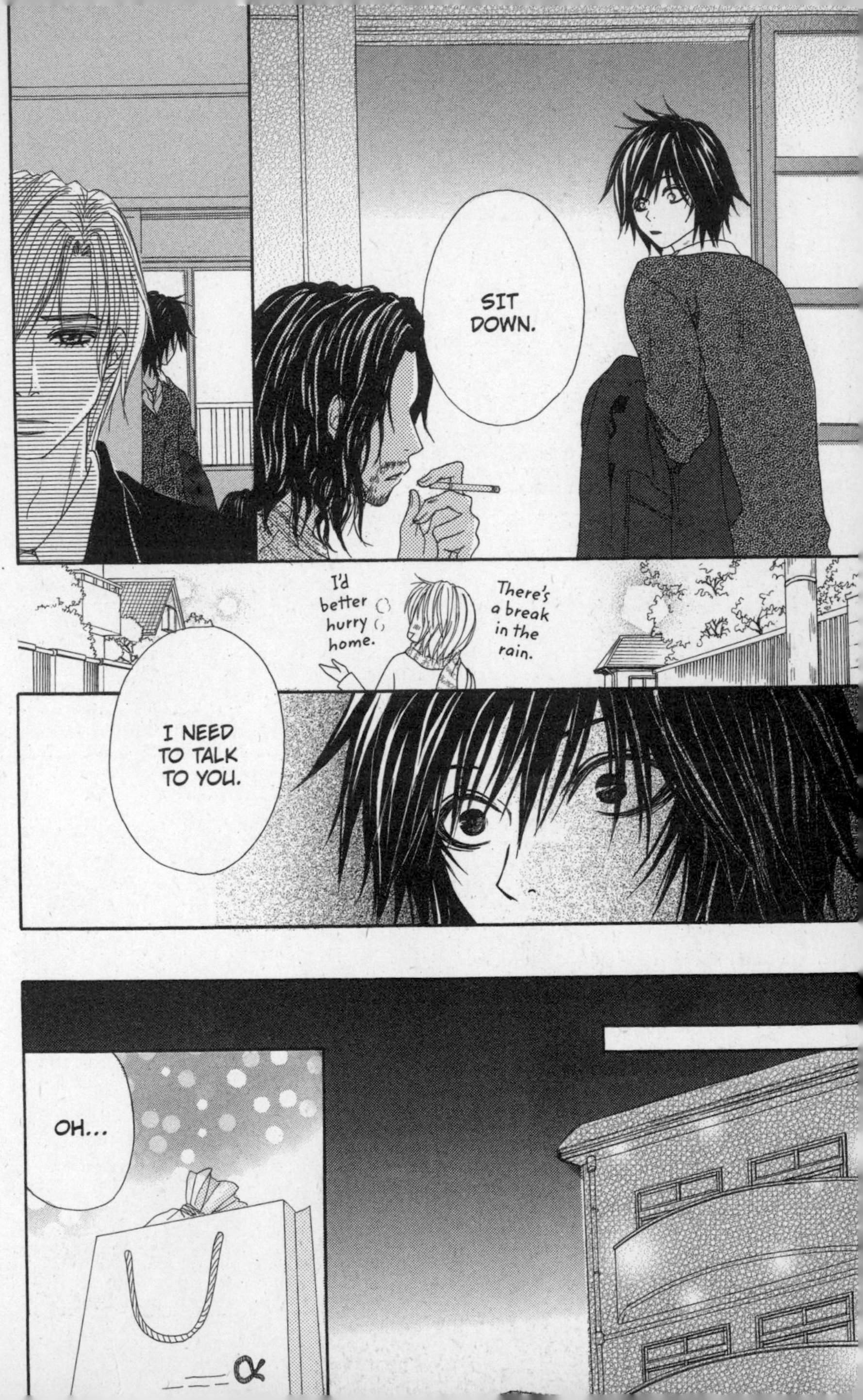
SIT DOWN.
There's a break in the rain.
I'd better hurry home.
I NEED TO TALK TO YOU.
OH...

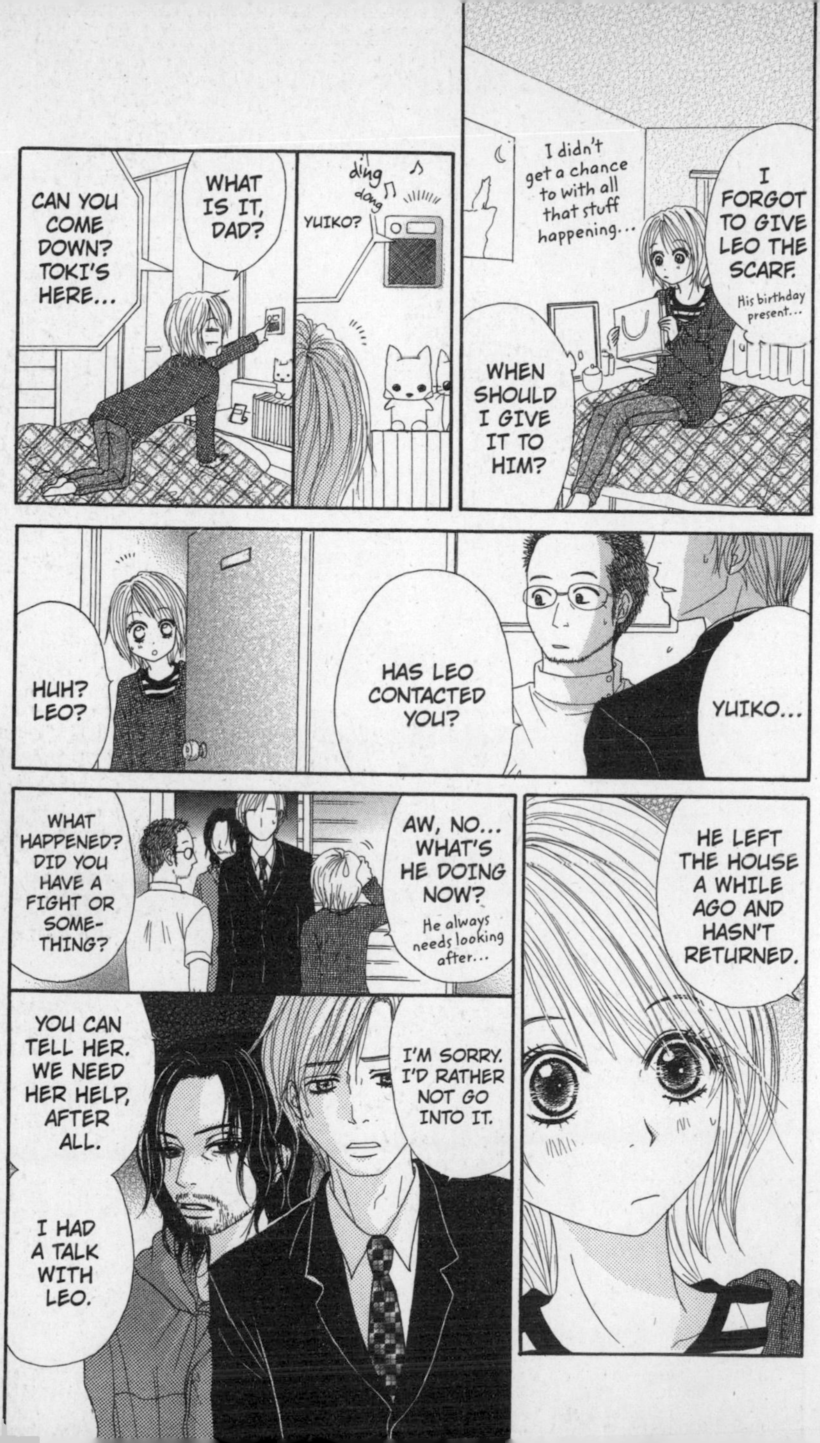
I FORGOT TO GIVE LEO THE SCARF.
His birthday present...
I didn't get a chance to with all that stuff happening...
WHEN SHOULD I GIVE IT TO HIM?
ding dong
YUIKO?
WHAT IS IT, DAD?
CAN YOU COME DOWN? TOKI'S HERE...
YUIKO...
HAS LEO CONTACTED YOU?
HUH? LEO?
HE LEFT THE HOUSE A WHILE AGO AND HASN'T RETURNED.
AW, NO... WHAT'S HE DOING NOW?
He always needs looking after...
WHAT HAPPENED? DID YOU HAVE A FIGHT OR SOME-THING?
I'M SORRY. I'D RATHER NOT GO INTO IT.
YOU CAN TELL HER. WE NEED HER HELP, AFTER ALL.
I HAD A TALK WITH LEO.

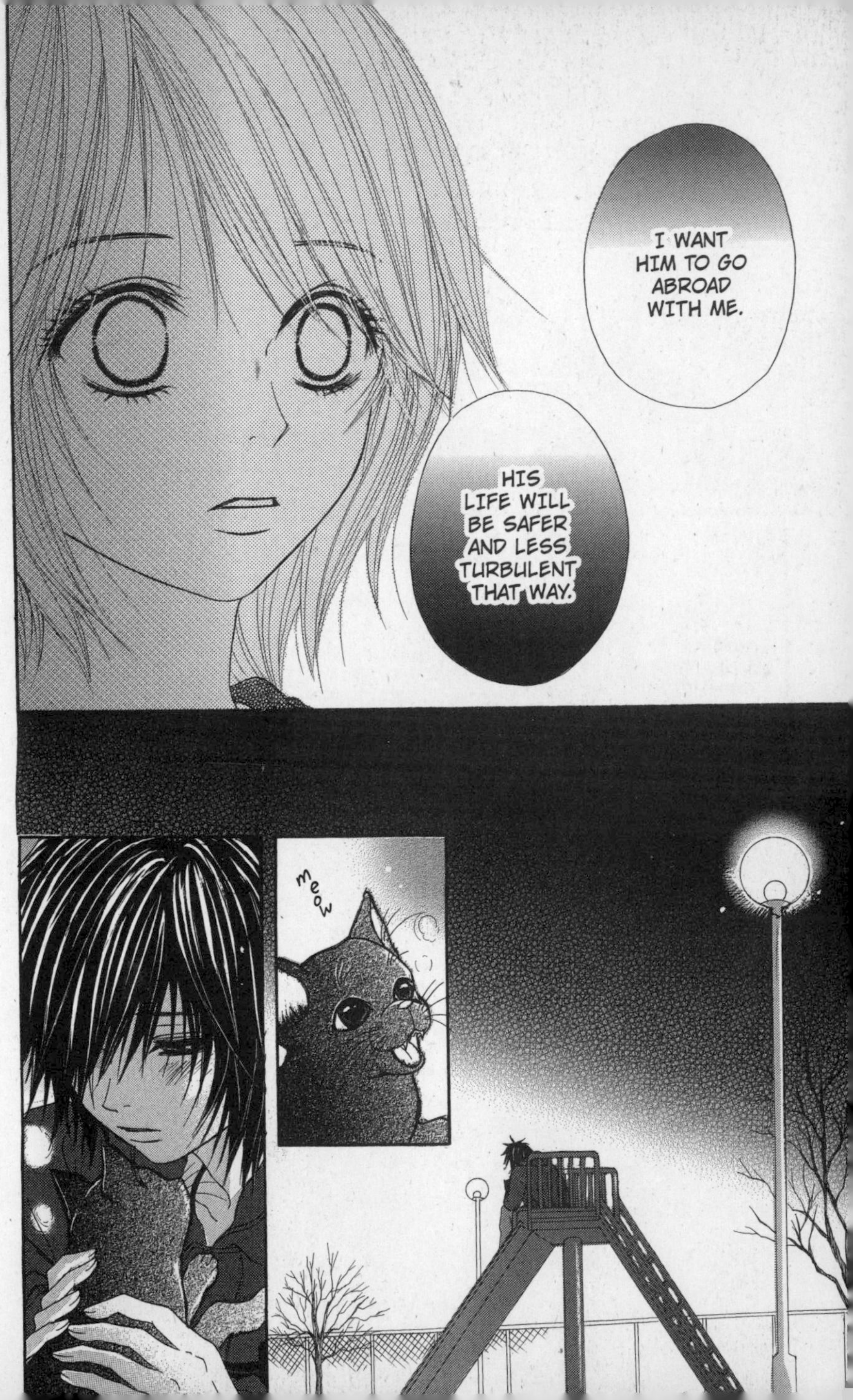
I WANT HIM TO GO ABROAD WITH ME.
HIS LIFE WILL BE SAFER AND LESS TURBULENT THAT WAY.
meow

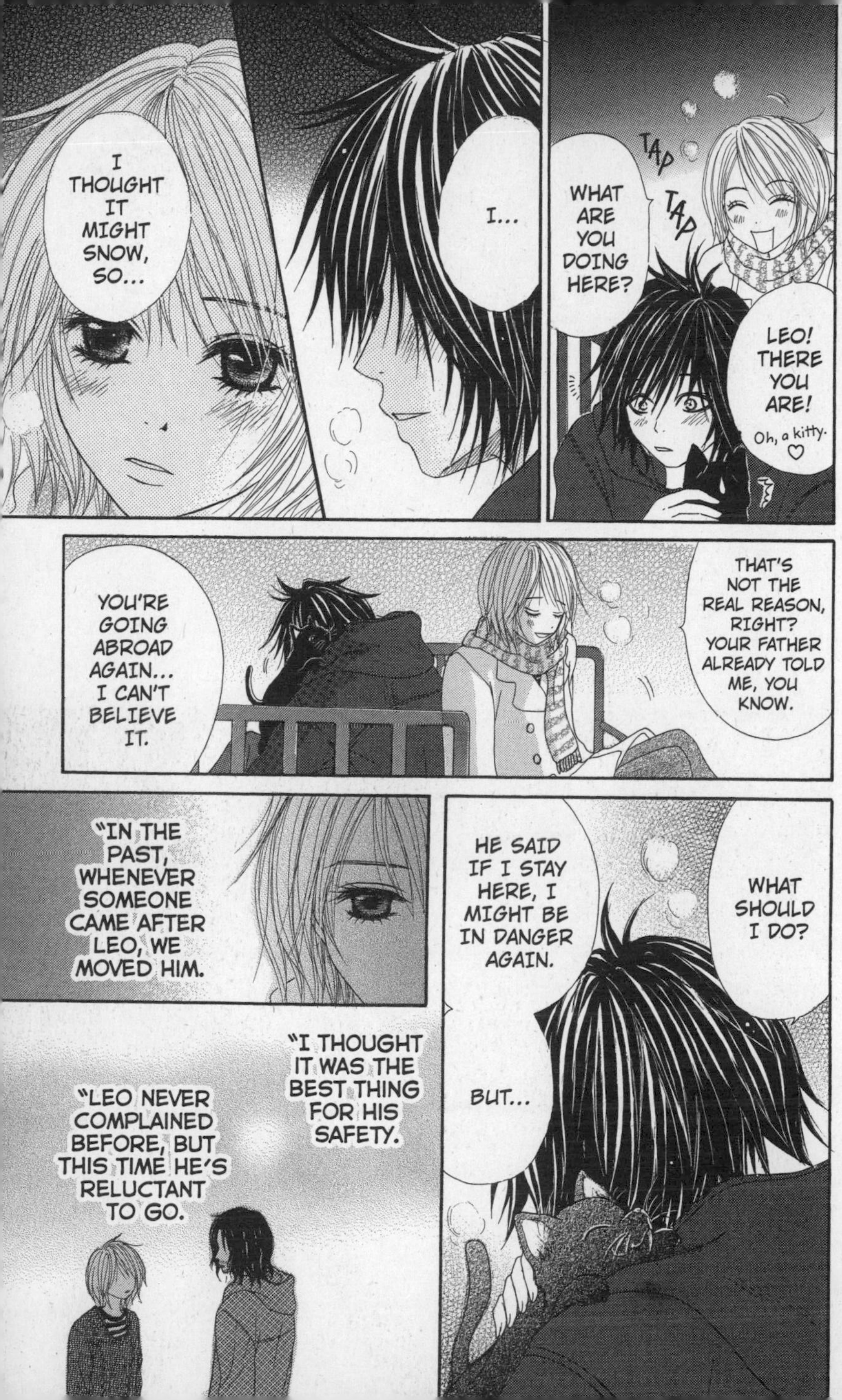
TAP
TAP
LEO! THERE YOU ARE!
Oh, a kitty. ♡
WHAT ARE YOU DOING HERE?
I...
I THOUGHT IT MIGHT SNOW, SO...
THAT'S NOT THE REAL REASON, RIGHT? YOUR FATHER ALREADY TOLD ME, YOU KNOW.
YOU'RE GOING ABROAD AGAIN... I CAN'T BELIEVE IT.
WHAT SHOULD I DO?
HE SAID IF I STAY HERE, I MIGHT BE IN DANGER AGAIN.
BUT...
"IN THE PAST, WHENEVER SOMEONE CAME AFTER LEO, WE MOVED HIM.
"I THOUGHT IT WAS THE BEST THING FOR HIS SAFETY.
"LEO NEVER COMPLAINED BEFORE, BUT THIS TIME HE'S RELUCTANT TO GO.

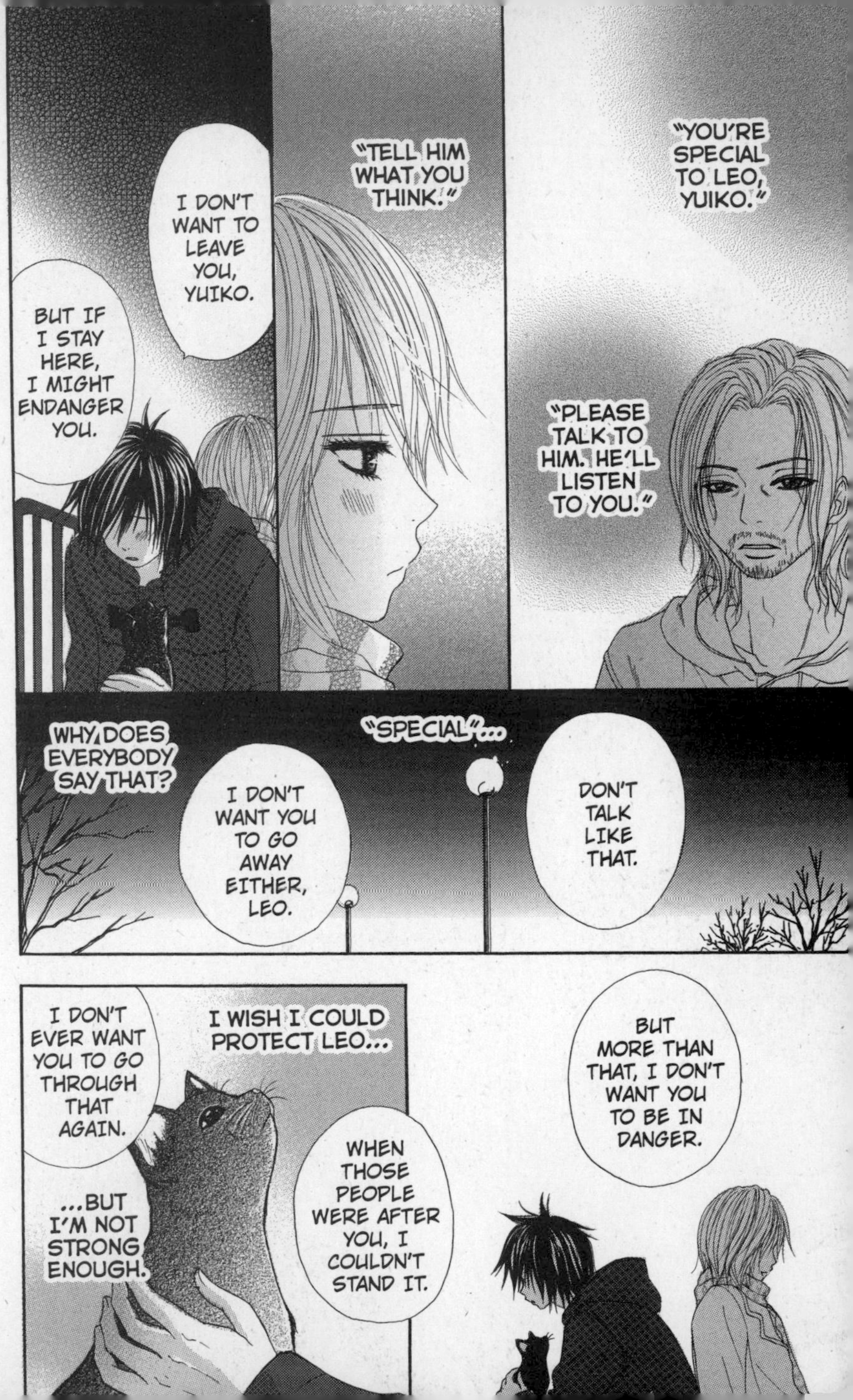
"YOU'RE SPECIAL TO LEO, YUIKO."
"PLEASE TALK TO HIM. HE'LL LISTEN TO YOU."
"TELL HIM WHAT YOU THINK."
I DON'T WANT TO LEAVE YOU, YUIKO.
BUT IF I STAY HERE, I MIGHT ENDANGER YOU.
DON'T TALK LIKE THAT.
"SPECIAL"...
WHY DOES EVERYBODY SAY THAT?
I DON'T WANT YOU TO GO AWAY EITHER, LEO.
BUT MORE THAN THAT, I DON'T WANT YOU TO BE IN DANGER.
I WISH I COULD PROTECT LEO...
WHEN THOSE PEOPLE WERE AFTER YOU, I COULDN'T STAND IT.
I DON'T EVER WANT YOU TO GO THROUGH THAT AGAIN.
...BUT I'M NOT STRONG ENOUGH.

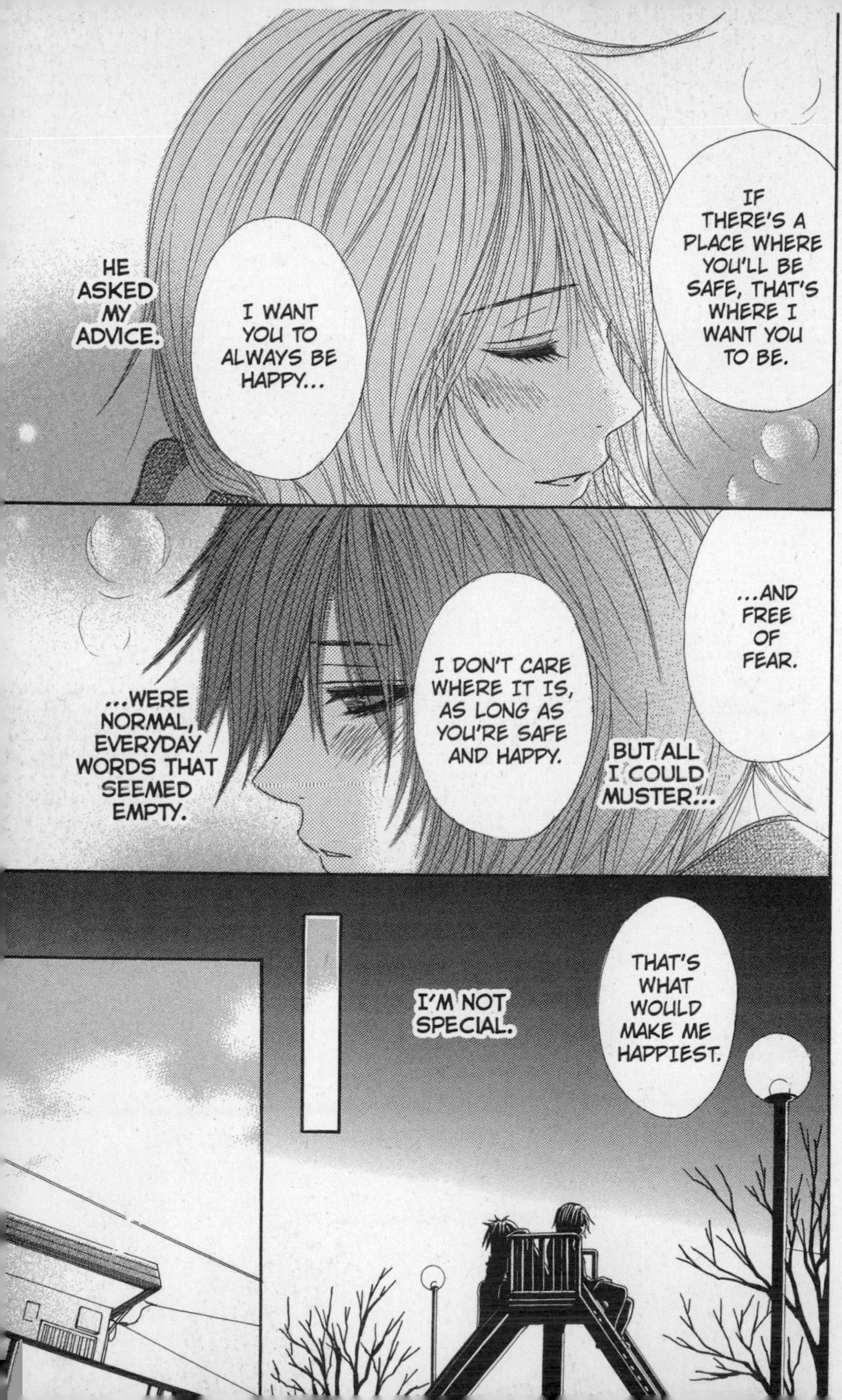
IF THERE'S A PLACE WHERE YOU'LL BE SAFE, THAT'S WHERE I WANT YOU TO BE.
I WANT YOU TO ALWAYS BE HAPPY...
HE ASKED MY ADVICE.
...AND FREE OF FEAR.
BUT ALL I COULD MUSTER...
I DON'T CARE WHERE IT IS, AS LONG AS YOU'RE SAFE AND HAPPY.
...WERE NORMAL, EVERYDAY WORDS THAT SEEMED EMPTY.
THAT'S WHAT WOULD MAKE ME HAPPIEST.
I'M NOT SPECIAL.

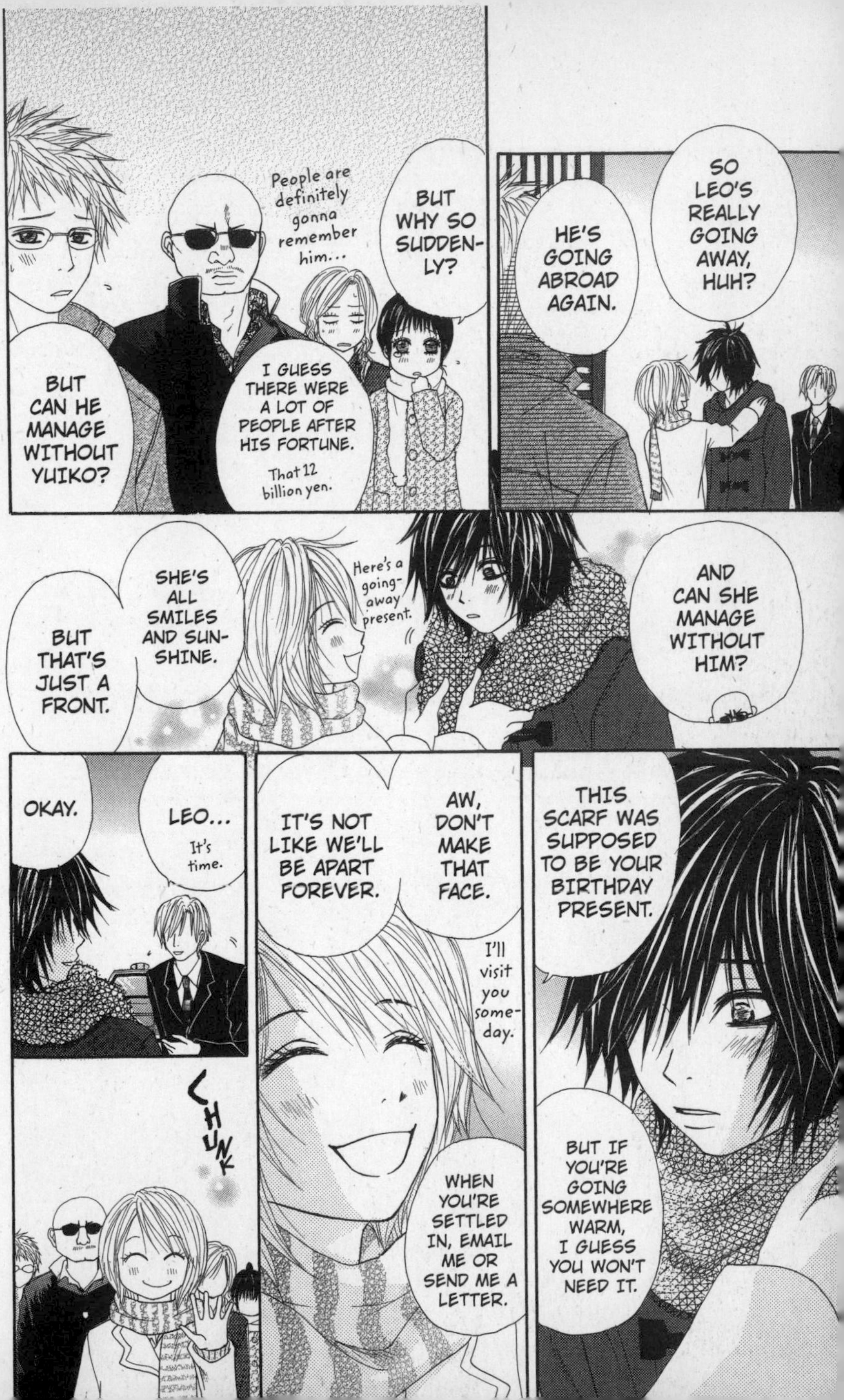
SO LEO'S REALLY GOING AWAY, HUH?
HE'S GOING ABROAD AGAIN.
BUT WHY SO SUDDEN-LY?
People are definitely gonna remember him...
I GUESS THERE WERE A LOT OF PEOPLE AFTER HIS FORTUNE.
That 12 billion yen.
BUT CAN HE MANAGE WITHOUT YUIKO?
AND CAN SHE MANAGE WITHOUT HIM?
Here's a going-away present.
SHE'S ALL SMILES AND SUN-SHINE.
BUT THAT'S JUST A FRONT.
THIS SCARF WAS SUPPOSED TO BE YOUR BIRTHDAY PRESENT.
BUT IF YOU'RE GOING SOMEWHERE WARM, I GUESS YOU WON'T NEED IT.
AW, DON'T MAKE THAT FACE.
IT'S NOT LIKE WE'LL BE APART FOREVER.
I'll visit you someday.
WHEN YOU'RE SETTLED IN, EMAIL ME OR SEND ME A LETTER.
LEO...
It's time.
OKAY.
CHUNK

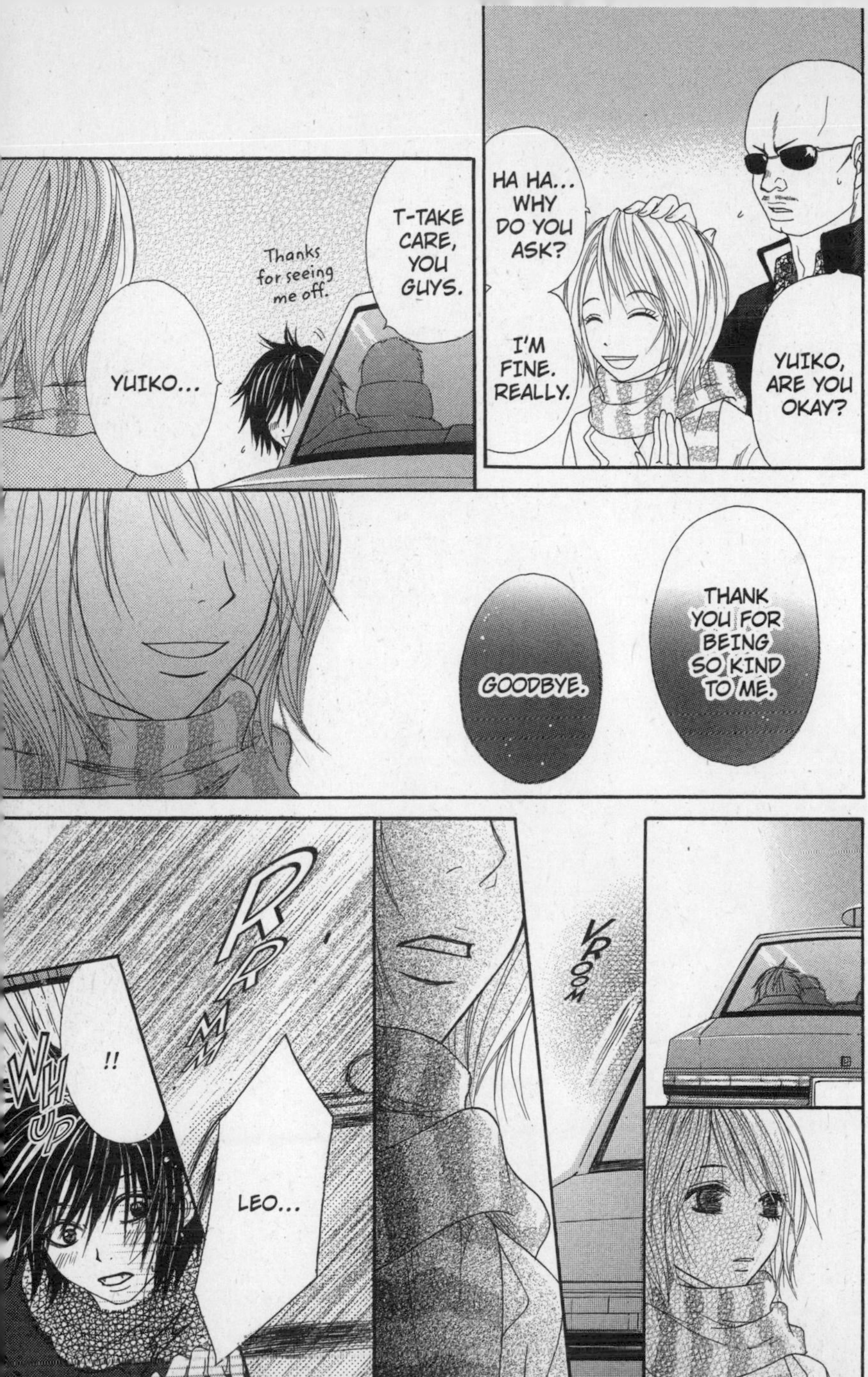
YUIKO, ARE YOU OKAY?
HA HA... WHY DO YOU ASK?
I'M FINE. REALLY.
T-TAKE CARE, YOU GUYS.
Thanks for seeing me off.
YUIKO...
THANK YOU FOR BEING SO KIND TO ME.
GOODBYE.
VROOM
RRRMMM
!!
WHUP
LEO...

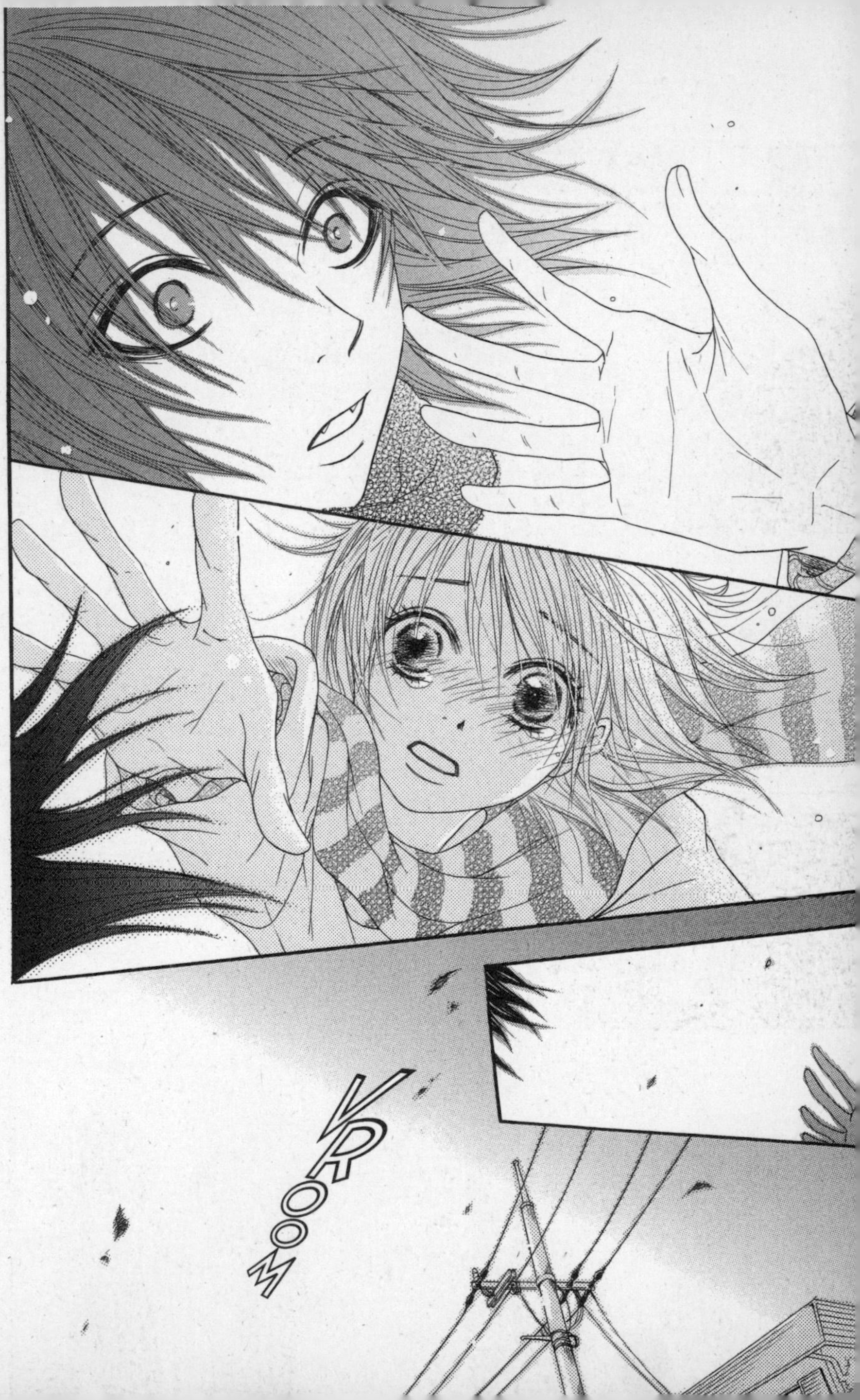
VROOM

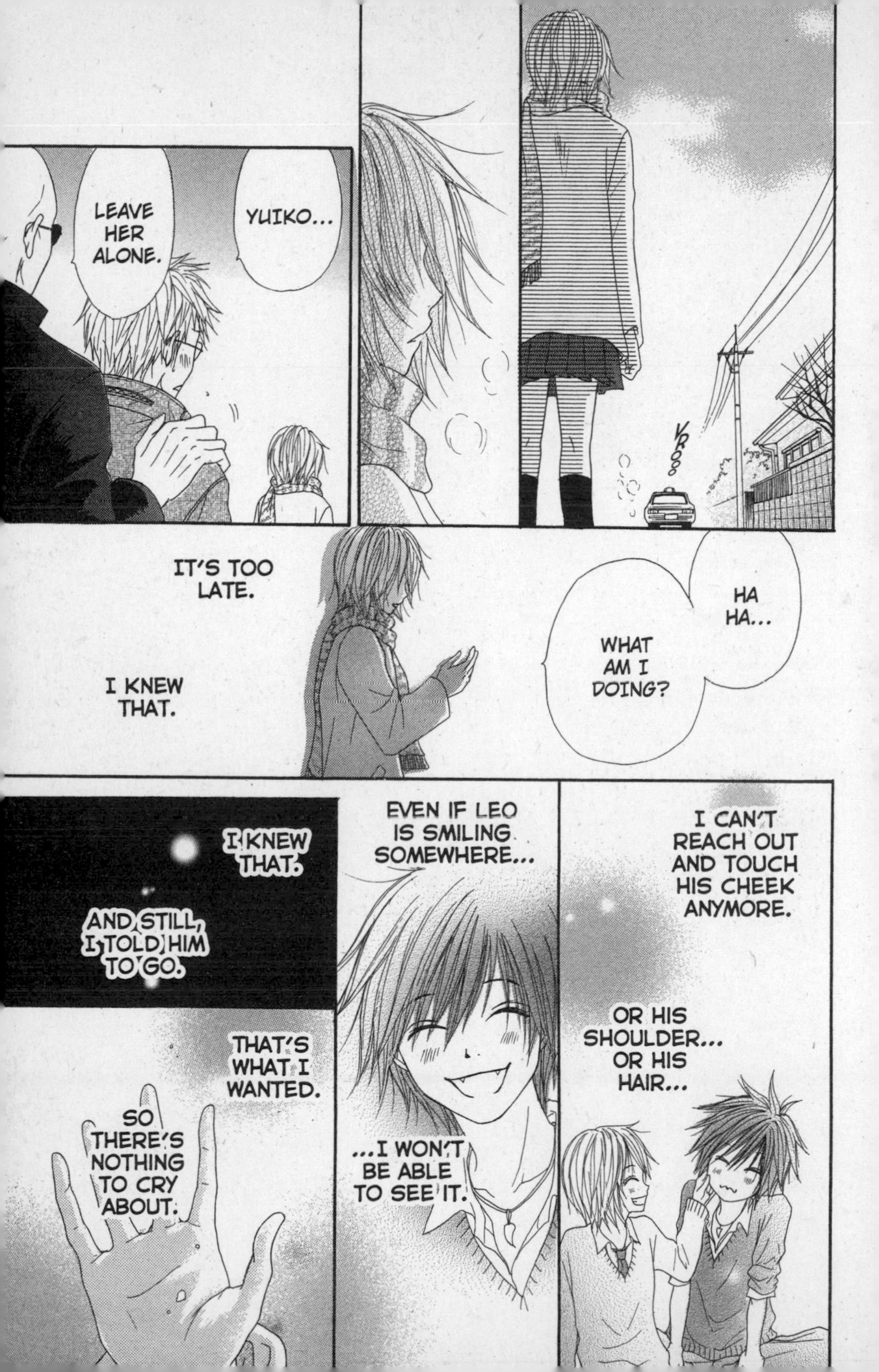
VROOO
YUIKO...
LEAVE HER ALONE.
HA HA...
WHAT AM I DOING?
IT'S TOO LATE.
I KNEW THAT.
I CAN'T REACH OUT AND TOUCH HIS CHEEK ANYMORE.
OR HIS SHOULDER... OR HIS HAIR...
EVEN IF LEO IS SMILING SOMEWHERE...
...I WON'T BE ABLE TO SEE IT.
I KNEW THAT.
AND STILL, I TOLD HIM TO GO.
THAT'S WHAT I WANTED.
SO THERE'S NOTHING TO CRY ABOUT.

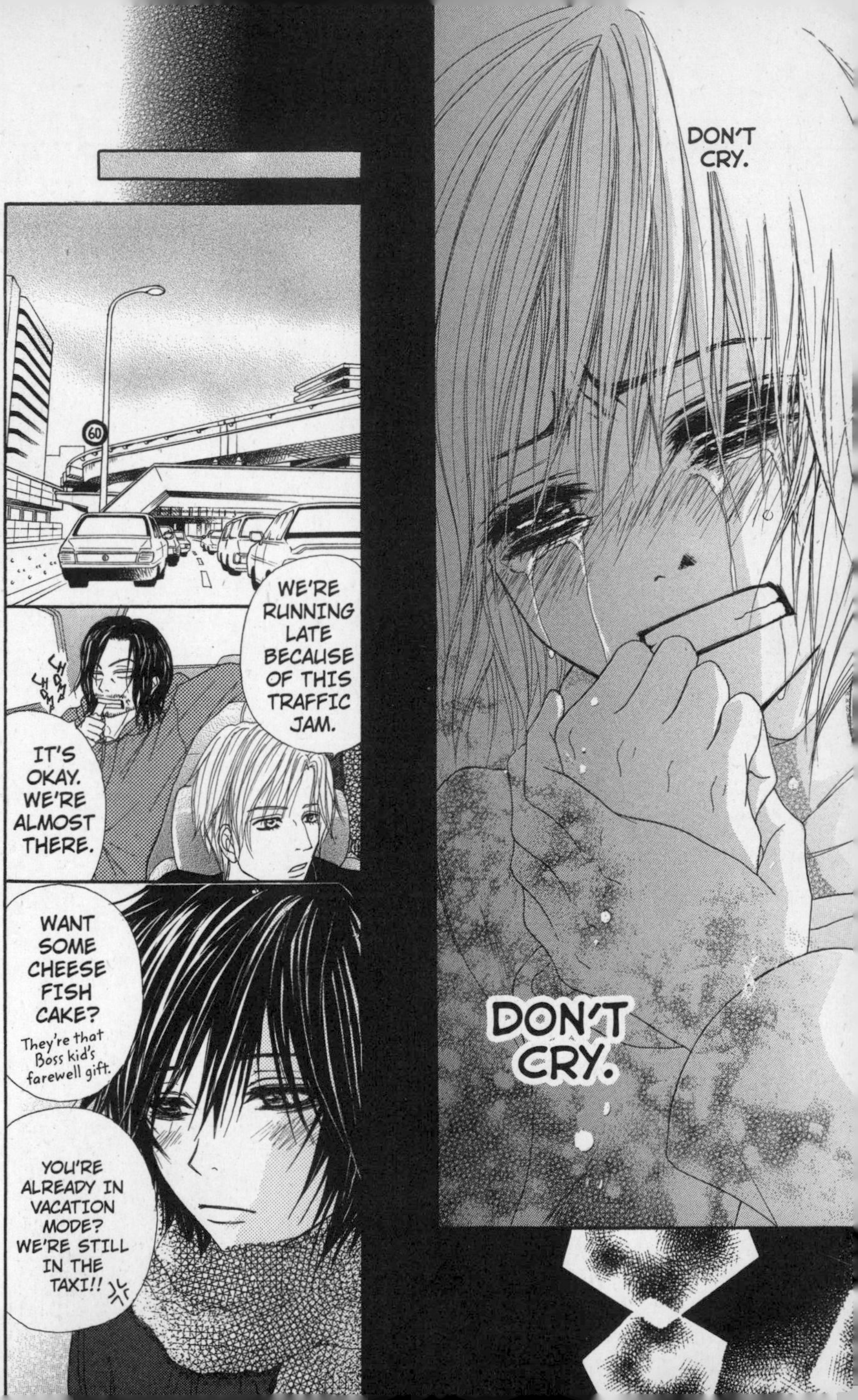
DON'T CRY.
DON'T CRY.
WE'RE RUNNING LATE BECAUSE OF THIS TRAFFIC JAM.
CHOMP CHOMP
IT'S OKAY. WE'RE ALMOST THERE.
WANT SOME CHEESE FISH CAKE?
They're that Boss kid's farewell gift.
YOU'RE ALREADY IN VACATION MODE? WE'RE STILL IN THE TAXI!!

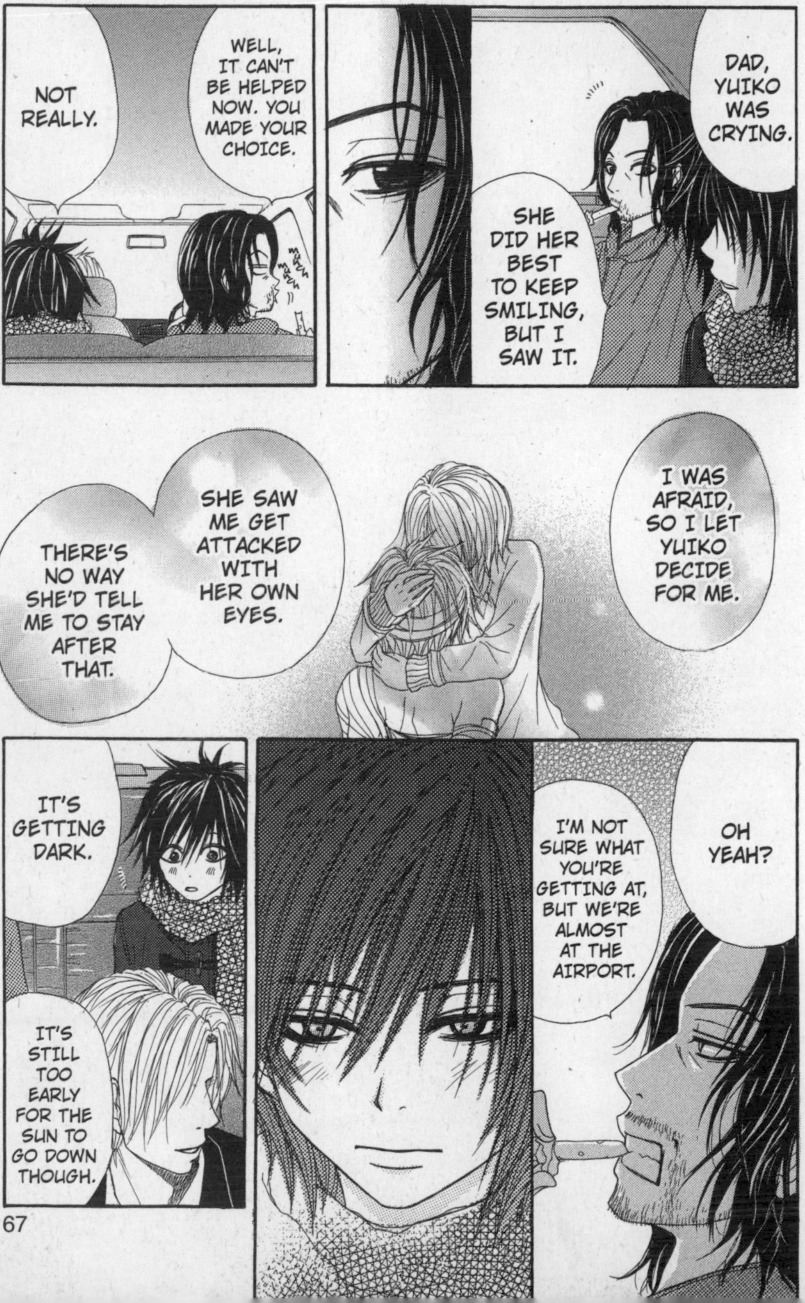
DAD, YUIKO WAS CRYING.
SHE DID HER BEST TO KEEP SMILING, BUT I SAW IT.
WELL, IT CAN'T BE HELPED NOW. YOU MADE YOUR CHOICE.
NOT REALLY.
I WAS AFRAID, SO I LET YUIKO DECIDE FOR ME.
SHE SAW ME GET ATTACKED WITH HER OWN EYES.
THERE'S NO WAY SHE'D TELL ME TO STAY AFTER THAT.
OH YEAH?
I'M NOT SURE WHAT YOU'RE GETTING AT, BUT WE'RE ALMOST AT THE AIRPORT.
IT'S GETTING DARK.
IT'S STILL TOO EARLY FOR THE SUN TO GO DOWN THOUGH.

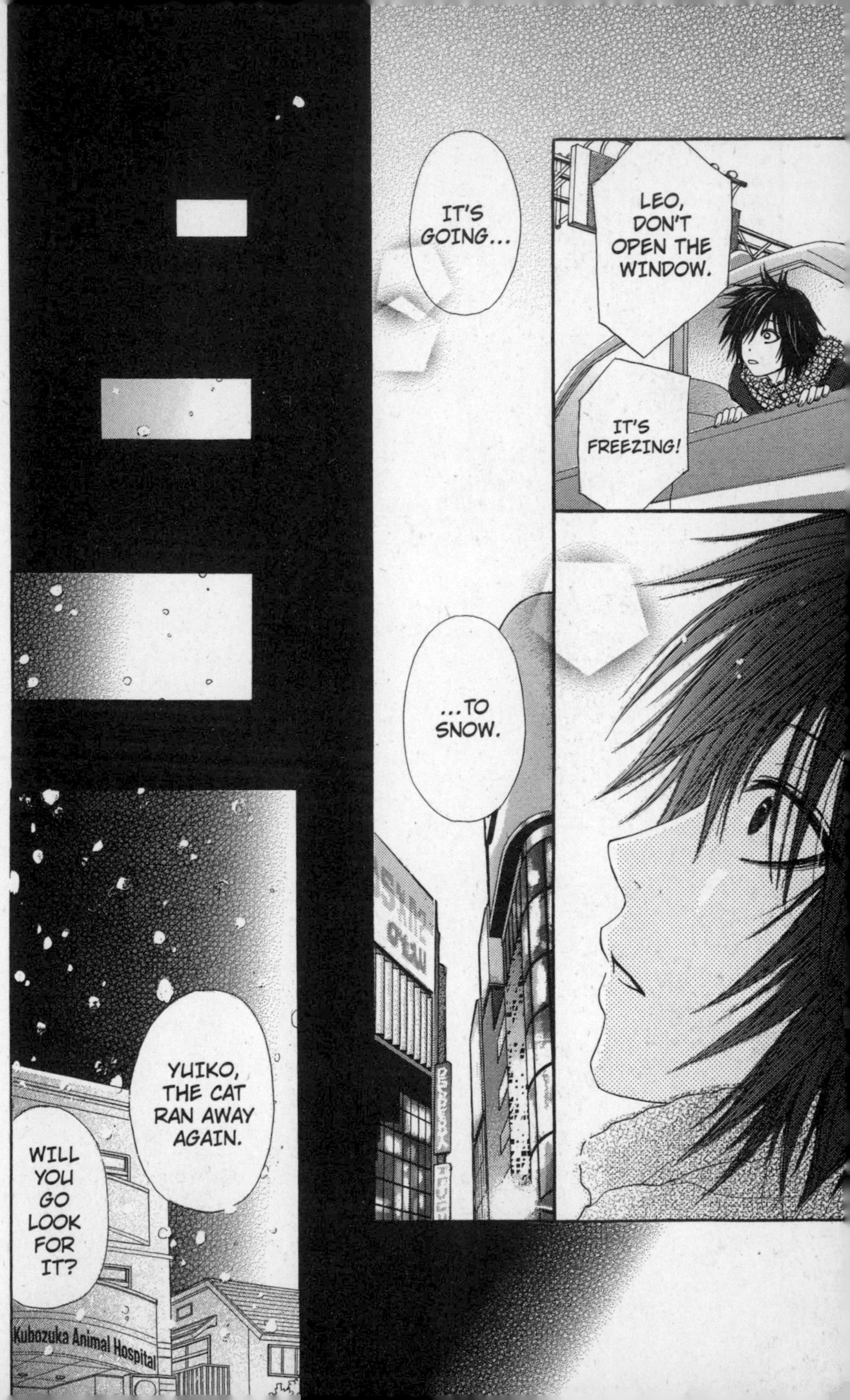
LEO, DON'T OPEN THE WINDOW.
IT'S FREEZING!
IT'S GOING...
...TO SNOW.
YUIKO, THE CAT RAN AWAY AGAIN.
WILL YOU GO LOOK FOR IT?
Kubozuka Animal Hospital

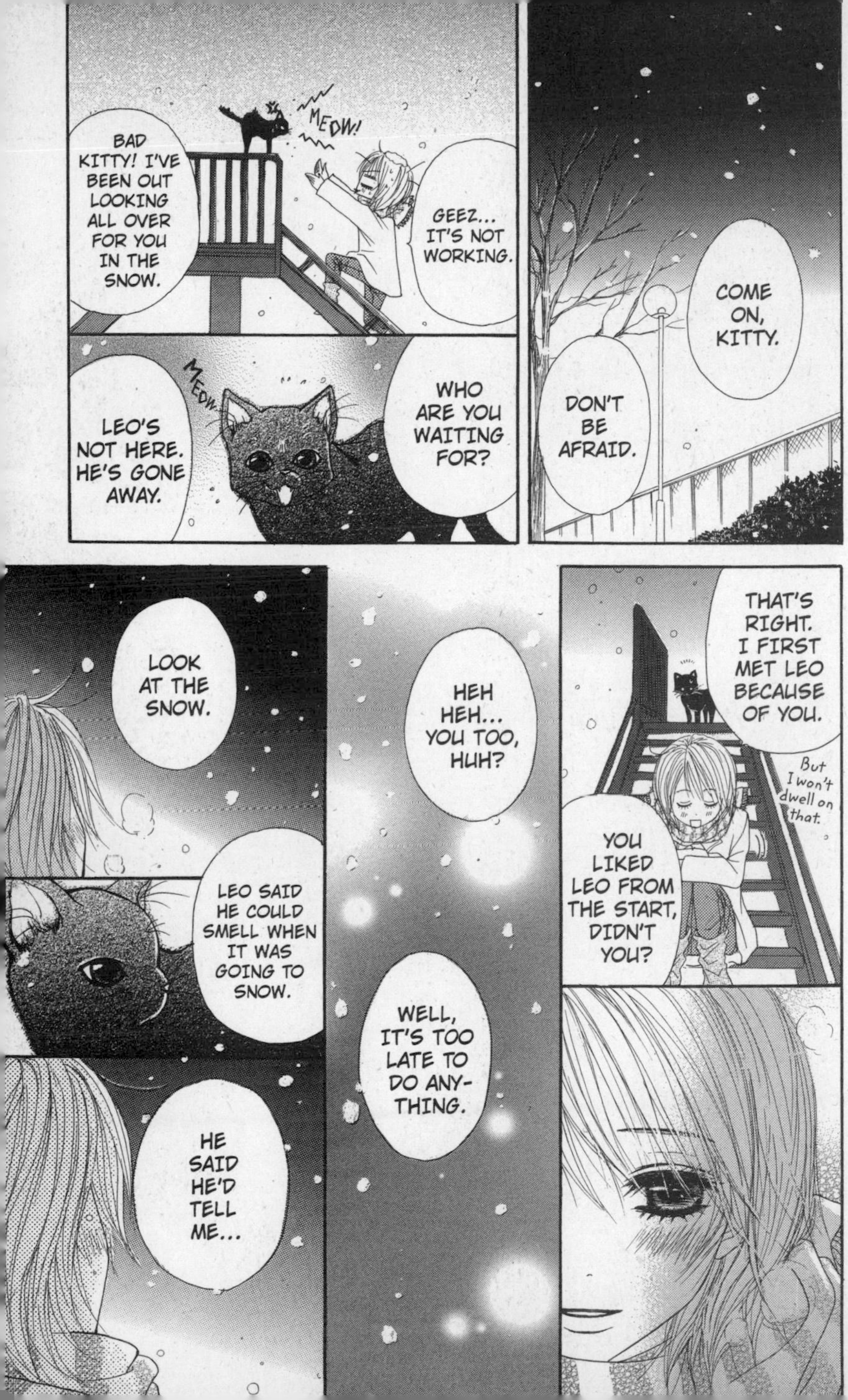
COME ON, KITTY.
DON'T BE AFRAID.
MEOW!
GEEZ... IT'S NOT WORKING.
BAD KITTY! I'VE BEEN OUT LOOKING ALL OVER FOR YOU IN THE SNOW.
WHO ARE YOU WAITING FOR?
MEOW
LEO'S NOT HERE. HE'S GONE AWAY.
THAT'S RIGHT. I FIRST MET LEO BECAUSE OF YOU.
But I won't dwell on that.
YOU LIKED LEO FROM THE START, DIDN'T YOU?
HEH HEH... YOU TOO, HUH?
WELL, IT'S TOO LATE TO DO ANY-THING.
LOOK AT THE SNOW.
LEO SAID HE COULD SMELL WHEN IT WAS GOING TO SNOW.
HE SAID HE'D TELL ME...

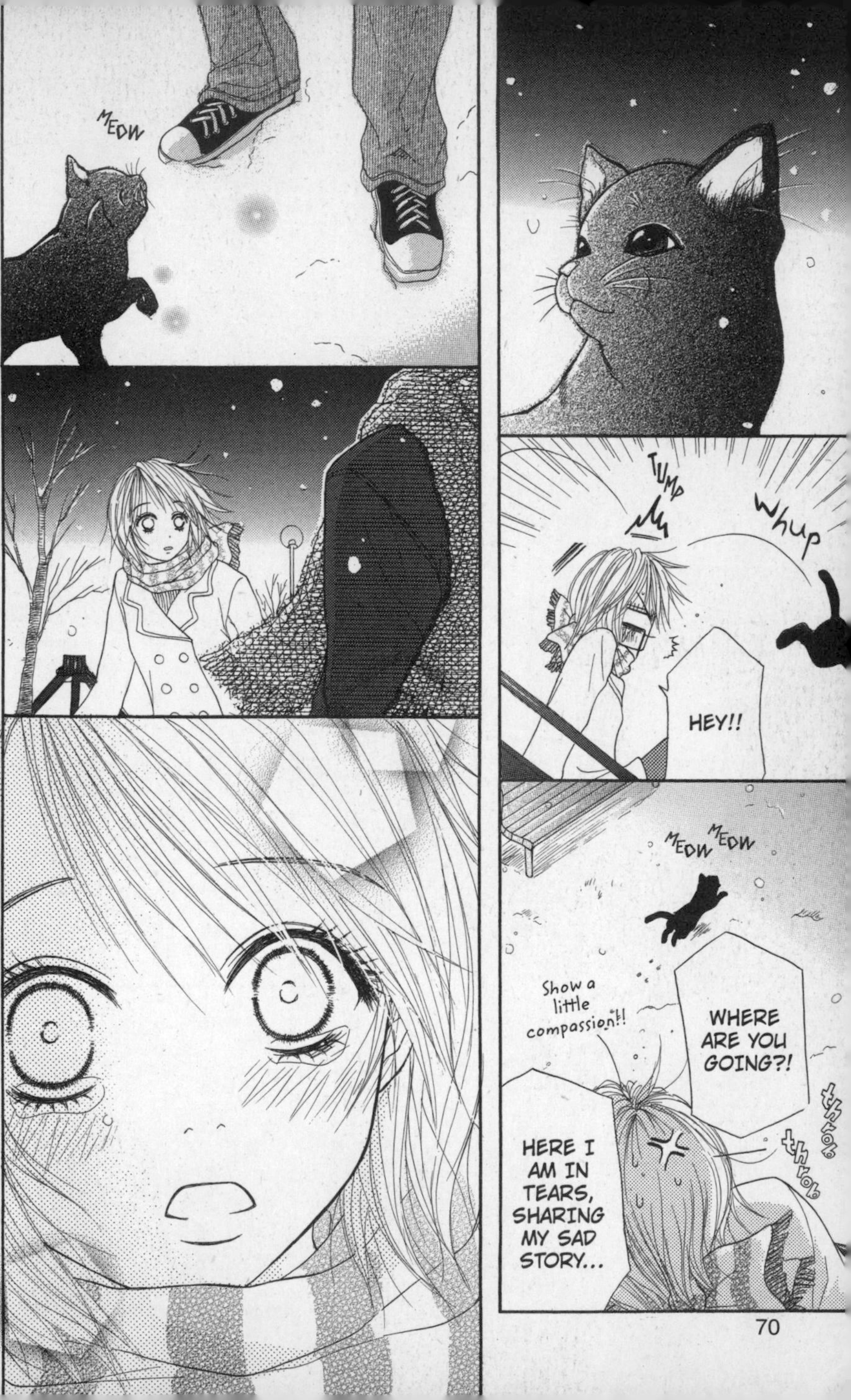
TUMP
whup
HEY!!
MEOW MEOW
WHERE ARE YOU GOING?!
Show a little compassion!!
HERE I AM IN TEARS, SHARING MY SAD STORY...
throb throb
MEOW

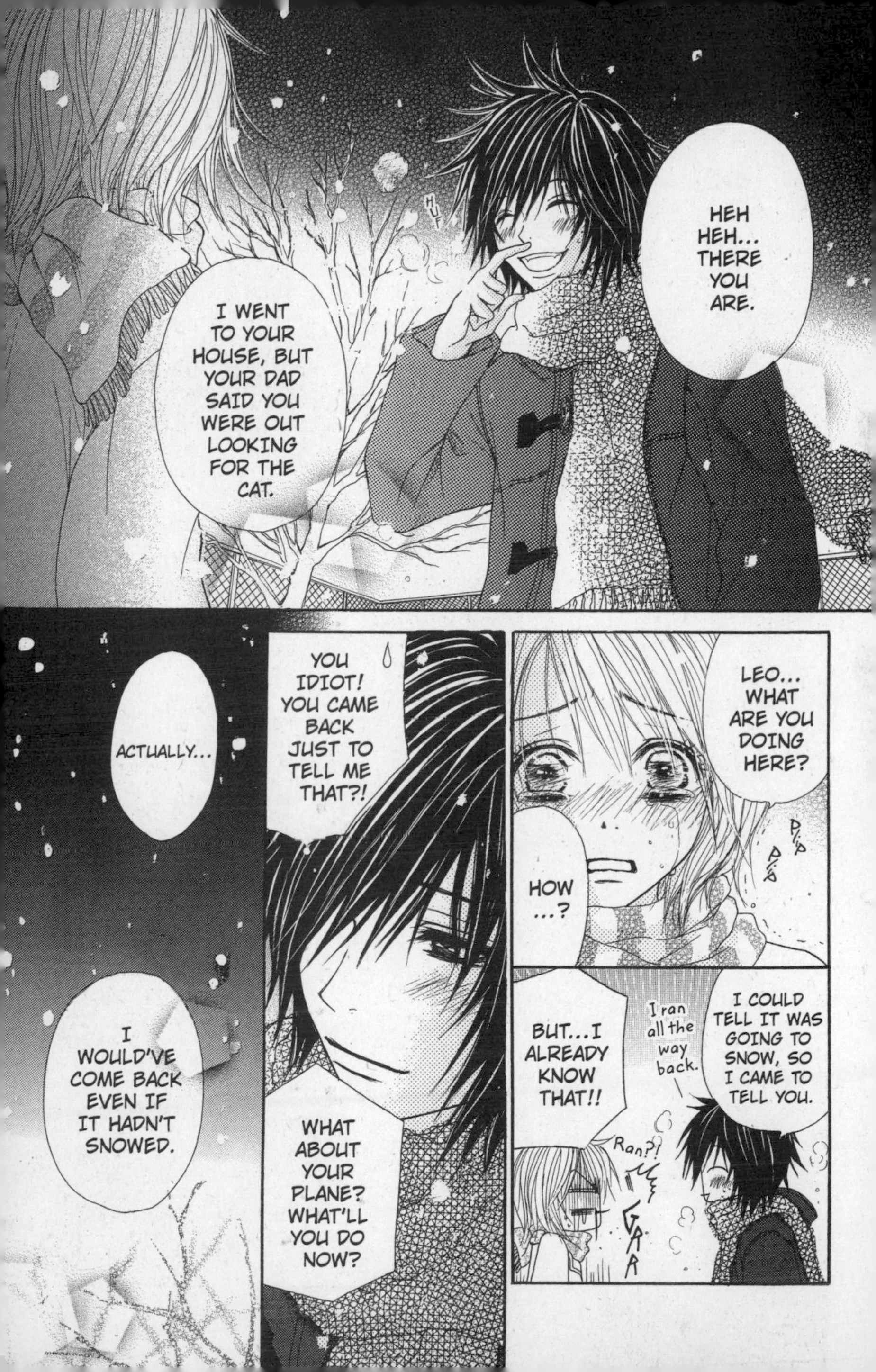
HEH HEH... THERE YOU ARE.
I WENT TO YOUR HOUSE, BUT YOUR DAD SAID YOU WERE OUT LOOKING FOR THE CAT.
LEO... WHAT ARE YOU DOING HERE?
HOW ...?
I COULD TELL IT WAS GOING TO SNOW, SO I CAME TO TELL YOU.
I ran all the way back.
BUT...I ALREADY KNOW THAT!!
Ran?!
GRR
YOU IDIOT! YOU CAME BACK JUST TO TELL ME THAT?!
WHAT ABOUT YOUR PLANE? WHAT'LL YOU DO NOW?
ACTUALLY...
I WOULD'VE COME BACK EVEN IF IT HADN'T SNOWED.

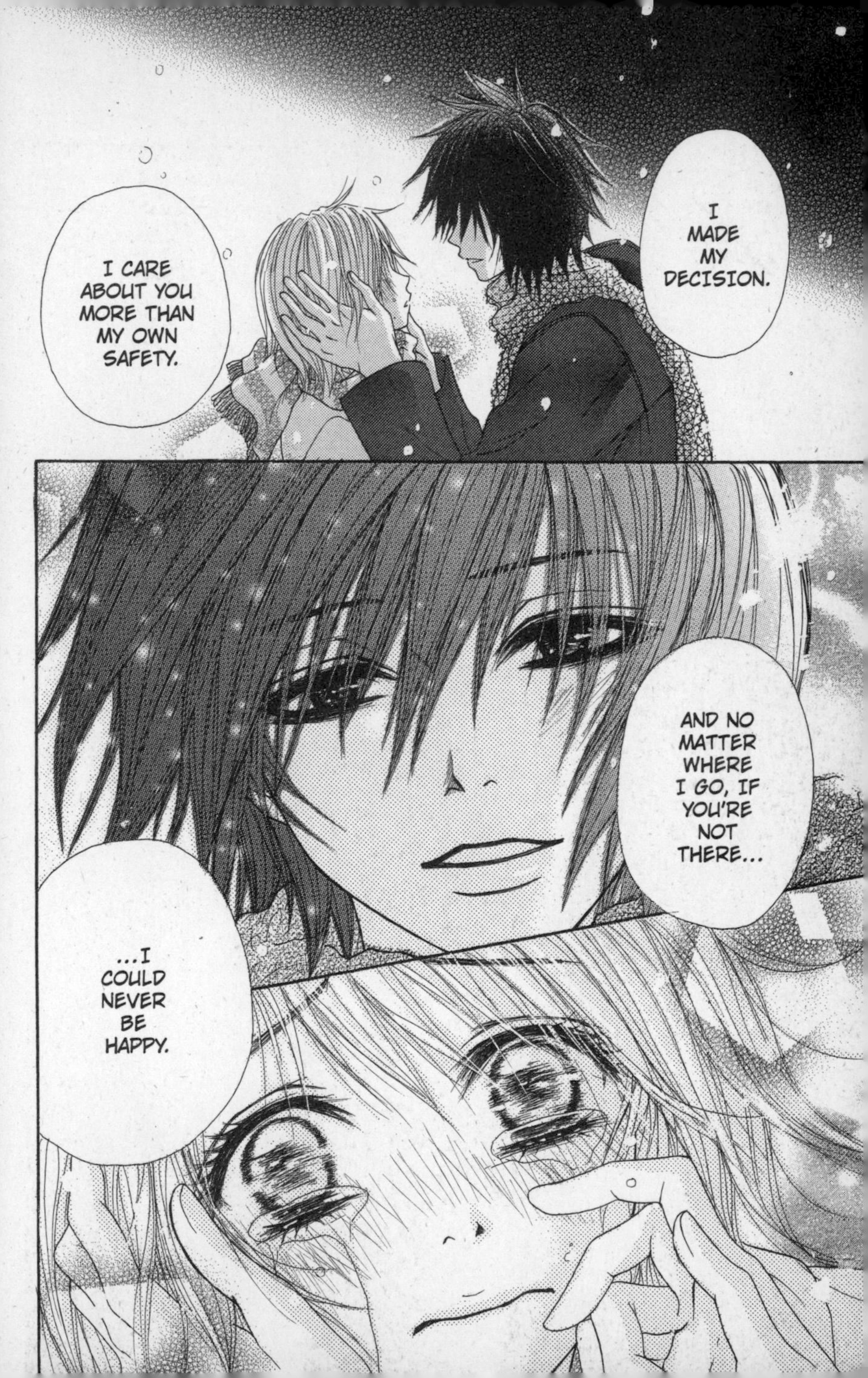
I MADE MY DECISION.
I CARE ABOUT YOU MORE THAN MY OWN SAFETY.
AND NO MATTER WHERE I GO, IF YOU'RE NOT THERE...
...I COULD NEVER BE HAPPY.

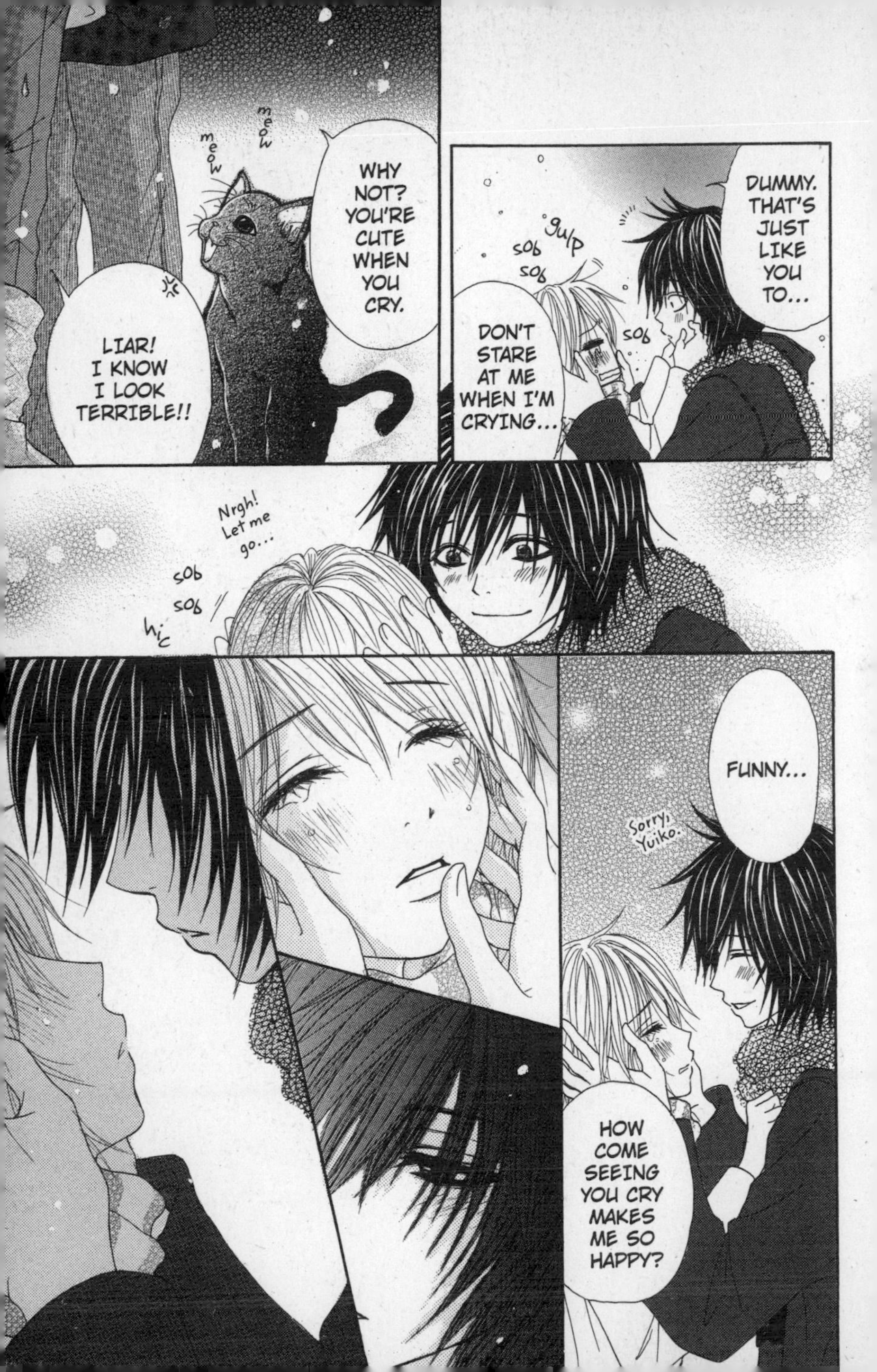
DUMMY. THAT'S JUST LIKE YOU TO...
gulp
sob
sob
sob
DON'T STARE AT ME WHEN I'M CRYING...
meow
meow
WHY NOT? YOU'RE CUTE WHEN YOU CRY.
LIAR! I KNOW I LOOK TERRIBLE!!
Nrgh! Let me go...
sob
sob
hic
FUNNY...
Sorry, Yuiko.
HOW COME SEEING YOU CRY MAKES ME SO HAPPY?

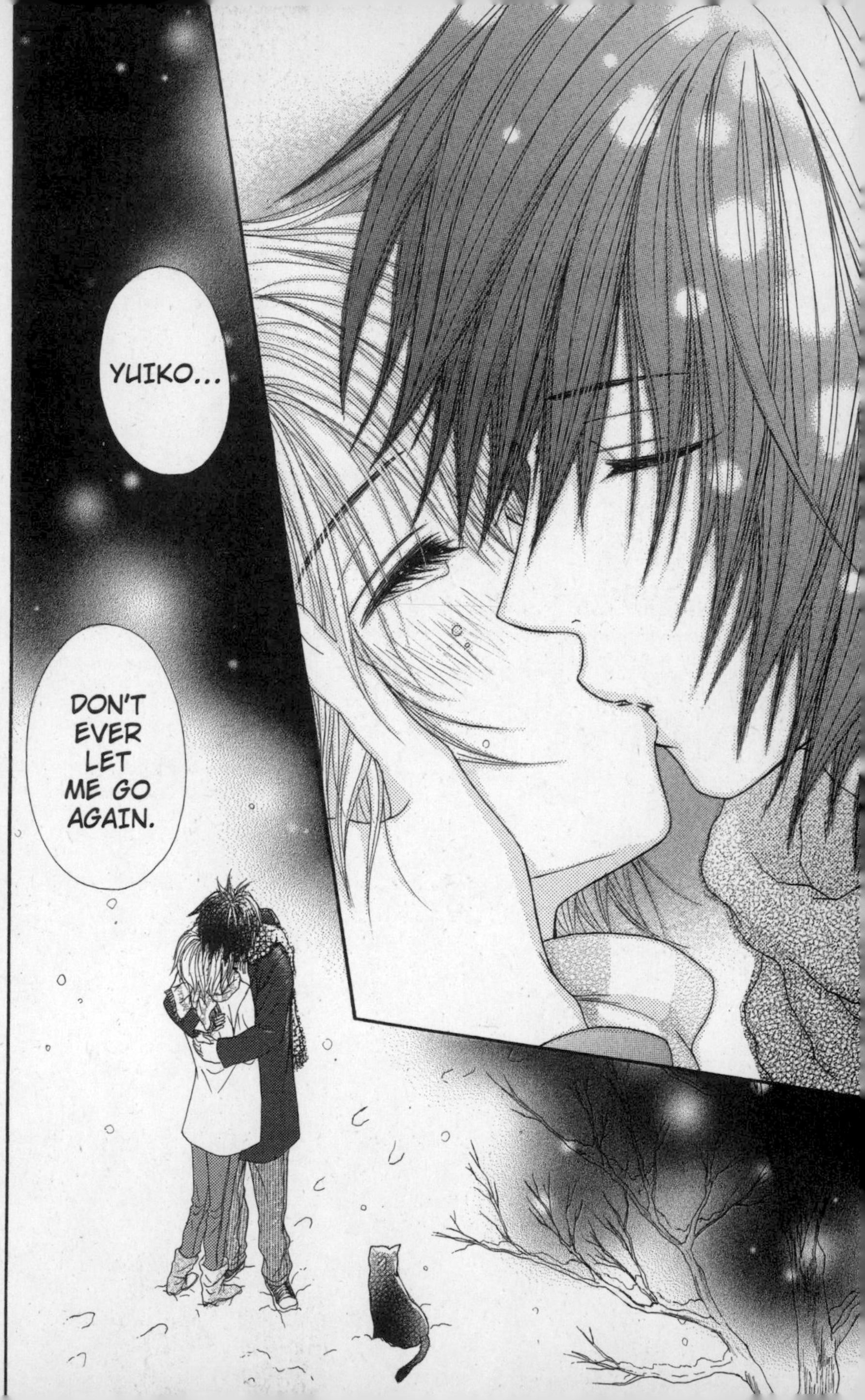
YUIKO...
DON'T EVER LET ME GO AGAIN.

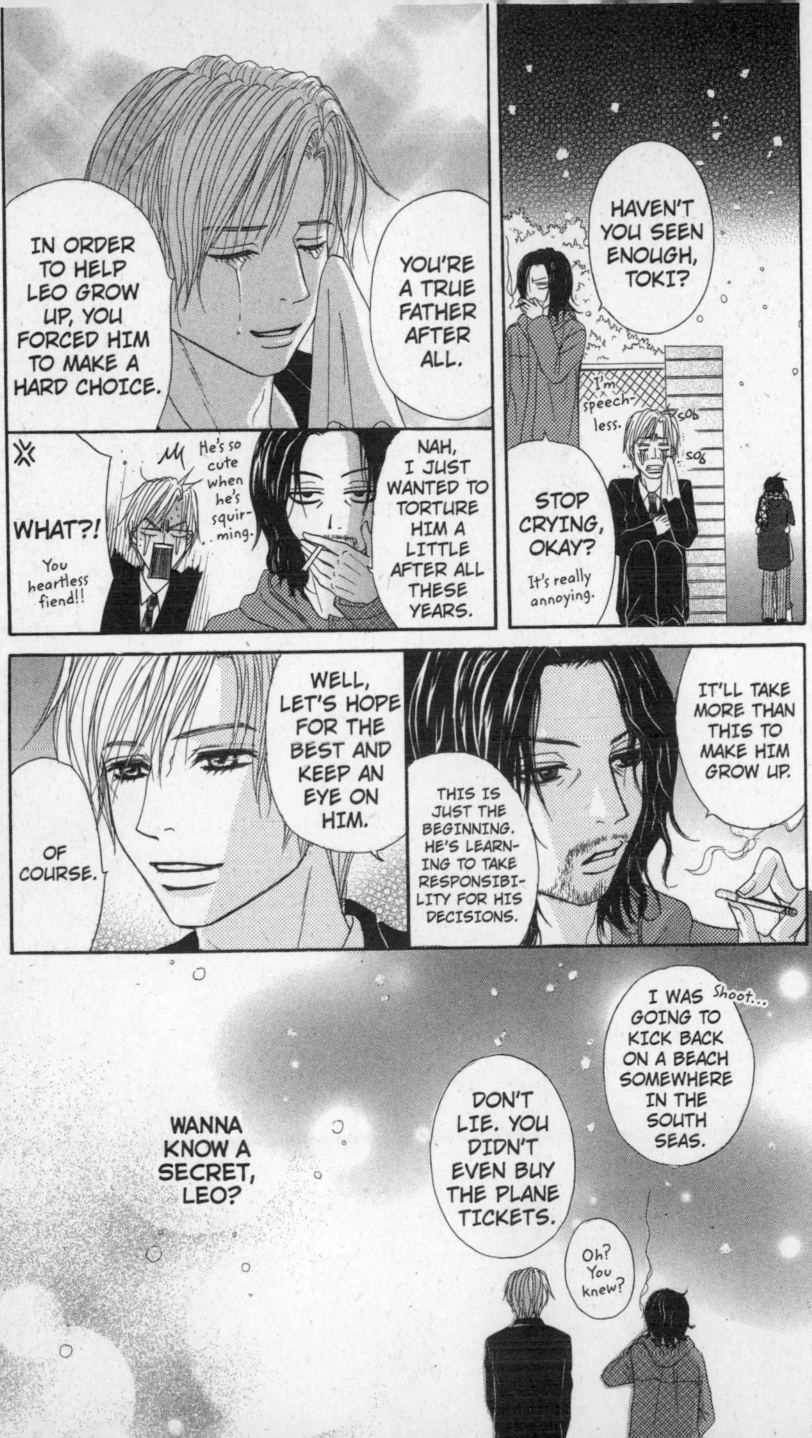
HAVEN'T YOU SEEN ENOUGH, TOKI?
I'm speechless.
sob
sob
STOP CRYING, OKAY?
It's really annoying.
YOU'RE A TRUE FATHER AFTER ALL.
IN ORDER TO HELP LEO GROW UP, YOU FORCED HIM TO MAKE A HARD CHOICE.
NAH, I JUST WANTED TO TORTURE HIM A LITTLE AFTER ALL THESE YEARS.
He's so cute when he's squirming.
WHAT?!
You heartless fiend!!
IT'LL TAKE MORE THAN THIS TO MAKE HIM GROW UP.
THIS IS JUST THE BEGINNING. HE'S LEARNING TO TAKE RESPONSIBILITY FOR HIS DECISIONS.
WELL, LET'S HOPE FOR THE BEST AND KEEP AN EYE ON HIM.
OF COURSE.
Shoot...
I WAS GOING TO KICK BACK ON A BEACH SOMEWHERE IN THE SOUTH SEAS.
DON'T LIE. YOU DIDN'T EVEN BUY THE PLANE TICKETS.
Oh? You knew?
WANNA KNOW A SECRET, LEO?

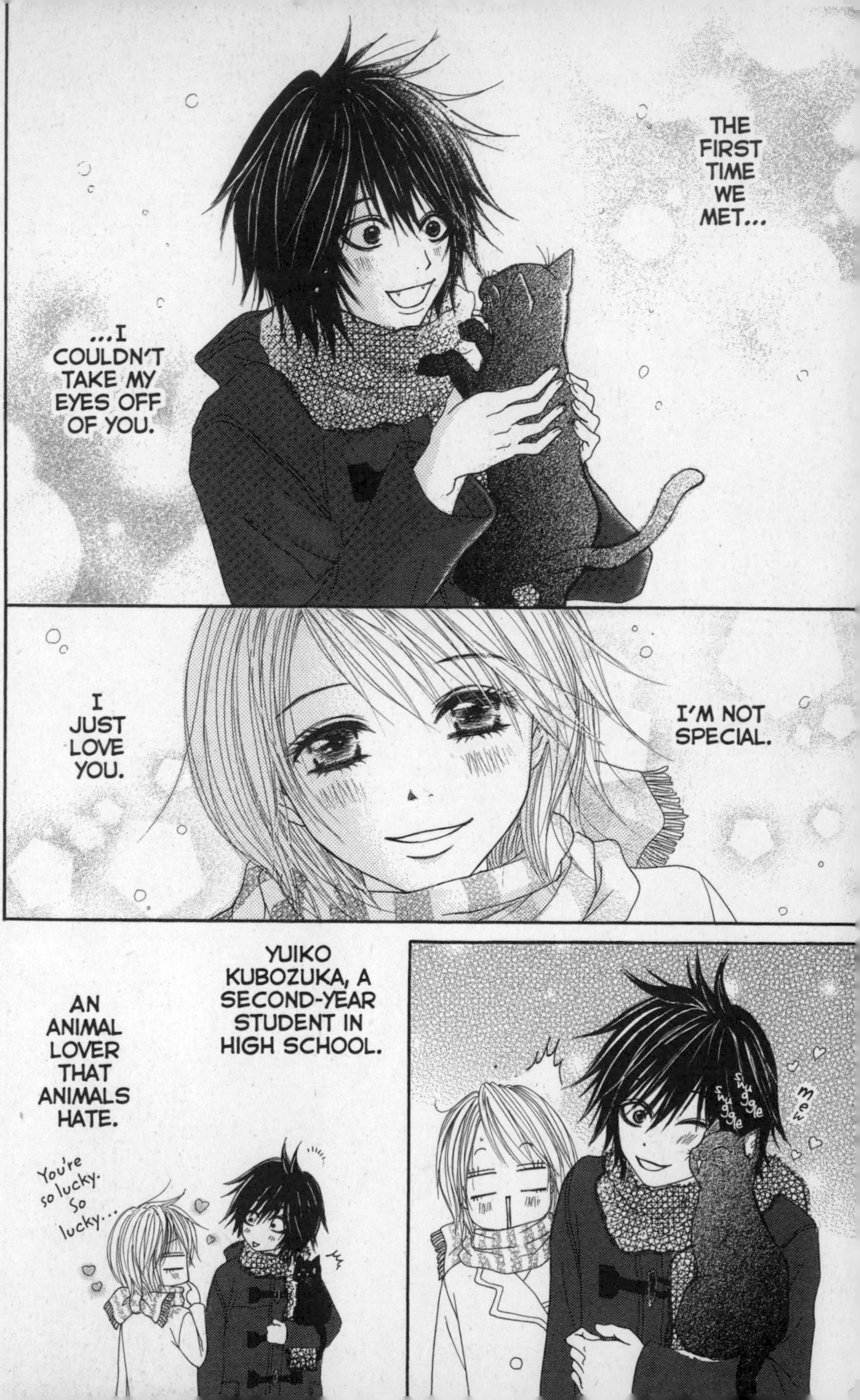
THE FIRST TIME WE MET...
...I COULDN'T TAKE MY EYES OFF OF YOU.
I'M NOT SPECIAL.
I JUST LOVE YOU.
swiggle swiggle
mew
YUIKO KUBOZUKA, A SECOND-YEAR STUDENT IN HIGH SCHOOL.
AN ANIMAL LOVER THAT ANIMALS HATE.
You're so lucky. So lucky...

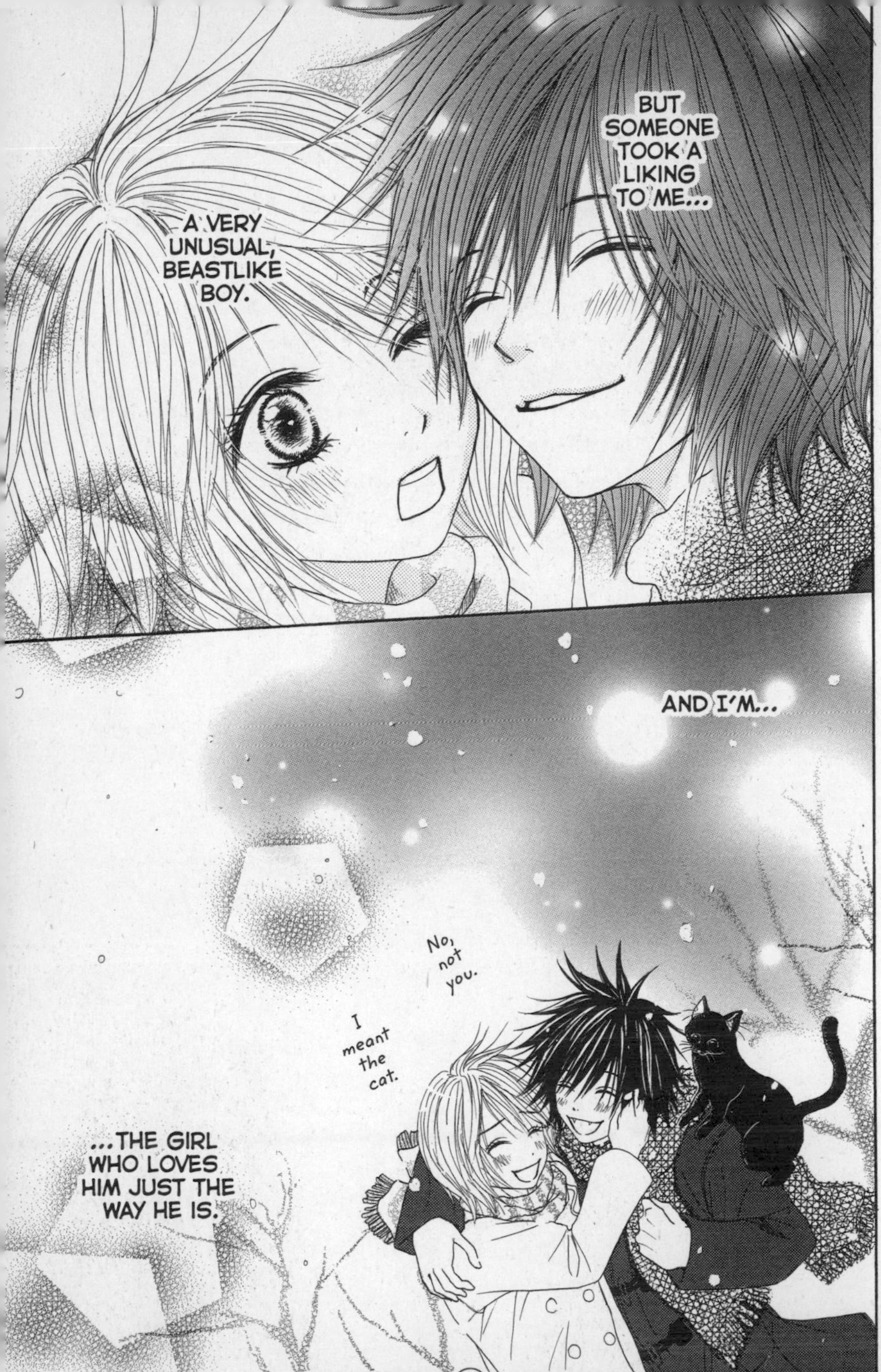
BUT SOMEONE TOOK A LIKING TO ME...
A VERY UNUSUAL, BEASTLIKE BOY.
AND I'M...
No, not you.
I meant the cat.
...THE GIRL WHO LOVES HIM JUST THE WAY HE IS.

Beast Master 2 *The End*

✿ A Note About Beast Master ✿

In chapter 5, I wrote that there is a beast inside each of us that protects the things we hold dear. This is why there are so many dangerous-looking characters—including Leo—in this manga.
But I believe everyone in the world, even the most ordinary people, go through life suppressing a wild madness that I call the "beast." Leo fears this beast and wishes it would go away, but that probably won't happen. The beast will be with him as long as he lives.

Even though the beast is always there, it can be tamed. It bares its fangs when something precious to it is threatened, but it can be persuaded by intelligence and reason.

Leo's "beast master" is Yuiko. That was the premise of this manga. But Leo will mature and be able to become his own master someday. I'm sure of it.

I'm a little embarrassed that I needed to add a postscript to explain my work. Thank you for reading my hard-to-understand sentences. May your beasts always be guided by your kind hearts.

← Uh... The bonus chapter begins on the next page. It's an epilogue to Leo and Yuiko's story. It contains things I drew that weren't part of the main story.

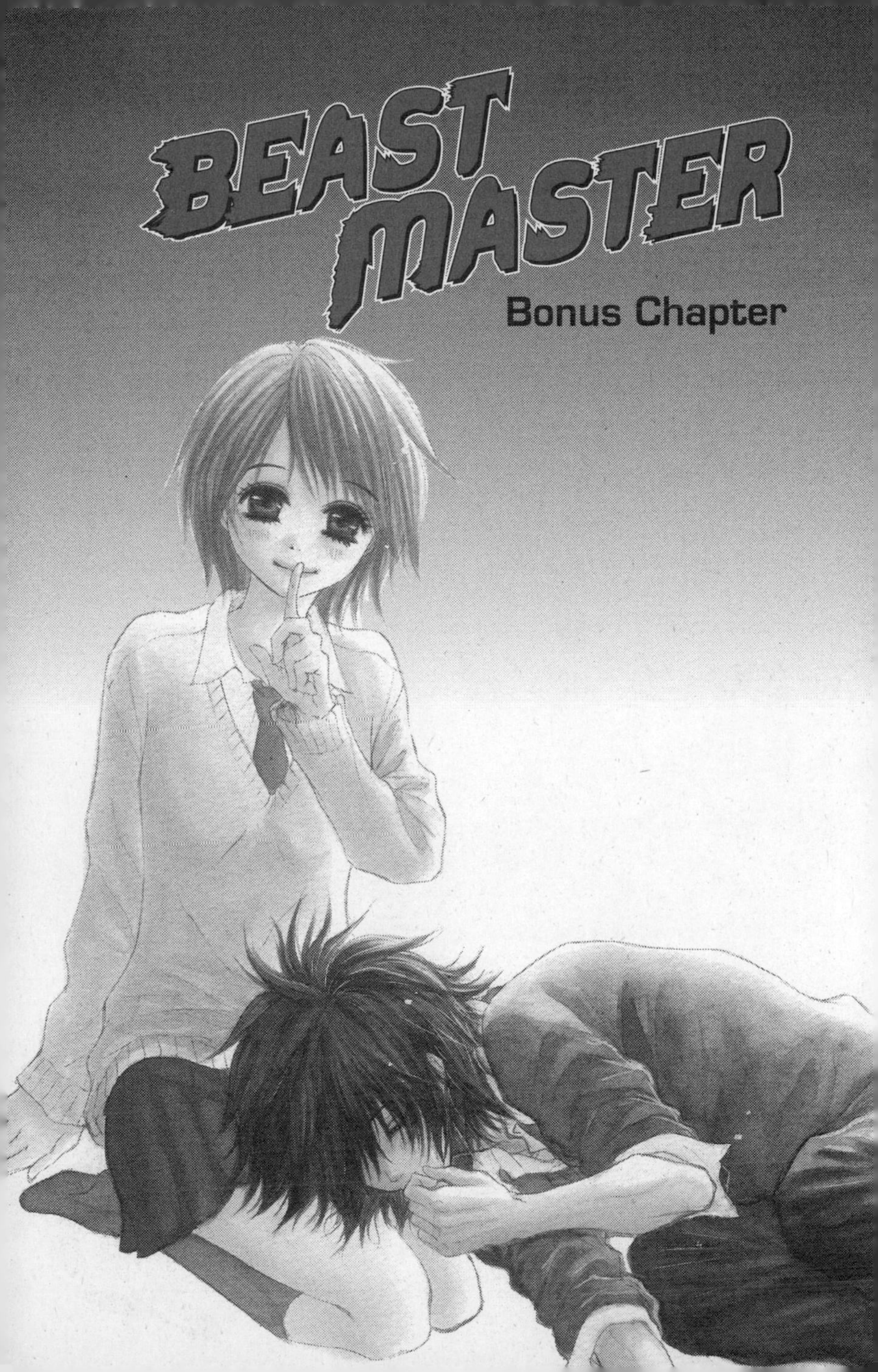
BEAST MASTER
Bonus Chapter

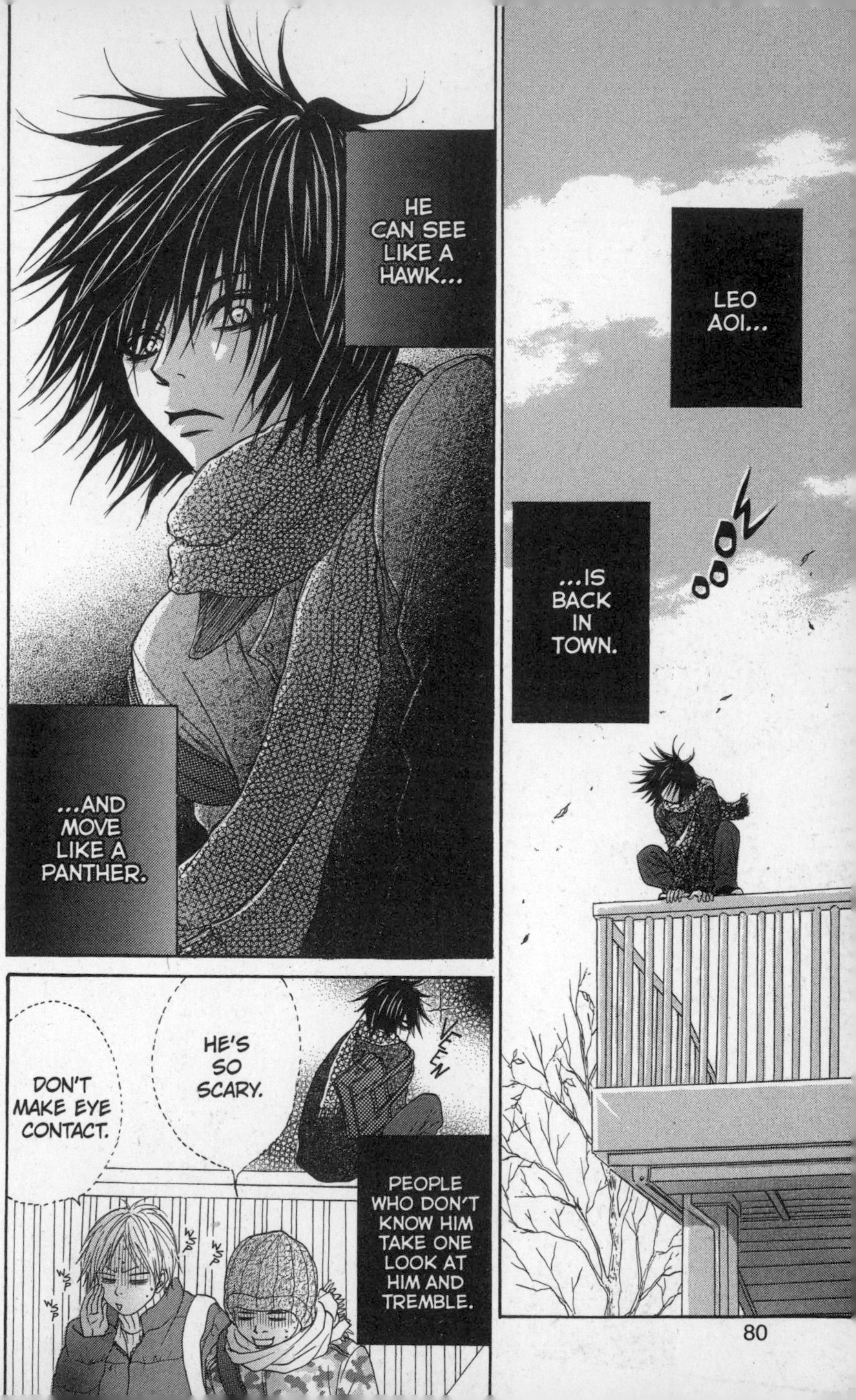
LEO AOI...
...IS BACK IN TOWN.
HE CAN SEE LIKE A HAWK...
...AND MOVE LIKE A PANTHER.
PEOPLE WHO DON'T KNOW HIM TAKE ONE LOOK AT HIM AND TREMBLE.
HE'S SO SCARY.
DON'T MAKE EYE CONTACT.
WSP
WSP
WSP
WSP

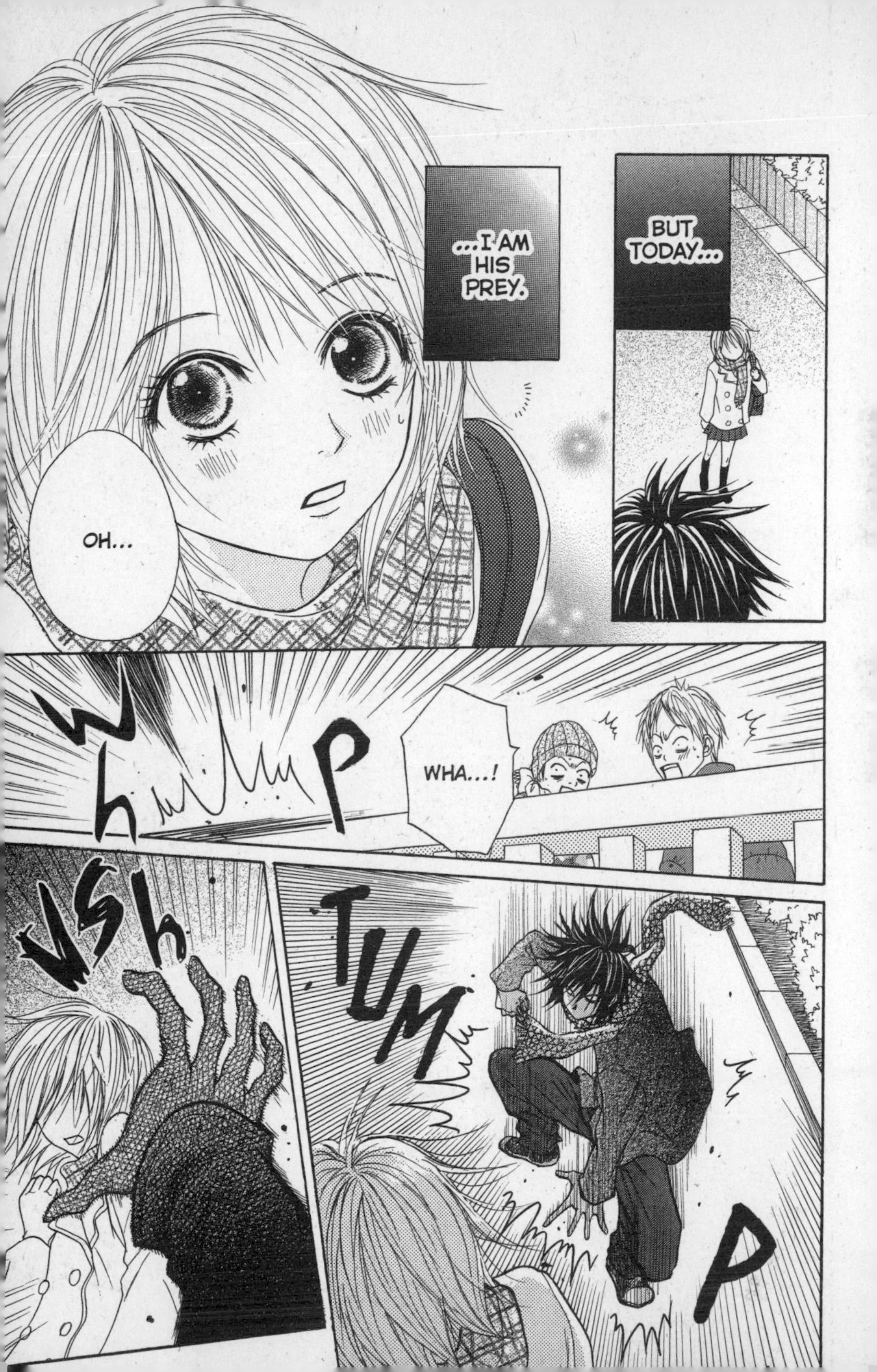
BUT TODAY...
...I AM HIS PREY.
OH...
WHA...!
WHUMP
TUMP
USH

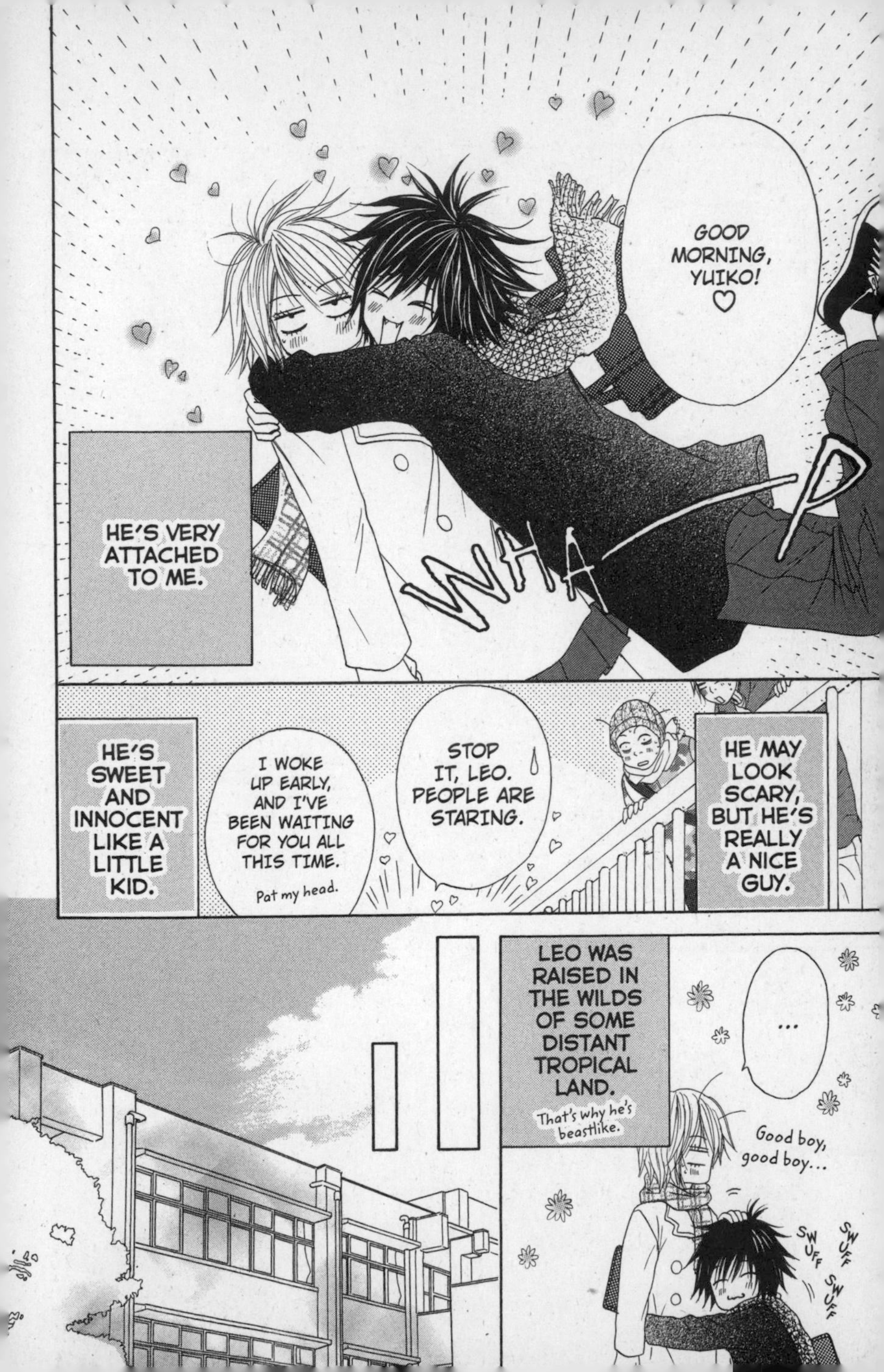
GOOD MORNING, YUIKO! ♡
WHAP
HE'S VERY ATTACHED TO ME.
HE MAY LOOK SCARY, BUT HE'S REALLY A NICE GUY.
STOP IT, LEO. PEOPLE ARE STARING.
I WOKE UP EARLY, AND I'VE BEEN WAITING FOR YOU ALL THIS TIME.
Pat my head.
HE'S SWEET AND INNOCENT LIKE A LITTLE KID.
LEO WAS RAISED IN THE WILDS OF SOME DISTANT TROPICAL LAND.
That's why he's beastlike.
...
Good boy, good boy...
SWUFF
SWUFF
SWUFF

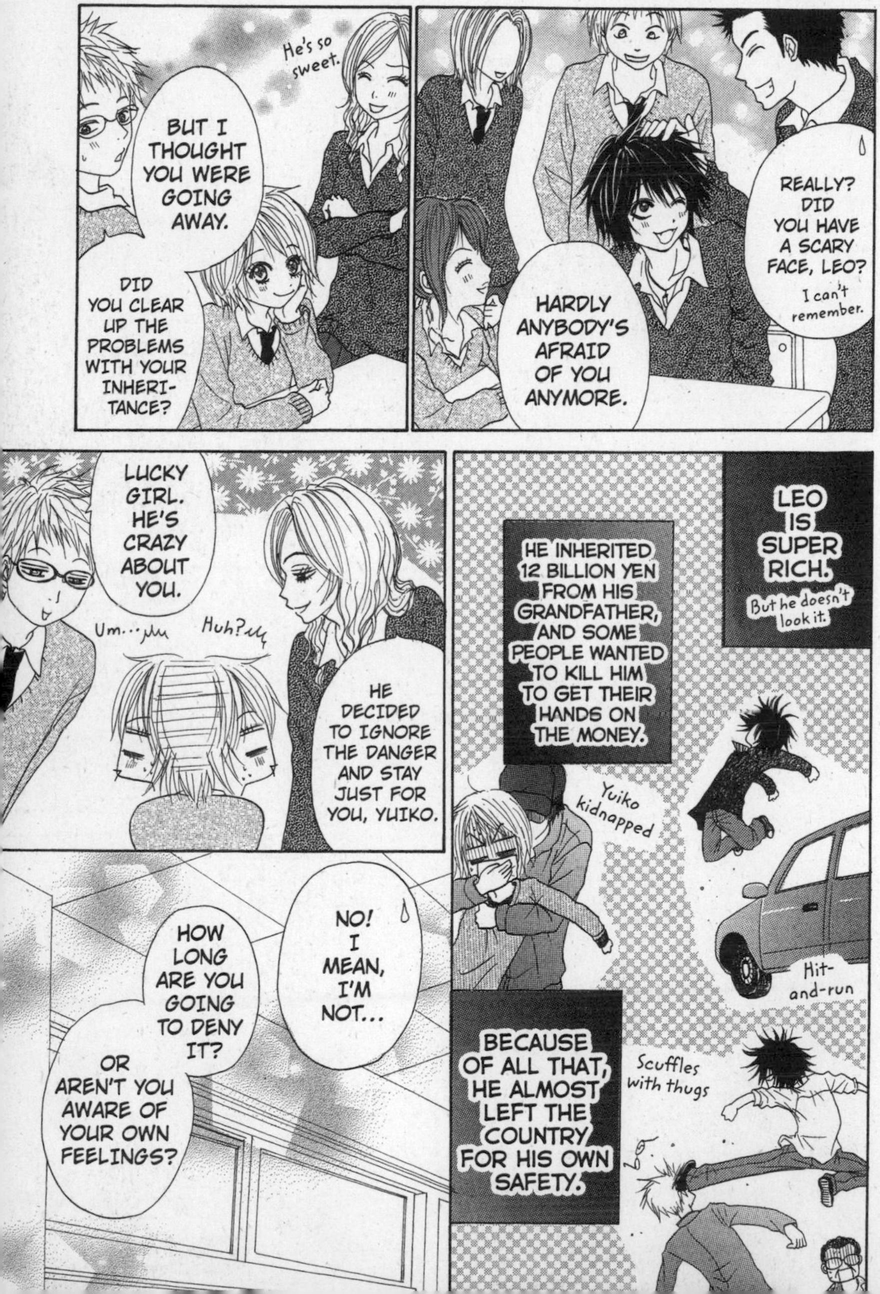
REALLY? DID YOU HAVE A SCARY FACE, LEO?
I can't remember.
HARDLY ANYBODY'S AFRAID OF YOU ANYMORE.
He's so sweet.
BUT I THOUGHT YOU WERE GOING AWAY.
DID YOU CLEAR UP THE PROBLEMS WITH YOUR INHERI-TANCE?
LEO IS SUPER RICH.
But he doesn't look it.
HE INHERITED 12 BILLION YEN FROM HIS GRANDFATHER, AND SOME PEOPLE WANTED TO KILL HIM TO GET THEIR HANDS ON THE MONEY.
Yuiko kidnapped
Hit-and-run
BECAUSE OF ALL THAT, HE ALMOST LEFT THE COUNTRY FOR HIS OWN SAFETY.
Scuffles with thugs
HE DECIDED TO IGNORE THE DANGER AND STAY JUST FOR YOU, YUIKO.
LUCKY GIRL. HE'S CRAZY ABOUT YOU.
Huh?
Um...
NO! I MEAN, I'M NOT...
HOW LONG ARE YOU GOING TO DENY IT?
OR AREN'T YOU AWARE OF YOUR OWN FEELINGS?

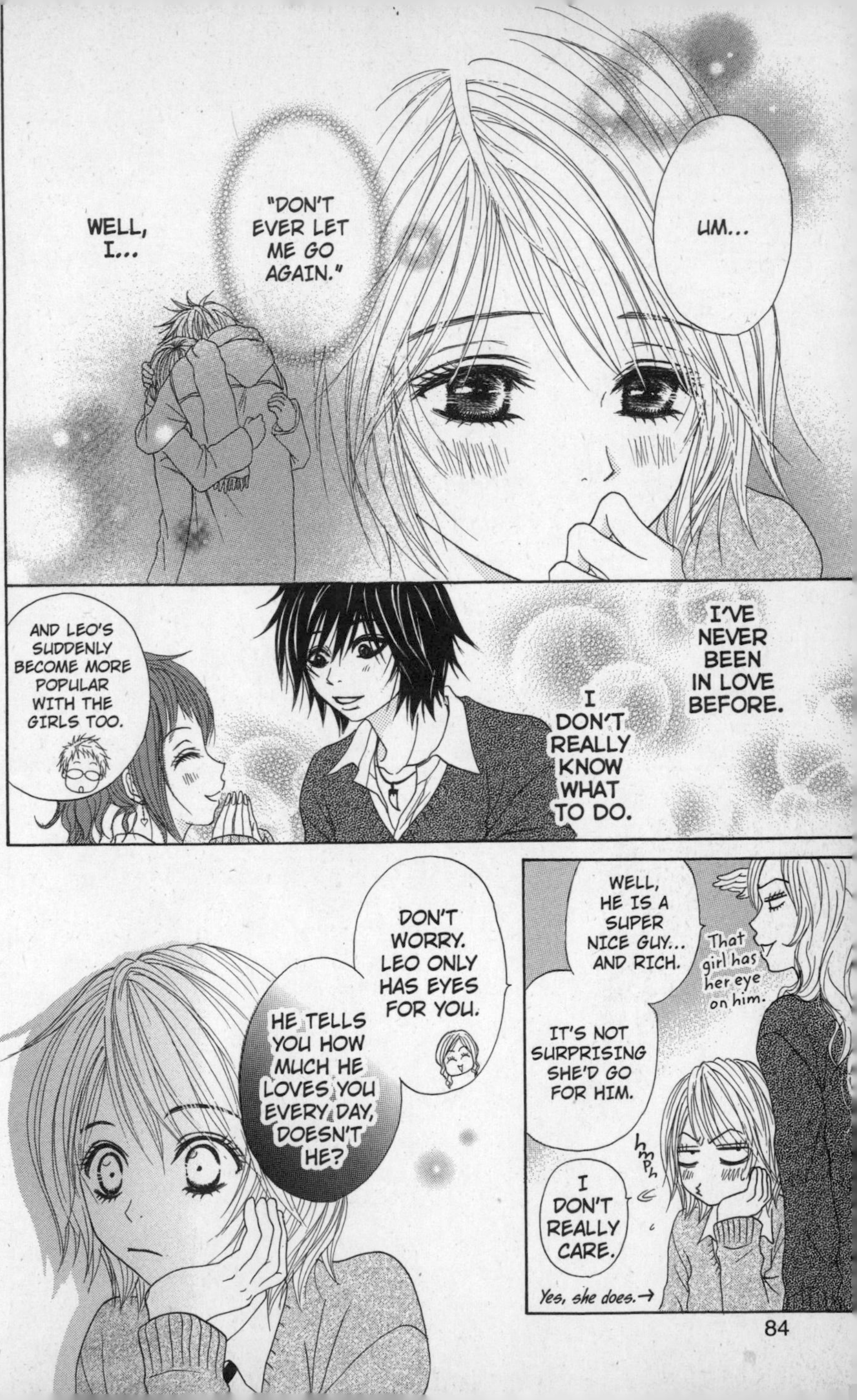
UM...
"DON'T EVER LET ME GO AGAIN."
WELL, I...
I'VE NEVER BEEN IN LOVE BEFORE.
I DON'T REALLY KNOW WHAT TO DO.
AND LEO'S SUDDENLY BECOME MORE POPULAR WITH THE GIRLS TOO.
WELL, HE IS A SUPER NICE GUY... AND RICH.
That girl has her eye on him.
IT'S NOT SURPRISING SHE'D GO FOR HIM.
hmph
I DON'T REALLY CARE.
Yes, she does.→
DON'T WORRY. LEO ONLY HAS EYES FOR YOU.
HE TELLS YOU HOW MUCH HE LOVES YOU EVERY DAY, DOESN'T HE?

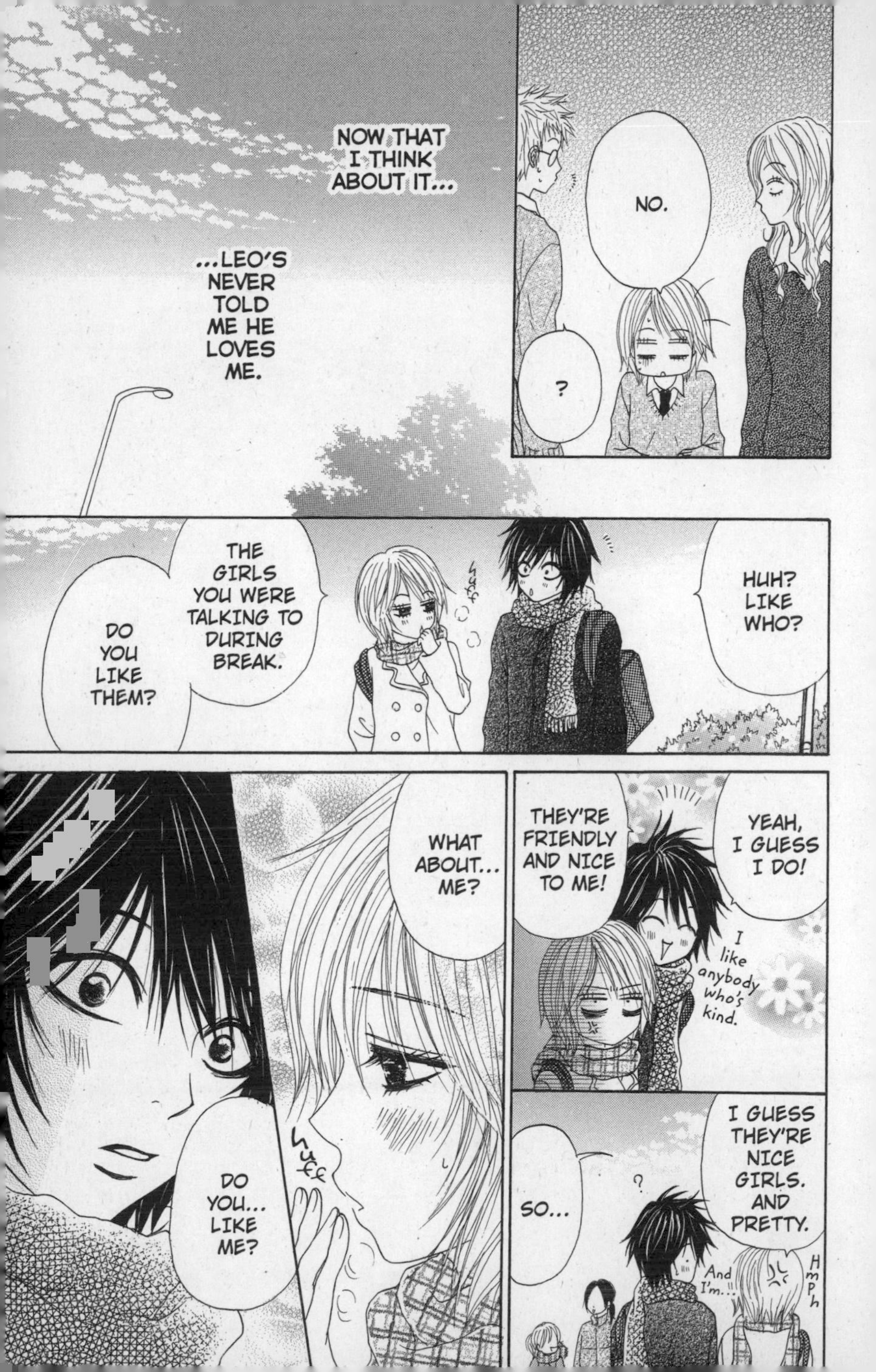
NO.
?
NOW THAT I THINK ABOUT IT...
...LEO'S NEVER TOLD ME HE LOVES ME.
HUH? LIKE WHO?
huff
THE GIRLS YOU WERE TALKING TO DURING BREAK.
DO YOU LIKE THEM?
YEAH, I GUESS I DO!
THEY'RE FRIENDLY AND NICE TO ME!
I like anybody who's kind.
I GUESS THEY'RE NICE GIRLS. AND PRETTY.
Hmph
And I'm...!!
?
SO...
WHAT ABOUT... ME?
huff
DO YOU... LIKE ME?

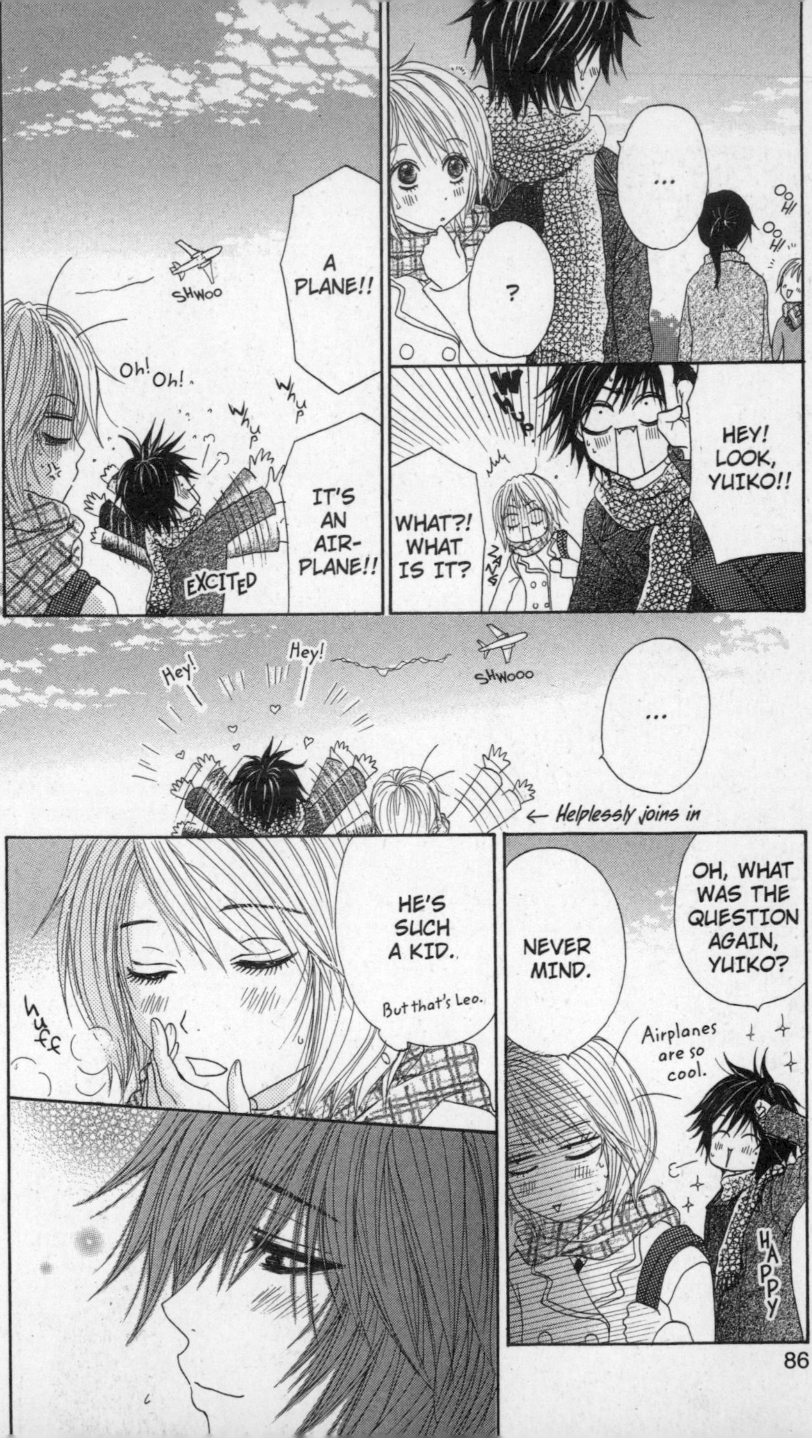
OOH!
OOH!
...
?
A PLANE!!
SHWOO
HEY! LOOK, YUIKO!!
WHUP
WHAT?! WHAT IS IT?
IT'S AN AIR-PLANE!!
Whup
Whup
Oh! Oh!
EXCITED
...
SHWOOO
Hey!
Hey!
← Helplessly joins in
OH, WHAT WAS THE QUESTION AGAIN, YUIKO?
NEVER MIND.
Airplanes are so cool.
HAPPY
HE'S SUCH A KID.
But that's Leo.
huff

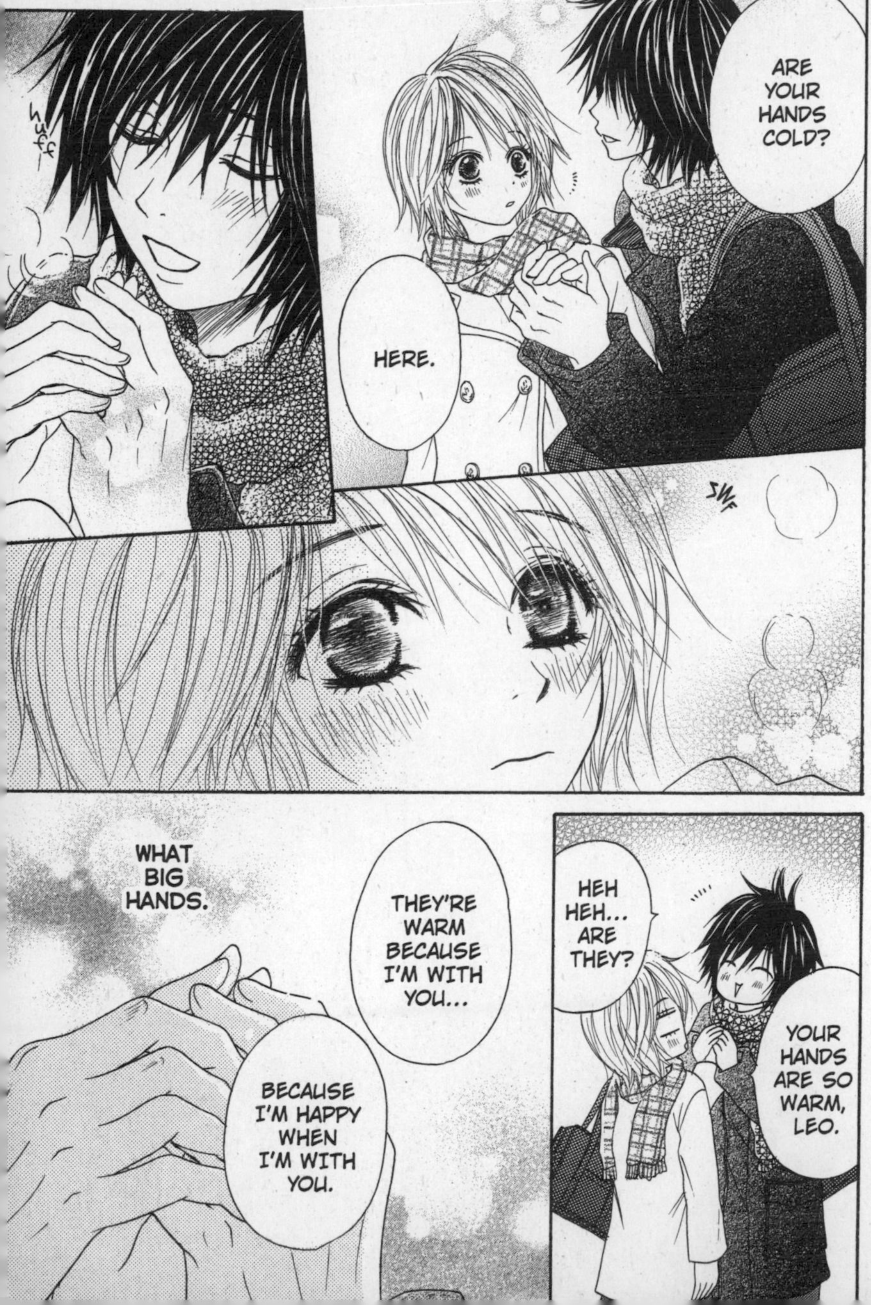
ARE YOUR HANDS COLD?
HERE.
huff
SWF
YOUR HANDS ARE SO WARM, LEO.
HEH HEH... ARE THEY?
WHAT BIG HANDS.
THEY'RE WARM BECAUSE I'M WITH YOU...
BECAUSE I'M HAPPY WHEN I'M WITH YOU.

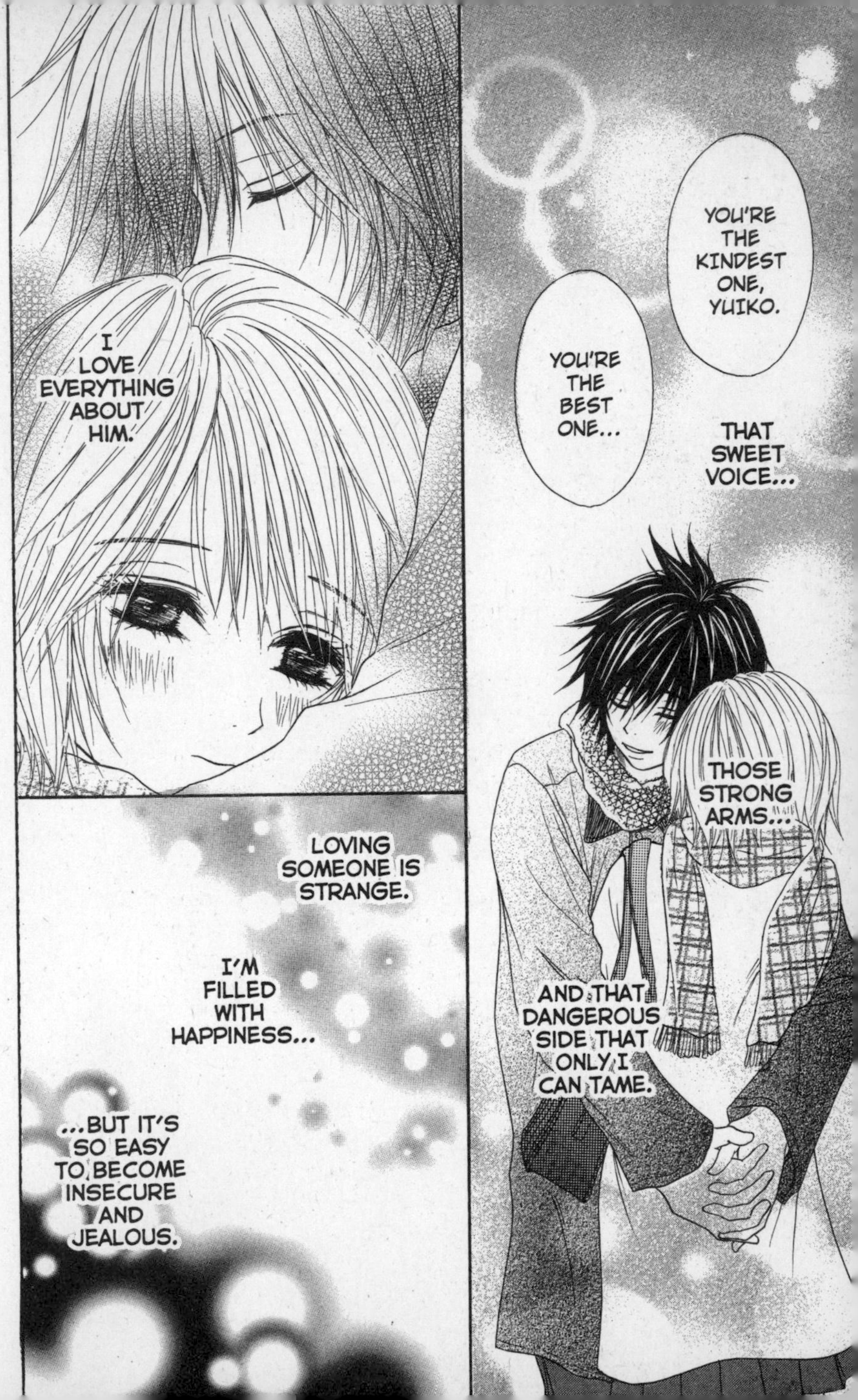
YOU'RE THE KINDEST ONE, YUIKO.
YOU'RE THE BEST ONE...
THAT SWEET VOICE...
THOSE STRONG ARMS...
AND THAT DANGEROUS SIDE THAT ONLY I CAN TAME.
I LOVE EVERYTHING ABOUT HIM.
LOVING SOMEONE IS STRANGE.
I'M FILLED WITH HAPPINESS...
...BUT IT'S SO EASY TO BECOME INSECURE AND JEALOUS.

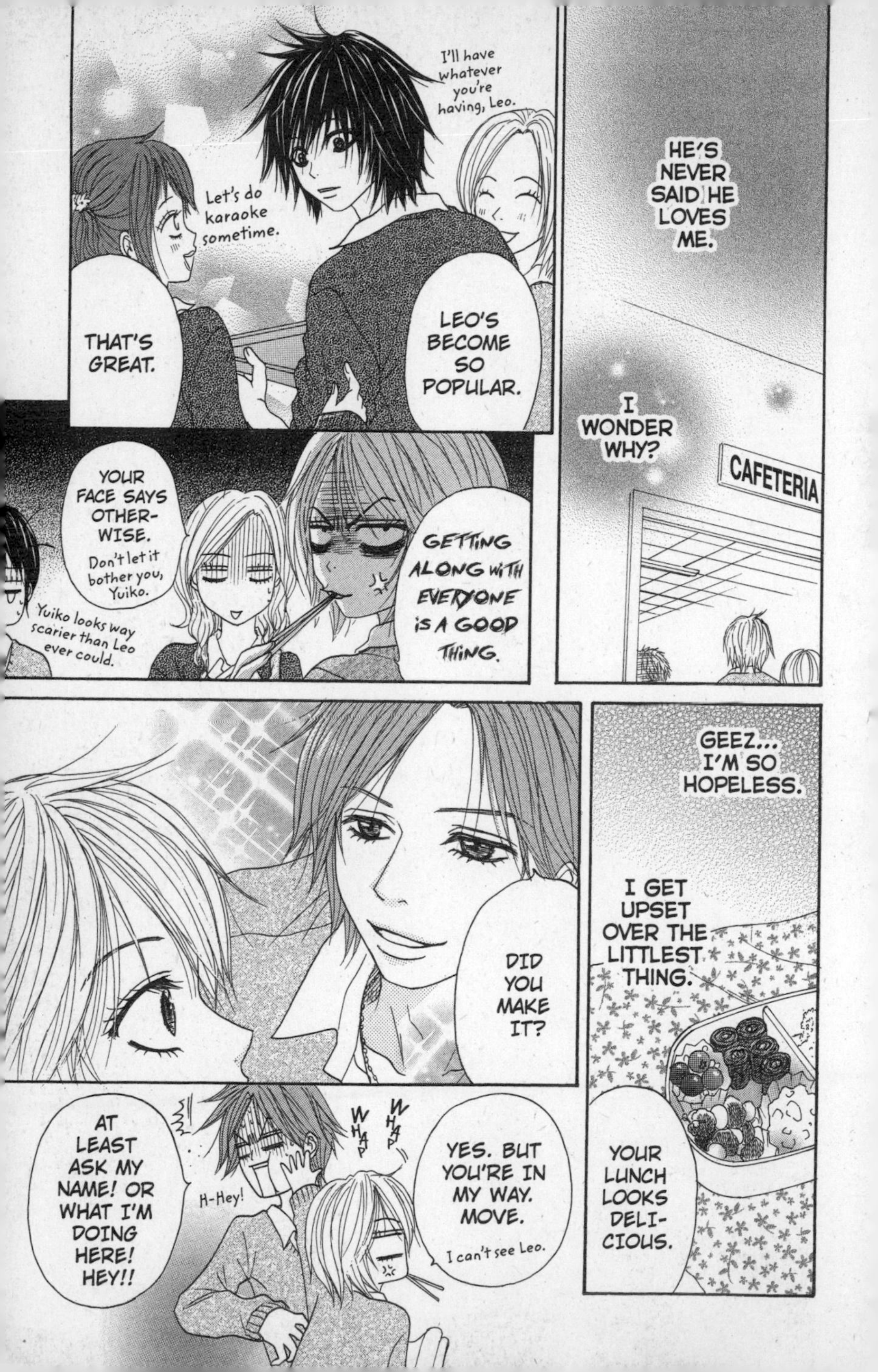
HE'S NEVER SAID HE LOVES ME.
I WONDER WHY?
CAFETERIA
I'll have whatever you're having, Leo.
Let's do karaoke sometime.
LEO'S BECOME SO POPULAR.
THAT'S GREAT.
GETTING ALONG WITH EVERYONE IS A GOOD THING.
YOUR FACE SAYS OTHER-WISE.
Don't let it bother you, Yuiko.
Yuiko looks way scarier than Leo ever could.
GEEZ... I'M SO HOPELESS.
I GET UPSET OVER THE LITTLEST THING.
YOUR LUNCH LOOKS DELI-CIOUS.
DID YOU MAKE IT?
WHAP
WHAP
YES. BUT YOU'RE IN MY WAY. MOVE.
I can't see Leo.
AT LEAST ASK MY NAME! OR WHAT I'M DOING HERE! HEY!!
H-Hey!

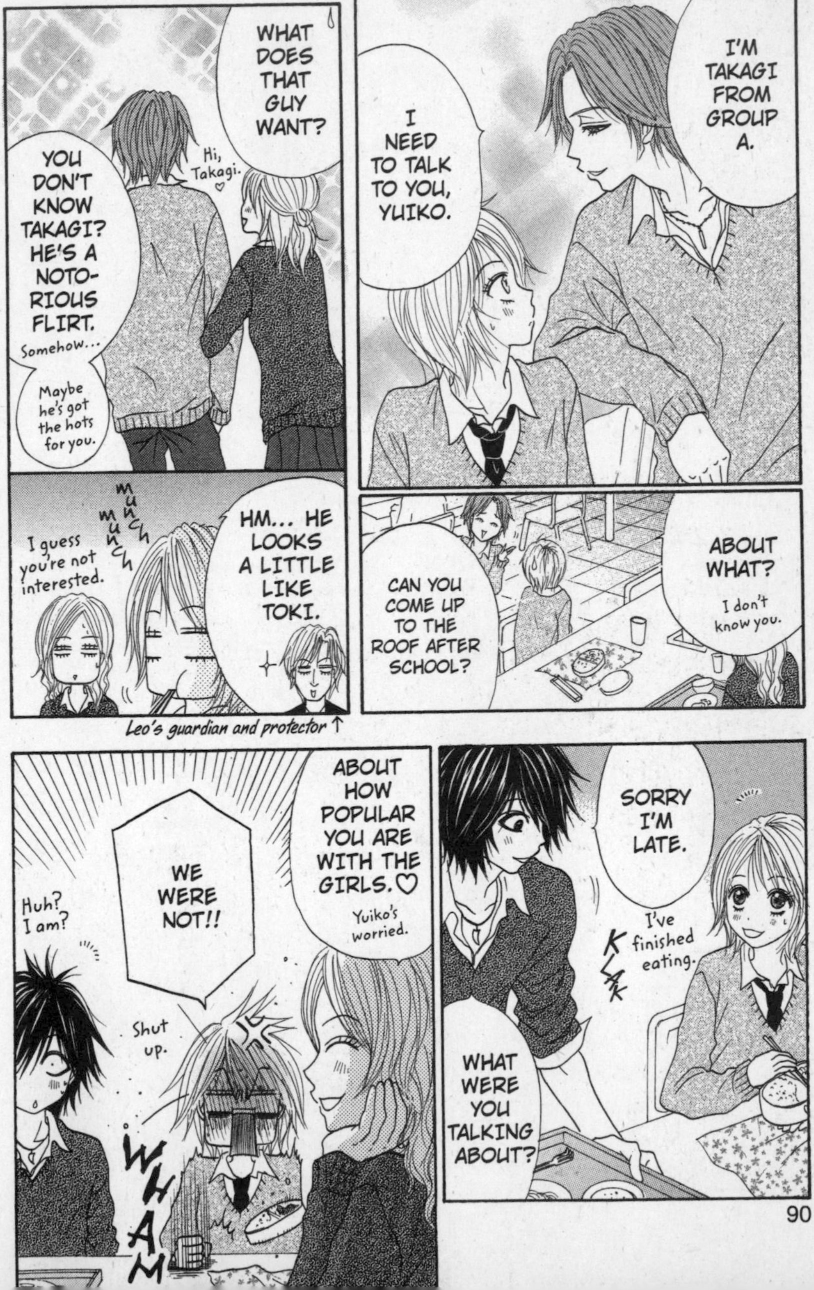
I'M TAKAGI FROM GROUP A.
I NEED TO TALK TO YOU, YUIKO.
WHAT DOES THAT GUY WANT?
Hi, Takagi. ♡
YOU DON'T KNOW TAKAGI? HE'S A NOTO-RIOUS FLIRT.
Somehow...
Maybe he's got the hots for you.
ABOUT WHAT?
I don't know you.
CAN YOU COME UP TO THE ROOF AFTER SCHOOL?
HM... HE LOOKS A LITTLE LIKE TOKI.
munch munch
I guess you're not interested.
Leo's guardian and protector ↑
SORRY I'M LATE.
I've finished eating.
KLAK
WHAT WERE YOU TALKING ABOUT?
ABOUT HOW POPULAR YOU ARE WITH THE GIRLS. ♡
Yuiko's worried.
WE WERE NOT!!
Huh? I am?
Shut up.
WHAM

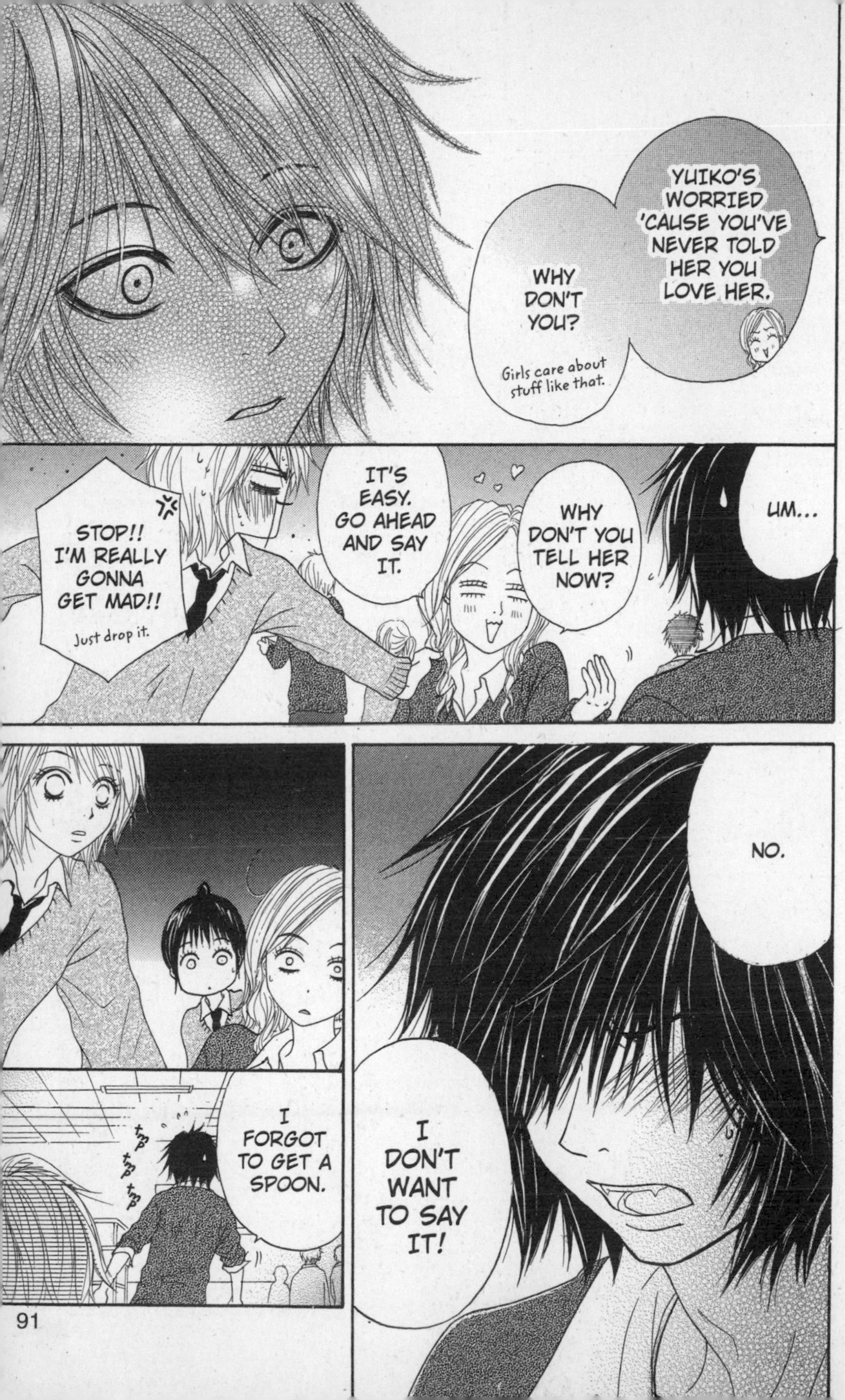
YUIKO'S WORRIED 'CAUSE YOU'VE NEVER TOLD HER YOU LOVE HER.
WHY DON'T YOU?
Girls care about stuff like that.
UM...
WHY DON'T YOU TELL HER NOW?
IT'S EASY. GO AHEAD AND SAY IT.
STOP!! I'M REALLY GONNA GET MAD!!
Just drop it.
NO.
I DON'T WANT TO SAY IT!
I FORGOT TO GET A SPOON.
tmp tmp tmp tmp

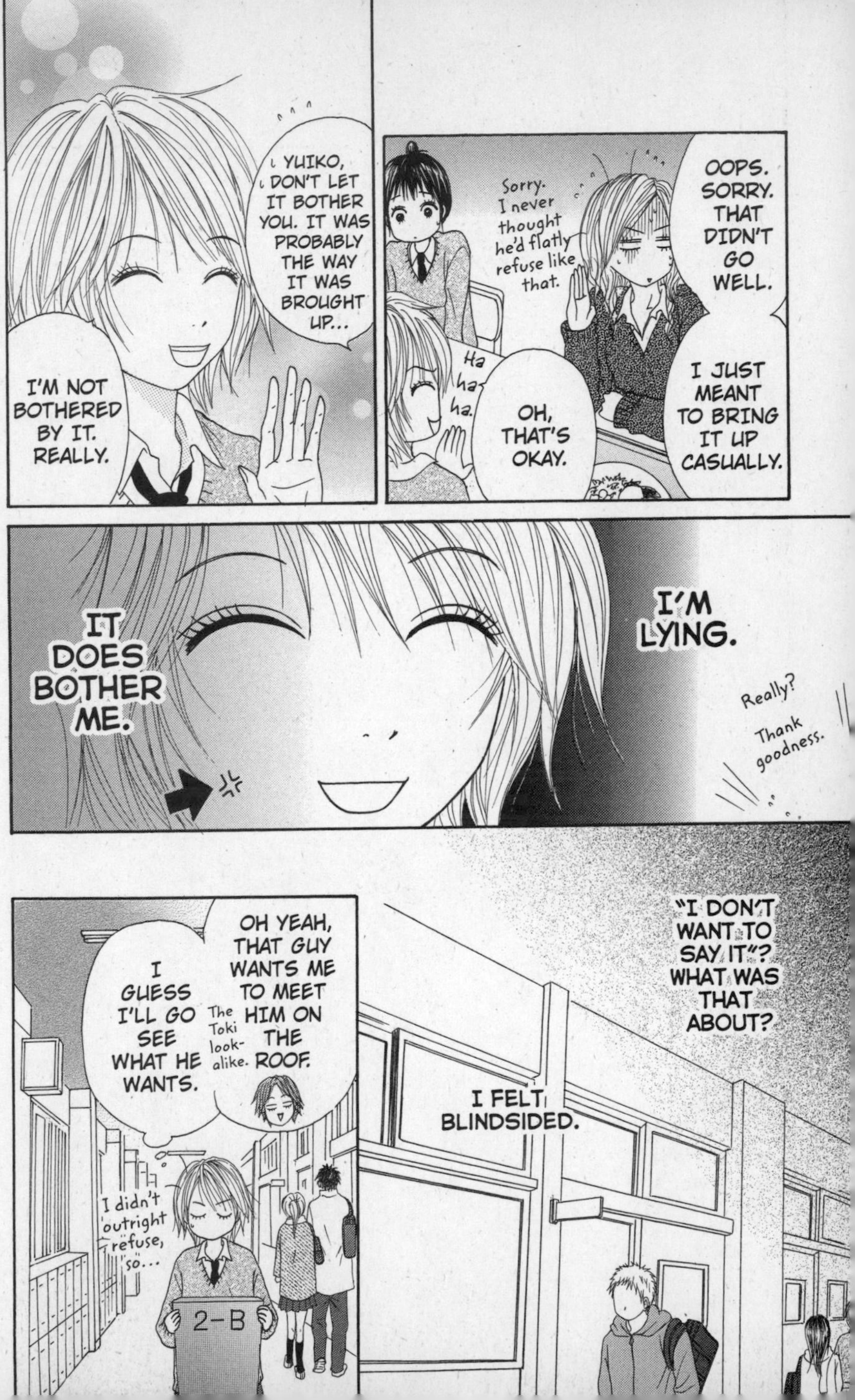
OOPS. SORRY. THAT DIDN'T GO WELL.
Sorry. I never thought he'd flatly refuse like that.
I JUST MEANT TO BRING IT UP CASUALLY.
Ha ha ha.
OH, THAT'S OKAY.
YUIKO, DON'T LET IT BOTHER YOU. IT WAS PROBABLY THE WAY IT WAS BROUGHT UP...
I'M NOT BOTHERED BY IT. REALLY.
I'M LYING.
Really? Thank goodness.
IT DOES BOTHER ME.
"I DON'T WANT TO SAY IT"? WHAT WAS THAT ABOUT?
I FELT BLINDSIDED.
OH YEAH, THAT GUY WANTS ME TO MEET HIM ON THE ROOF.
The Toki look-alike.
I GUESS I'LL GO SEE WHAT HE WANTS.
I didn't outright refuse, so...
2-B

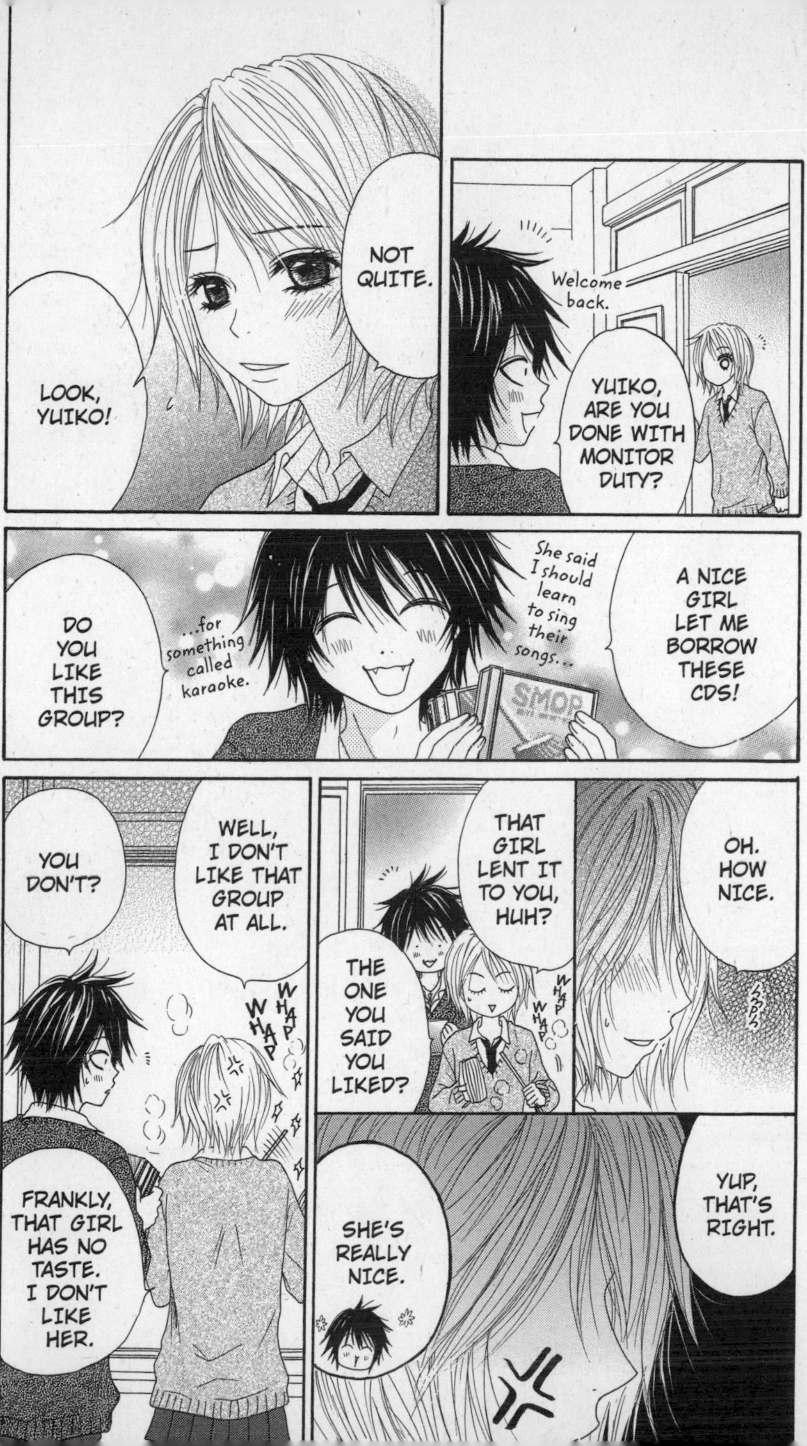
Welcome back.
YUIKO, ARE YOU DONE WITH MONITOR DUTY?
NOT QUITE.
LOOK, YUIKO!
A NICE GIRL LET ME BORROW THESE CDS!
She said I should learn to sing their songs...
...for something called karaoke.
SMOP
DO YOU LIKE THIS GROUP?
OH. HOW NICE.
THAT GIRL LENT IT TO YOU, HUH?
WHAP WHAP
THE ONE YOU SAID YOU LIKED?
YUP, THAT'S RIGHT.
SHE'S REALLY NICE.
WELL, I DON'T LIKE THAT GROUP AT ALL.
YOU DON'T?
WHAP WHAP
FRANKLY, THAT GIRL HAS NO TASTE. I DON'T LIKE HER.

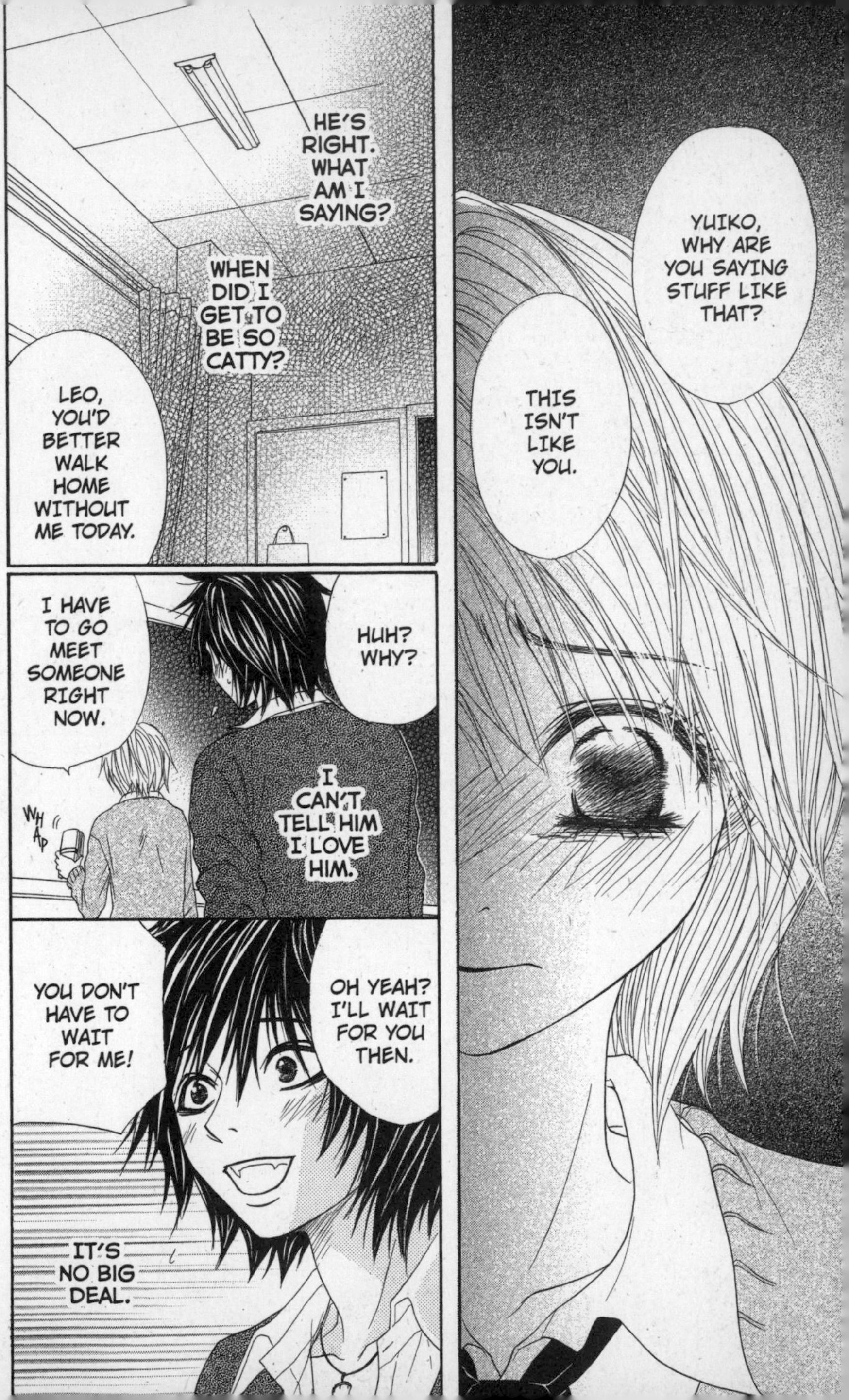
YUIKO, WHY ARE YOU SAYING STUFF LIKE THAT?
THIS ISN'T LIKE YOU.
HE'S RIGHT. WHAT AM I SAYING?
WHEN DID I GET TO BE SO CATTY?
LEO, YOU'D BETTER WALK HOME WITHOUT ME TODAY.
HUH? WHY?
I HAVE TO GO MEET SOMEONE RIGHT NOW.
I CAN'T TELL HIM I LOVE HIM.
WHAP
OH YEAH? I'LL WAIT FOR YOU THEN.
YOU DON'T HAVE TO WAIT FOR ME!
IT'S NO BIG DEAL.

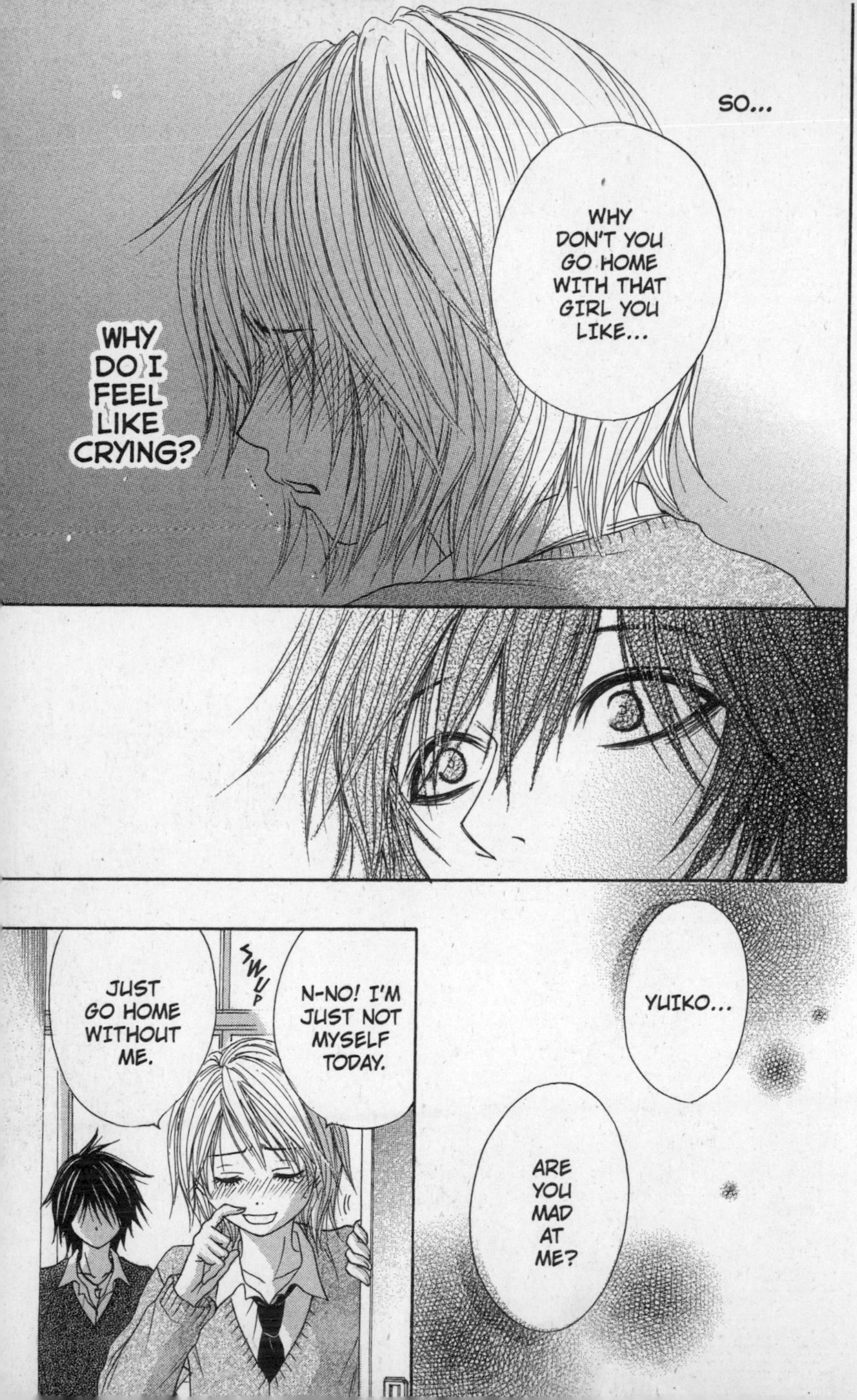
SO...
WHY DON'T YOU GO HOME WITH THAT GIRL YOU LIKE...
WHY DO I FEEL LIKE CRYING?
YUIKO...
ARE YOU MAD AT ME?
N-NO! I'M JUST NOT MYSELF TODAY.
SWUP
JUST GO HOME WITHOUT ME.

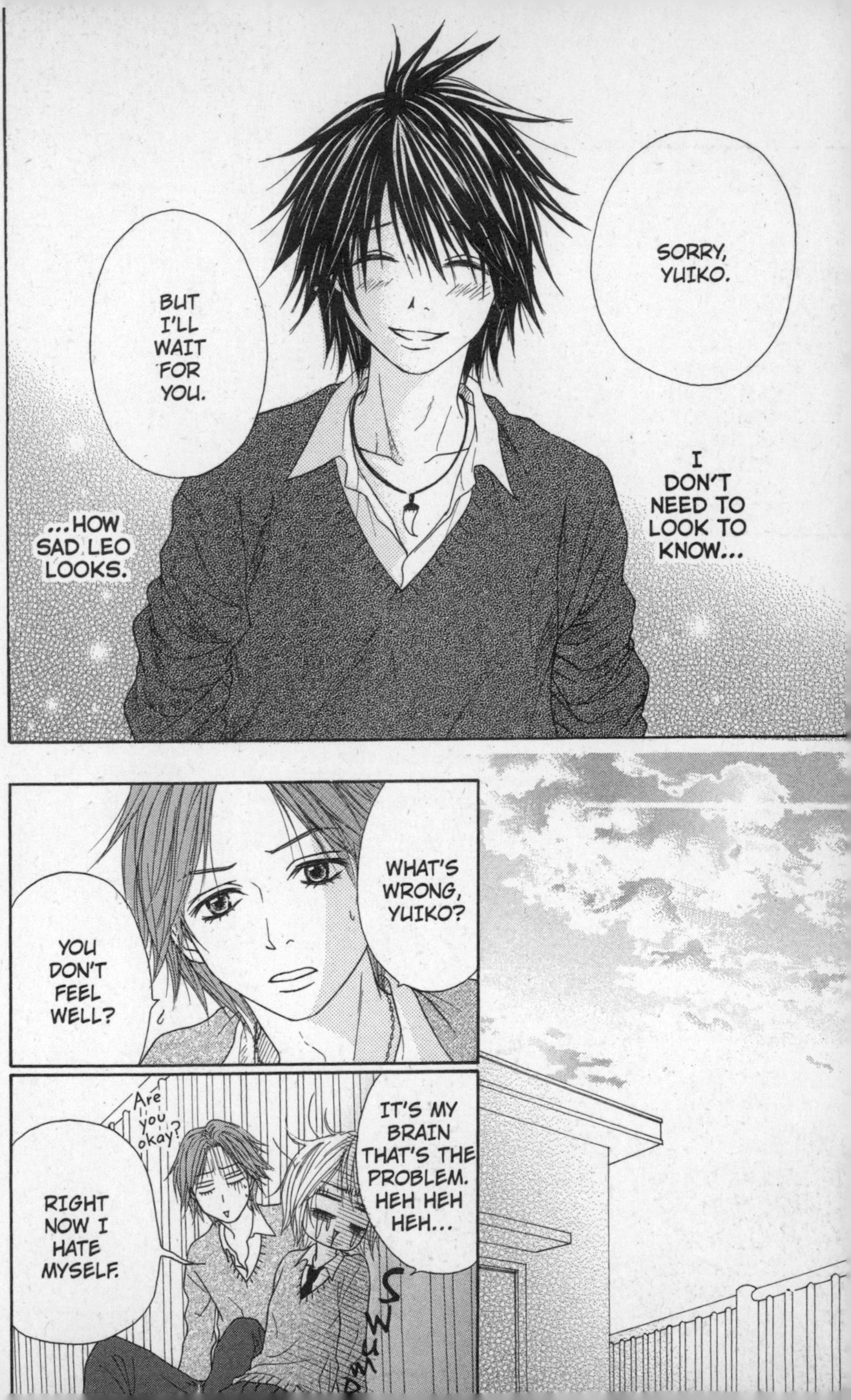

SORRY, YUIKO.
BUT I'LL WAIT FOR YOU.
I DON'T NEED TO LOOK TO KNOW...
...HOW SAD LEO LOOKS.
WHAT'S WRONG, YUIKO?
YOU DON'T FEEL WELL?
IT'S MY BRAIN THAT'S THE PROBLEM. HEH HEH HEH...
SWUMP
Are you okay?
RIGHT NOW I HATE MYSELF.

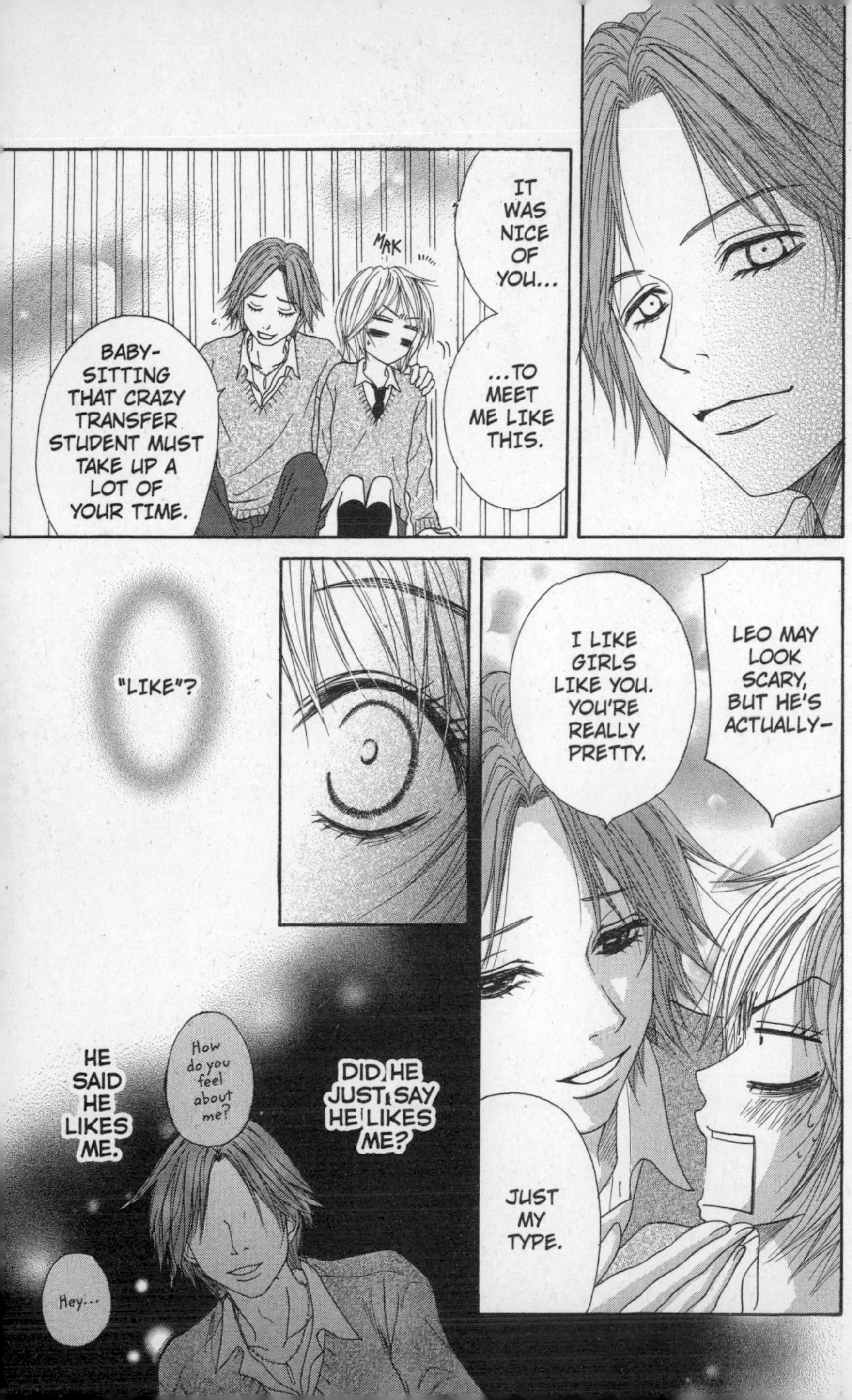
IT WAS NICE OF YOU...
MAK
...TO MEET ME LIKE THIS.
BABY-SITTING THAT CRAZY TRANSFER STUDENT MUST TAKE UP A LOT OF YOUR TIME.
LEO MAY LOOK SCARY, BUT HE'S ACTUALLY—
I LIKE GIRLS LIKE YOU. YOU'RE REALLY PRETTY.
JUST MY TYPE.
"LIKE"?
DID HE JUST SAY HE LIKES ME?
How do you feel about me?
HE SAID HE LIKES ME.
Hey...

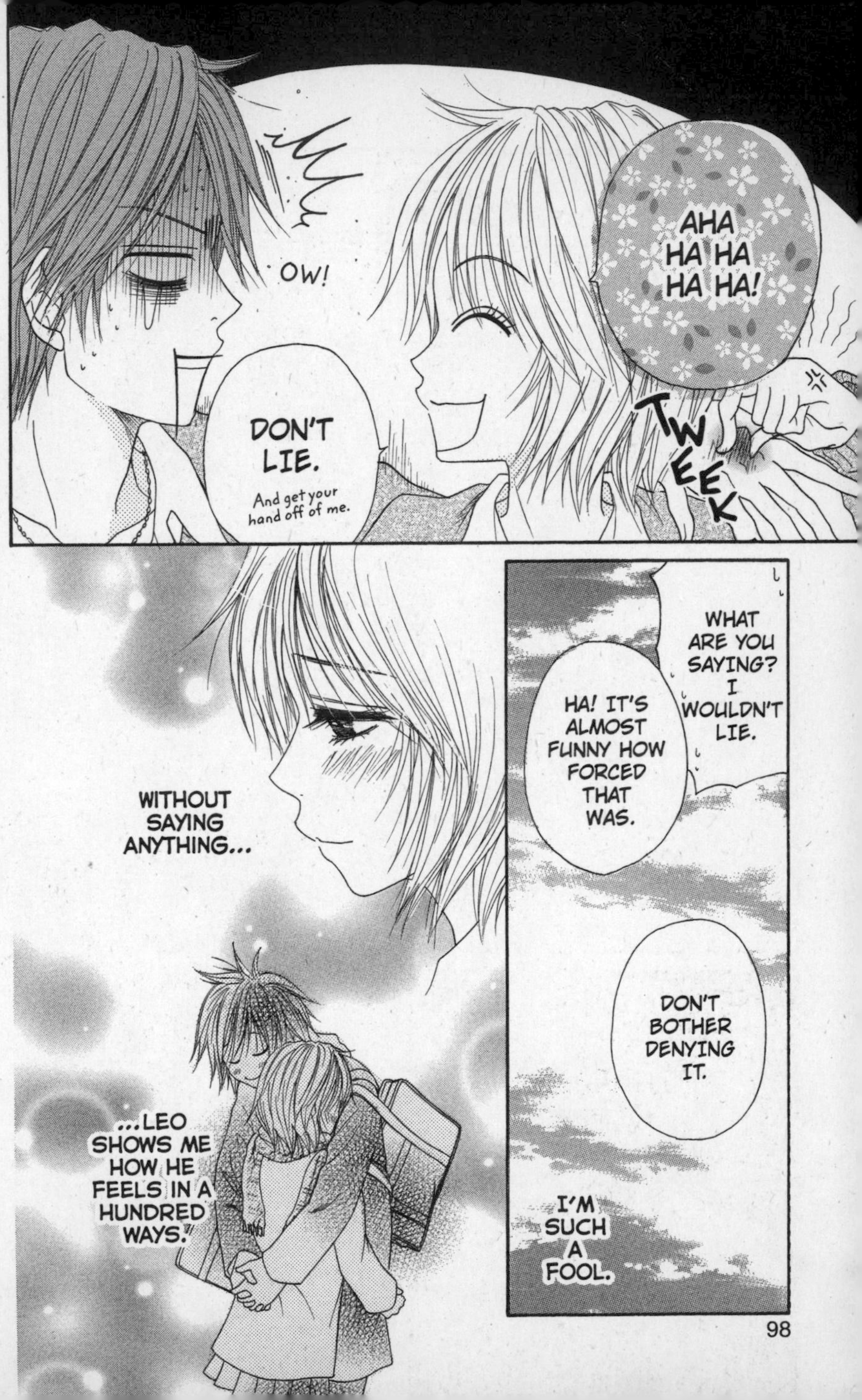

AHA HA HA HA HA!
TWEEK
OW!
DON'T LIE.
And get your hand off of me.
WHAT ARE YOU SAYING? I WOULDN'T LIE.
HA! IT'S ALMOST FUNNY HOW FORCED THAT WAS.
DON'T BOTHER DENYING IT.
I'M SUCH A FOOL.
WITHOUT SAYING ANYTHING...
...LEO SHOWS ME HOW HE FEELS IN A HUNDRED WAYS.

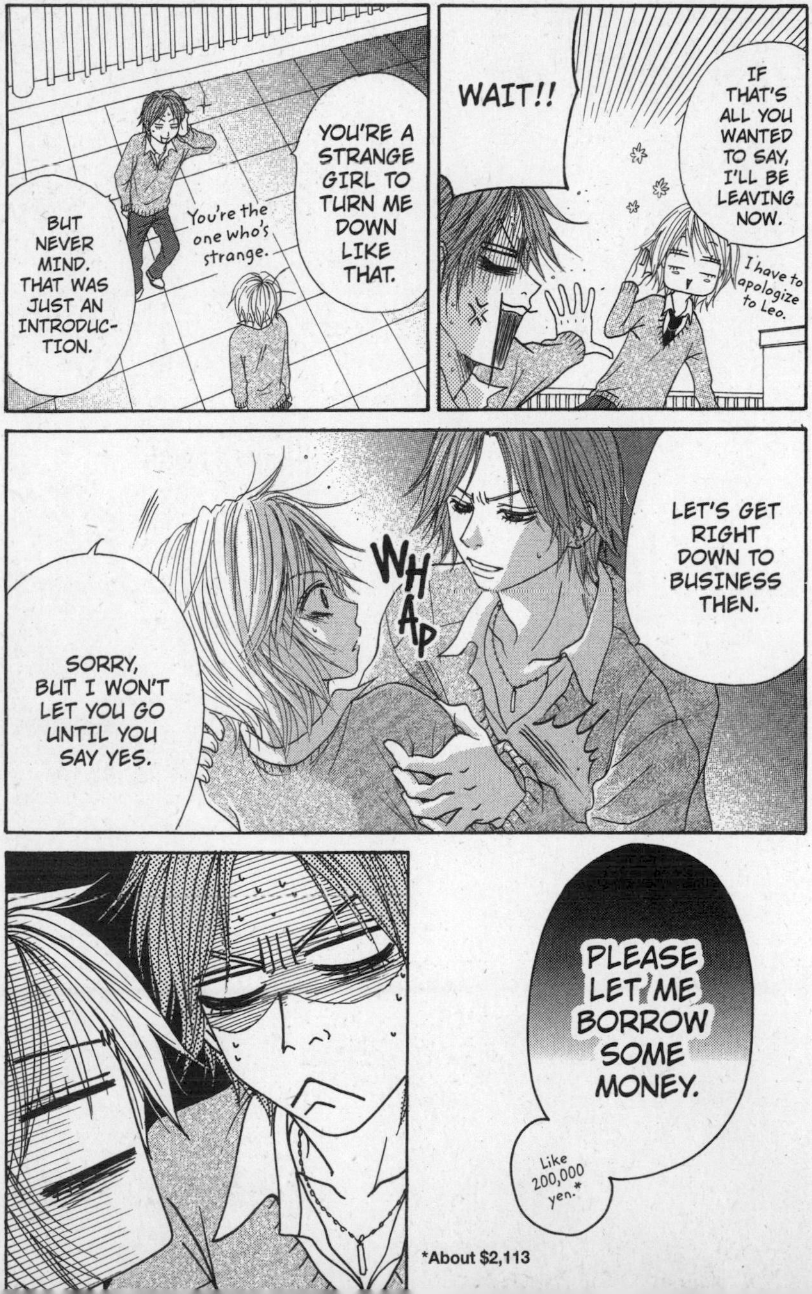
IF THAT'S ALL YOU WANTED TO SAY, I'LL BE LEAVING NOW.
I have to apologize to Leo.
WAIT!!
YOU'RE A STRANGE GIRL TO TURN ME DOWN LIKE THAT.
You're the one who's strange.
BUT NEVER MIND. THAT WAS JUST AN INTRODUC-TION.
LET'S GET RIGHT DOWN TO BUSINESS THEN.
WHAP
SORRY, BUT I WON'T LET YOU GO UNTIL YOU SAY YES.
PLEASE LET ME BORROW SOME MONEY.
Like 200,000 yen.*

*About $2,113

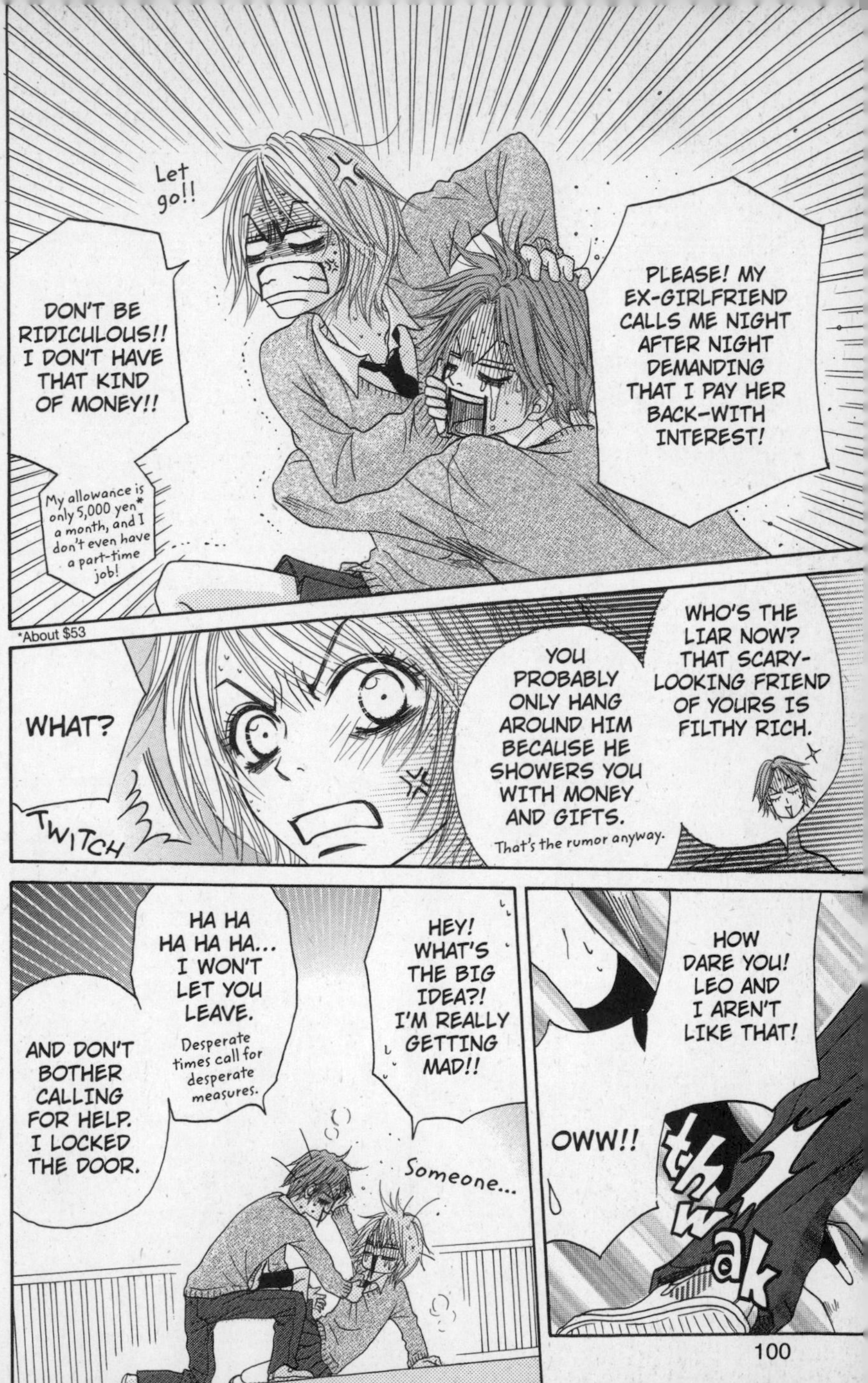
PLEASE! MY EX-GIRLFRIEND CALLS ME NIGHT AFTER NIGHT DEMANDING THAT I PAY HER BACK—WITH INTEREST!
Let go!!
DON'T BE RIDICULOUS!! I DON'T HAVE THAT KIND OF MONEY!!
My allowance is only 5,000 yen* a month, and I don't even have a part-time job!
WHO'S THE LIAR NOW? THAT SCARY-LOOKING FRIEND OF YOURS IS FILTHY RICH.
YOU PROBABLY ONLY HANG AROUND HIM BECAUSE HE SHOWERS YOU WITH MONEY AND GIFTS.
That's the rumor anyway.
WHAT?
TWITCH
HOW DARE YOU! LEO AND I AREN'T LIKE THAT!
OWW!!
thwak
HEY! WHAT'S THE BIG IDEA?! I'M REALLY GETTING MAD!!
Someone...
HA HA HA HA HA... I WON'T LET YOU LEAVE.
Desperate times call for desperate measures.
AND DON'T BOTHER CALLING FOR HELP. I LOCKED THE DOOR.

*About $53

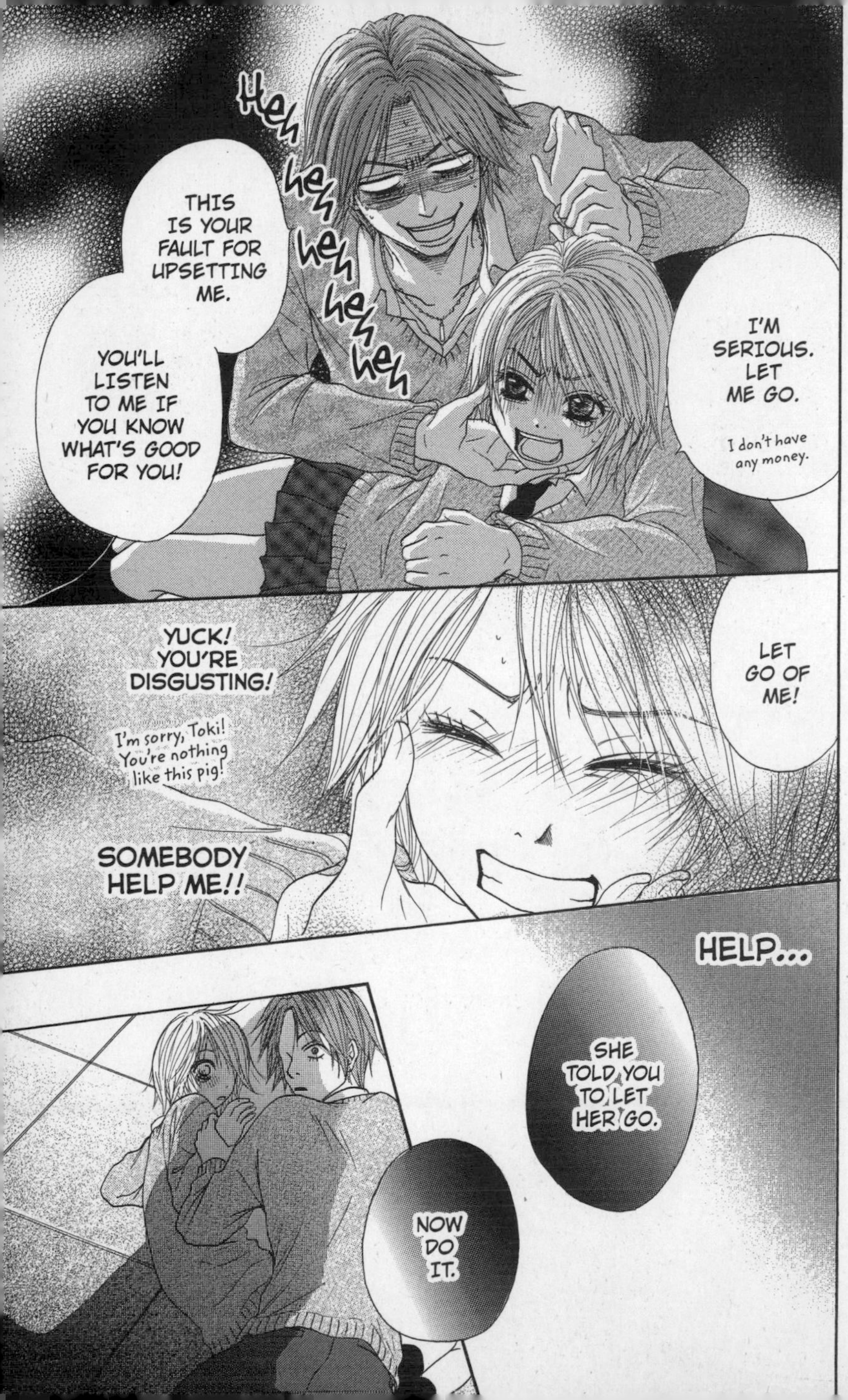
I'M SERIOUS. LET ME GO.
I don't have any money.
Heh heh heh heh heh
THIS IS YOUR FAULT FOR UPSETTING ME.
YOU'LL LISTEN TO ME IF YOU KNOW WHAT'S GOOD FOR YOU!
LET GO OF ME!
YUCK! YOU'RE DISGUSTING!
I'm sorry, Toki! You're nothing like this pig!
SOMEBODY HELP ME!!
HELP...
SHE TOLD YOU TO LET HER GO.
NOW DO IT.

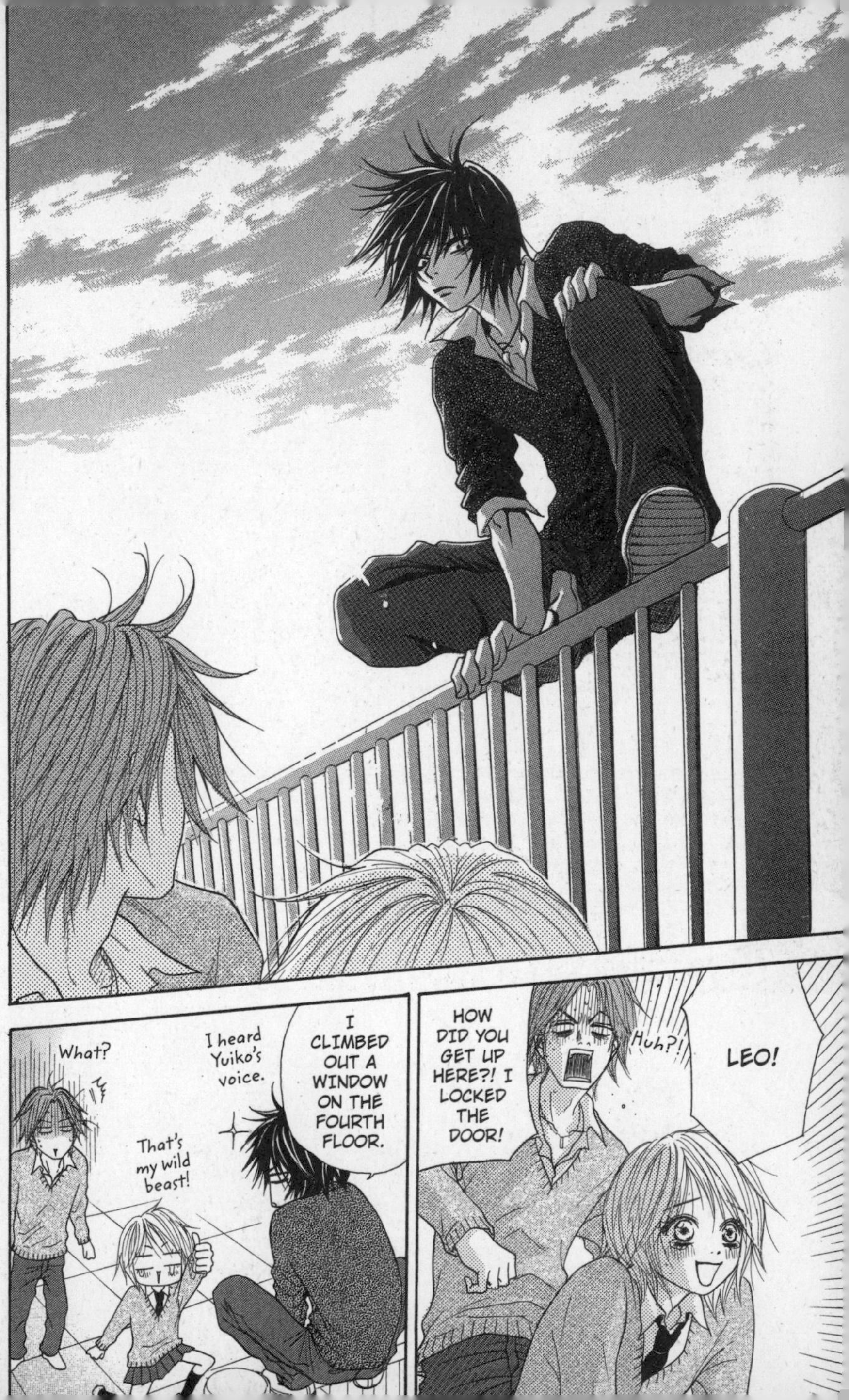
LEO!
Huh?!
HOW DID YOU GET UP HERE?! I LOCKED THE DOOR!
I CLIMBED OUT A WINDOW ON THE FOURTH FLOOR.
I heard Yuiko's voice.
What?
That's my wild beast!

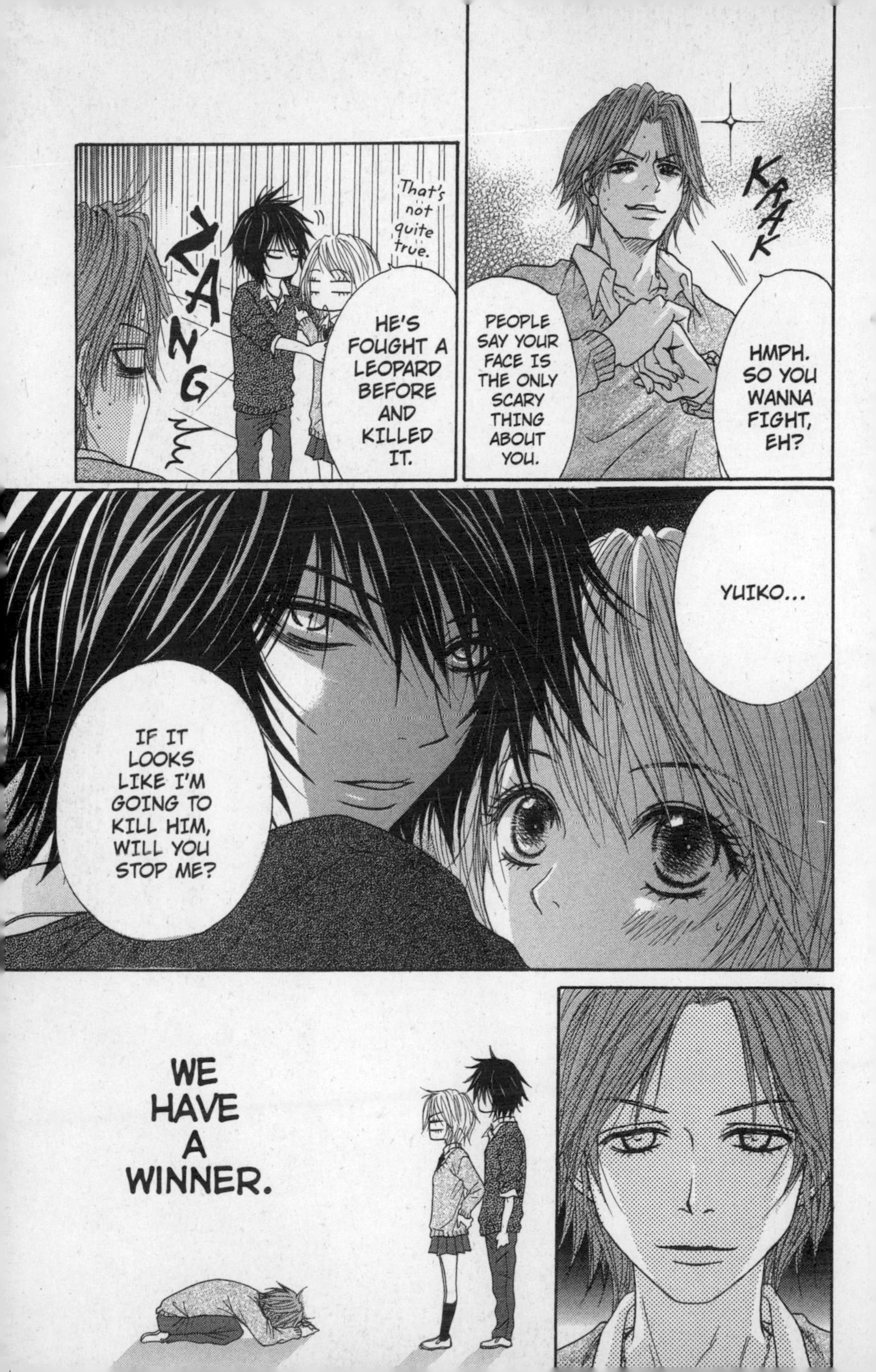
KRAK
HMPH. SO YOU WANNA FIGHT, EH?
PEOPLE SAY YOUR FACE IS THE ONLY SCARY THING ABOUT YOU.
That's not quite true.
HE'S FOUGHT A LEOPARD BEFORE AND KILLED IT.
ZANG
YUIKO...
IF IT LOOKS LIKE I'M GOING TO KILL HIM, WILL YOU STOP ME?
WE HAVE A WINNER.

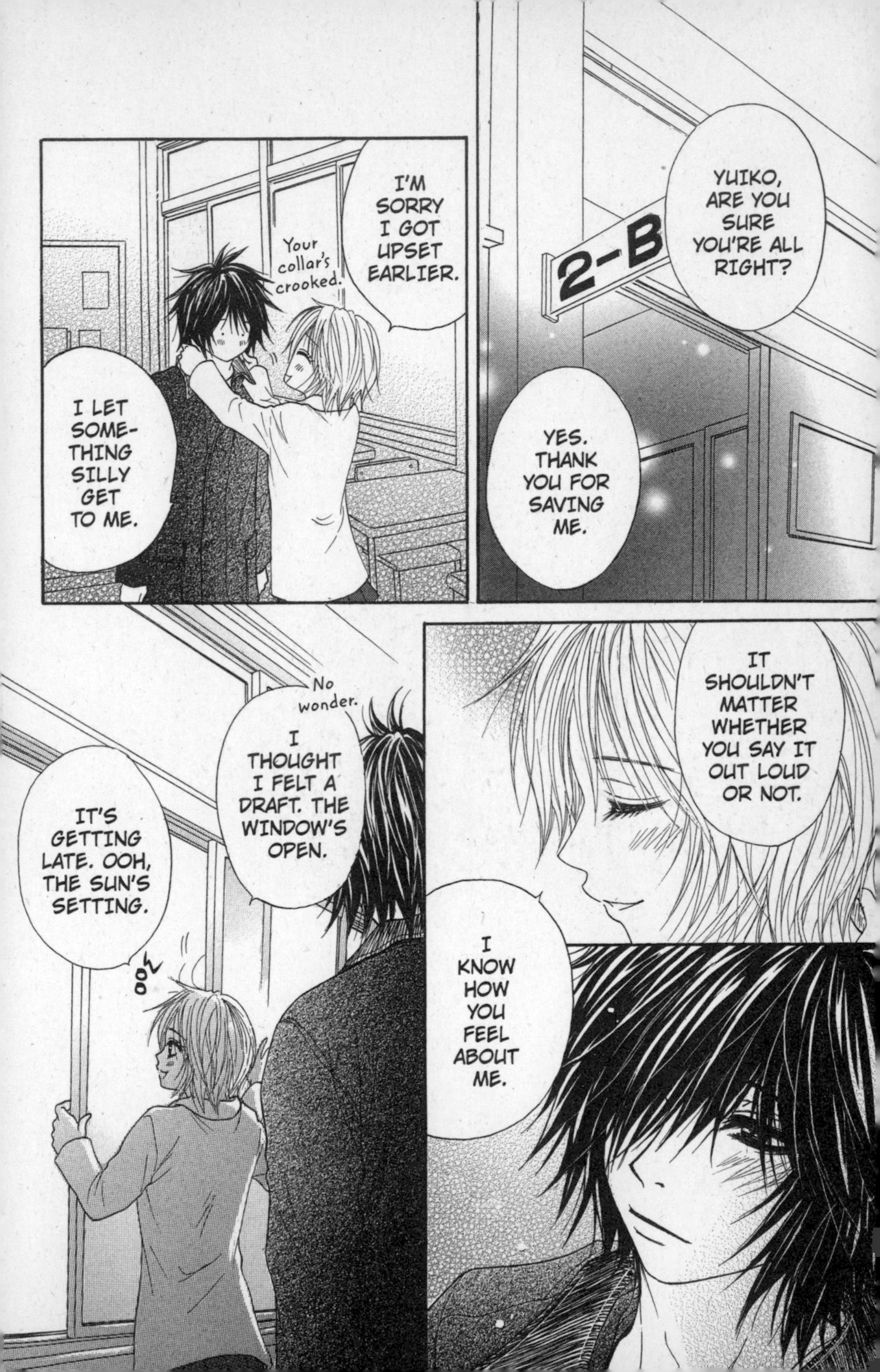
2-B
YUIKO, ARE YOU SURE YOU'RE ALL RIGHT?
YES. THANK YOU FOR SAVING ME.
I'M SORRY I GOT UPSET EARLIER.
Your collar's crooked.
I LET SOME-THING SILLY GET TO ME.
IT SHOULDN'T MATTER WHETHER YOU SAY IT OUT LOUD OR NOT.
I KNOW HOW YOU FEEL ABOUT ME.
No wonder.
I THOUGHT I FELT A DRAFT. THE WINDOW'S OPEN.
IT'S GETTING LATE. OOH, THE SUN'S SETTING.

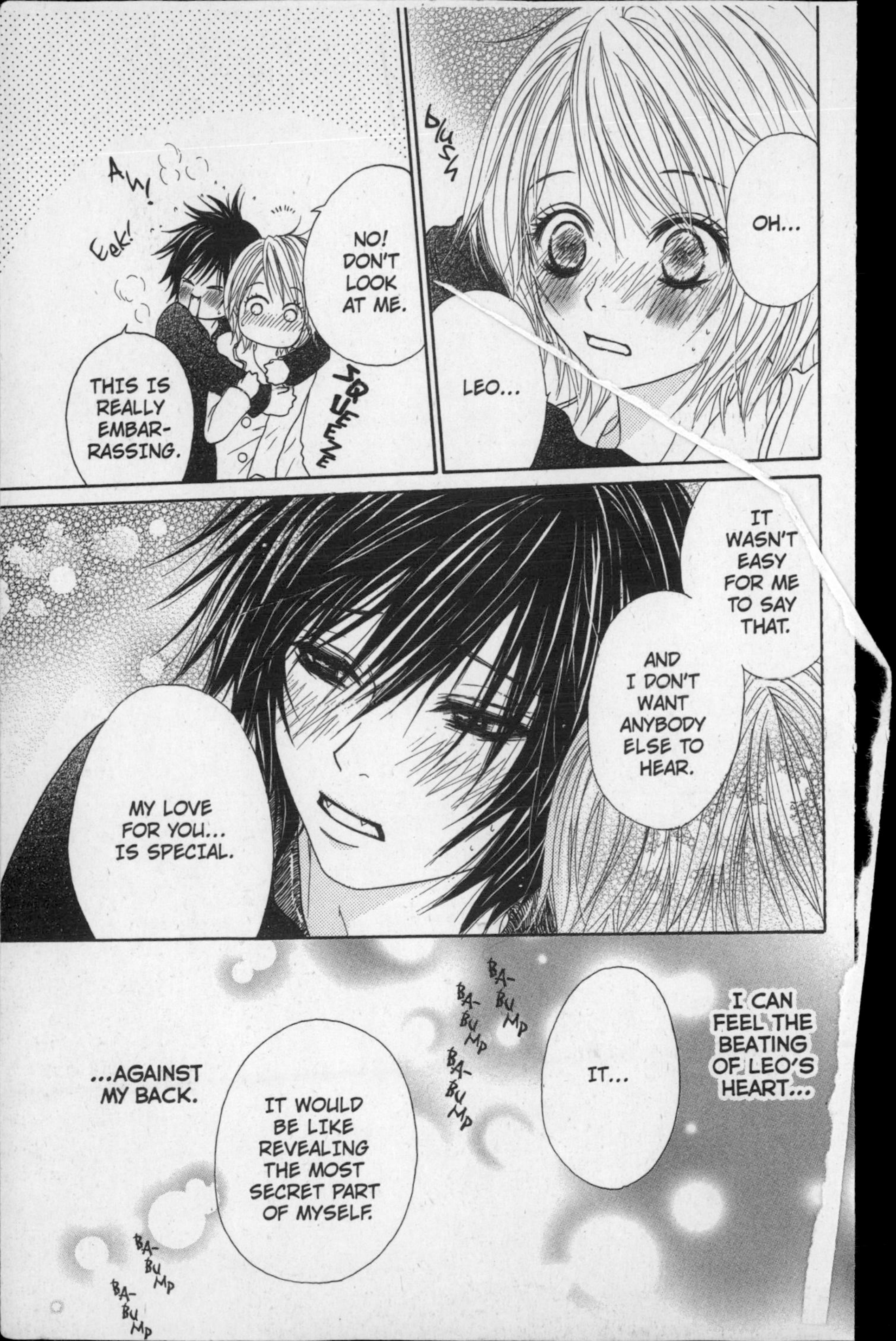
blush
OH...
LEO...
NO! DON'T LOOK AT ME.
Aw!
Eek!
THIS IS REALLY EMBAR-RASSING.
SQUEEZE
IT WASN'T EASY FOR ME TO SAY THAT.
AND I DON'T WANT ANYBODY ELSE TO HEAR.
MY LOVE FOR YOU... IS SPECIAL.
I CAN FEEL THE BEATING OF LEO'S HEART...
IT...
BA-BUMP BA-BUMP BA-BUMP
IT WOULD BE LIKE REVEALING THE MOST SECRET PART OF MYSELF.
...AGAINST MY BACK.
BA-BUMP BA-BUMP

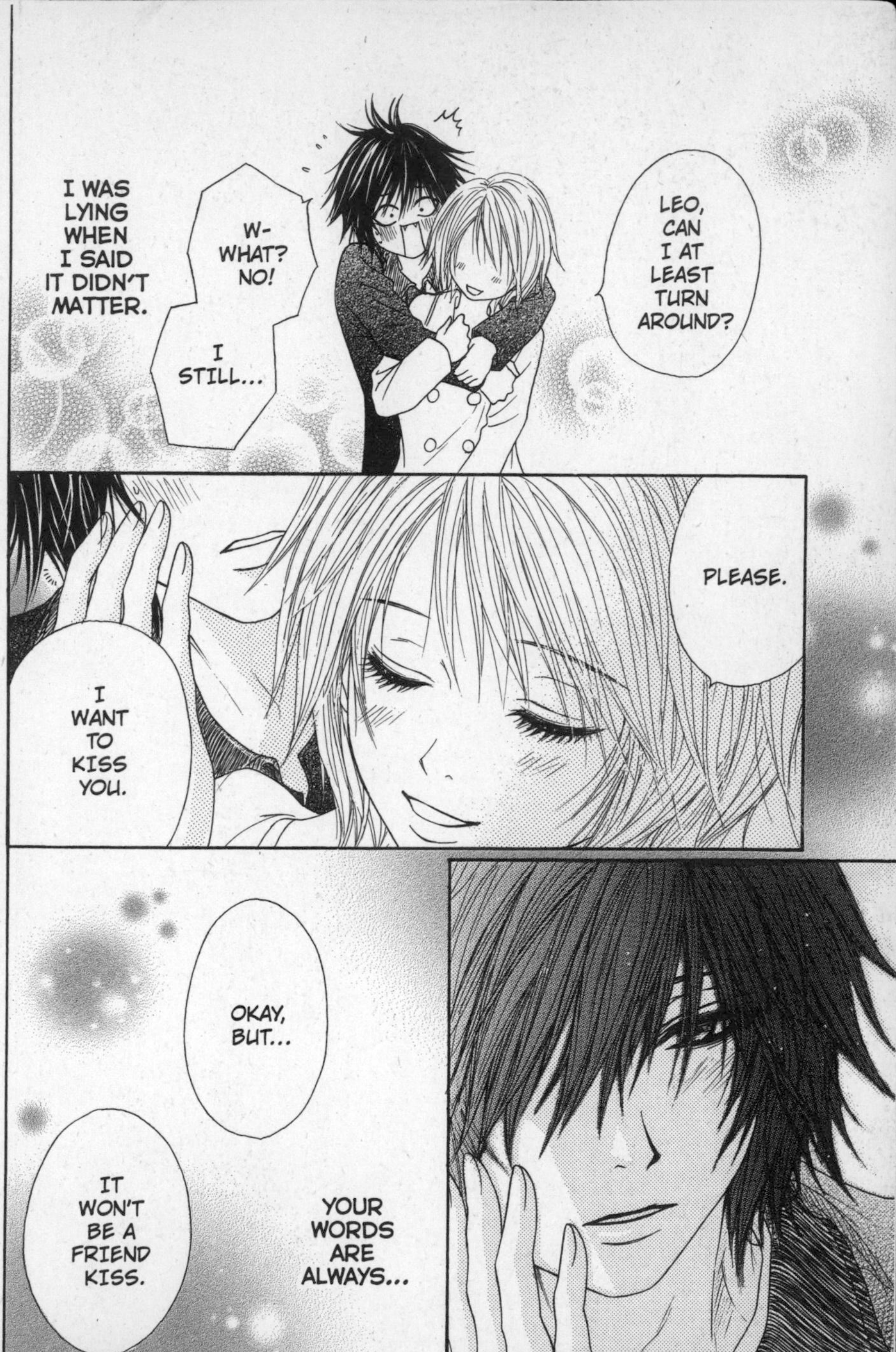
LEO, CAN I AT LEAST TURN AROUND?
W-WHAT? NO!
I STILL...
I WAS LYING WHEN I SAID IT DIDN'T MATTER.
PLEASE.
I WANT TO KISS YOU.
OKAY, BUT...
YOUR WORDS ARE ALWAYS...
IT WON'T BE A FRIEND KISS.

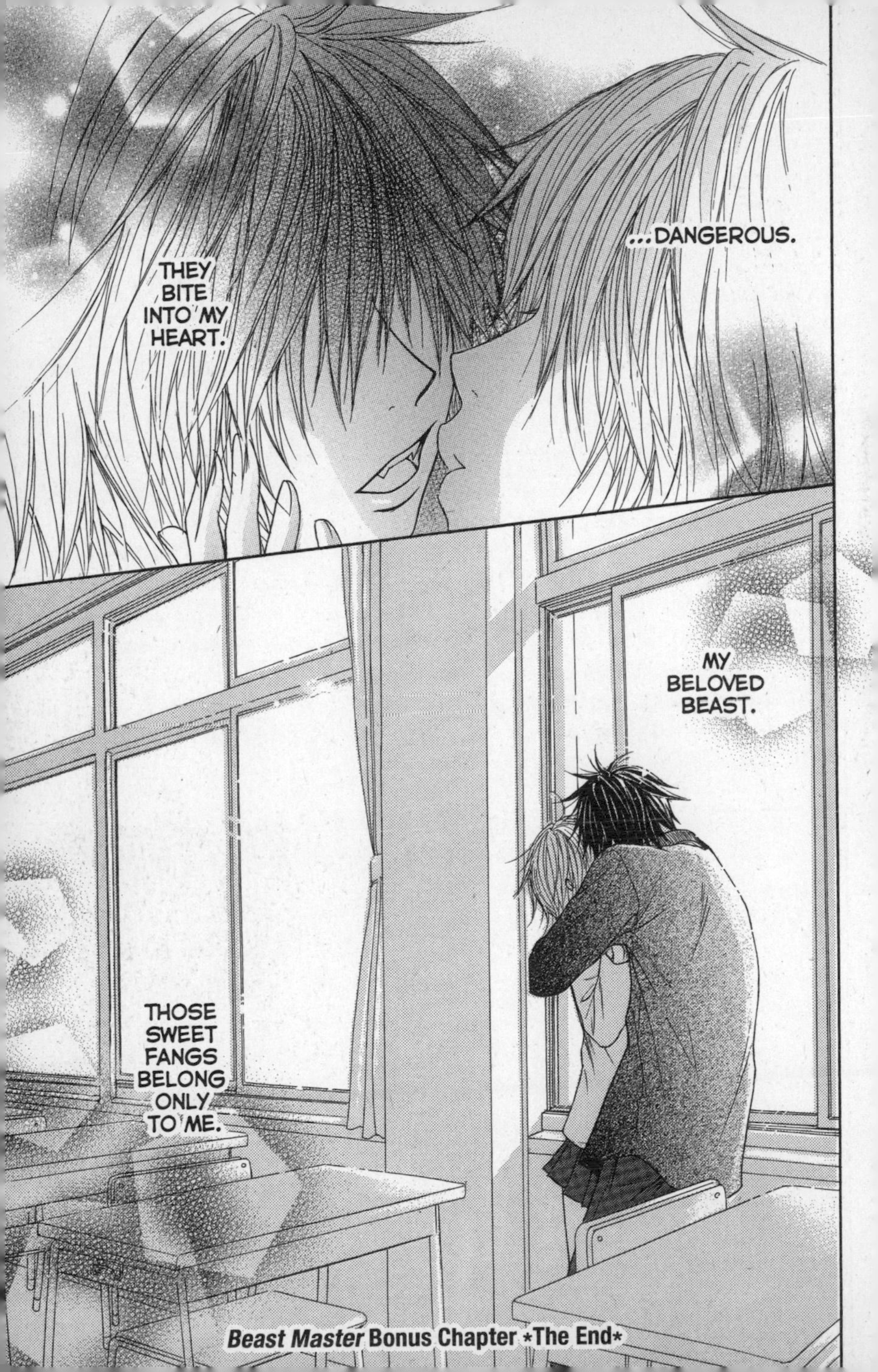
...DANGEROUS.
THEY BITE INTO MY HEART.
MY BELOVED BEAST.
THOSE SWEET FANGS BELONG ONLY TO ME.
Beast Master Bonus Chapter ⋆The End⋆

About "Cactus Summer Surprise"

"What? There's no commentary on the bonus story?" Are any of you thinking that? Of course not. I mean, you read it and understood it, right? It's hard for me to write anything about it!! (I'm too embarrassed!)

Okay, about "Cactus Summer Surprise." I wrote this short story while I was working on Beast Master. It holds many memories for me. What memories? Well, this manga is 80 pages long. Lots of manga artists do that many pages all the time, but for a slow drawer like me, this was a real monster. It was so monstrous I don't remember how I beat it. (After saying how memorable it was...) Anyway, more than the usual number of people helped me with this, and I spent a lot of time drawing it. I even did some research for it. (Ise is really great. I want to go there again. Ise Shrine is truly a powerful place. If you're ever feeling weary, go there!!)

This unexpectedly turned out to be my first fantasy story, and there are more crazy characters than usual. So it's not just the number of pages that made it memorable for me.

As for the human-faced cactus that appears throughout the story, several people have told me that it looks like a self-portrait.
I think so too.

• Also appearing in the story is Kansuke Yamamoto, who I inserted simply because I needed a historical character. I was surprised that he was the central figure in this year's NHK Taiga drama though.

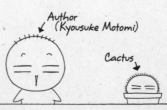

Author
(Kyousuke Motomi)
Cactus

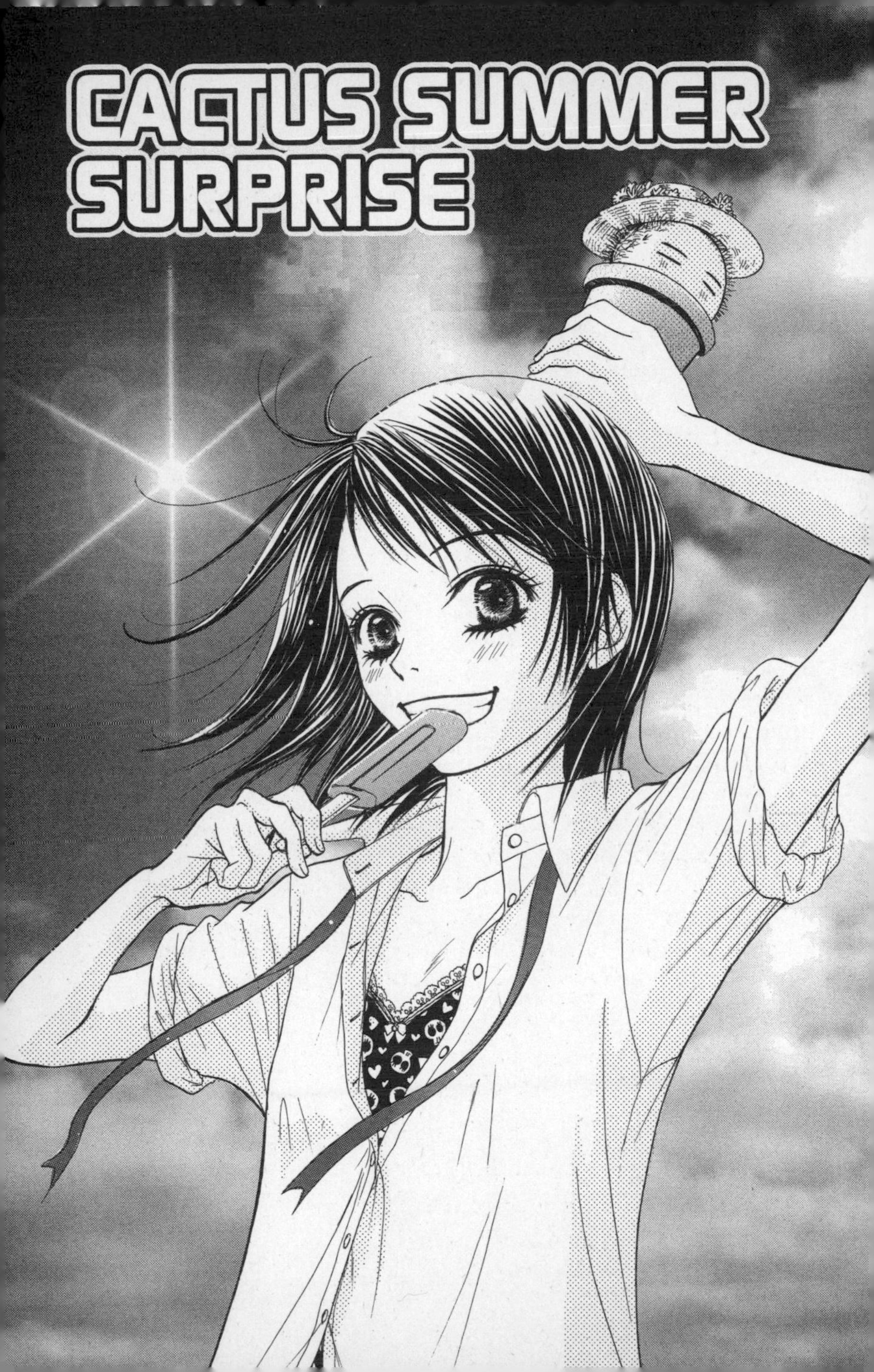
CACTUS SUMMER SURPRISE

IT IS SAID THAT CACTUSES HAVE MYSTERIOUS POWERS.

I ONLY HALF BELIEVED THAT BEFORE.

THIS IS THE STORY OF MY UNUSUAL SUMMER.

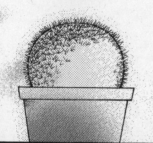

CHAPTER 1: A BALL OF SPIKES SNEAKS UP

SHHK

EXCUSE ME!

WHAT'S THE MATTER, AKIRA?

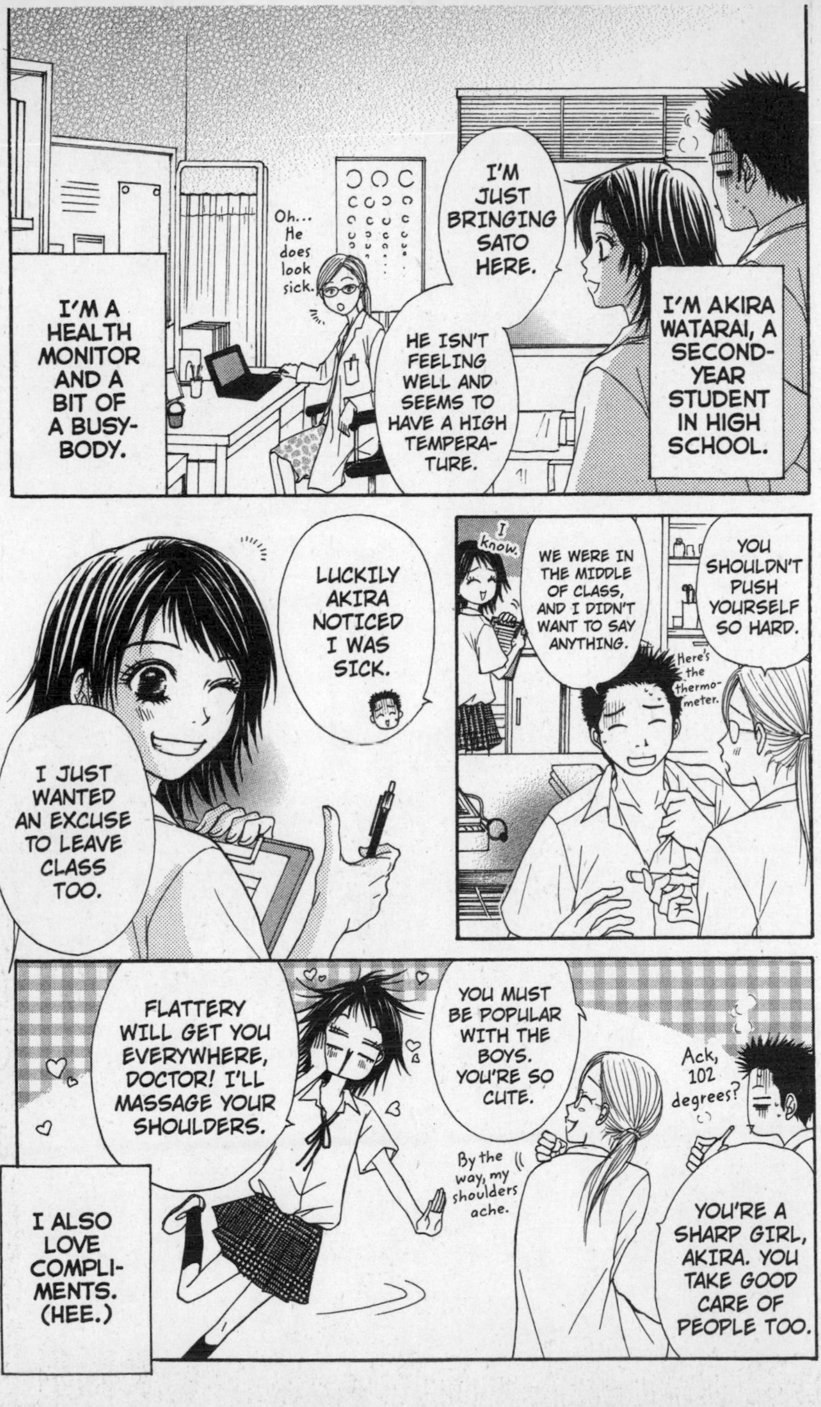
I'M AKIRA WATARAI, A SECOND-YEAR STUDENT IN HIGH SCHOOL.
I'M JUST BRINGING SATO HERE.
HE ISN'T FEELING WELL AND SEEMS TO HAVE A HIGH TEMPERA-TURE.
Oh... He does look sick.
I'M A HEALTH MONITOR AND A BIT OF A BUSY-BODY.
YOU SHOULDN'T PUSH YOURSELF SO HARD.
Here's the thermo-meter.
WE WERE IN THE MIDDLE OF CLASS, AND I DIDN'T WANT TO SAY ANYTHING.
I know.
LUCKILY AKIRA NOTICED I WAS SICK.
I JUST WANTED AN EXCUSE TO LEAVE CLASS TOO.
Ack, 102 degrees?
YOU'RE A SHARP GIRL, AKIRA. YOU TAKE GOOD CARE OF PEOPLE TOO.
YOU MUST BE POPULAR WITH THE BOYS. YOU'RE SO CUTE.
FLATTERY WILL GET YOU EVERYWHERE, DOCTOR! I'LL MASSAGE YOUR SHOULDERS.
By the way, my shoulders ache.
I ALSO LOVE COMPLI-MENTS. (HEE.)

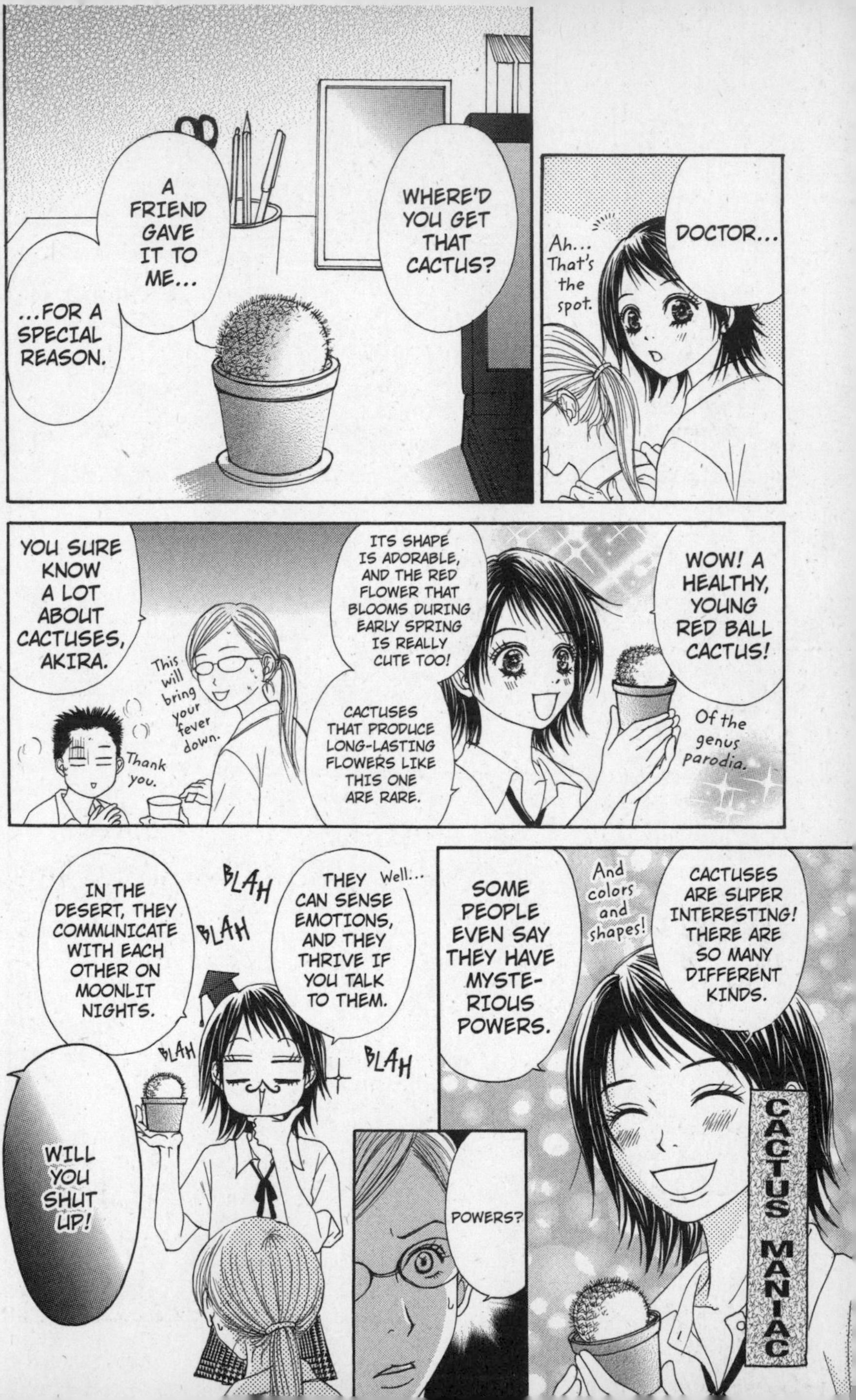
DOCTOR...
Ah... That's the spot.
WHERE'D YOU GET THAT CACTUS?
A FRIEND GAVE IT TO ME...
...FOR A SPECIAL REASON.
WOW! A HEALTHY, YOUNG RED BALL CACTUS!
Of the genus parodia.
ITS SHAPE IS ADORABLE, AND THE RED FLOWER THAT BLOOMS DURING EARLY SPRING IS REALLY CUTE TOO!
CACTUSES THAT PRODUCE LONG-LASTING FLOWERS LIKE THIS ONE ARE RARE.
This will bring your fever down.
Thank you.
YOU SURE KNOW A LOT ABOUT CACTUSES, AKIRA.
CACTUSES ARE SUPER INTERESTING! THERE ARE SO MANY DIFFERENT KINDS.
And colors and shapes!
SOME PEOPLE EVEN SAY THEY HAVE MYSTE-RIOUS POWERS.
CACTUS MANIAC
POWERS?
THEY CAN SENSE EMOTIONS, AND THEY THRIVE IF YOU TALK TO THEM.
Well...
IN THE DESERT, THEY COMMUNICATE WITH EACH OTHER ON MOONLIT NIGHTS.
BLAH
BLAH
BLAH
BLAH
WILL YOU SHUT UP!

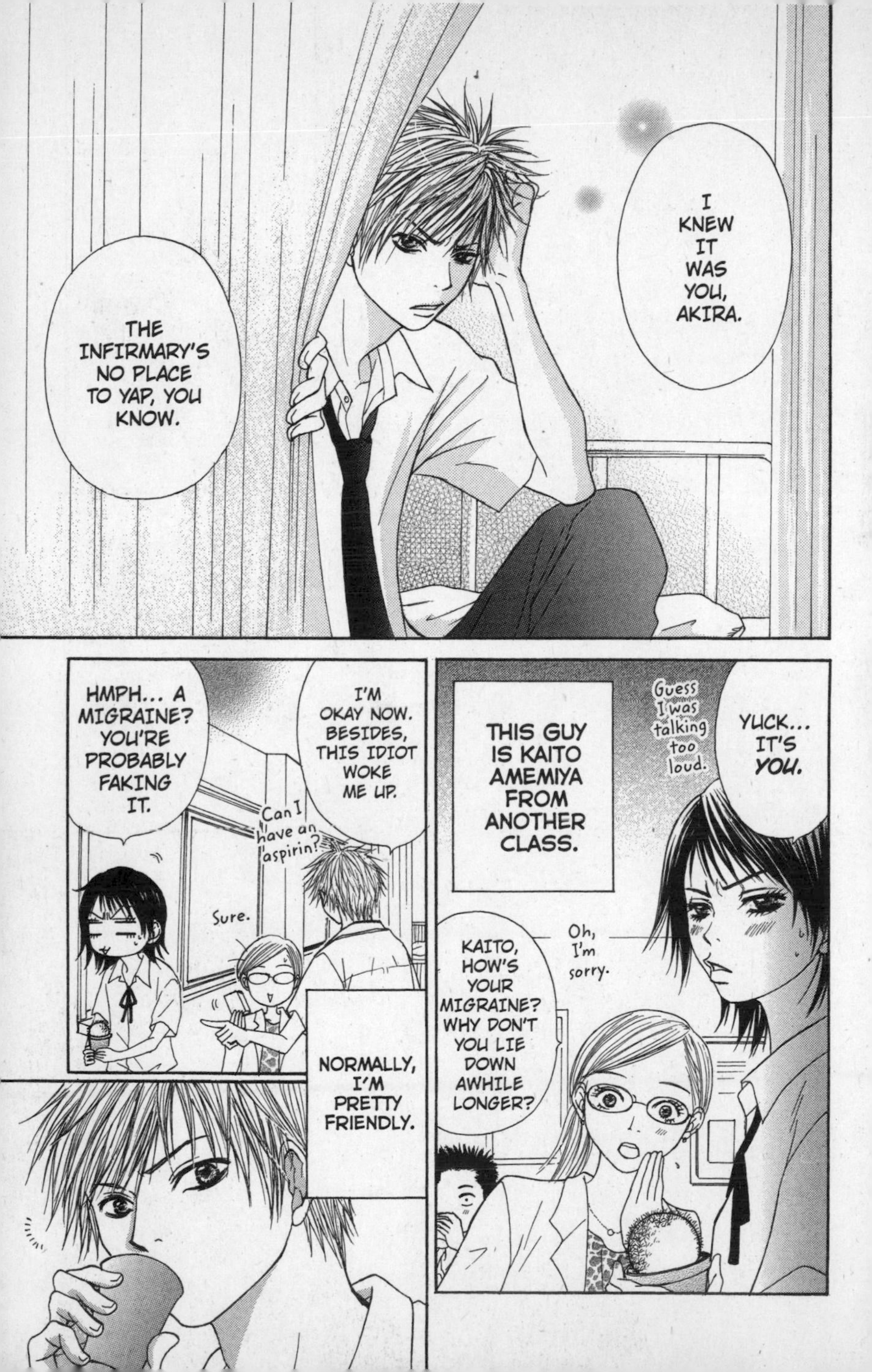
I KNEW IT WAS YOU, AKIRA.
THE INFIRMARY'S NO PLACE TO YAP, YOU KNOW.
YUCK... IT'S YOU.
Guess I was talking too loud.
THIS GUY IS KAITO AMEMIYA FROM ANOTHER CLASS.
Oh, I'm sorry.
KAITO, HOW'S YOUR MIGRAINE? WHY DON'T YOU LIE DOWN AWHILE LONGER?
I'M OKAY NOW. BESIDES, THIS IDIOT WOKE ME UP.
Can I have an aspirin?
HMPH... A MIGRAINE? YOU'RE PROBABLY FAKING IT.
Sure.
NORMALLY, I'M PRETTY FRIENDLY.

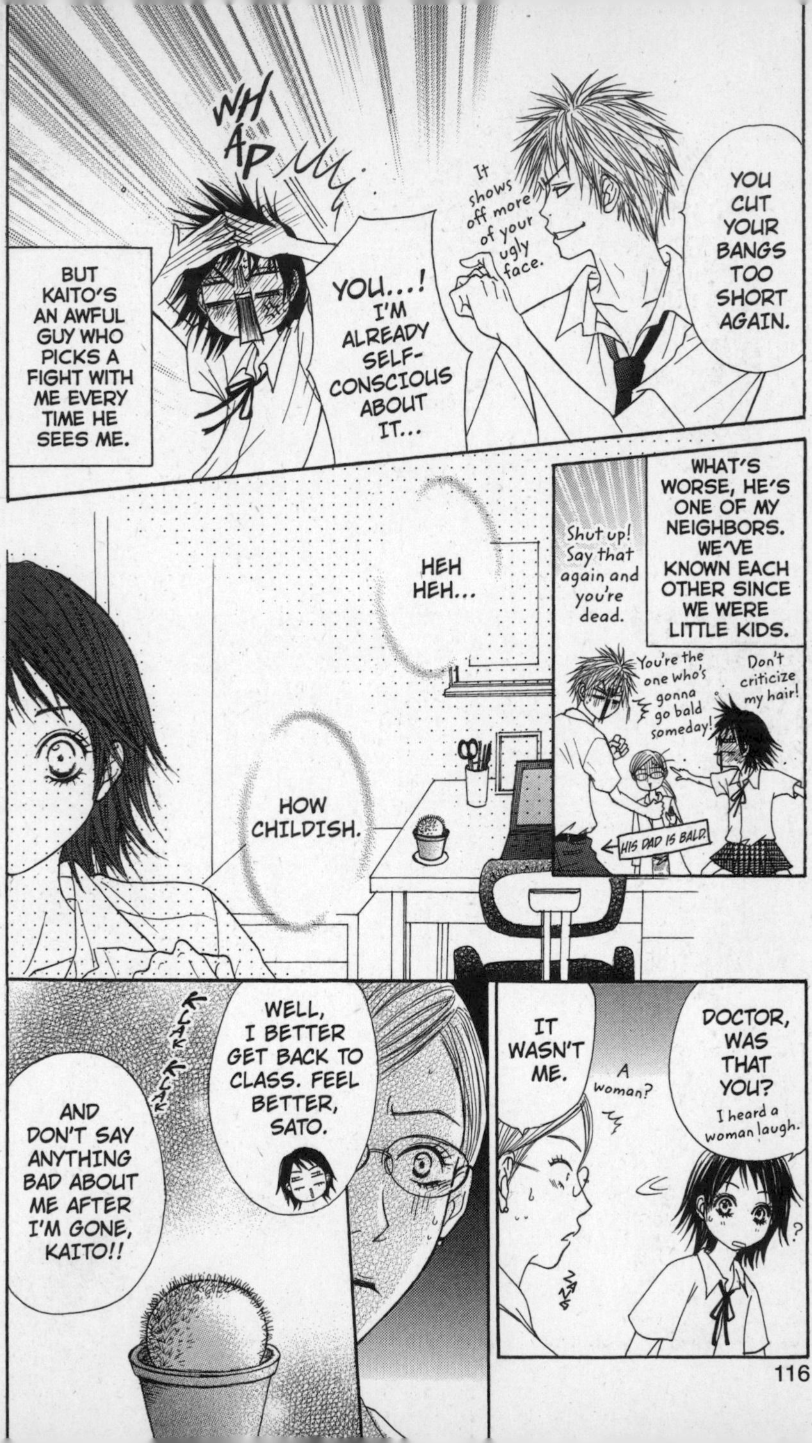
YOU CUT YOUR BANGS TOO SHORT AGAIN.
It shows off more of your ugly face.
WHAP
YOU...! I'M ALREADY SELF-CONSCIOUS ABOUT IT...
BUT KAITO'S AN AWFUL GUY WHO PICKS A FIGHT WITH ME EVERY TIME HE SEES ME.
WHAT'S WORSE, HE'S ONE OF MY NEIGHBORS. WE'VE KNOWN EACH OTHER SINCE WE WERE LITTLE KIDS.
Shut up! Say that again and you're dead.
Don't criticize my hair!
You're the one who's gonna go bald someday!
HIS DAD IS BALD.
HEH HEH...
HOW CHILDISH.
DOCTOR, WAS THAT YOU?
I heard a woman laugh.
IT WASN'T ME.
A woman?
WELL, I BETTER GET BACK TO CLASS. FEEL BETTER, SATO.
KLAK KLAK
AND DON'T SAY ANYTHING BAD ABOUT ME AFTER I'M GONE, KAITO!!

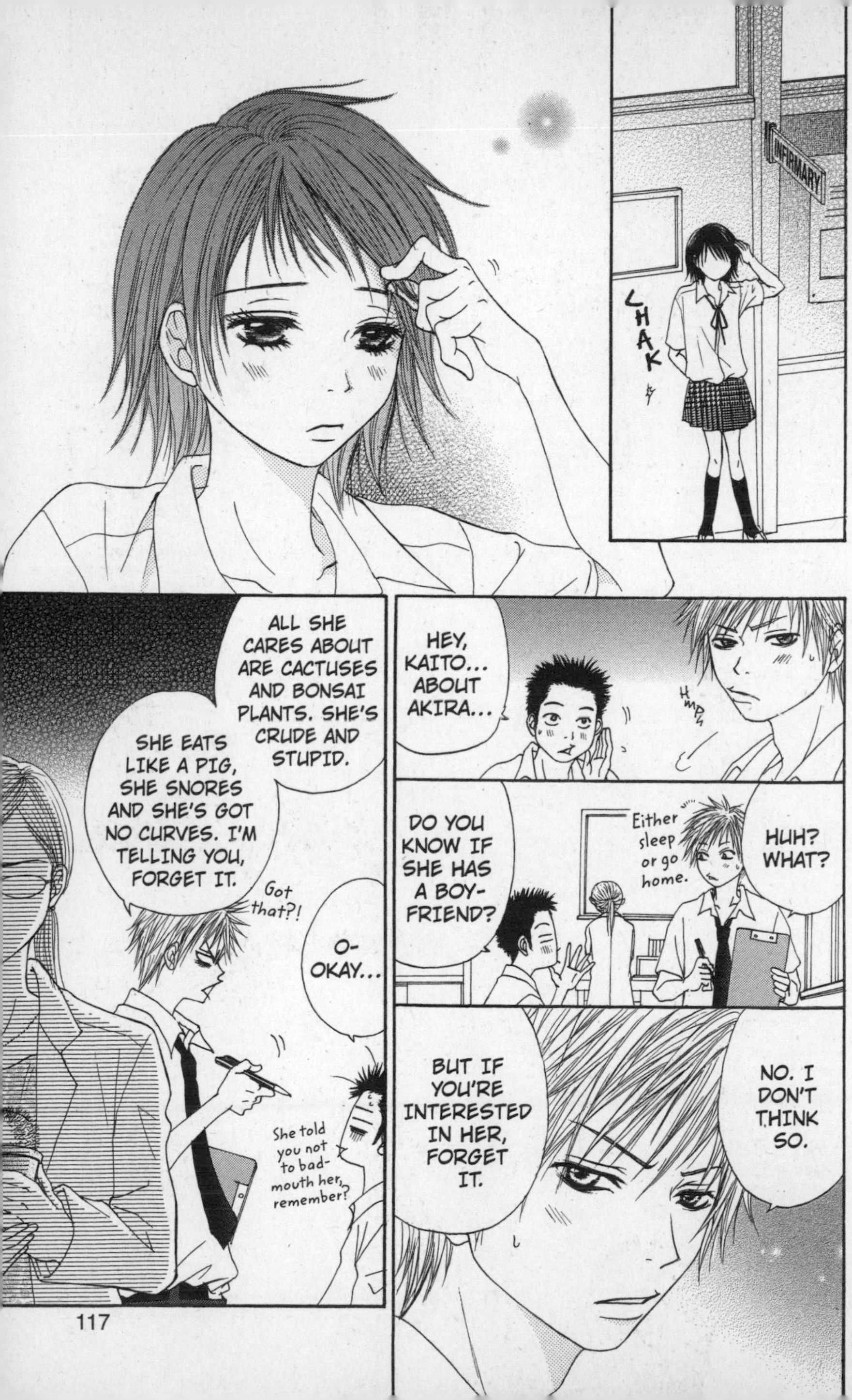
INFIRMARY
CHAK
HEY, KAITO... ABOUT AKIRA...
HMPH
HUH? WHAT?
Either sleep or go home.
DO YOU KNOW IF SHE HAS A BOY-FRIEND?
NO. I DON'T THINK SO.
BUT IF YOU'RE INTERESTED IN HER, FORGET IT.
ALL SHE CARES ABOUT ARE CACTUSES AND BONSAI PLANTS. SHE'S CRUDE AND STUPID.
SHE EATS LIKE A PIG, SHE SNORES AND SHE'S GOT NO CURVES. I'M TELLING YOU, FORGET IT.
Got that?!
O-OKAY...
She told you not to bad-mouth her, remember?

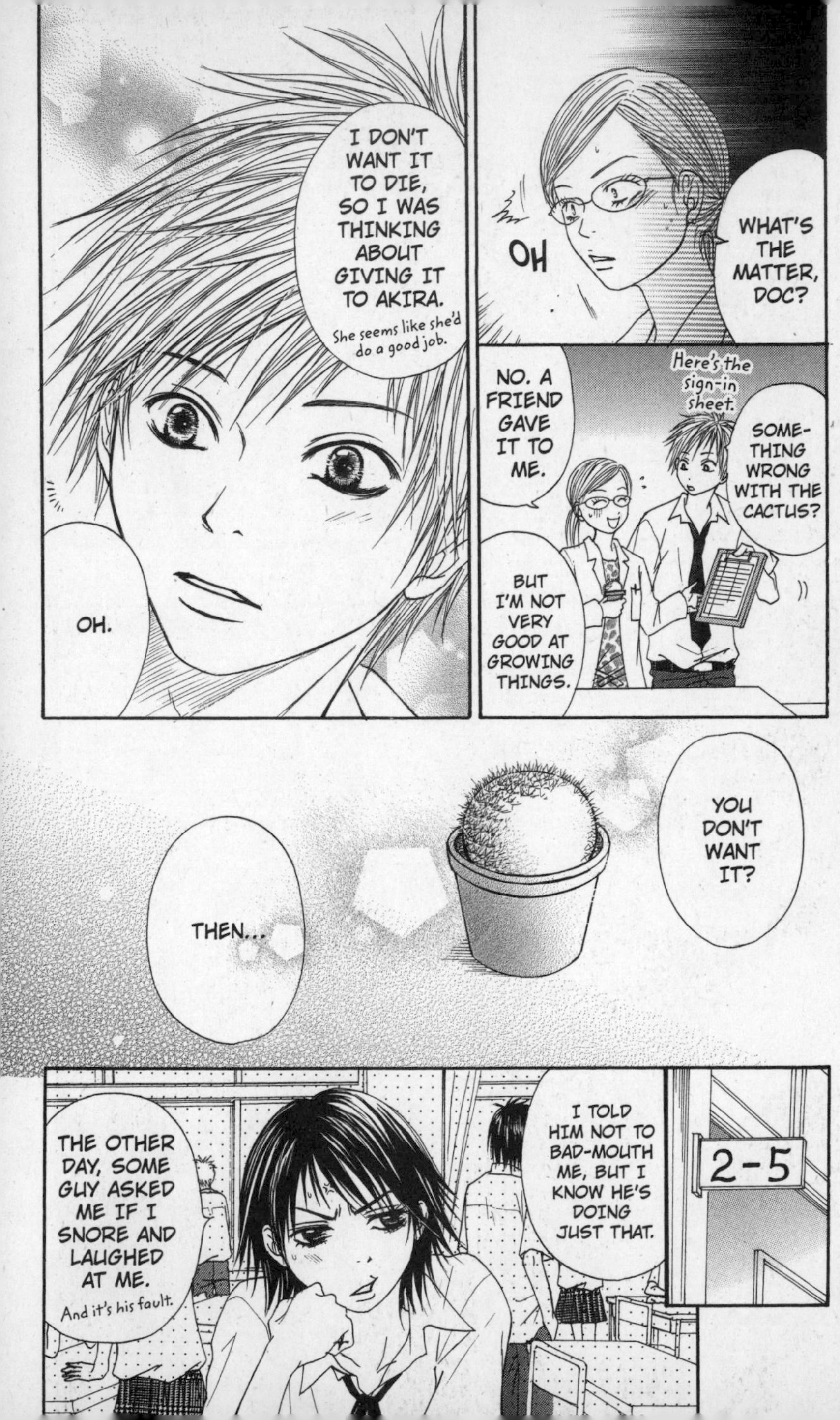
WHAT'S THE MATTER, DOC?
OH
Here's the sign-in sheet.
SOMETHING WRONG WITH THE CACTUS?
NO. A FRIEND GAVE IT TO ME.
BUT I'M NOT VERY GOOD AT GROWING THINGS.
I DON'T WANT IT TO DIE, SO I WAS THINKING ABOUT GIVING IT TO AKIRA.
She seems like she'd do a good job.
OH.
YOU DON'T WANT IT?
THEN...
2-5
I TOLD HIM NOT TO BAD-MOUTH ME, BUT I KNOW HE'S DOING JUST THAT.
THE OTHER DAY, SOME GUY ASKED ME IF I SNORE AND LAUGHED AT ME.
And it's his fault.

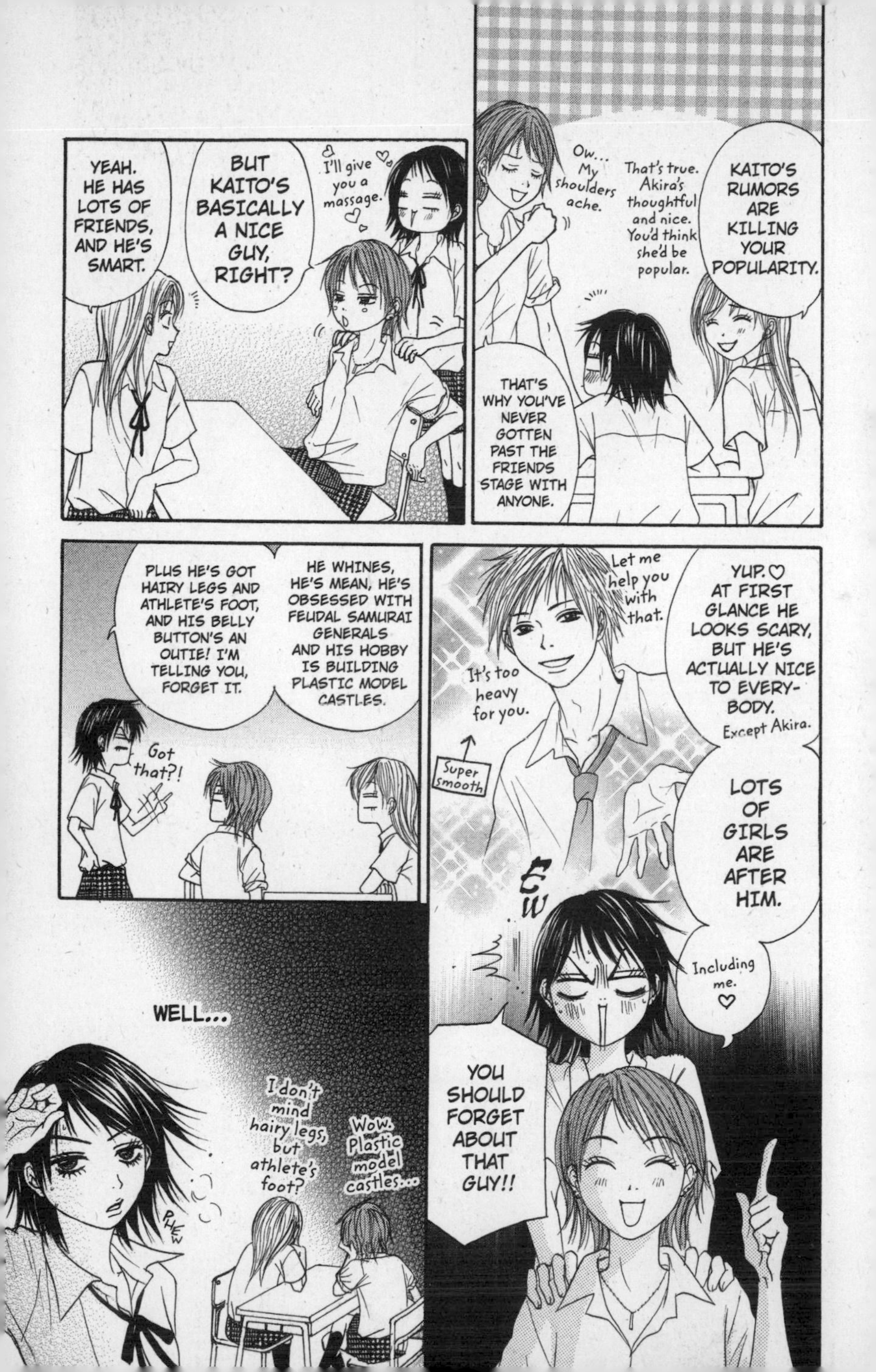
KAITO'S RUMORS ARE KILLING YOUR POPULARITY.
That's true. Akira's thoughtful and nice. You'd think she'd be popular.
Ow... My shoulders ache.
THAT'S WHY YOU'VE NEVER GOTTEN PAST THE FRIENDS STAGE WITH ANYONE.
I'll give you a massage.
BUT KAITO'S BASICALLY A NICE GUY, RIGHT?
YEAH. HE HAS LOTS OF FRIENDS, AND HE'S SMART.
YUP. ♡ AT FIRST GLANCE HE LOOKS SCARY, BUT HE'S ACTUALLY NICE TO EVERYBODY.
Except Akira.
Let me help you with that.
It's too heavy for you.
Super smooth
LOTS OF GIRLS ARE AFTER HIM.
Including me. ♡
EW
YOU SHOULD FORGET ABOUT THAT GUY!!
HE WHINES, HE'S MEAN, HE'S OBSESSED WITH FEUDAL SAMURAI GENERALS AND HIS HOBBY IS BUILDING PLASTIC MODEL CASTLES.
PLUS HE'S GOT HAIRY LEGS AND ATHLETE'S FOOT, AND HIS BELLY BUTTON'S AN OUTIE! I'M TELLING YOU, FORGET IT.
Got that?!
WELL...
Wow. Plastic model castles...
I don't mind hairy legs, but athlete's foot?
PHEW

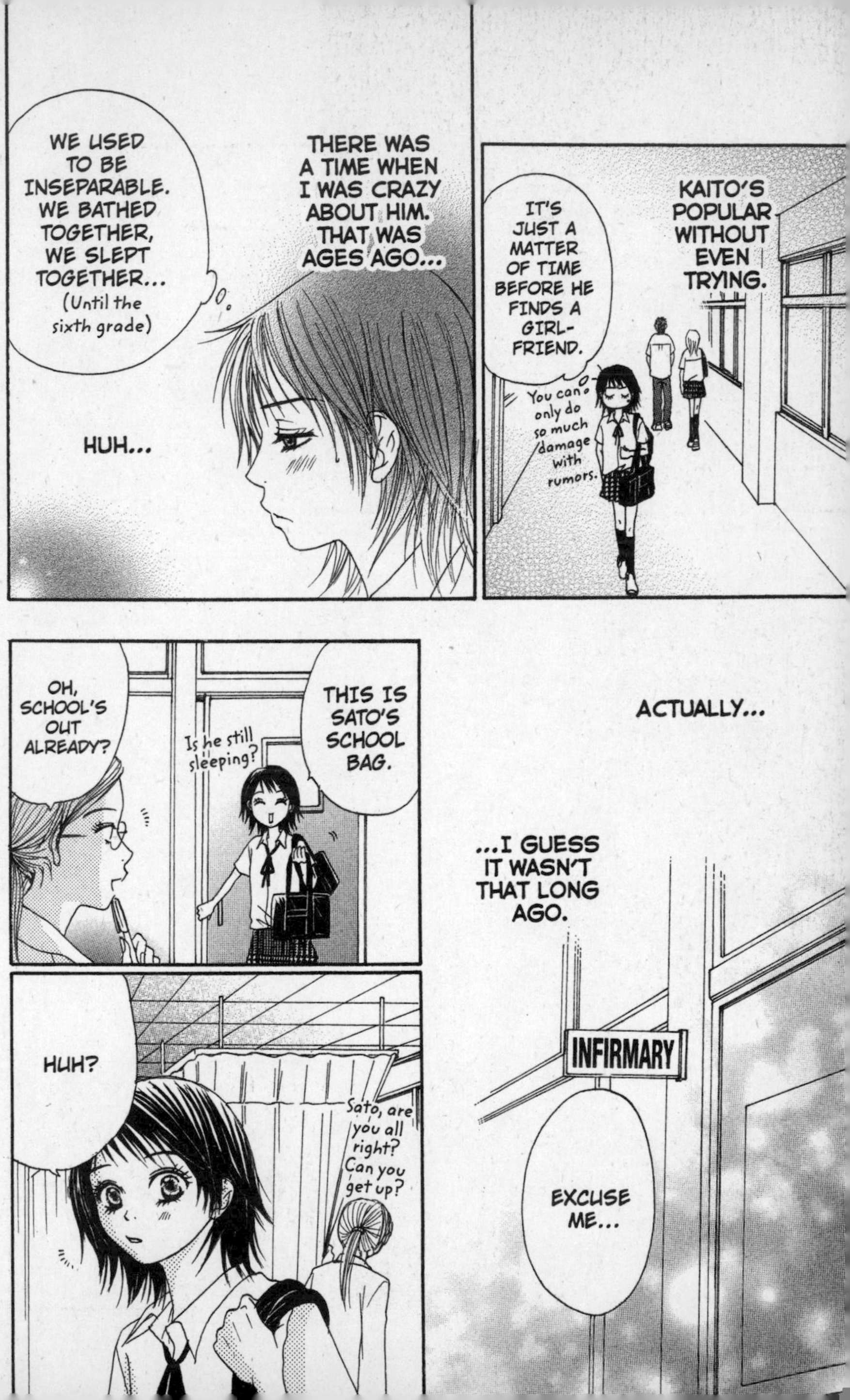
KAITO'S POPULAR WITHOUT EVEN TRYING.
IT'S JUST A MATTER OF TIME BEFORE HE FINDS A GIRLFRIEND.
You can only do so much damage with rumors.
THERE WAS A TIME WHEN I WAS CRAZY ABOUT HIM. THAT WAS AGES AGO...
WE USED TO BE INSEPARABLE. WE BATHED TOGETHER, WE SLEPT TOGETHER...
(Until the sixth grade)
HUH...
ACTUALLY...
...I GUESS IT WASN'T THAT LONG AGO.
INFIRMARY
EXCUSE ME...
THIS IS SATO'S SCHOOL BAG.
Is he still sleeping?
OH, SCHOOL'S OUT ALREADY?
Sato, are you all right? Can you get up?
HUH?

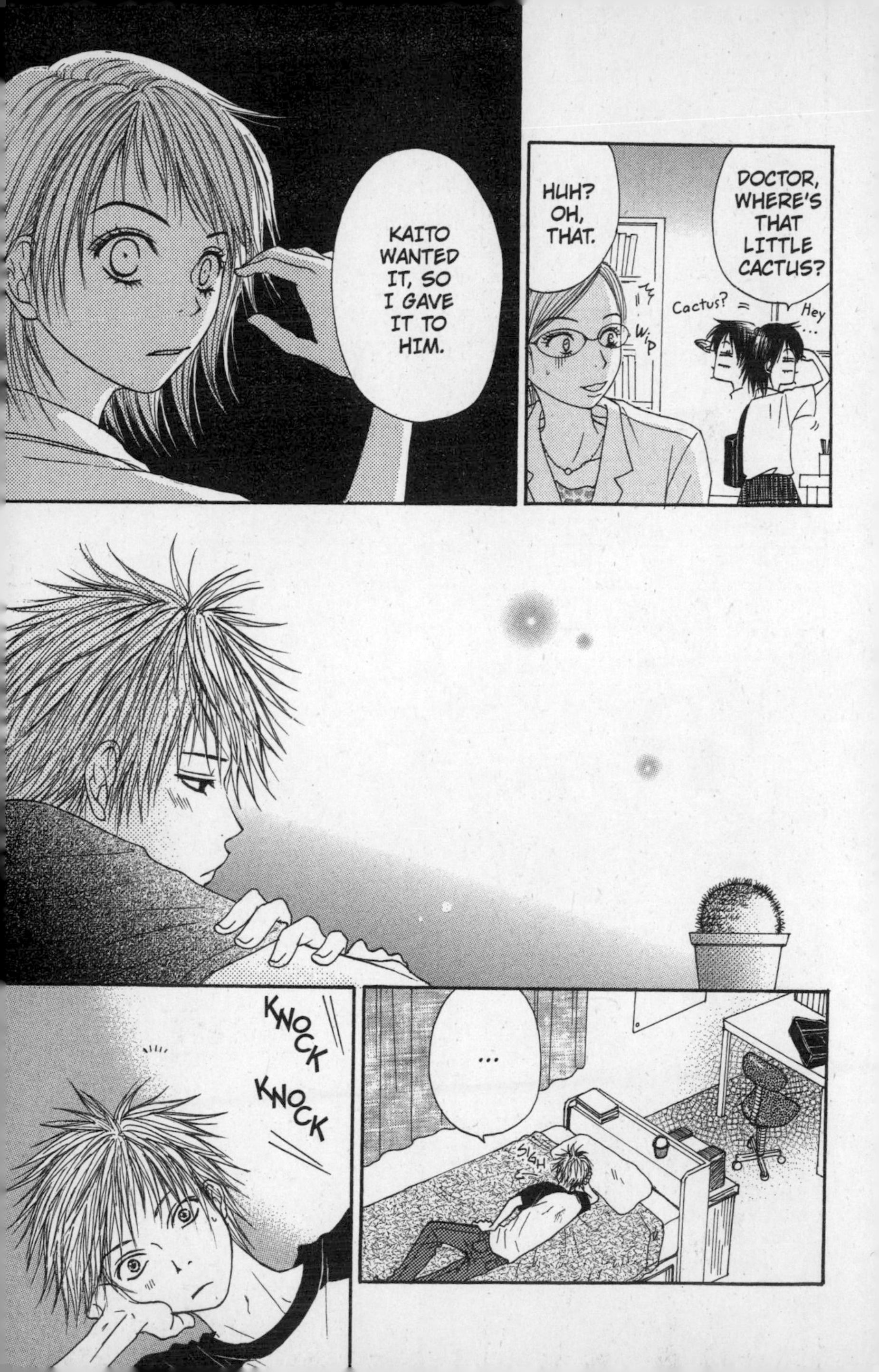
DOCTOR, WHERE'S THAT LITTLE CACTUS?
Hey...
Cactus?
HUH? OH, THAT.
Wip
KAITO WANTED IT, SO I GAVE IT TO HIM.
...
SIGH
KNOCK
KNOCK

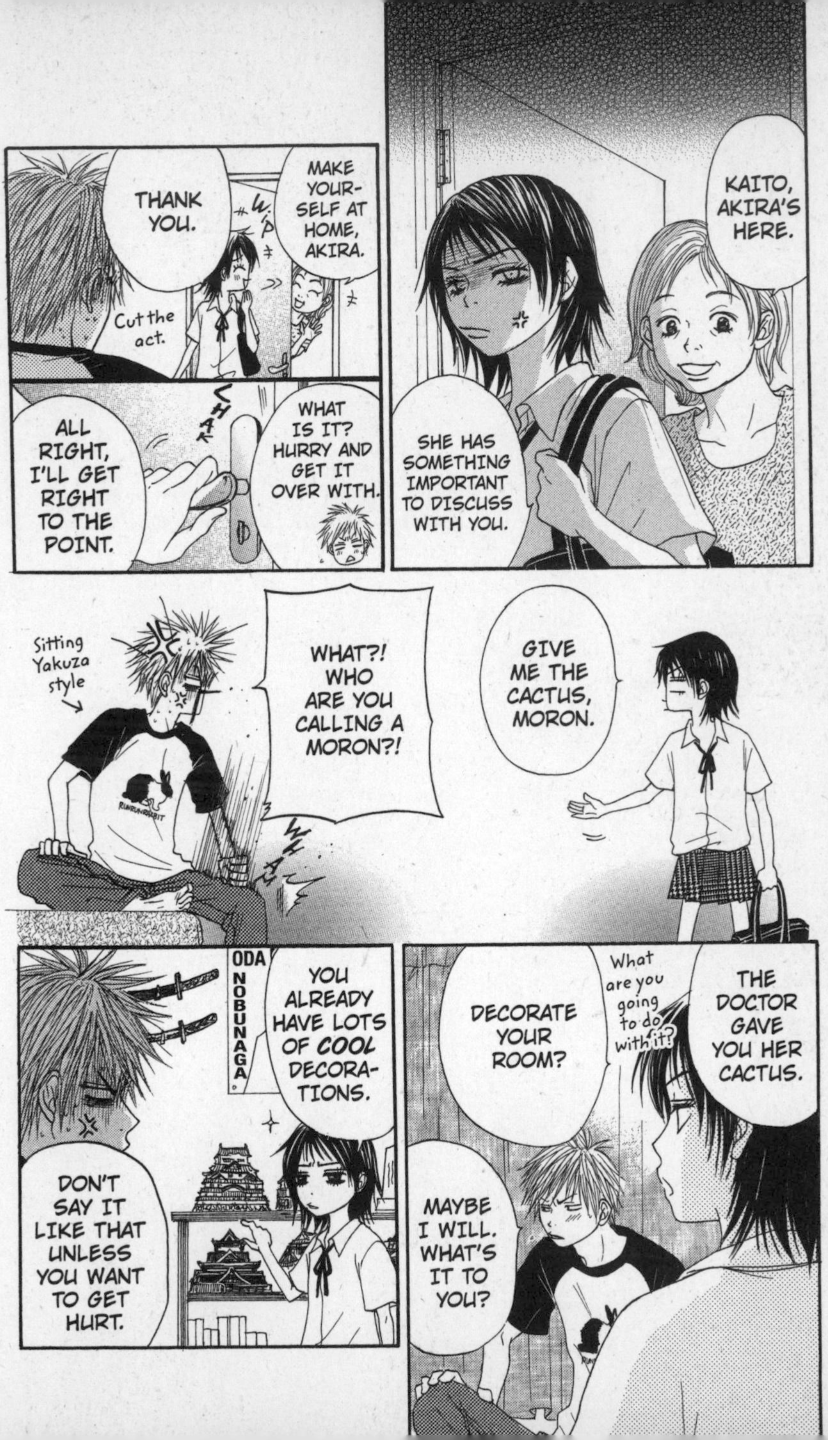
KAITO, AKIRA'S HERE.
SHE HAS SOMETHING IMPORTANT TO DISCUSS WITH YOU.
MAKE YOUR-SELF AT HOME, AKIRA.
THANK YOU.
Cut the act.
WHAT IS IT? HURRY AND GET IT OVER WITH.
ALL RIGHT, I'LL GET RIGHT TO THE POINT.
GIVE ME THE CACTUS, MORON.
WHAT?! WHO ARE YOU CALLING A MORON?!
Sitting Yakuza style
THE DOCTOR GAVE YOU HER CACTUS.
What are you going to do with it?
DECORATE YOUR ROOM?
MAYBE I WILL. WHAT'S IT TO YOU?
YOU ALREADY HAVE LOTS OF COOL DECORA-TIONS.
ODA NOBUNAGA
DON'T SAY IT LIKE THAT UNLESS YOU WANT TO GET HURT.

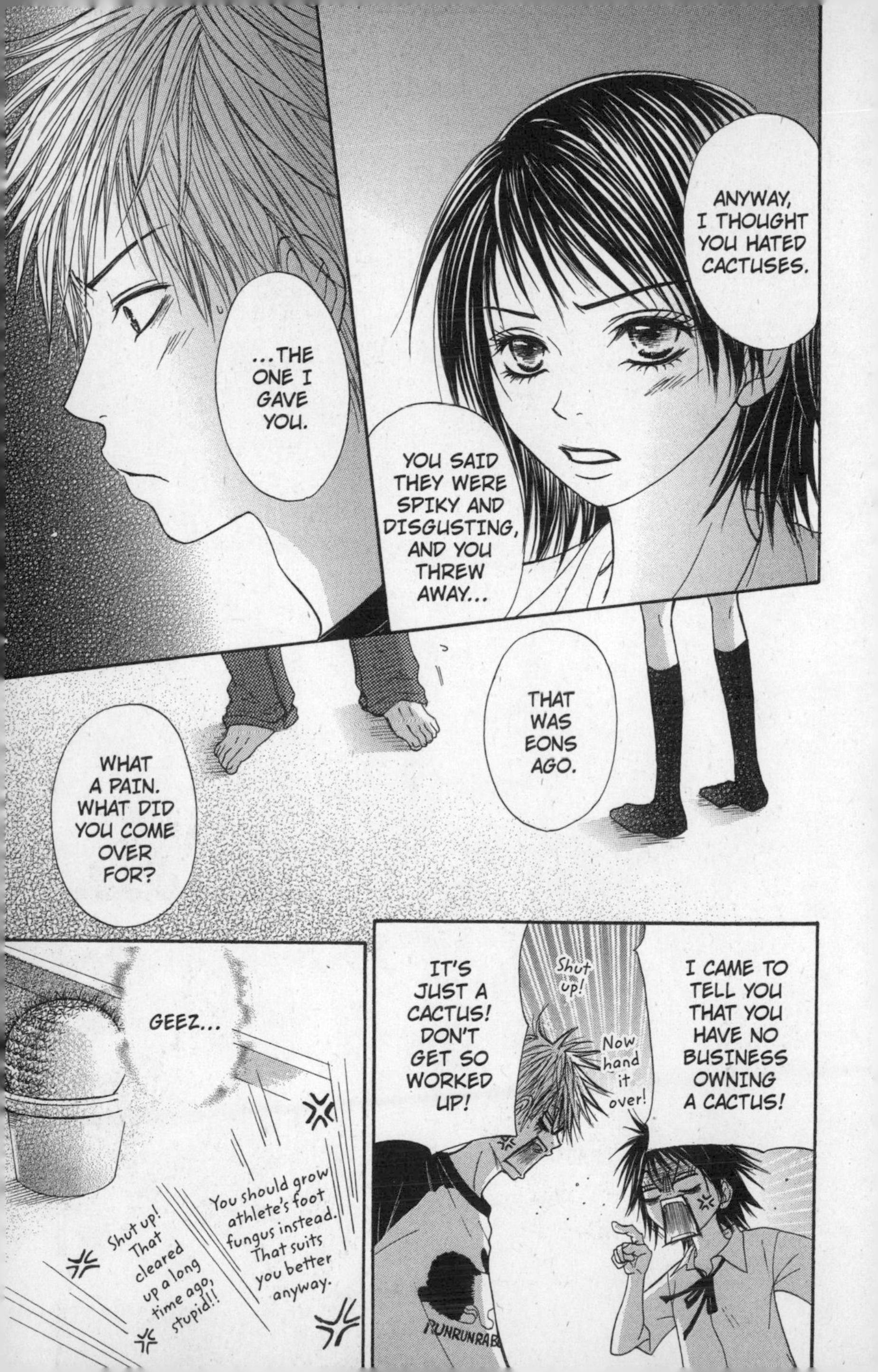
ANYWAY, I THOUGHT YOU HATED CACTUSES.
YOU SAID THEY WERE SPIKY AND DISGUSTING, AND YOU THREW AWAY...
...THE ONE I GAVE YOU.
THAT WAS EONS AGO.
WHAT A PAIN. WHAT DID YOU COME OVER FOR?
I CAME TO TELL YOU THAT YOU HAVE NO BUSINESS OWNING A CACTUS!
Now hand it over!
Shut up!
IT'S JUST A CACTUS! DON'T GET SO WORKED UP!
GEEZ...
You should grow athlete's foot fungus instead. That suits you better anyway.
Shut up! That cleared up a long time ago, stupid!!

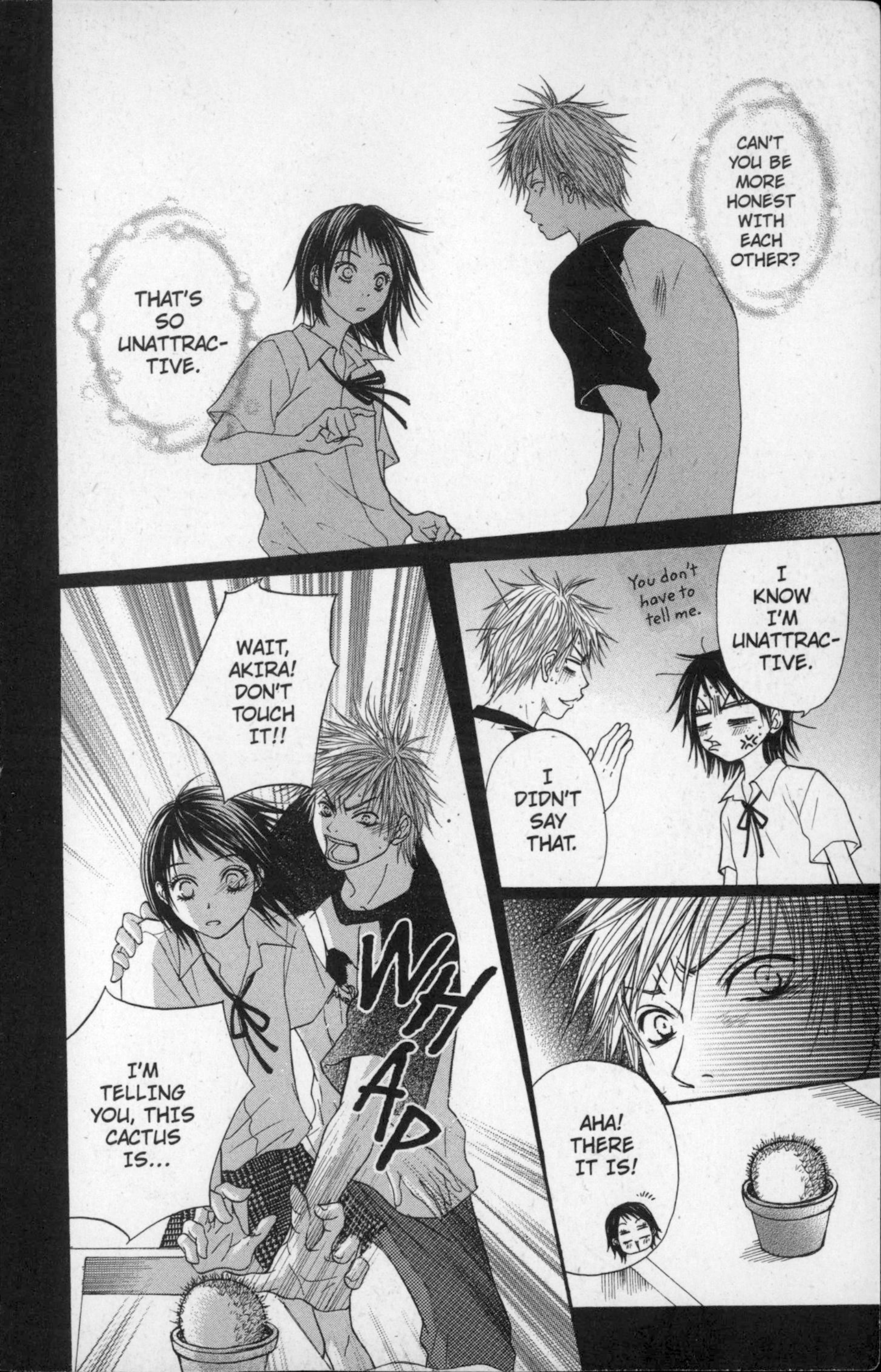
CAN'T YOU BE MORE HONEST WITH EACH OTHER?
THAT'S SO UNATTRAC-TIVE.
I KNOW I'M UNATTRAC-TIVE.
You don't have to tell me.
I DIDN'T SAY THAT.
AHA! THERE IT IS!
WAIT, AKIRA! DON'T TOUCH IT!!
WHAP
I'M TELLING YOU, THIS CACTUS IS...

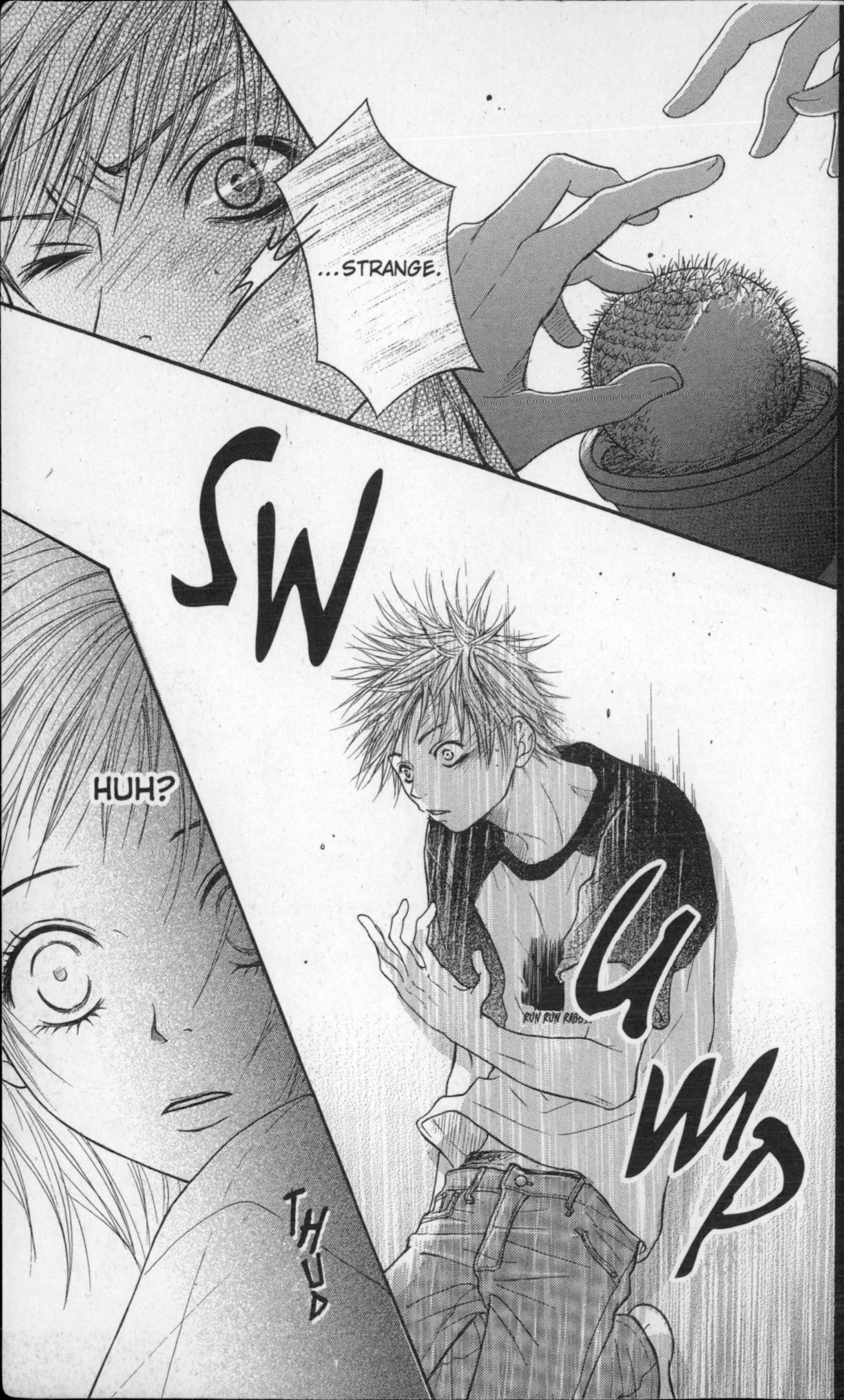
...STRANGE.
SWUMP
HUH?
THUD

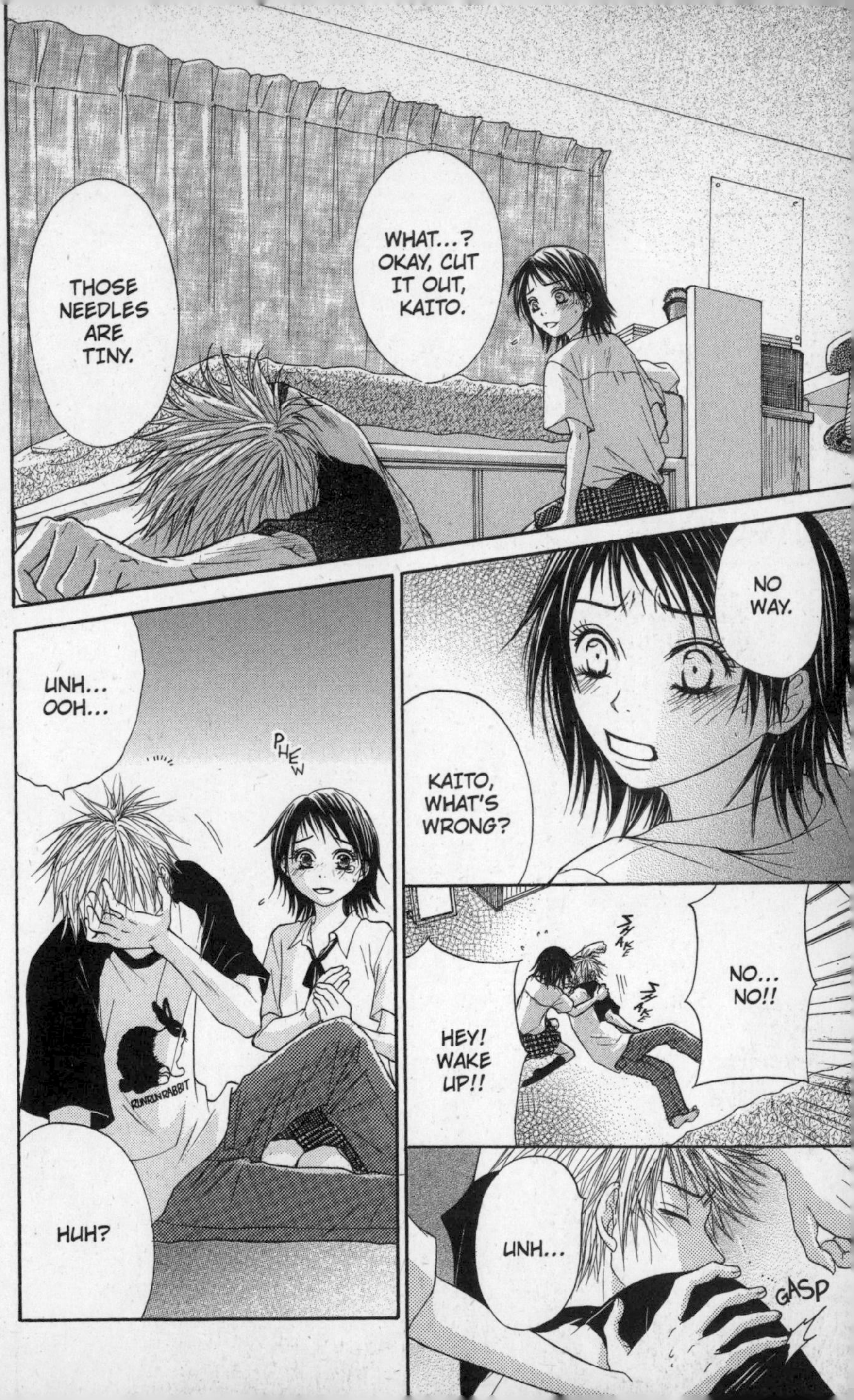
WHAT...? OKAY, CUT IT OUT, KAITO.
THOSE NEEDLES ARE TINY.
NO WAY.
KAITO, WHAT'S WRONG?
NO... NO!!
SHAKE
SHAKE
HEY! WAKE UP!!
GASP
UNH...
UNH... OOH...
PHEW
RUNRUNRABBIT
HUH?

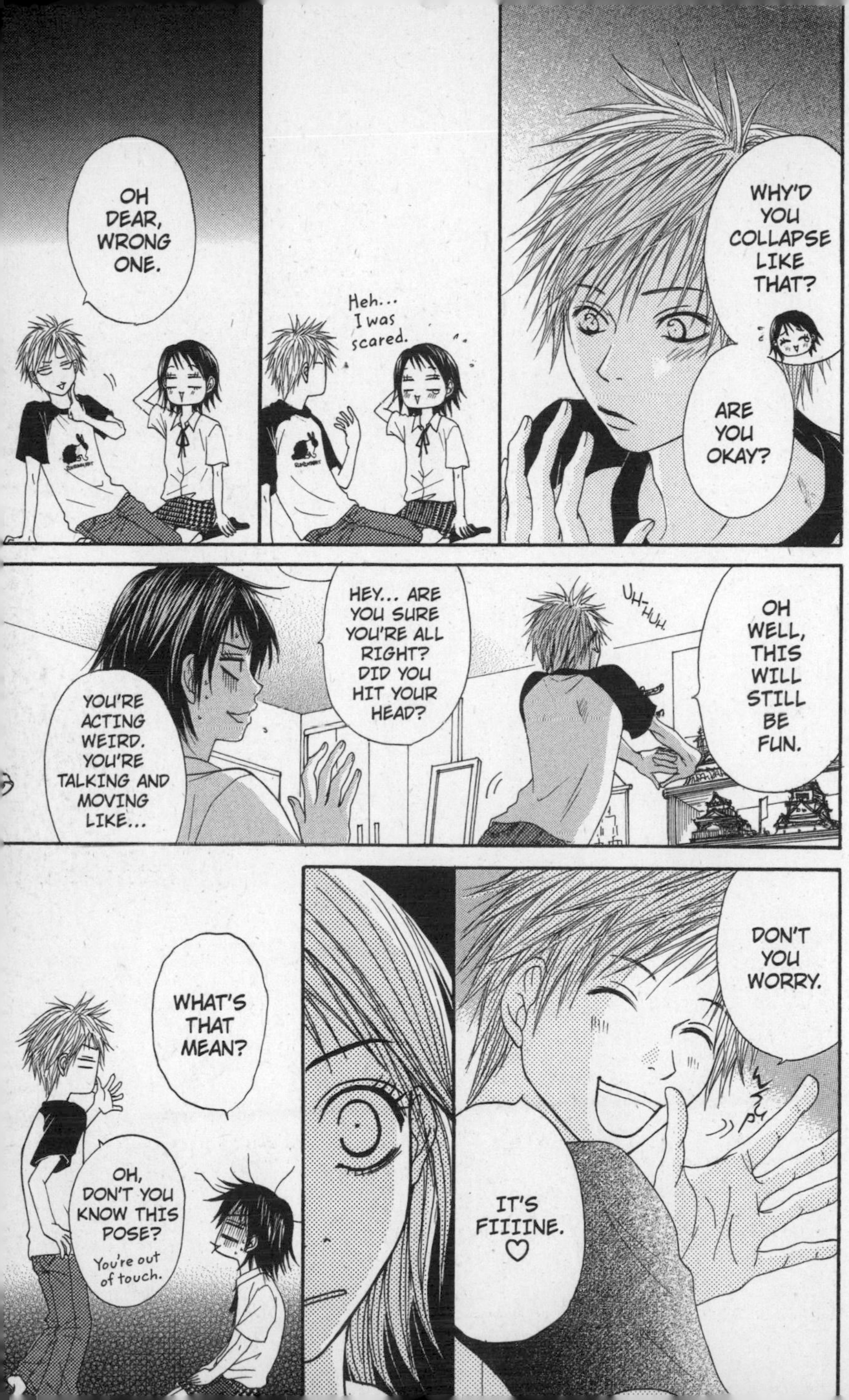
WHY'D YOU COLLAPSE LIKE THAT?
ARE YOU OKAY?
Heh... I was scared.
OH DEAR, WRONG ONE.
OH WELL, THIS WILL STILL BE FUN.
UH-HUH.
HEY... ARE YOU SURE YOU'RE ALL RIGHT? DID YOU HIT YOUR HEAD?
YOU'RE ACTING WEIRD. YOU'RE TALKING AND MOVING LIKE...
DON'T YOU WORRY.
IT'S FIIIINE. ♡
WHAT'S THAT MEAN?
OH, DON'T YOU KNOW THIS POSE?
You're out of touch.

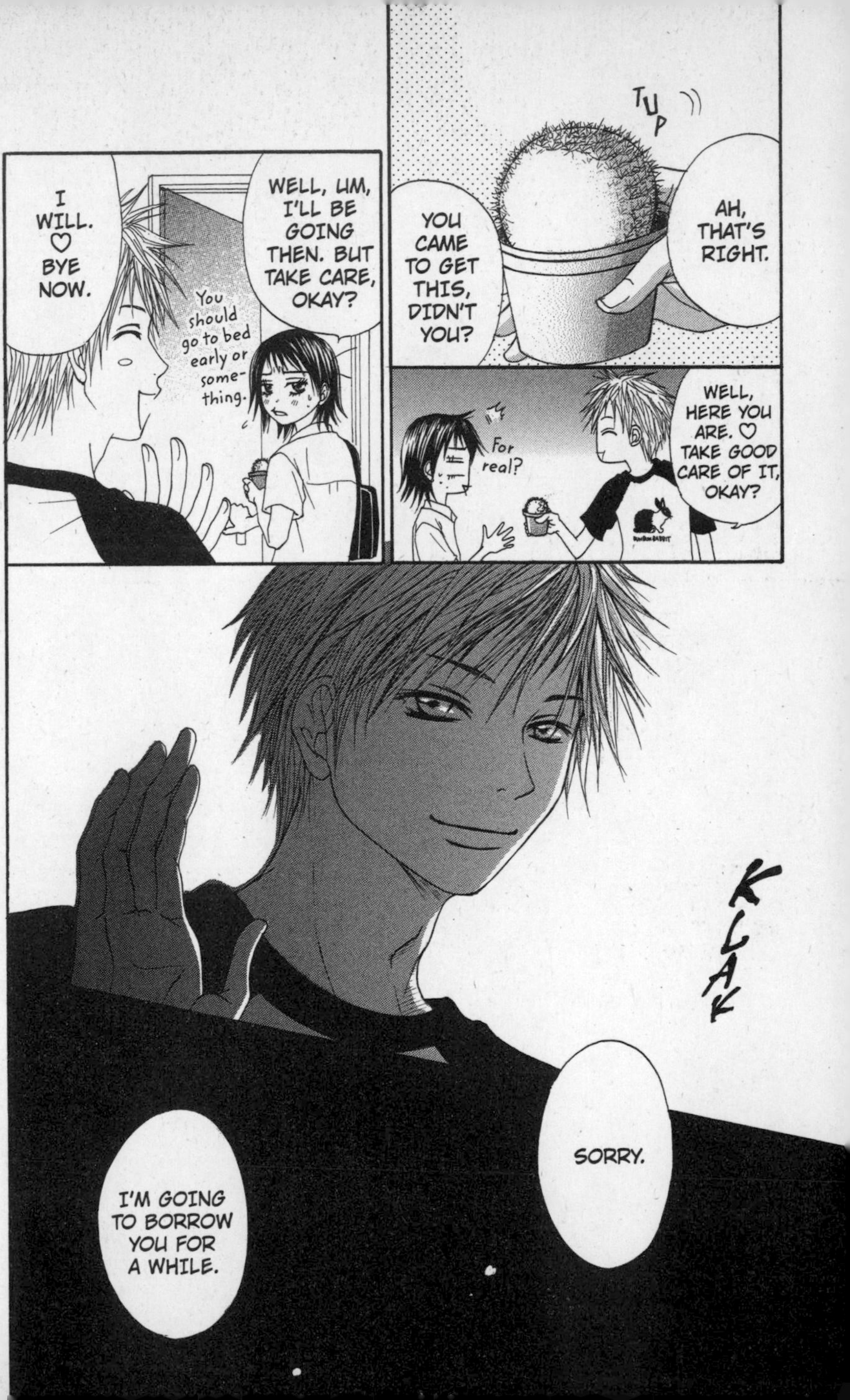
TUP
AH, THAT'S RIGHT.
YOU CAME TO GET THIS, DIDN'T YOU?
WELL, HERE YOU ARE. ♡ TAKE GOOD CARE OF IT, OKAY?
For real?
WELL, UM, I'LL BE GOING THEN. BUT TAKE CARE, OKAY?
You should go to bed early or something.
I WILL. ♡ BYE NOW.
KLAK
SORRY.
I'M GOING TO BORROW YOU FOR A WHILE.

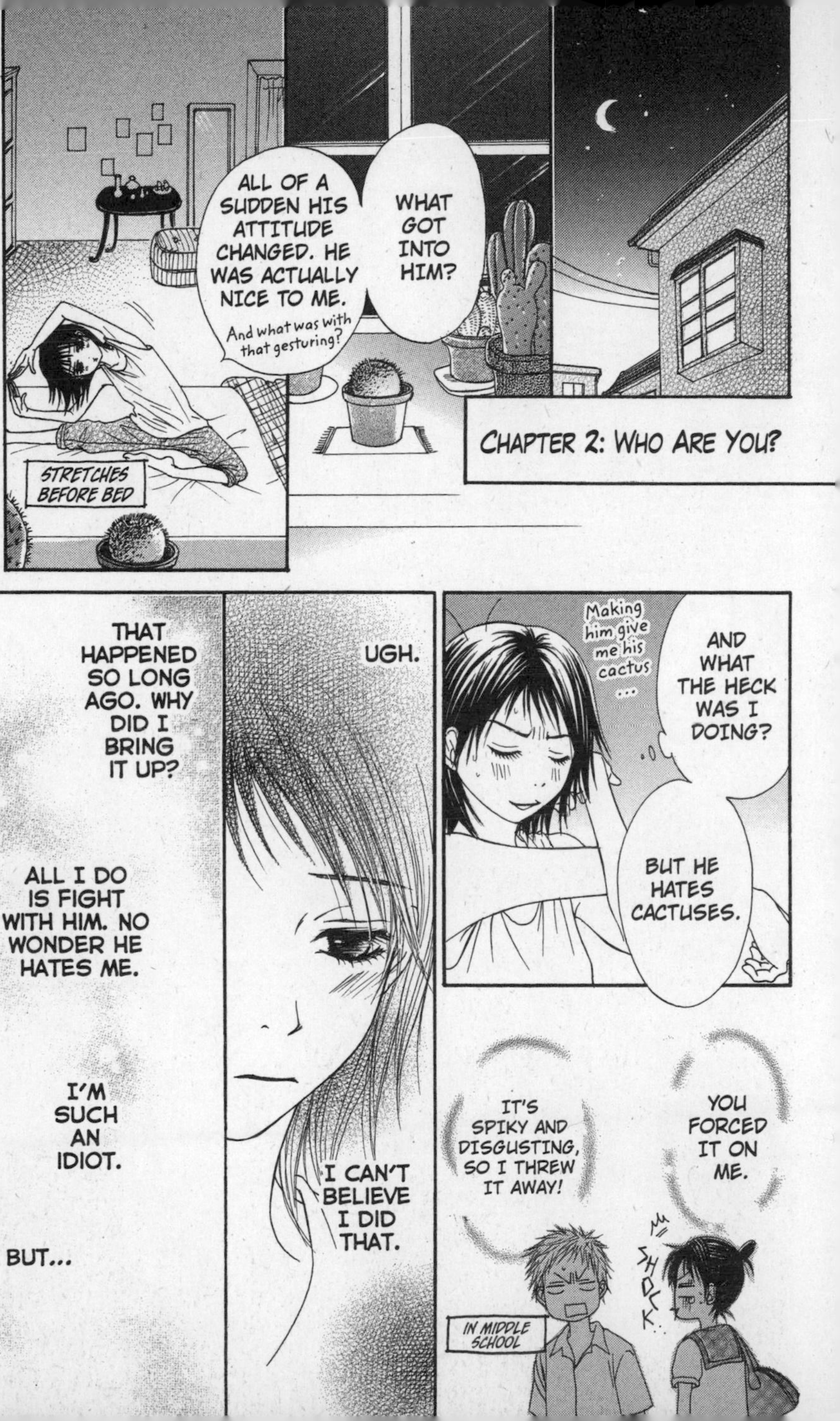
WHAT GOT INTO HIM?
ALL OF A SUDDEN HIS ATTITUDE CHANGED. HE WAS ACTUALLY NICE TO ME.
And what was with that gesturing?
CHAPTER 2: WHO ARE YOU?
STRETCHES BEFORE BED
AND WHAT THE HECK WAS I DOING?
Making him give me his cactus...
BUT HE HATES CACTUSES.
YOU FORCED IT ON ME.
IT'S SPIKY AND DISGUSTING, SO I THREW IT AWAY!
SHOCK
IN MIDDLE SCHOOL
UGH.
I CAN'T BELIEVE I DID THAT.
THAT HAPPENED SO LONG AGO. WHY DID I BRING IT UP?
ALL I DO IS FIGHT WITH HIM. NO WONDER HE HATES ME.
I'M SUCH AN IDIOT.
BUT...

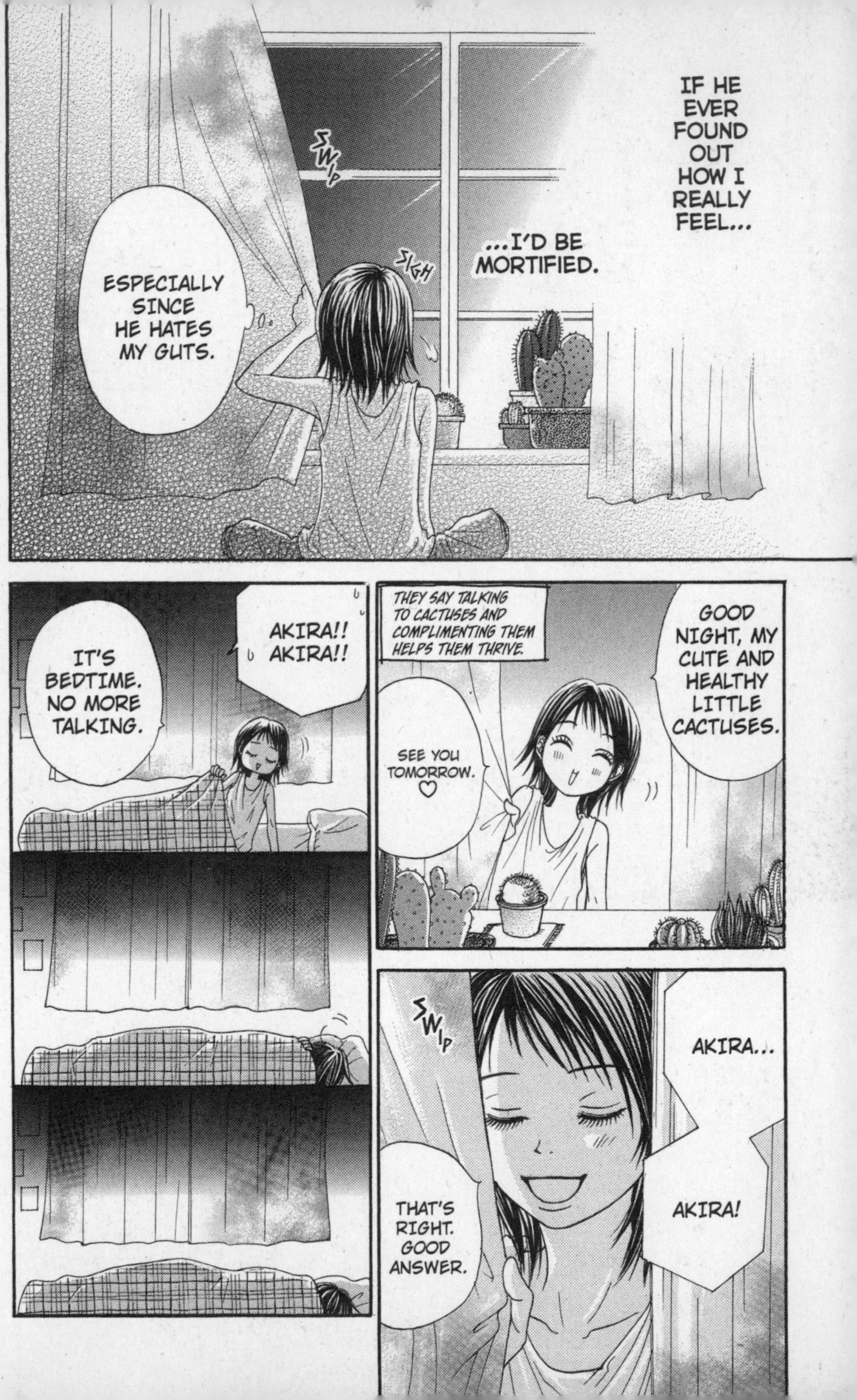
IF HE EVER FOUND OUT HOW I REALLY FEEL...
...I'D BE MORTIFIED.
SWIP
SIGH
ESPECIALLY SINCE HE HATES MY GUTS.
THEY SAY TALKING TO CACTUSES AND COMPLIMENTING THEM HELPS THEM THRIVE.
GOOD NIGHT, MY CUTE AND HEALTHY LITTLE CACTUSES.
SEE YOU TOMORROW. ♡
SWIP
AKIRA...
AKIRA!
THAT'S RIGHT. GOOD ANSWER.
AKIRA!! AKIRA!!
IT'S BEDTIME. NO MORE TALKING.

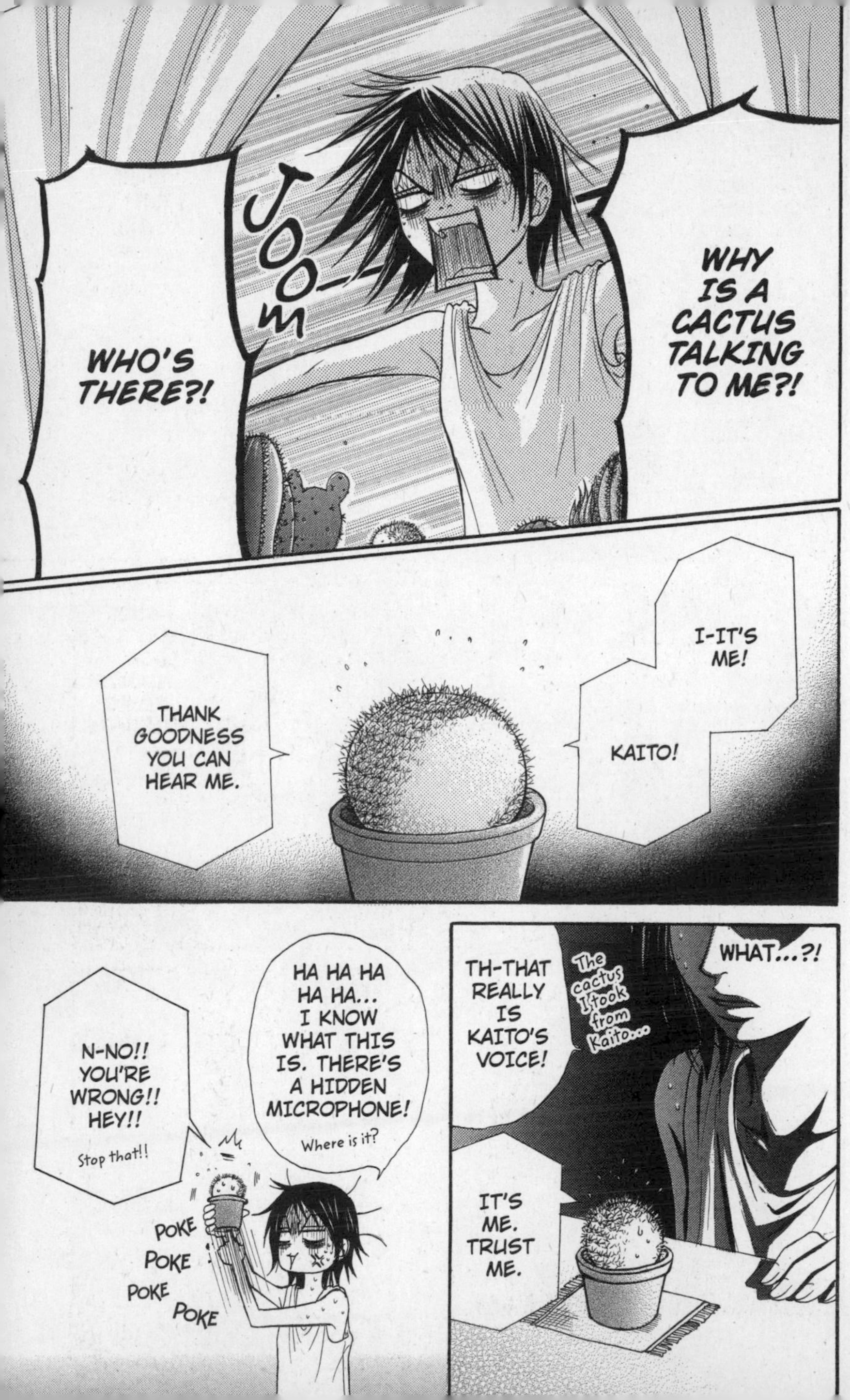
WHY IS A CACTUS TALKING TO ME?!
JOOOM
WHO'S THERE?!
I-IT'S ME!
KAITO!
THANK GOODNESS YOU CAN HEAR ME.
WHAT...?!
TH-THAT REALLY IS KAITO'S VOICE!
The cactus I took from Kaito...
IT'S ME. TRUST ME.
HA HA HA HA HA... I KNOW WHAT THIS IS. THERE'S A HIDDEN MICROPHONE!
Where is it?
N-NO!! YOU'RE WRONG!! HEY!!
Stop that!!
POKE
POKE
POKE
POKE

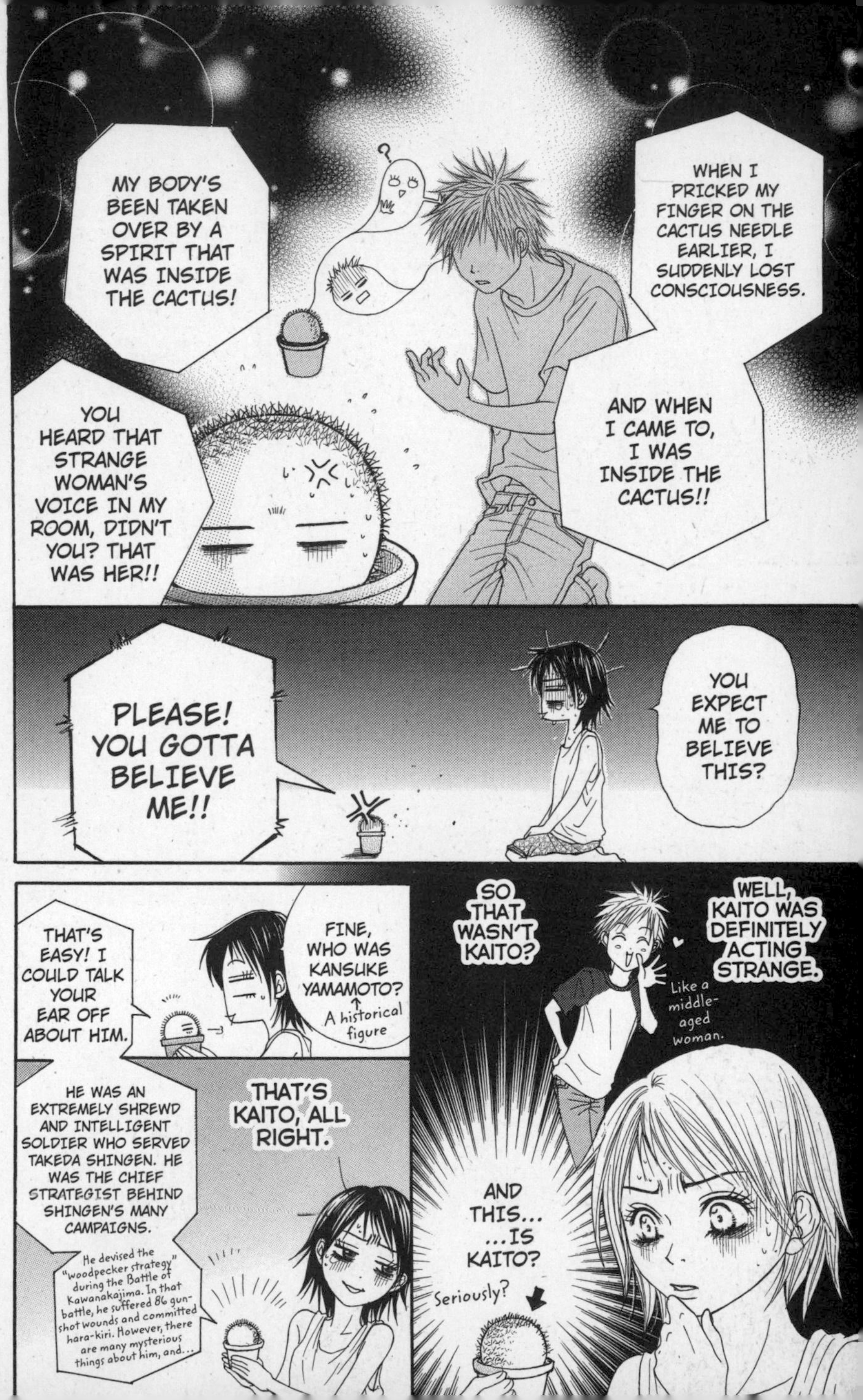
WHEN I PRICKED MY FINGER ON THE CACTUS NEEDLE EARLIER, I SUDDENLY LOST CONSCIOUSNESS.
AND WHEN I CAME TO, I WAS INSIDE THE CACTUS!!
MY BODY'S BEEN TAKEN OVER BY A SPIRIT THAT WAS INSIDE THE CACTUS!
YOU HEARD THAT STRANGE WOMAN'S VOICE IN MY ROOM, DIDN'T YOU? THAT WAS HER!!
YOU EXPECT ME TO BELIEVE THIS?
PLEASE! YOU GOTTA BELIEVE ME!!
WELL, KAITO WAS DEFINITELY ACTING STRANGE.
Like a middle-aged woman.
SO THAT WASN'T KAITO?
AND THIS... ...IS KAITO?
Seriously?
FINE, WHO WAS KANSUKE YAMAMOTO?
A historical figure
THAT'S EASY! I COULD TALK YOUR EAR OFF ABOUT HIM.
THAT'S KAITO, ALL RIGHT.
HE WAS AN EXTREMELY SHREWD AND INTELLIGENT SOLDIER WHO SERVED TAKEDA SHINGEN. HE WAS THE CHIEF STRATEGIST BEHIND SHINGEN'S MANY CAMPAIGNS.
He devised the "woodpecker strategy" during the Battle of Kawanakajima. In that battle, he suffered 86 gunshot wounds and committed hara-kiri. However, there are many mysterious things about him, and...

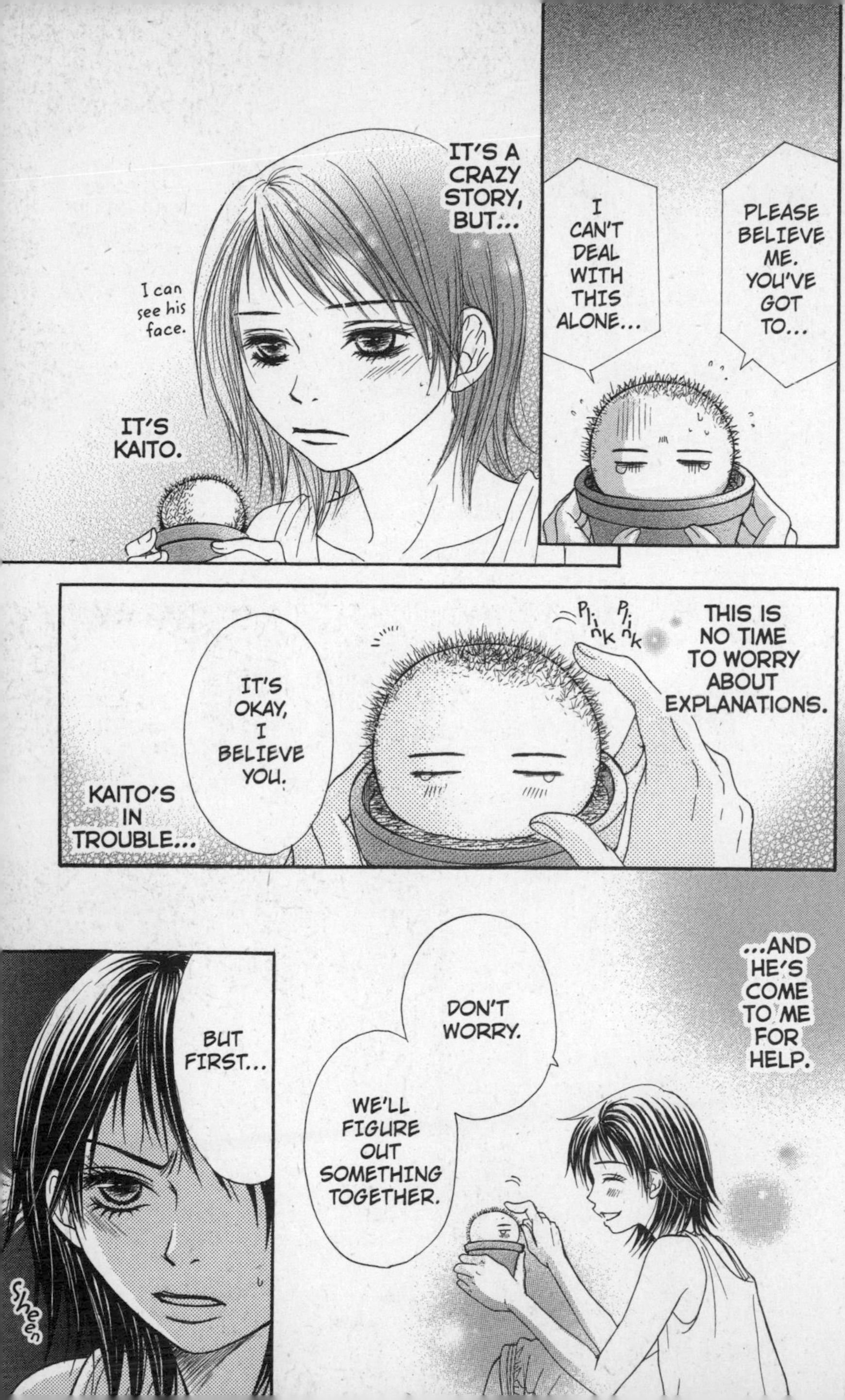
PLEASE BELIEVE ME. YOU'VE GOT TO...
I CAN'T DEAL WITH THIS ALONE...
IT'S A CRAZY STORY, BUT...
I can see his face.
IT'S KAITO.
THIS IS NO TIME TO WORRY ABOUT EXPLANATIONS.
Plink Plink
IT'S OKAY, I BELIEVE YOU.
KAITO'S IN TROUBLE...
...AND HE'S COME TO ME FOR HELP.
DON'T WORRY.
WE'LL FIGURE OUT SOMETHING TOGETHER.
BUT FIRST...
Sheen

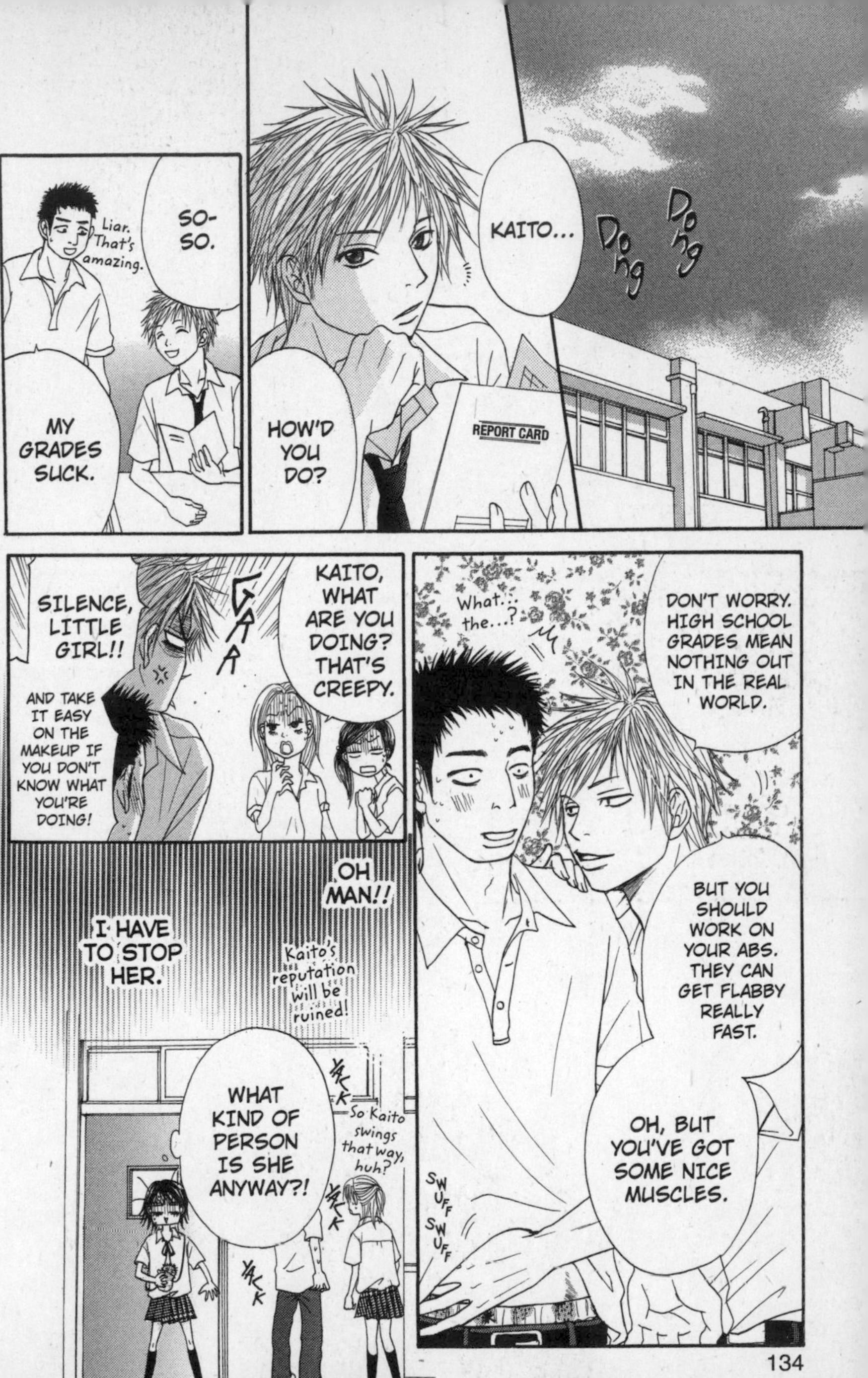
Dong Dong
KAITO...
HOW'D YOU DO?
REPORT CARD
SO-SO.
Liar. That's amazing.
MY GRADES SUCK.
What... the...?
DON'T WORRY. HIGH SCHOOL GRADES MEAN NOTHING OUT IN THE REAL WORLD.
BUT YOU SHOULD WORK ON YOUR ABS. THEY CAN GET FLABBY REALLY FAST.
OH, BUT YOU'VE GOT SOME NICE MUSCLES.
SWUFF SWUFF
KAITO, WHAT ARE YOU DOING? THAT'S CREEPY.
GAR
SILENCE, LITTLE GIRL!!
AND TAKE IT EASY ON THE MAKEUP IF YOU DON'T KNOW WHAT YOU'RE DOING!
OH MAN!!
I HAVE TO STOP HER.
Kaito's reputation will be ruined!
YACK
So Kaito swings that way, huh?
YACK
WHAT KIND OF PERSON IS SHE ANYWAY?!
YACK

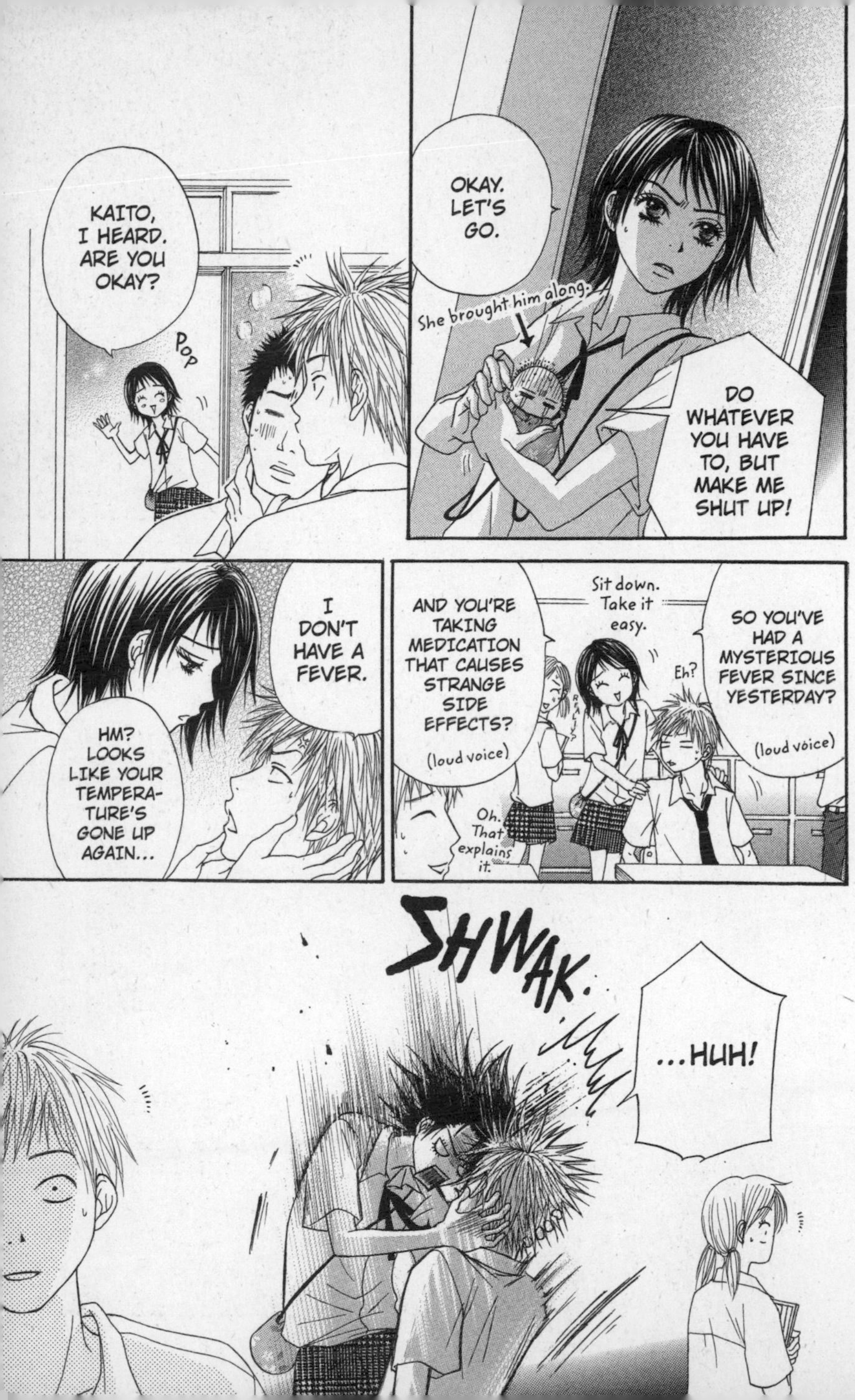
OKAY. LET'S GO.
She brought him along.
DO WHATEVER YOU HAVE TO, BUT MAKE ME SHUT UP!
KAITO, I HEARD. ARE YOU OKAY?
POP
SO YOU'VE HAD A MYSTERIOUS FEVER SINCE YESTERDAY? (loud voice)
Eh?
Sit down. Take it easy.
AND YOU'RE TAKING MEDICATION THAT CAUSES STRANGE SIDE EFFECTS? (loud voice)
Oh. That explains it.
I DON'T HAVE A FEVER.
HM? LOOKS LIKE YOUR TEMPERATURE'S GONE UP AGAIN...
SHWAK.
MMM
...HUH!

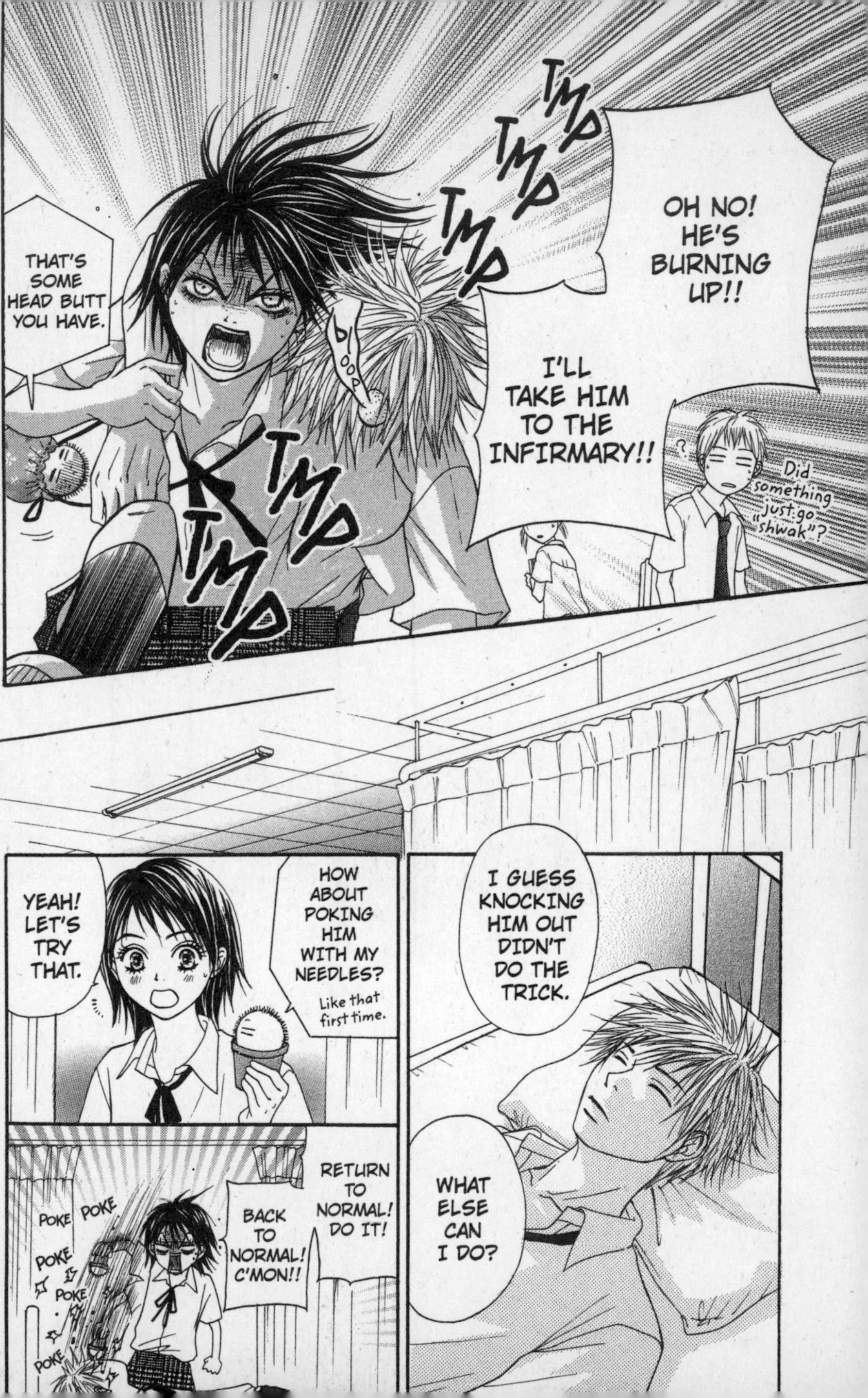
OH NO! HE'S BURNING UP!!
I'LL TAKE HIM TO THE INFIRMARY!!
TMP TMP TMP
Did something just go "shwak"?
DLOOP
THAT'S SOME HEAD BUTT YOU HAVE.
TMP TMP
I GUESS KNOCKING HIM OUT DIDN'T DO THE TRICK.
WHAT ELSE CAN I DO?
HOW ABOUT POKING HIM WITH MY NEEDLES?
Like that first time.
YEAH! LET'S TRY THAT.
RETURN TO NORMAL! DO IT!
BACK TO NORMAL! C'MON!!
POKE POKE
POKE
POKE
POKE

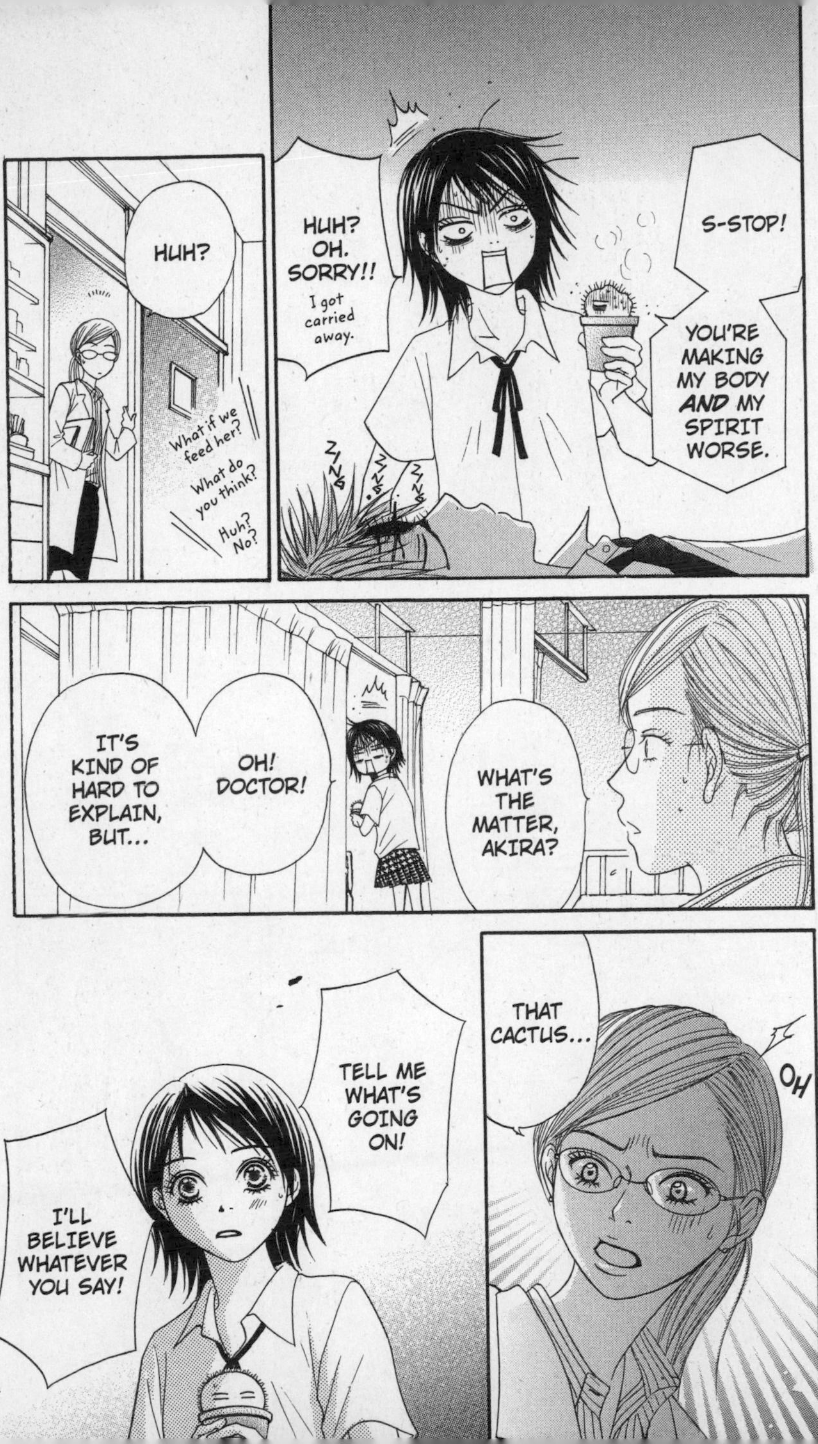
S-STOP!
YOU'RE MAKING MY BODY **AND** MY SPIRIT WORSE.
HUH? OH. SORRY!! I got carried away.
ZING ZING ZING
HUH?
What if we feed her?
What do you think?
Huh? No?
WHAT'S THE MATTER, AKIRA?
OH! DOCTOR!
IT'S KIND OF HARD TO EXPLAIN, BUT...
OH
THAT CACTUS...
TELL ME WHAT'S GOING ON!
I'LL BELIEVE WHATEVER YOU SAY!

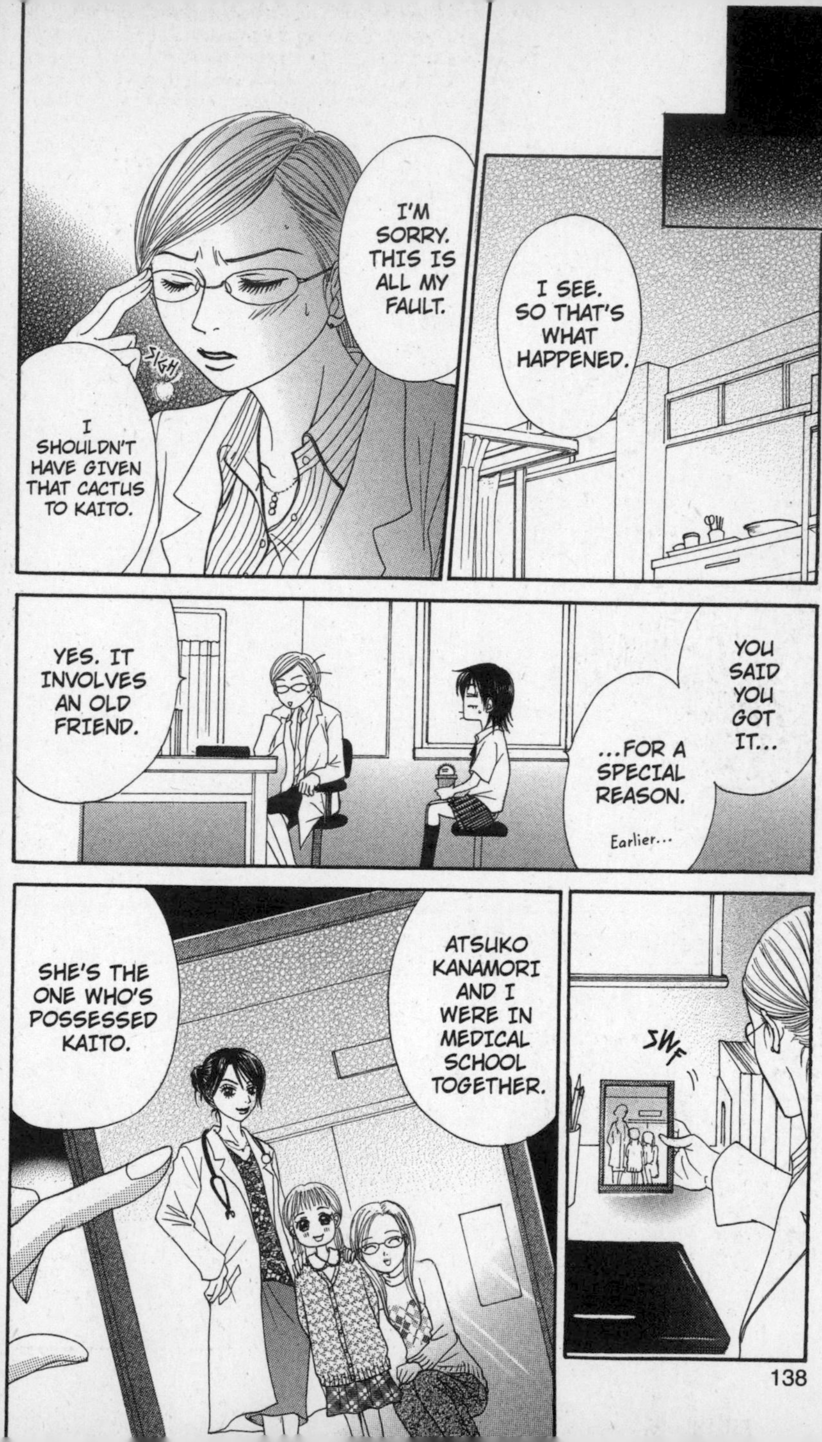
I SEE. SO THAT'S WHAT HAPPENED.
I'M SORRY. THIS IS ALL MY FAULT.
SIGH
I SHOULDN'T HAVE GIVEN THAT CACTUS TO KAITO.
YOU SAID YOU GOT IT...
...FOR A SPECIAL REASON.
Earlier...
YES. IT INVOLVES AN OLD FRIEND.
SWF
ATSUKO KANAMORI AND I WERE IN MEDICAL SCHOOL TOGETHER.
SHE'S THE ONE WHO'S POSSESSED KAITO.

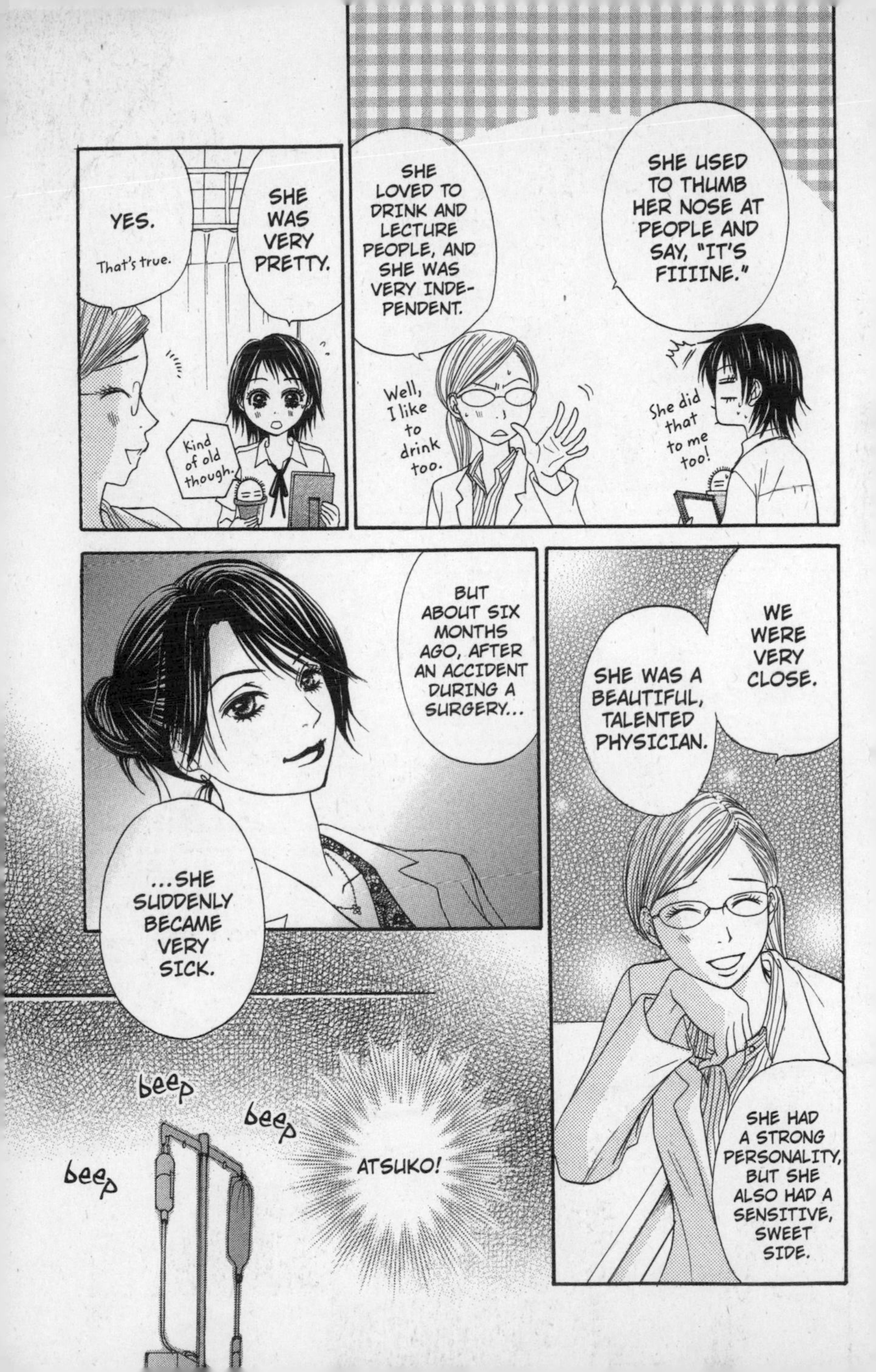
SHE USED TO THUMB HER NOSE AT PEOPLE AND SAY, "IT'S FIIINE."
SHE LOVED TO DRINK AND LECTURE PEOPLE, AND SHE WAS VERY INDE-PENDENT.
She did that to me too!
Well, I like to drink too.
SHE WAS VERY PRETTY.
YES.
That's true.
Kind of old though.
WE WERE VERY CLOSE.
SHE WAS A BEAUTIFUL, TALENTED PHYSICIAN.
SHE HAD A STRONG PERSONALITY, BUT SHE ALSO HAD A SENSITIVE, SWEET SIDE.
BUT ABOUT SIX MONTHS AGO, AFTER AN ACCIDENT DURING A SURGERY...
...SHE SUDDENLY BECAME VERY SICK.
beep
beep
ATSUKO!
beep

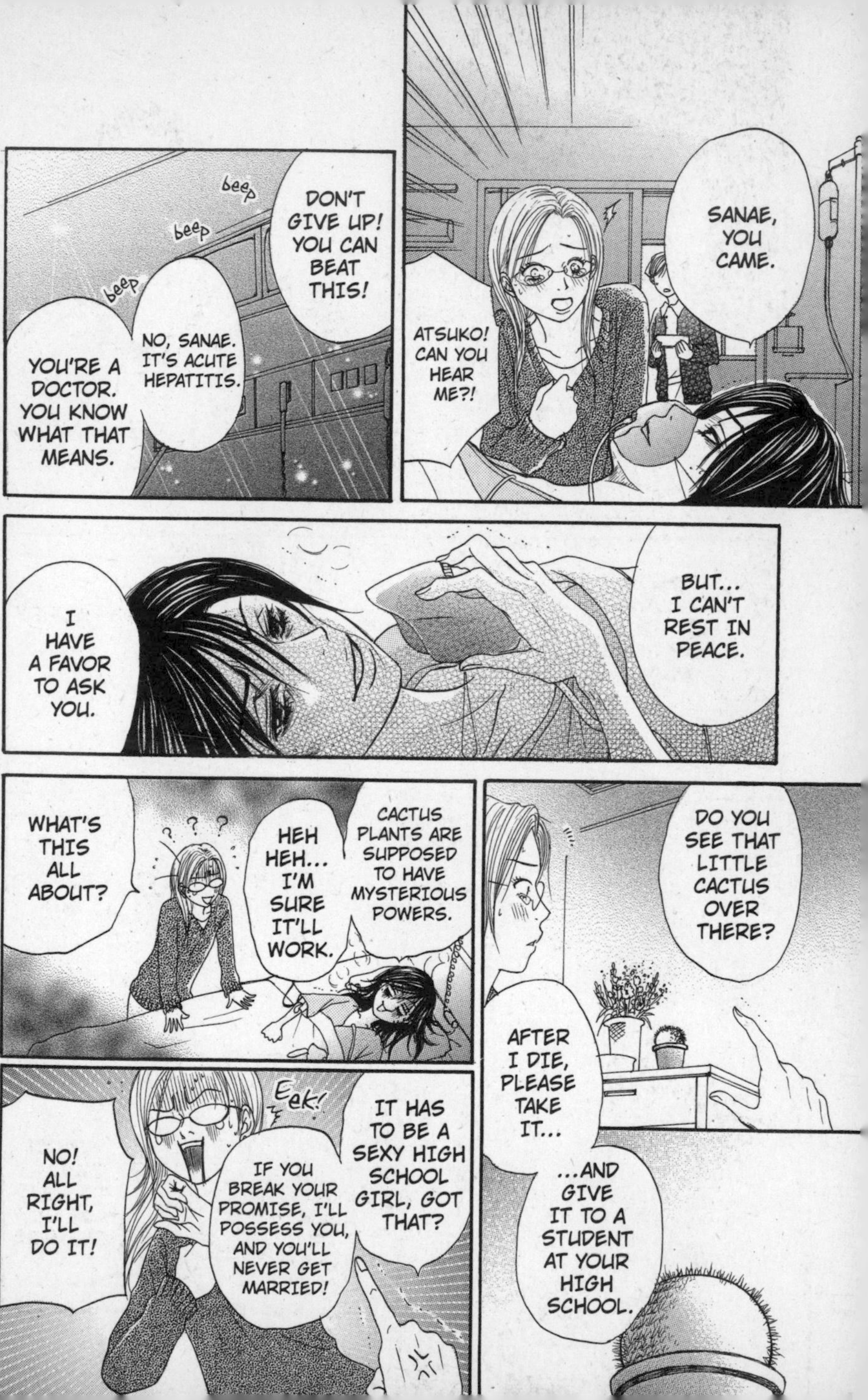
SANAE, YOU CAME.
ATSUKO! CAN YOU HEAR ME?!
DON'T GIVE UP! YOU CAN BEAT THIS!
beep
beep
beep
NO, SANAE. IT'S ACUTE HEPATITIS.
YOU'RE A DOCTOR. YOU KNOW WHAT THAT MEANS.
BUT... I CAN'T REST IN PEACE.
I HAVE A FAVOR TO ASK YOU.
DO YOU SEE THAT LITTLE CACTUS OVER THERE?
AFTER I DIE, PLEASE TAKE IT...
...AND GIVE IT TO A STUDENT AT YOUR HIGH SCHOOL.
CACTUS PLANTS ARE SUPPOSED TO HAVE MYSTERIOUS POWERS.
HEH HEH... I'M SURE IT'LL WORK.
WHAT'S THIS ALL ABOUT?
IT HAS TO BE A SEXY HIGH SCHOOL GIRL, GOT THAT?
IF YOU BREAK YOUR PROMISE, I'LL POSSESS YOU, AND YOU'LL NEVER GET MARRIED!
Eek!
NO! ALL RIGHT, I'LL DO IT!

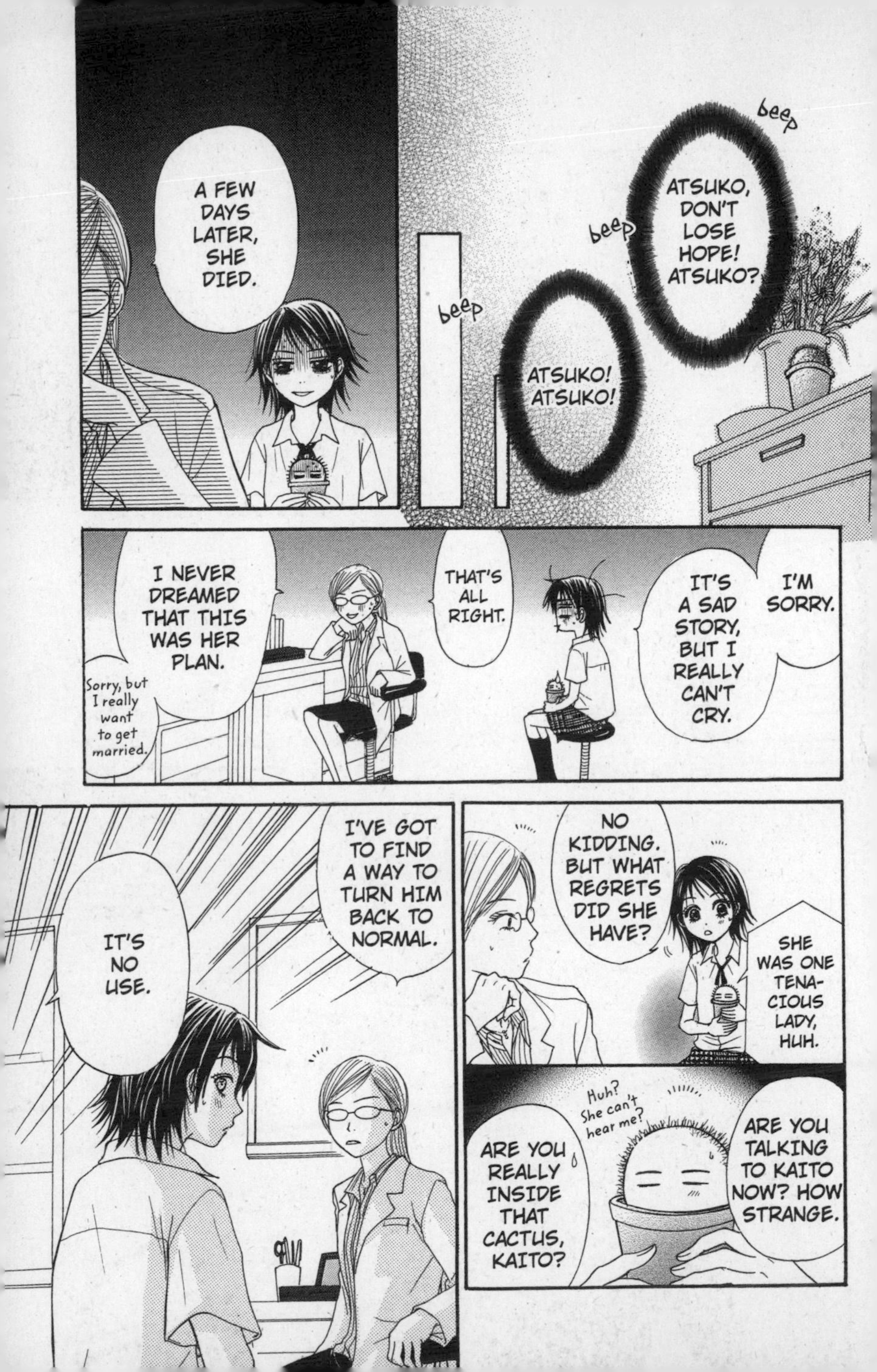
beep
ATSUKO, DON'T LOSE HOPE! ATSUKO?
beep
beep
ATSUKO! ATSUKO!
A FEW DAYS LATER, SHE DIED.
I'M SORRY.
IT'S A SAD STORY, BUT I REALLY CAN'T CRY.
THAT'S ALL RIGHT.
I NEVER DREAMED THAT THIS WAS HER PLAN.
Sorry, but I really want to get married.
SHE WAS ONE TENACIOUS LADY, HUH.
NO KIDDING. BUT WHAT REGRETS DID SHE HAVE?
ARE YOU TALKING TO KAITO NOW? HOW STRANGE.
Huh? She can't hear me?
ARE YOU REALLY INSIDE THAT CACTUS, KAITO?
I'VE GOT TO FIND A WAY TO TURN HIM BACK TO NORMAL.
IT'S NO USE.

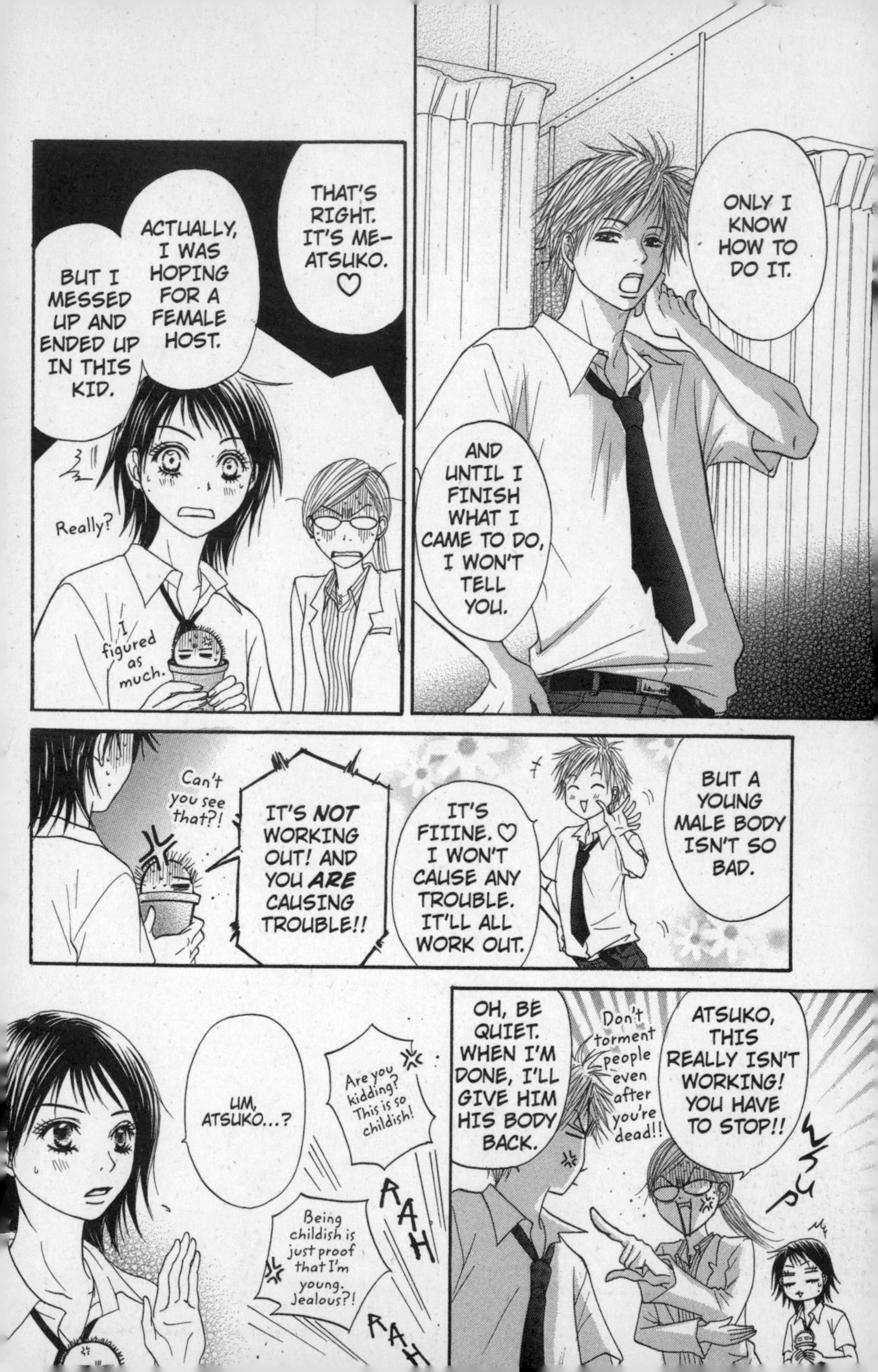
ONLY I KNOW HOW TO DO IT.
AND UNTIL I FINISH WHAT I CAME TO DO, I WON'T TELL YOU.
THAT'S RIGHT. IT'S ME-ATSUKO. ♡
ACTUALLY, I WAS HOPING FOR A FEMALE HOST.
BUT I MESSED UP AND ENDED UP IN THIS KID.
Really?
I figured as much.
BUT A YOUNG MALE BODY ISN'T SO BAD.
IT'S FIIINE. ♡ I WON'T CAUSE ANY TROUBLE. IT'LL ALL WORK OUT.
IT'S **NOT** WORKING OUT! AND YOU **ARE** CAUSING TROUBLE!!
Can't you see that?!
ATSUKO, THIS REALLY ISN'T WORKING! YOU HAVE TO STOP!!
WHUP
Don't torment people even after you're dead!!
OH, BE QUIET. WHEN I'M DONE, I'LL GIVE HIM HIS BODY BACK.
Are you kidding? This is so childish!
RAH
Being childish is just proof that I'm young. Jealous?!
RAH
UM, ATSUKO...?

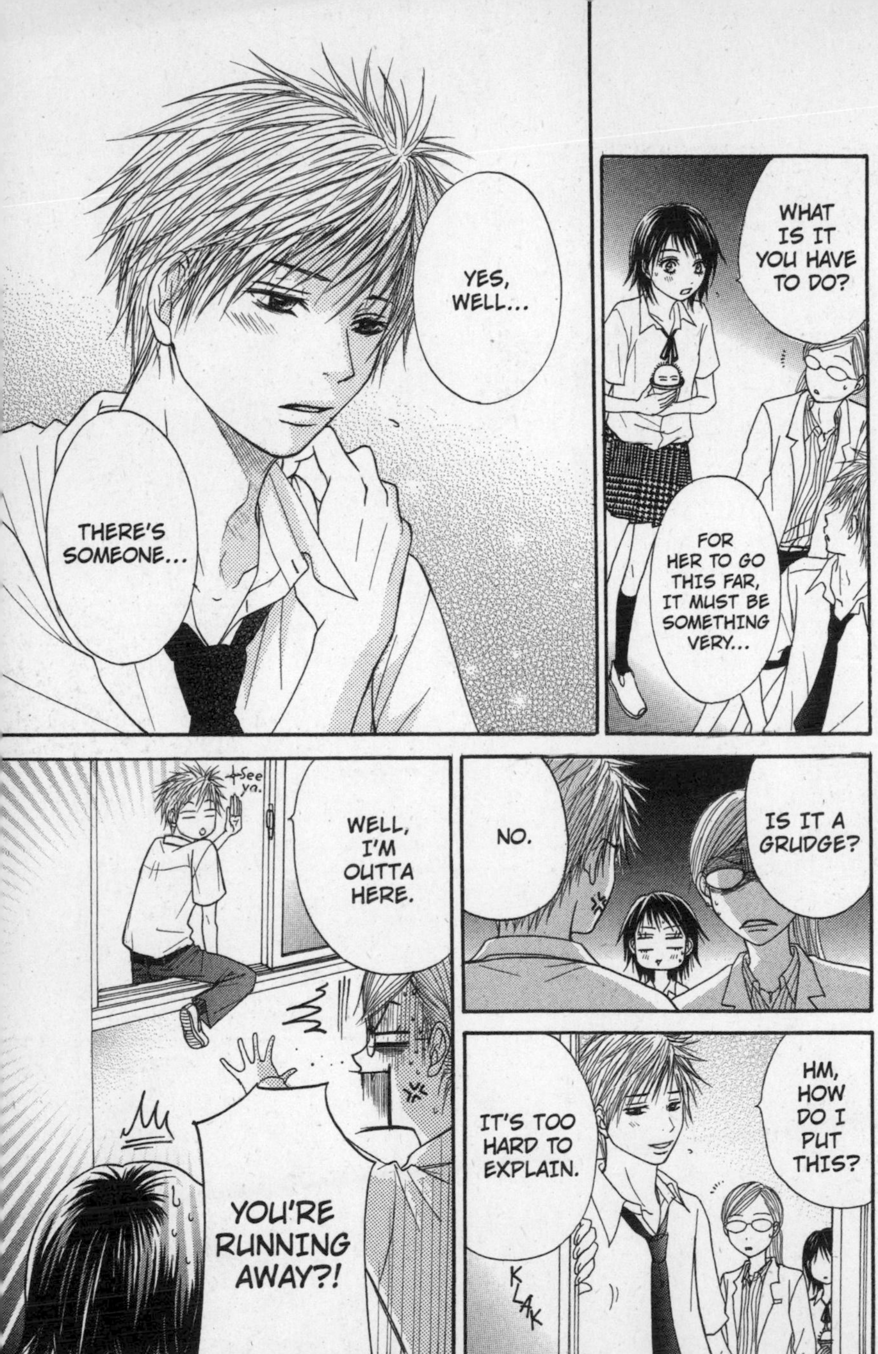
WHAT IS IT YOU HAVE TO DO?
FOR HER TO GO THIS FAR, IT MUST BE SOMETHING VERY...
YES, WELL...
THERE'S SOMEONE...
IS IT A GRUDGE?
NO.
HM, HOW DO I PUT THIS?
IT'S TOO HARD TO EXPLAIN.
KLAK
See ya.
WELL, I'M OUTTA HERE.
YOU'RE RUNNING AWAY?!

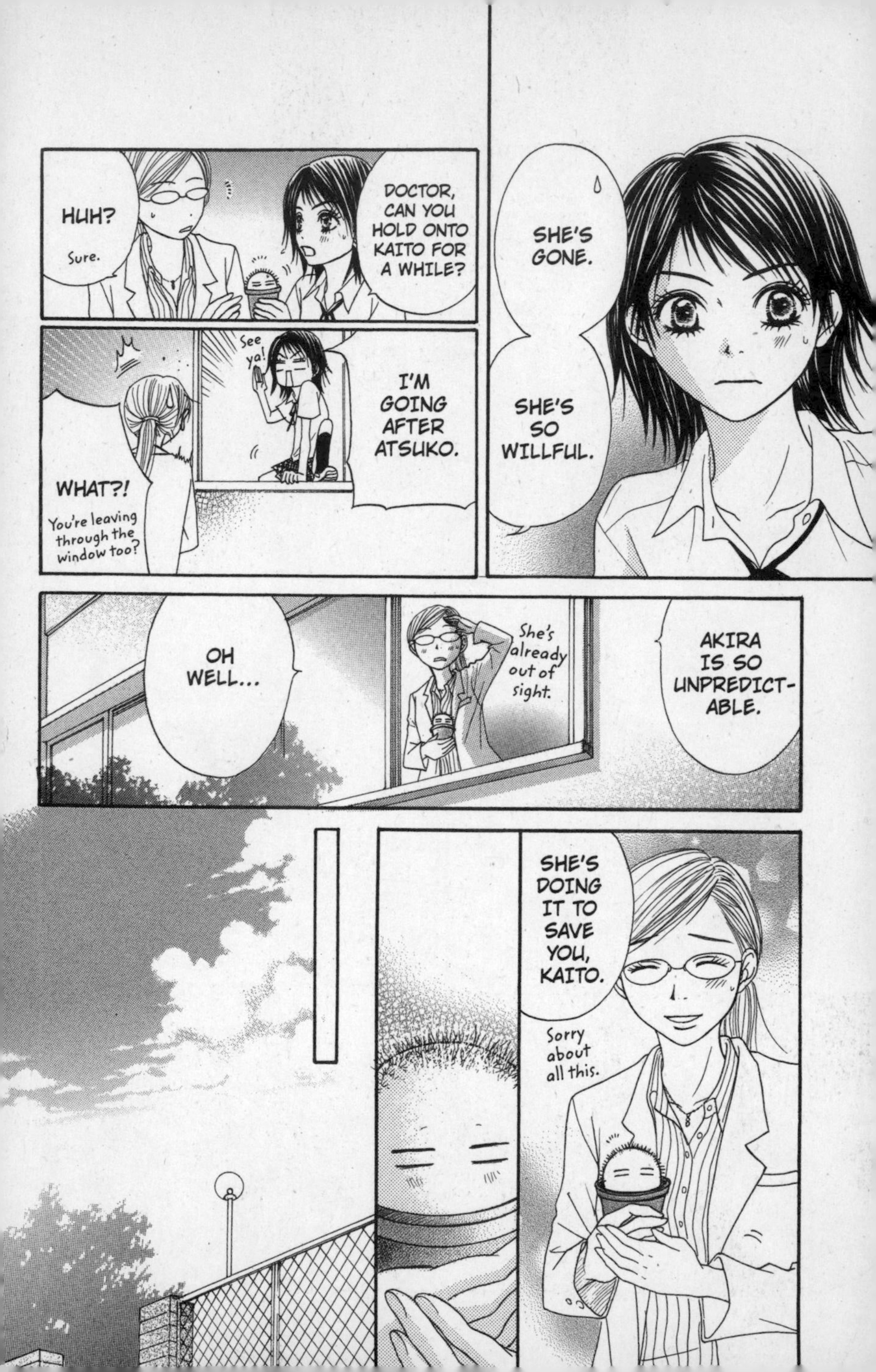
SHE'S GONE.
SHE'S SO WILLFUL.
DOCTOR, CAN YOU HOLD ONTO KAITO FOR A WHILE?
HUH?
Sure.
I'M GOING AFTER ATSUKO.
See ya!
WHAT?!
You're leaving through the window too?
AKIRA IS SO UNPREDICT-ABLE.
She's already out of sight.
OH WELL...
SHE'S DOING IT TO SAVE YOU, KAITO.
Sorry about all this.

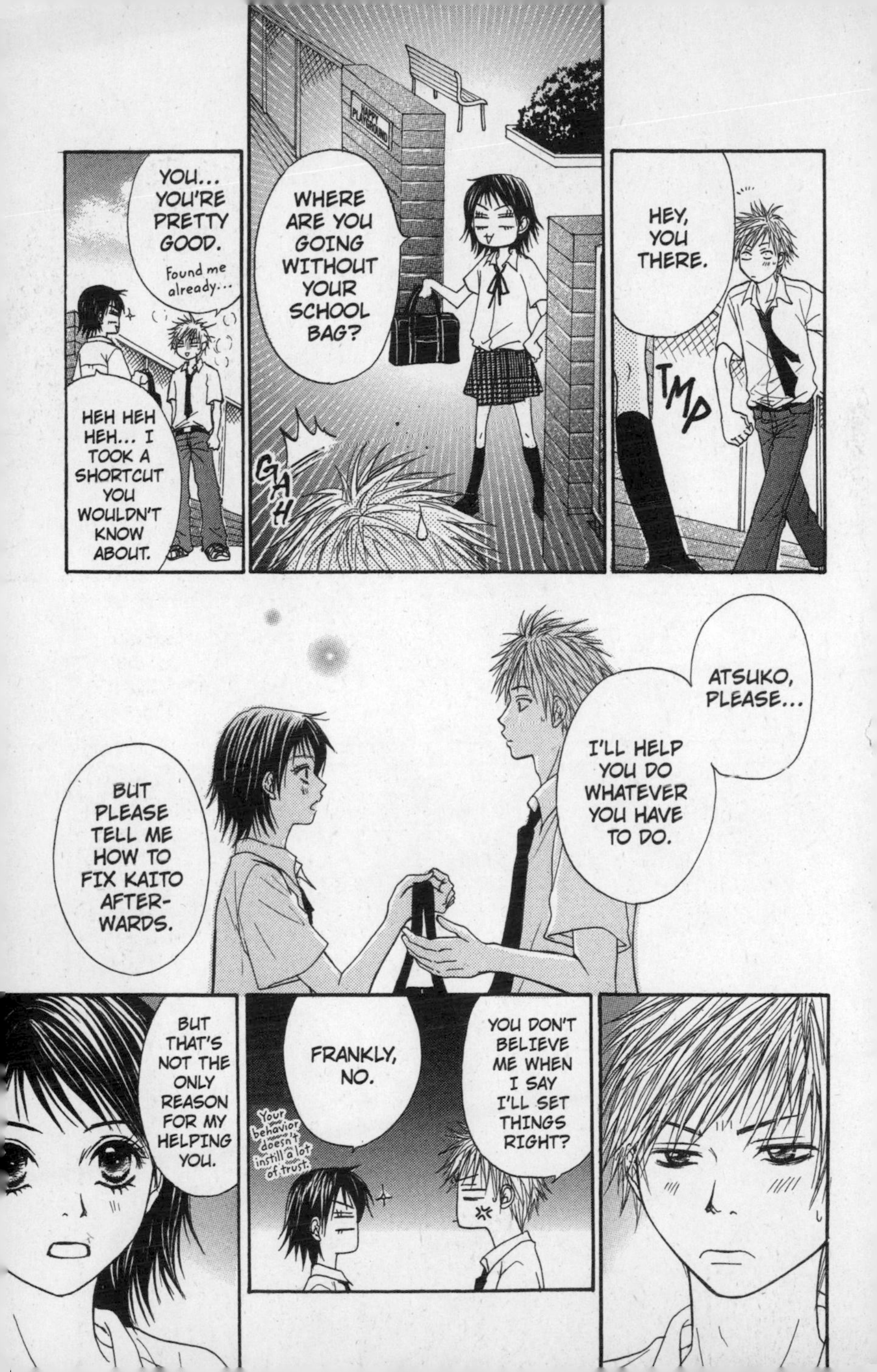
HEY, YOU THERE.
TMP
HAPPY PLAYGROUND
WHERE ARE YOU GOING WITHOUT YOUR SCHOOL BAG?
GAH
YOU... YOU'RE PRETTY GOOD.
Found me already...
HEH HEH HEH... I TOOK A SHORTCUT YOU WOULDN'T KNOW ABOUT.
ATSUKO, PLEASE...
I'LL HELP YOU DO WHATEVER YOU HAVE TO DO.
BUT PLEASE TELL ME HOW TO FIX KAITO AFTER-WARDS.
YOU DON'T BELIEVE ME WHEN I SAY I'LL SET THINGS RIGHT?
FRANKLY, NO.
Your behavior doesn't instill a lot of trust.
BUT THAT'S NOT THE ONLY REASON FOR MY HELPING YOU.

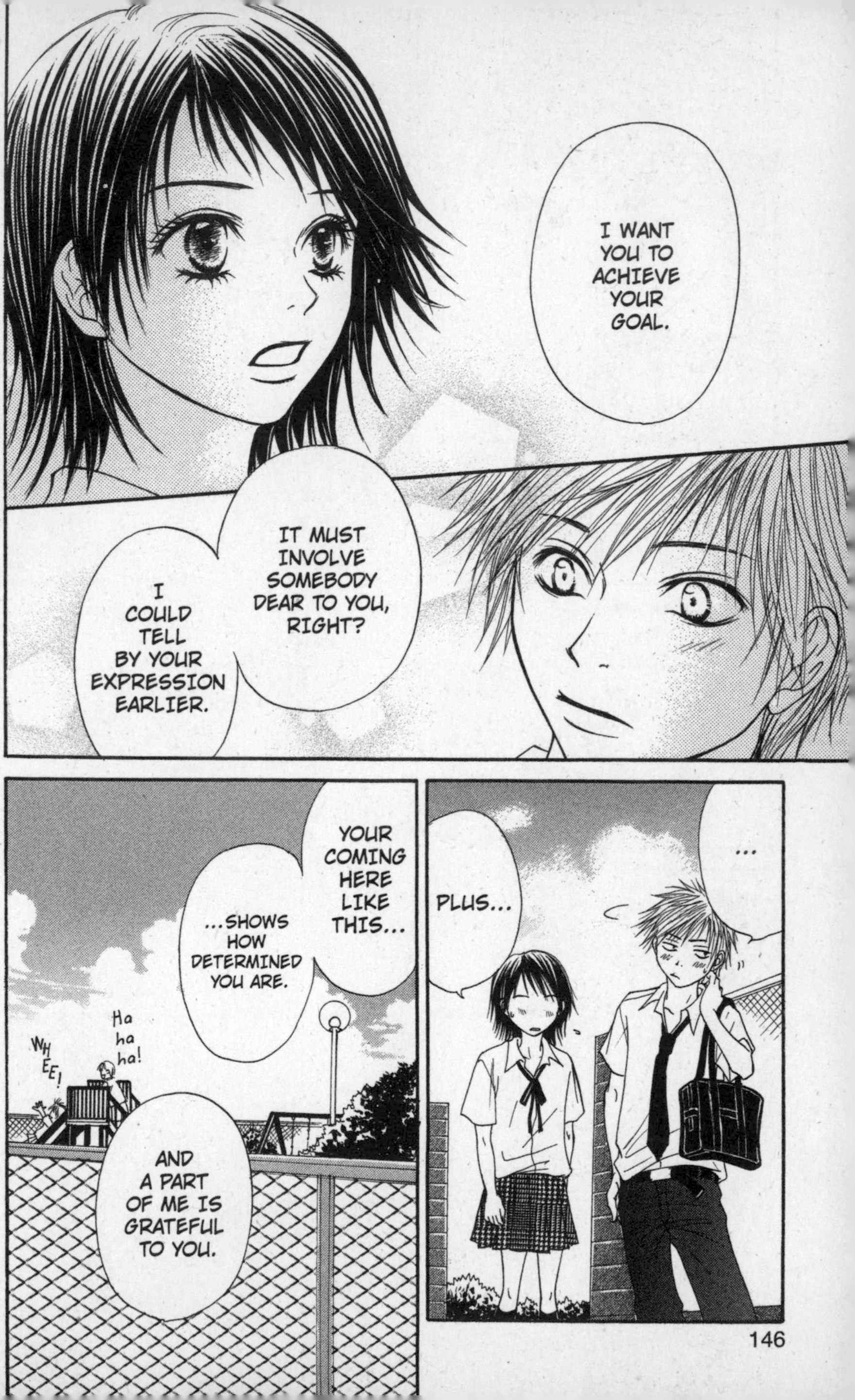
I WANT YOU TO ACHIEVE YOUR GOAL.
IT MUST INVOLVE SOMEBODY DEAR TO YOU, RIGHT?
I COULD TELL BY YOUR EXPRESSION EARLIER.
...
PLUS...
YOUR COMING HERE LIKE THIS...
...SHOWS HOW DETERMINED YOU ARE.
Ha ha ha!
WHEE!
AND A PART OF ME IS GRATEFUL TO YOU.

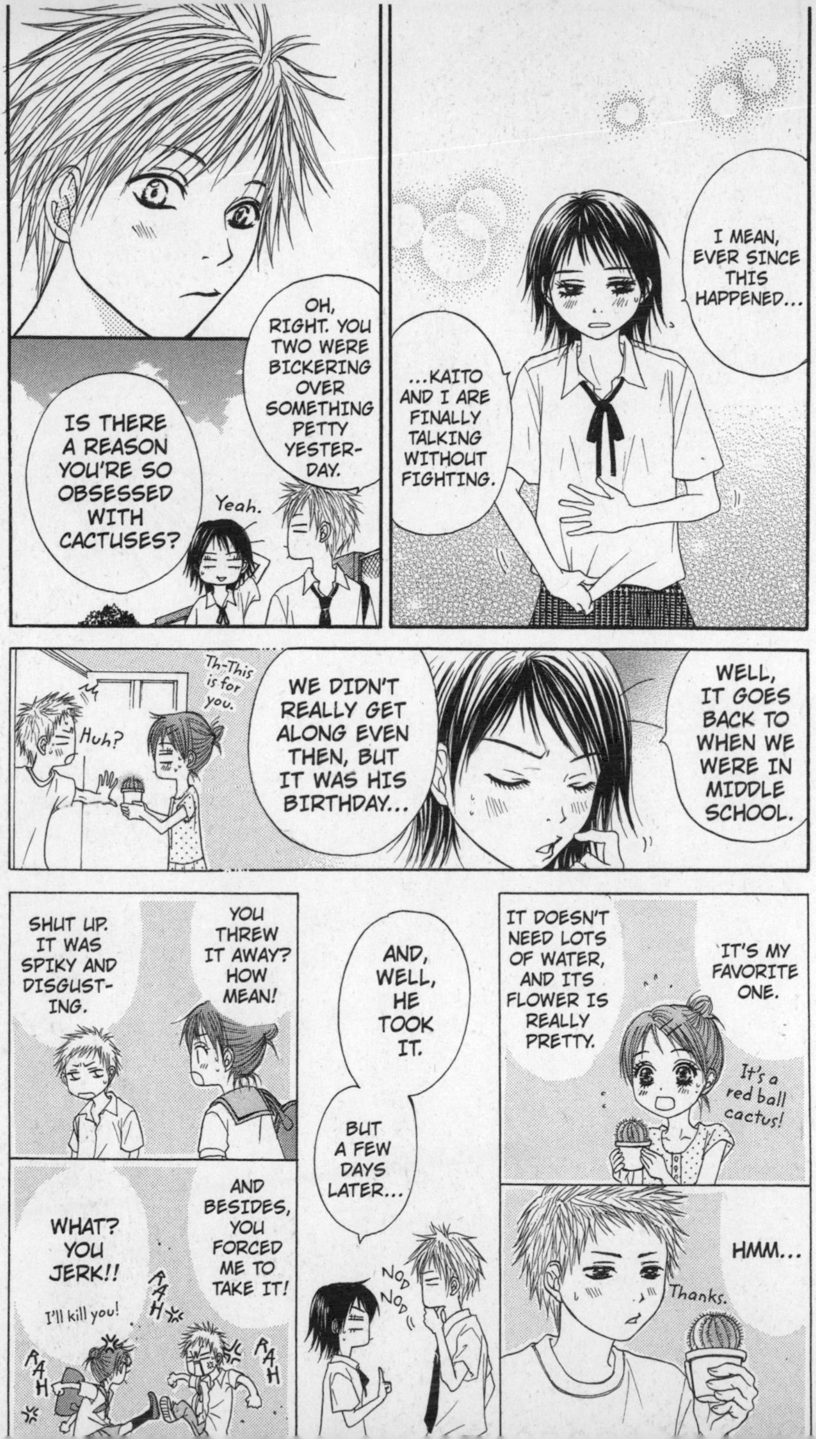
I MEAN, EVER SINCE THIS HAPPENED...
...KAITO AND I ARE FINALLY TALKING WITHOUT FIGHTING.
OH, RIGHT. YOU TWO WERE BICKERING OVER SOMETHING PETTY YESTER-DAY.
Yeah.
IS THERE A REASON YOU'RE SO OBSESSED WITH CACTUSES?
WELL, IT GOES BACK TO WHEN WE WERE IN MIDDLE SCHOOL.
WE DIDN'T REALLY GET ALONG EVEN THEN, BUT IT WAS HIS BIRTHDAY...
Th-This is for you.
Huh?
IT'S MY FAVORITE ONE.
IT DOESN'T NEED LOTS OF WATER, AND ITS FLOWER IS REALLY PRETTY.
It's a red ball cactus!
HMM...
Thanks.
AND, WELL, HE TOOK IT.
BUT A FEW DAYS LATER...
NOD NOD
YOU THREW IT AWAY? HOW MEAN!
SHUT UP. IT WAS SPIKY AND DISGUST-ING.
AND BESIDES, YOU FORCED ME TO TAKE IT!
WHAT? YOU JERK!!
RAH
I'll kill you!
RAH
RAH

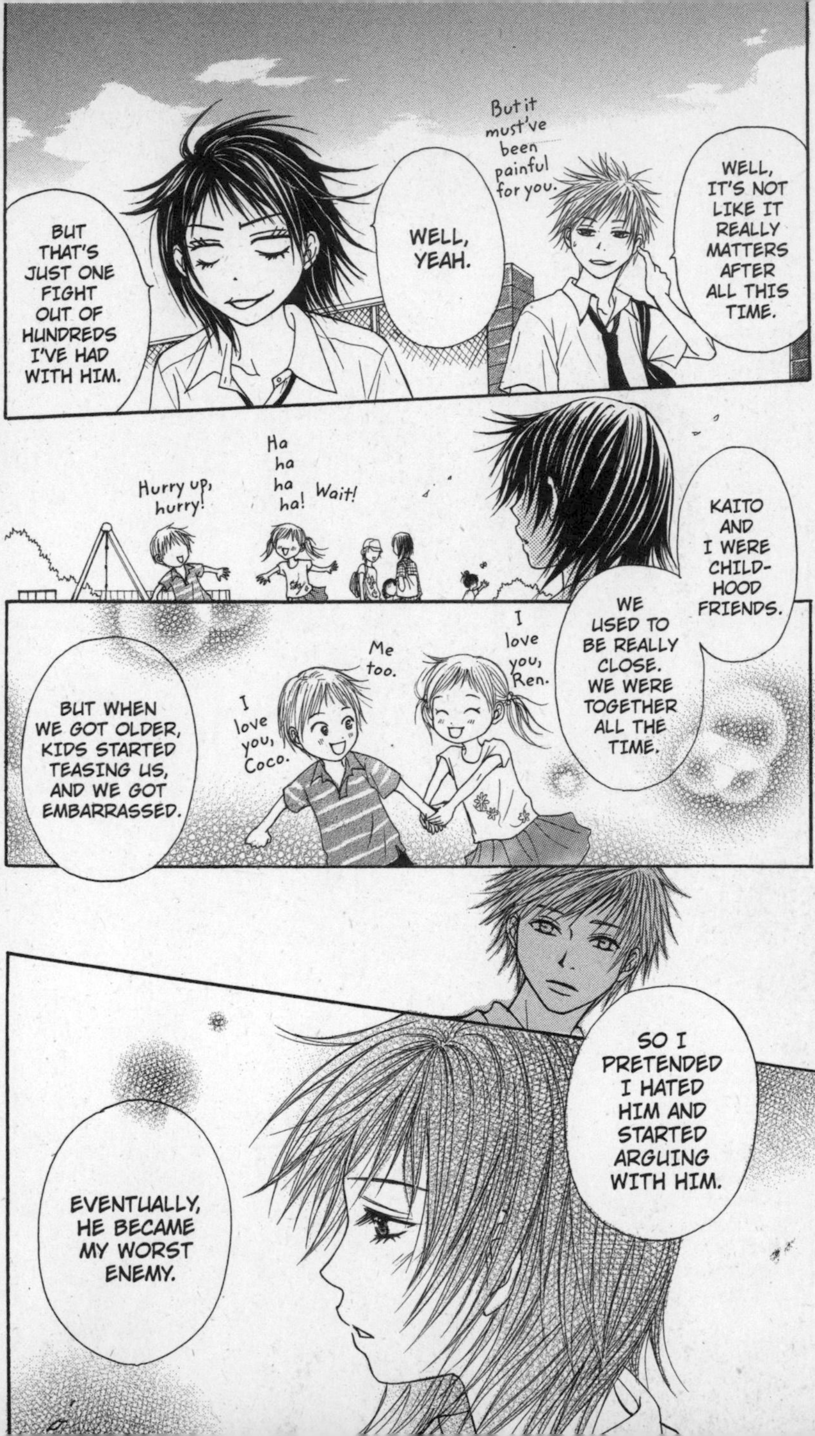
WELL, IT'S NOT LIKE IT REALLY MATTERS AFTER ALL THIS TIME.
But it must've been painful for you.
WELL, YEAH.
BUT THAT'S JUST ONE FIGHT OUT OF HUNDREDS I'VE HAD WITH HIM.
KAITO AND I WERE CHILD-HOOD FRIENDS.
Wait!
Ha ha ha ha!
Hurry up, hurry!
WE USED TO BE REALLY CLOSE. WE WERE TOGETHER ALL THE TIME.
I love you, Ren.
Me too.
I love you, Coco.
BUT WHEN WE GOT OLDER, KIDS STARTED TEASING US, AND WE GOT EMBARRASSED.
SO I PRETENDED I HATED HIM AND STARTED ARGUING WITH HIM.
EVENTUALLY, HE BECAME MY WORST ENEMY.

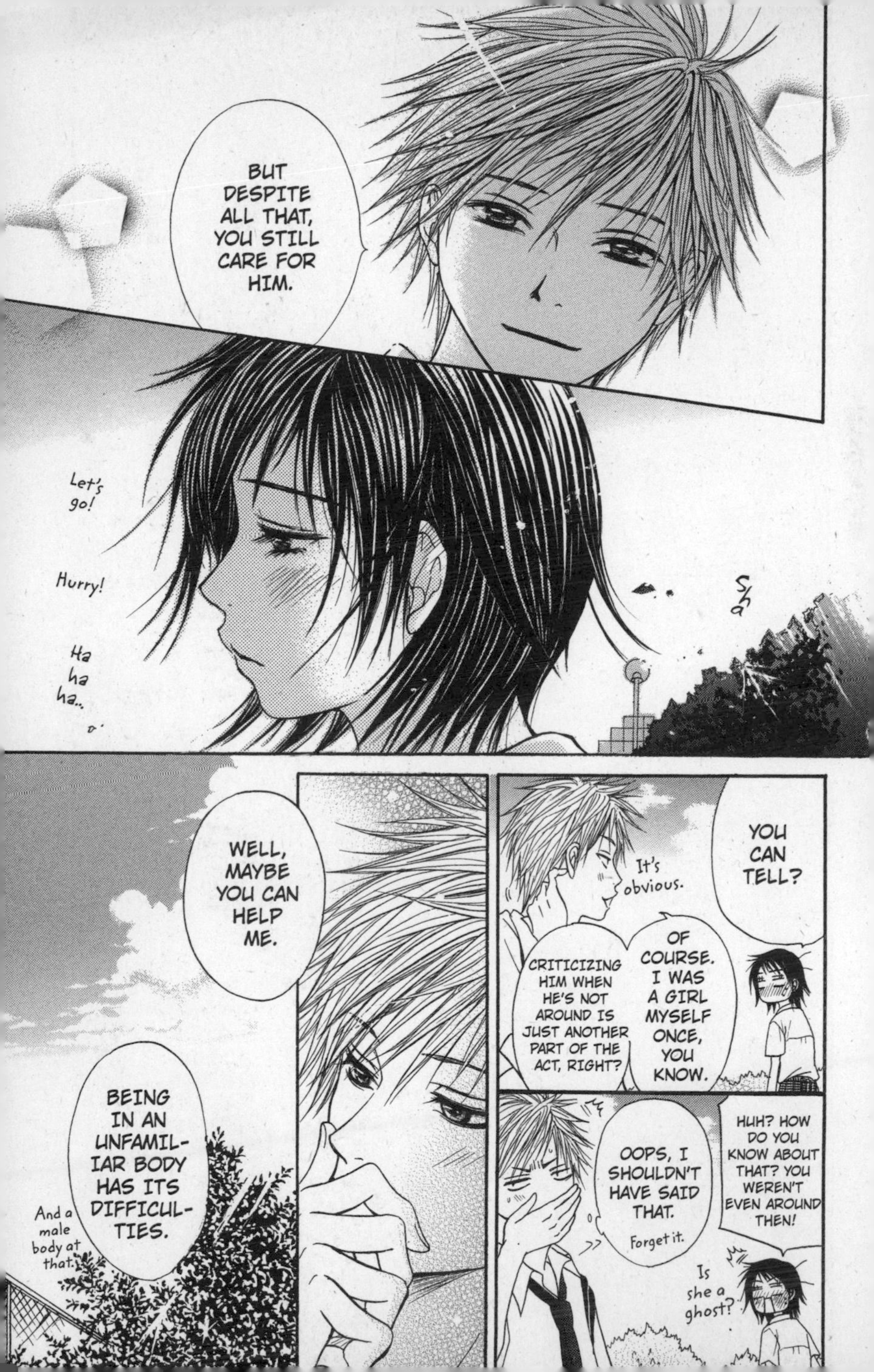
BUT DESPITE ALL THAT, YOU STILL CARE FOR HIM.
Sha
Let's go!
Hurry!
Ha ha ha..
YOU CAN TELL?
It's obvious.
OF COURSE. I WAS A GIRL MYSELF ONCE, YOU KNOW.
CRITICIZING HIM WHEN HE'S NOT AROUND IS JUST ANOTHER PART OF THE ACT, RIGHT?
HUH? HOW DO YOU KNOW ABOUT THAT? YOU WEREN'T EVEN AROUND THEN!
OOPS, I SHOULDN'T HAVE SAID THAT.
Forget it.
Is she a ghost?
WELL, MAYBE YOU CAN HELP ME.
BEING IN AN UNFAMIL-IAR BODY HAS ITS DIFFICUL-TIES.
And a male body at that.

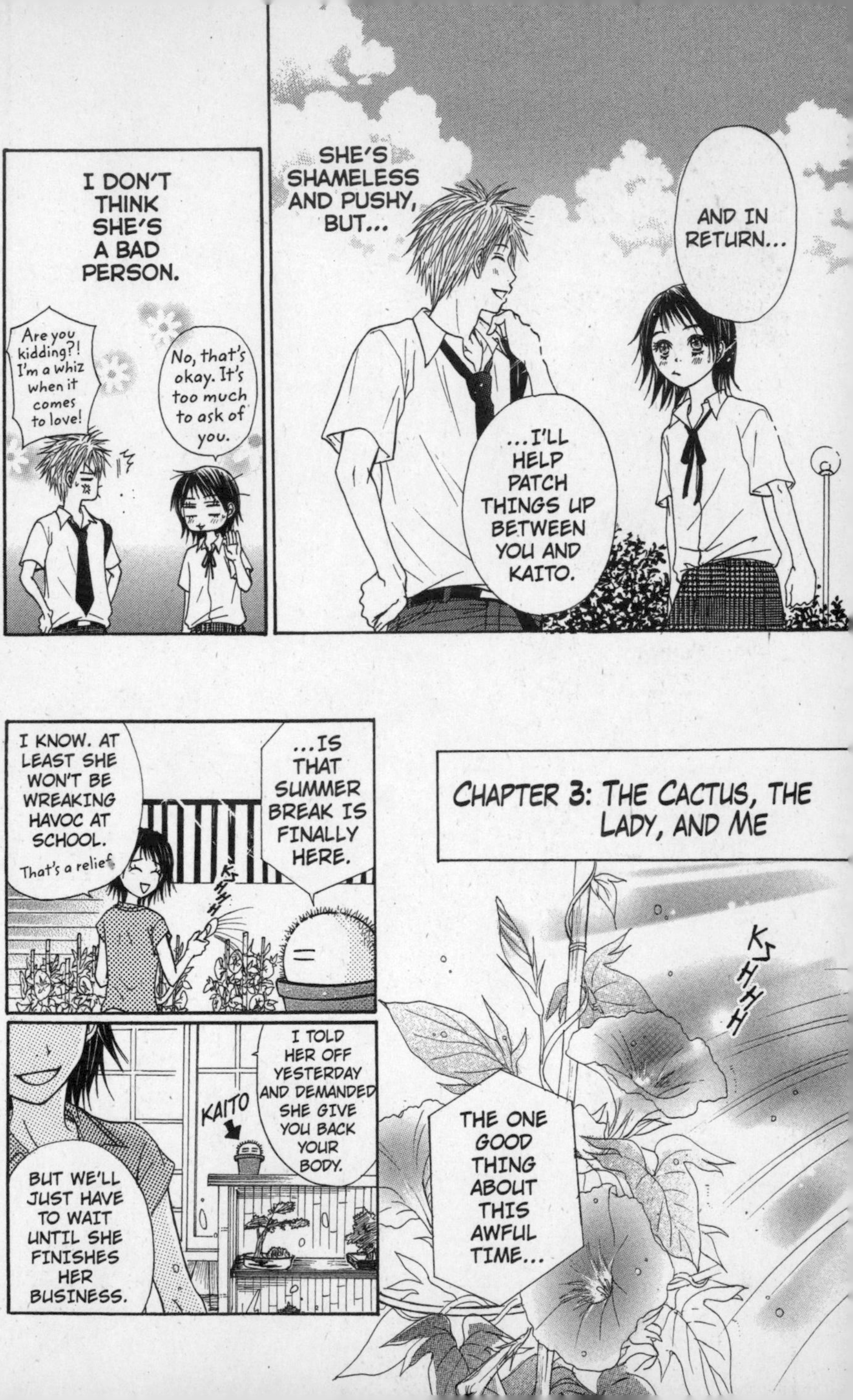
AND IN RETURN...
...I'LL HELP PATCH THINGS UP BETWEEN YOU AND KAITO.
SHE'S SHAMELESS AND PUSHY, BUT...
I DON'T THINK SHE'S A BAD PERSON.
No, that's okay. It's too much to ask of you.
Are you kidding?! I'm a whiz when it comes to love!
CHAPTER 3: THE CACTUS, THE LADY, AND ME
KSHHHH
THE ONE GOOD THING ABOUT THIS AWFUL TIME...
...IS THAT SUMMER BREAK IS FINALLY HERE.
I KNOW. AT LEAST SHE WON'T BE WREAKING HAVOC AT SCHOOL.
That's a relief
KSHHHH
I TOLD HER OFF YESTERDAY AND DEMANDED SHE GIVE YOU BACK YOUR BODY.
KAITO
BUT WE'LL JUST HAVE TO WAIT UNTIL SHE FINISHES HER BUSINESS.

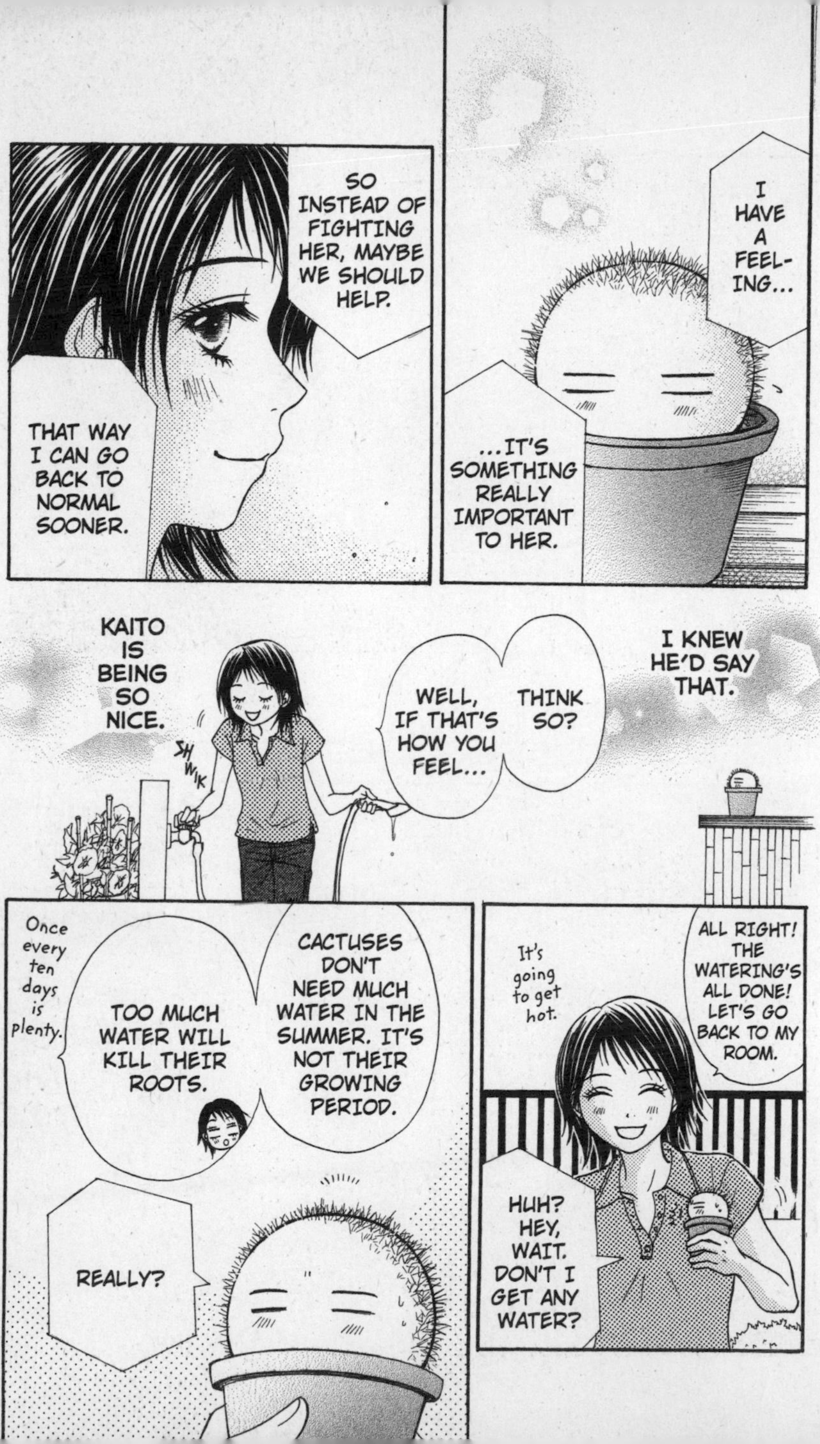
I HAVE A FEELING...
...IT'S SOMETHING REALLY IMPORTANT TO HER.
SO INSTEAD OF FIGHTING HER, MAYBE WE SHOULD HELP.
THAT WAY I CAN GO BACK TO NORMAL SOONER.
I KNEW HE'D SAY THAT.
THINK SO?
WELL, IF THAT'S HOW YOU FEEL...
KAITO IS BEING SO NICE.
SHWIK
ALL RIGHT! THE WATERING'S ALL DONE! LET'S GO BACK TO MY ROOM.
It's going to get hot.
HUH? HEY, WAIT. DON'T I GET ANY WATER?
CACTUSES DON'T NEED MUCH WATER IN THE SUMMER. IT'S NOT THEIR GROWING PERIOD.
TOO MUCH WATER WILL KILL THEIR ROOTS.
Once every ten days is plenty.
REALLY?

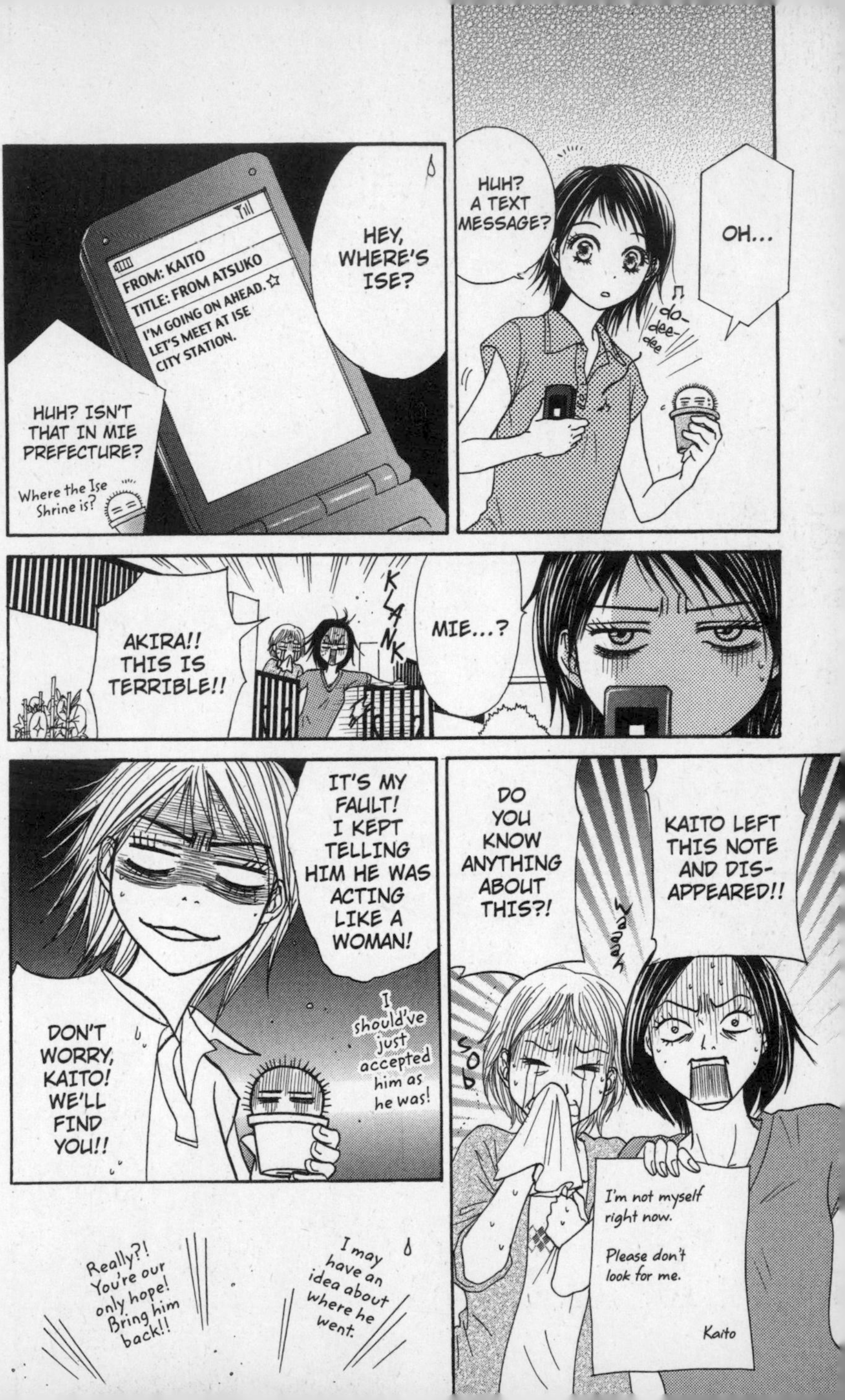
HUH? A TEXT MESSAGE?
do-dee-dee
OH...
FROM: KAITO
TITLE: FROM ATSUKO ☆
I'M GOING ON AHEAD. ☆ LET'S MEET AT ISE CITY STATION.
HEY, WHERE'S ISE?
HUH? ISN'T THAT IN MIE PREFECTURE?
Where the Ise Shrine is?
MIE...?
KLANK
AKIRA!! THIS IS TERRIBLE!!
KAITO LEFT THIS NOTE AND DIS-APPEARED!!
DO YOU KNOW ANYTHING ABOUT THIS?!
SOB
I'm not myself right now.
Please don't look for me.
Kaito
IT'S MY FAULT! I KEPT TELLING HIM HE WAS ACTING LIKE A WOMAN!
I should've just accepted him as he was!
DON'T WORRY, KAITO! WE'LL FIND YOU!!
I may have an idea about where he went.
Really?! You're our only hope! Bring him back!!

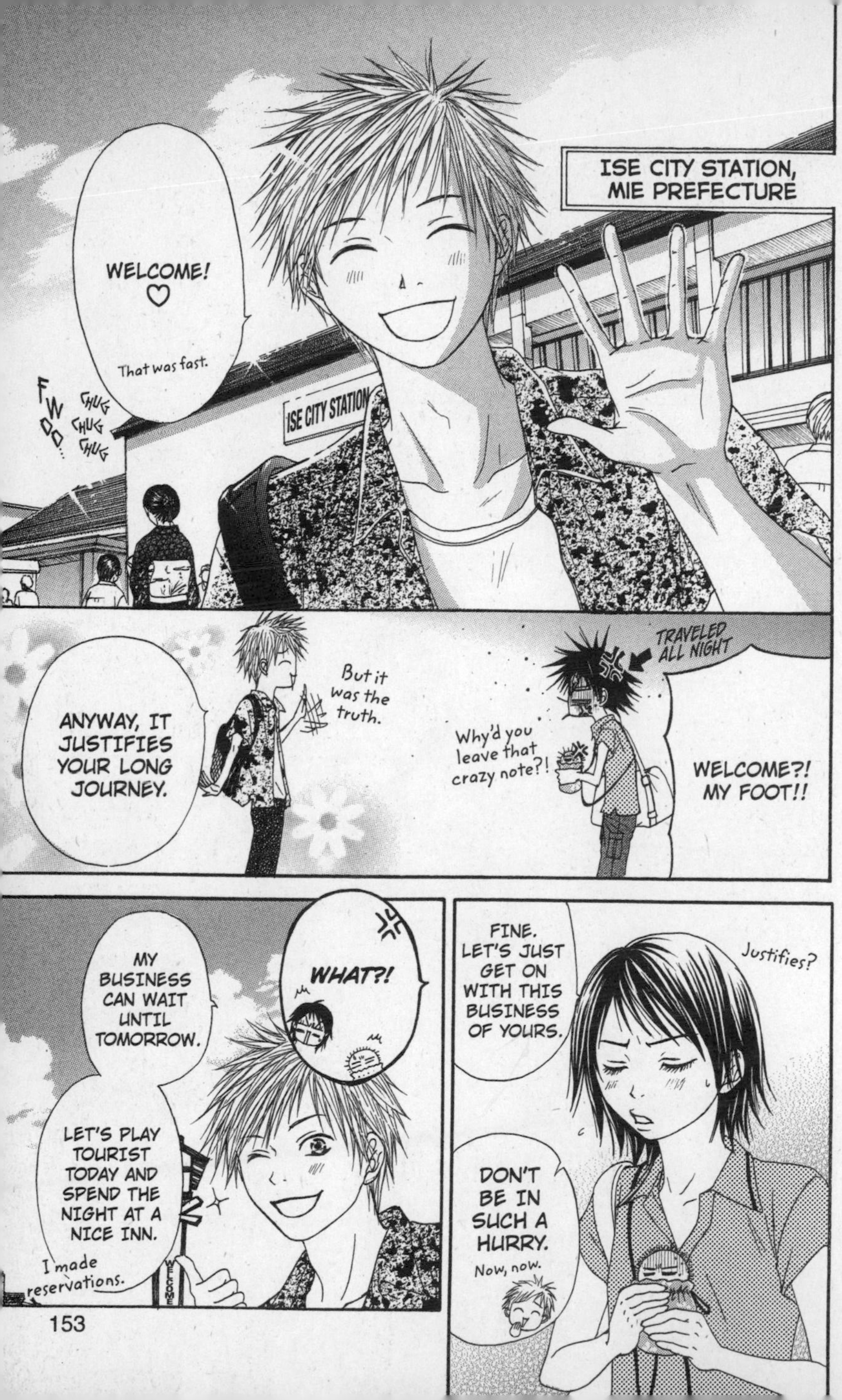
ISE CITY STATION, MIE PREFECTURE
WELCOME! ♡
That was fast.
ISE CITY STATION
FWOO...
CHUG CHUG CHUG
TRAVELED ALL NIGHT
WELCOME?! MY FOOT!!
Why'd you leave that crazy note?!
But it was the truth.
ANYWAY, IT JUSTIFIES YOUR LONG JOURNEY.
Justifies?
FINE. LET'S JUST GET ON WITH THIS BUSINESS OF YOURS.
DON'T BE IN SUCH A HURRY.
Now, now.
WHAT?!
MY BUSINESS CAN WAIT UNTIL TOMORROW.
LET'S PLAY TOURIST TODAY AND SPEND THE NIGHT AT A NICE INN.
I made reservations.
WELCOME

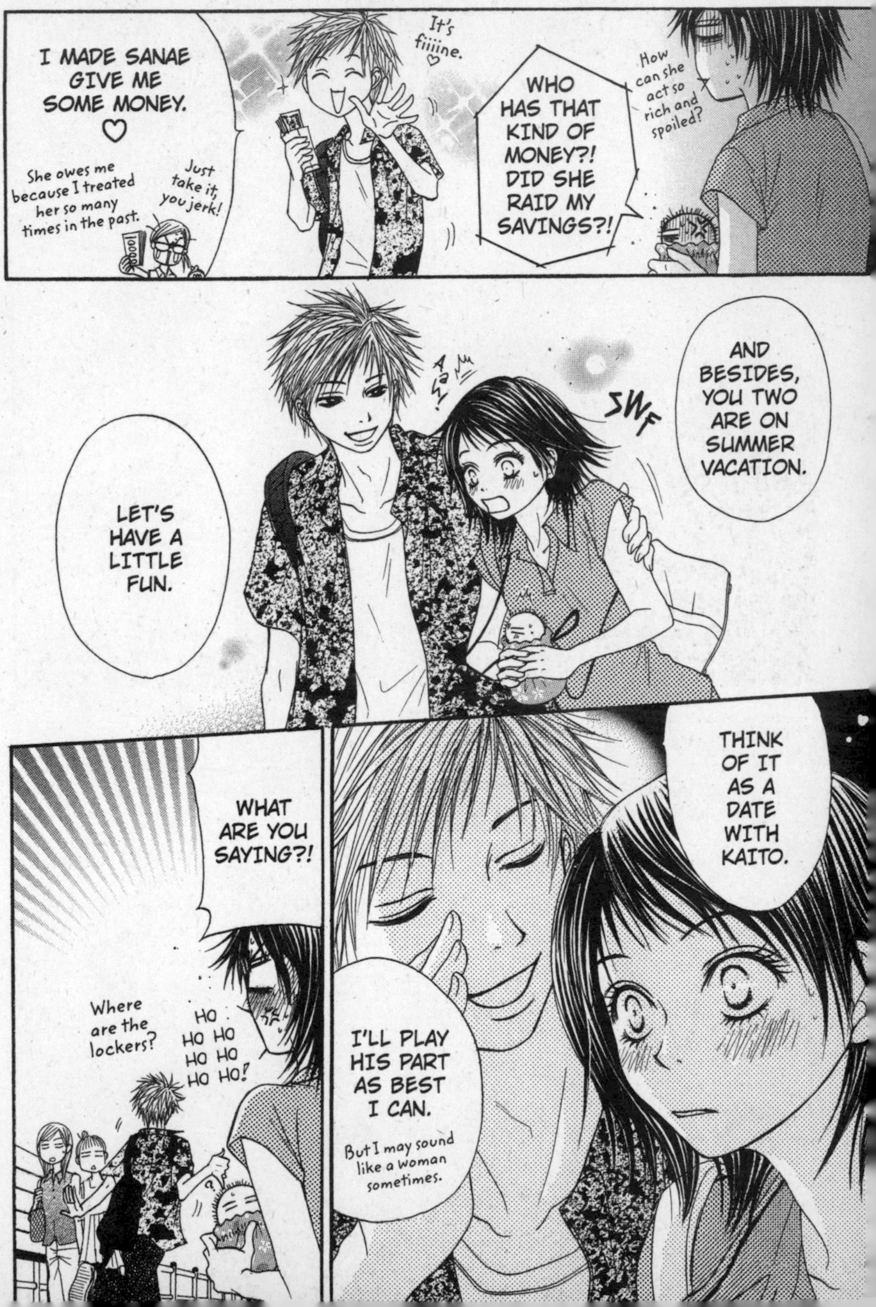
How can she act so rich and spoiled?
WHO HAS THAT KIND OF MONEY?! DID SHE RAID MY SAVINGS?!
It's fiiiine. ♡
I MADE SANAE GIVE ME SOME MONEY. ♡
Just take it, you jerk!
She owes me because I treated her so many times in the past.
AND BESIDES, YOU TWO ARE ON SUMMER VACATION.
SWF
LET'S HAVE A LITTLE FUN.
THINK OF IT AS A DATE WITH KAITO.
I'LL PLAY HIS PART AS BEST I CAN.
But I may sound like a woman sometimes.
WHAT ARE YOU SAYING?!
HO HO HO HO HO HO HO!
Where are the lockers?

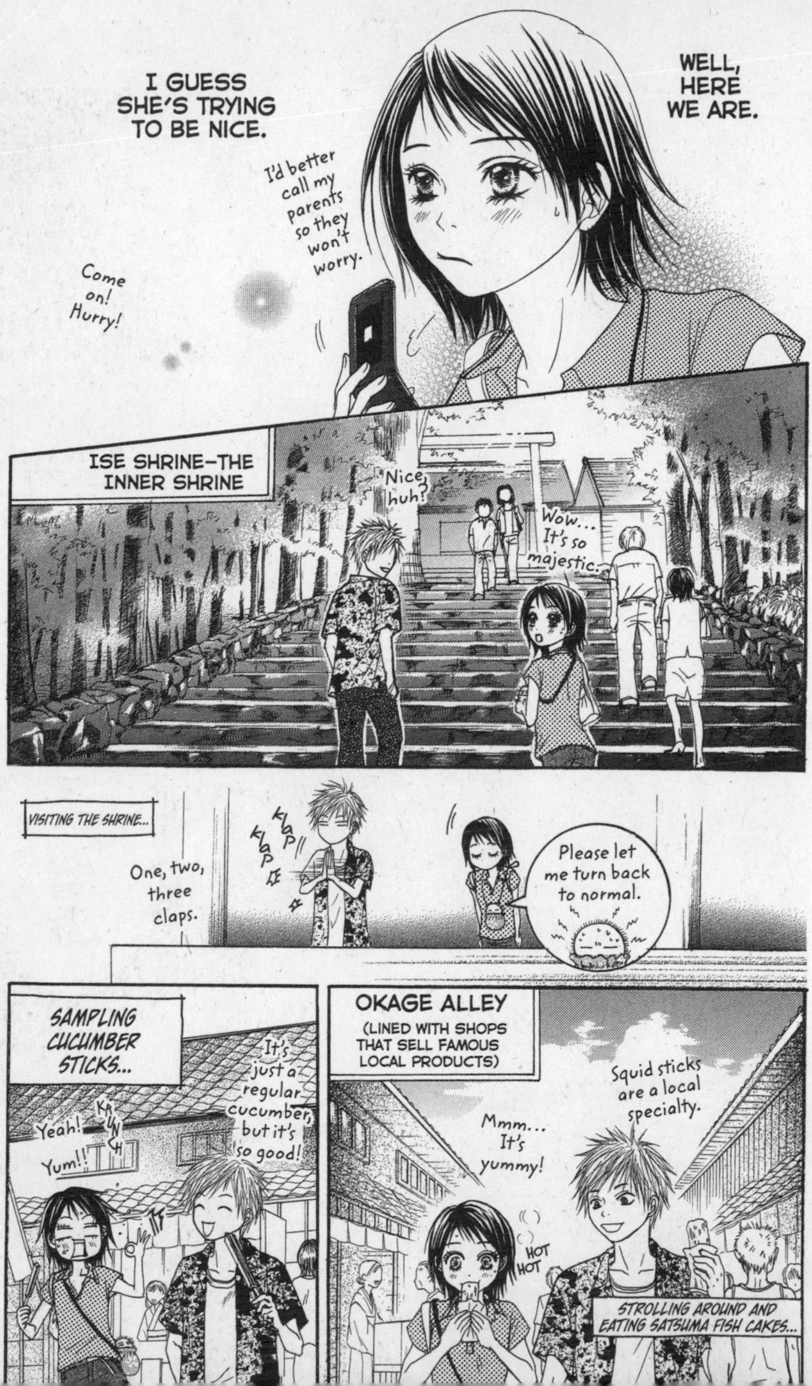
WELL, HERE WE ARE.
I GUESS SHE'S TRYING TO BE NICE.
I'd better call my parents so they won't worry.
Come on! Hurry!
ISE SHRINE—THE INNER SHRINE
Nice, huh?
Wow... It's so majestic.
VISITING THE SHRINE...
One, two, three claps.
KLAP KLAP
Please let me turn back to normal.
OKAGE ALLEY
(LINED WITH SHOPS THAT SELL FAMOUS LOCAL PRODUCTS)
Squid sticks are a local specialty.
Mmm... It's yummy!
HOT HOT
STROLLING AROUND AND EATING SATSUMA FISH CAKES...
SAMPLING CUCUMBER STICKS...
It's just a regular cucumber, but it's so good!
KRUNCH
Yeah!
Yum!!

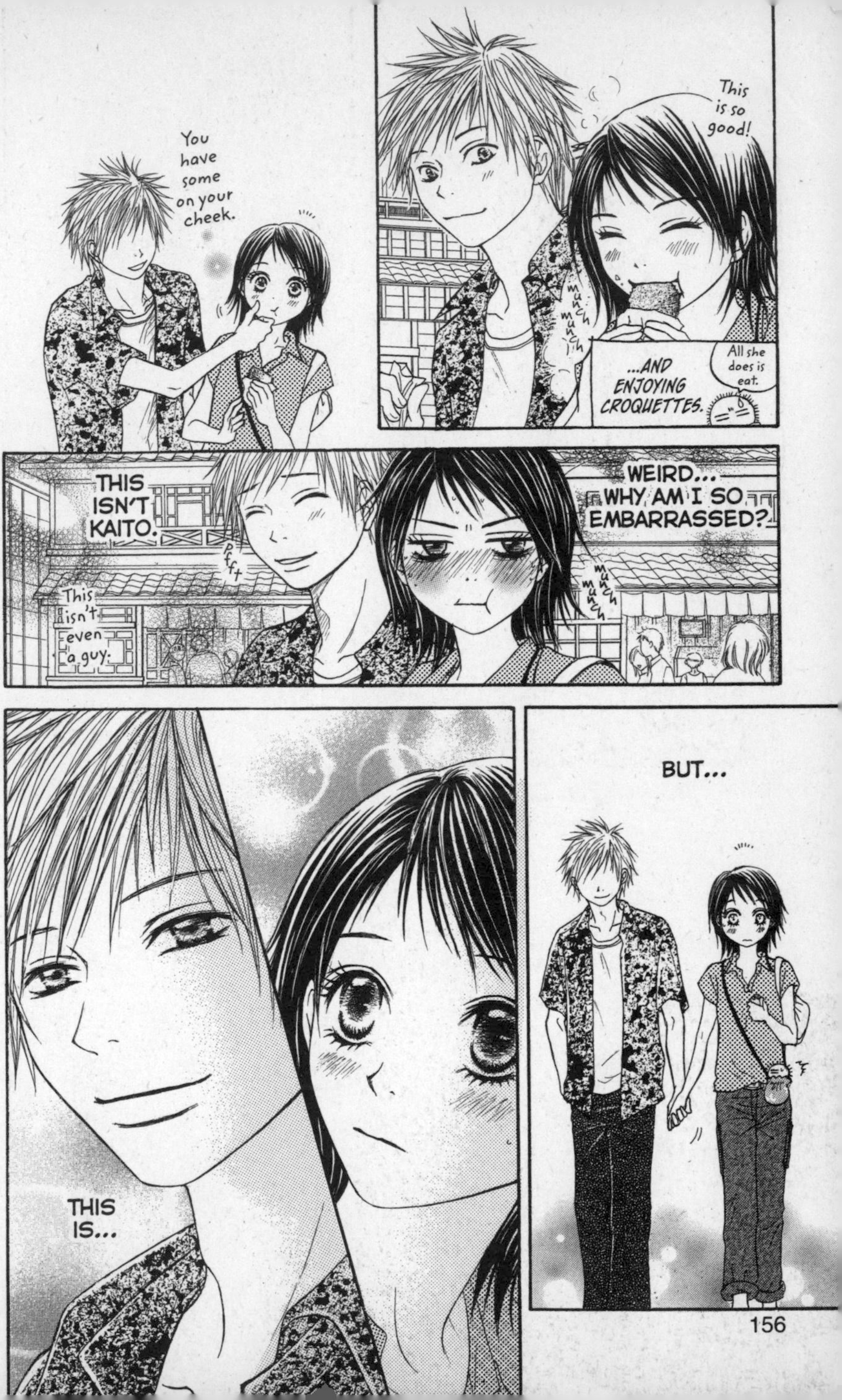
This is so good!
munch munch
...AND ENJOYING CROQUETTES.
All she does is eat.
You have some on your cheek.
WEIRD... WHY AM I SO EMBARRASSED?
munch munch
Pfft
THIS ISN'T KAITO.
This isn't even a guy.
BUT...
THIS IS...

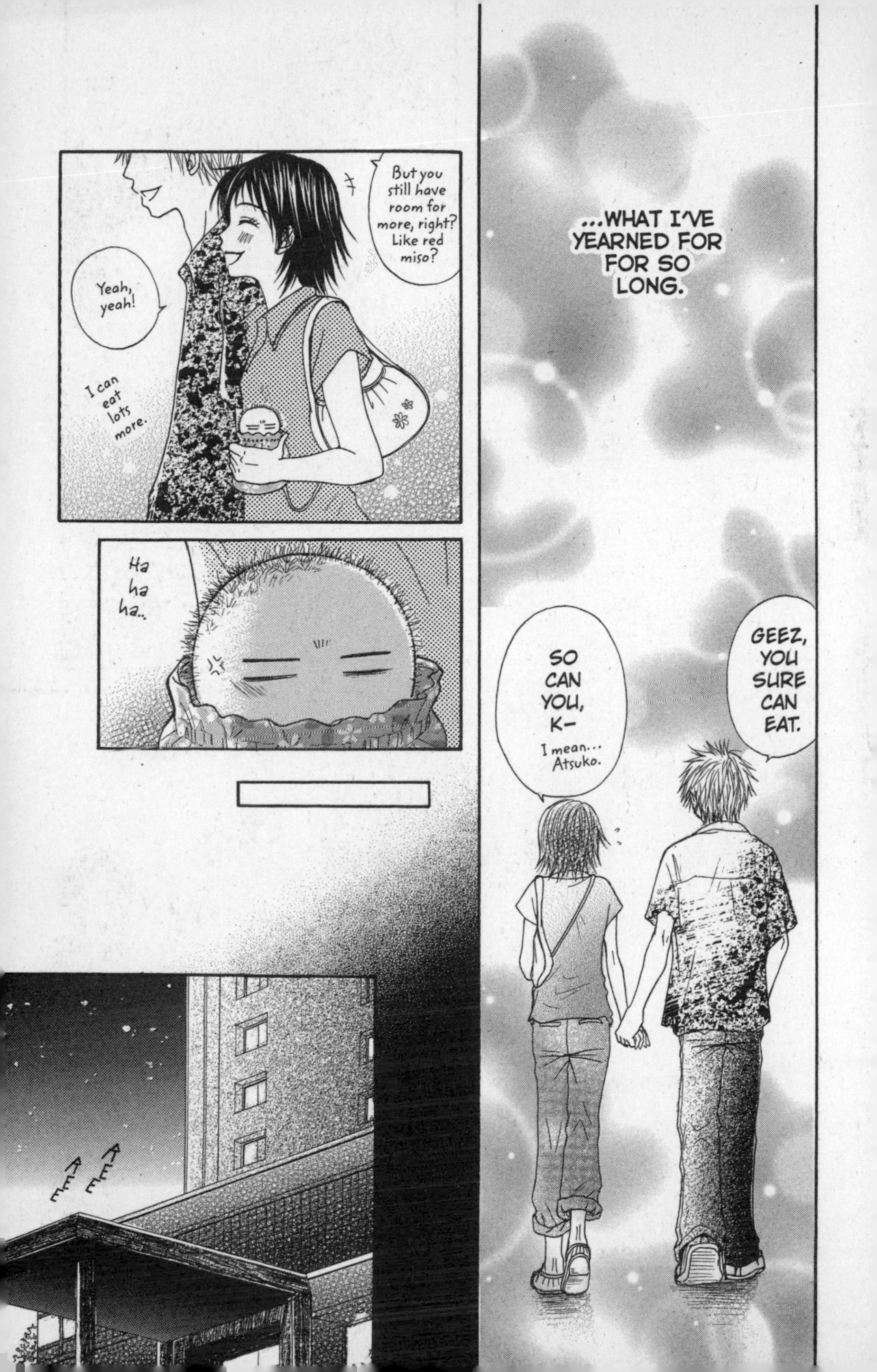
...WHAT I'VE YEARNED FOR FOR SO LONG.
GEEZ, YOU SURE CAN EAT.
SO CAN YOU, K—
I mean... Atsuko.
But you still have room for more, right? Like red miso?
Yeah, yeah!
I can eat lots more.
Ha ha ha..

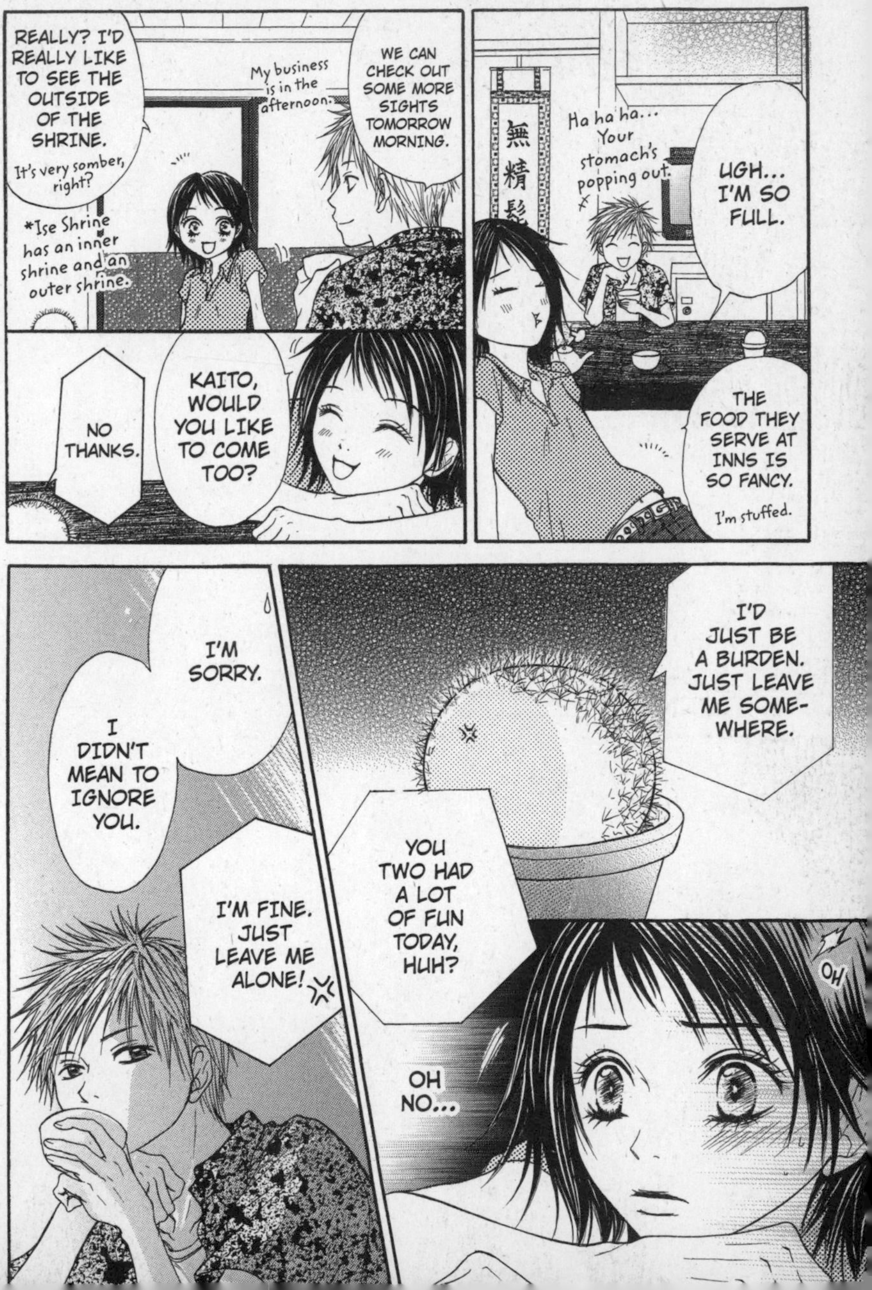
UGH... I'M SO FULL.
Ha ha ha... Your stomach's popping out.
THE FOOD THEY SERVE AT INNS IS SO FANCY.
I'm stuffed.
WE CAN CHECK OUT SOME MORE SIGHTS TOMORROW MORNING.
My business is in the afternoon.
REALLY? I'D REALLY LIKE TO SEE THE OUTSIDE OF THE SHRINE.
It's very somber, right?
*Ise Shrine has an inner shrine and an outer shrine.
KAITO, WOULD YOU LIKE TO COME TOO?
NO THANKS.
I'D JUST BE A BURDEN. JUST LEAVE ME SOME-WHERE.
OH
YOU TWO HAD A LOT OF FUN TODAY, HUH?
OH NO...
I'M SORRY.
I DIDN'T MEAN TO IGNORE YOU.
I'M FINE. JUST LEAVE ME ALONE!

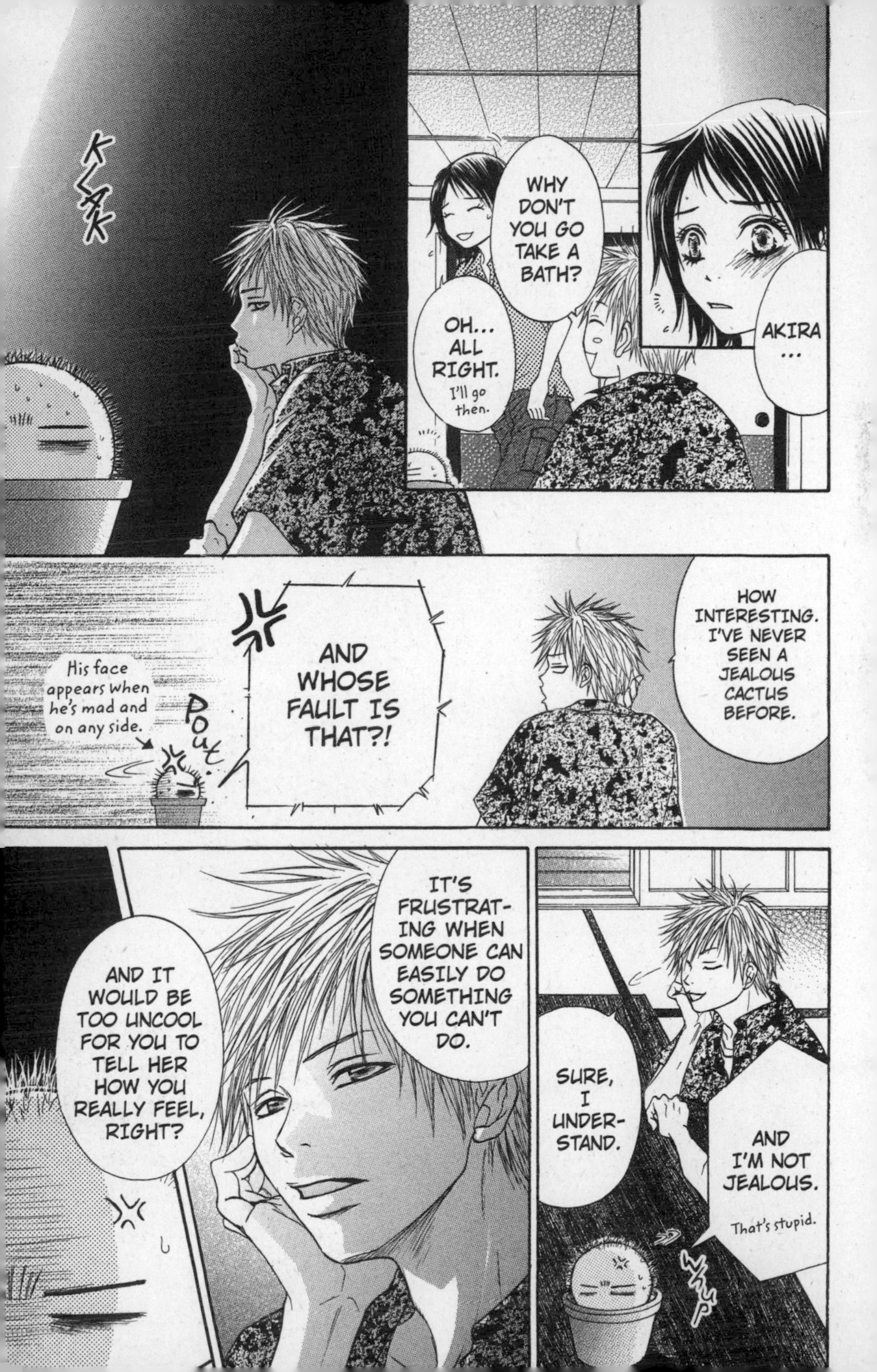
AKIRA ...
WHY DON'T YOU GO TAKE A BATH?
OH... ALL RIGHT. I'll go then.
KLAK
HOW INTERESTING. I'VE NEVER SEEN A JEALOUS CACTUS BEFORE.
AND WHOSE FAULT IS THAT?!
Pout.
His face appears when he's mad and on any side.
SURE, I UNDERSTAND.
AND I'M NOT JEALOUS.
That's stupid.
WHAP
IT'S FRUSTRATING WHEN SOMEONE CAN EASILY DO SOMETHING YOU CAN'T DO.
AND IT WOULD BE TOO UNCOOL FOR YOU TO TELL HER HOW YOU REALLY FEEL, RIGHT?

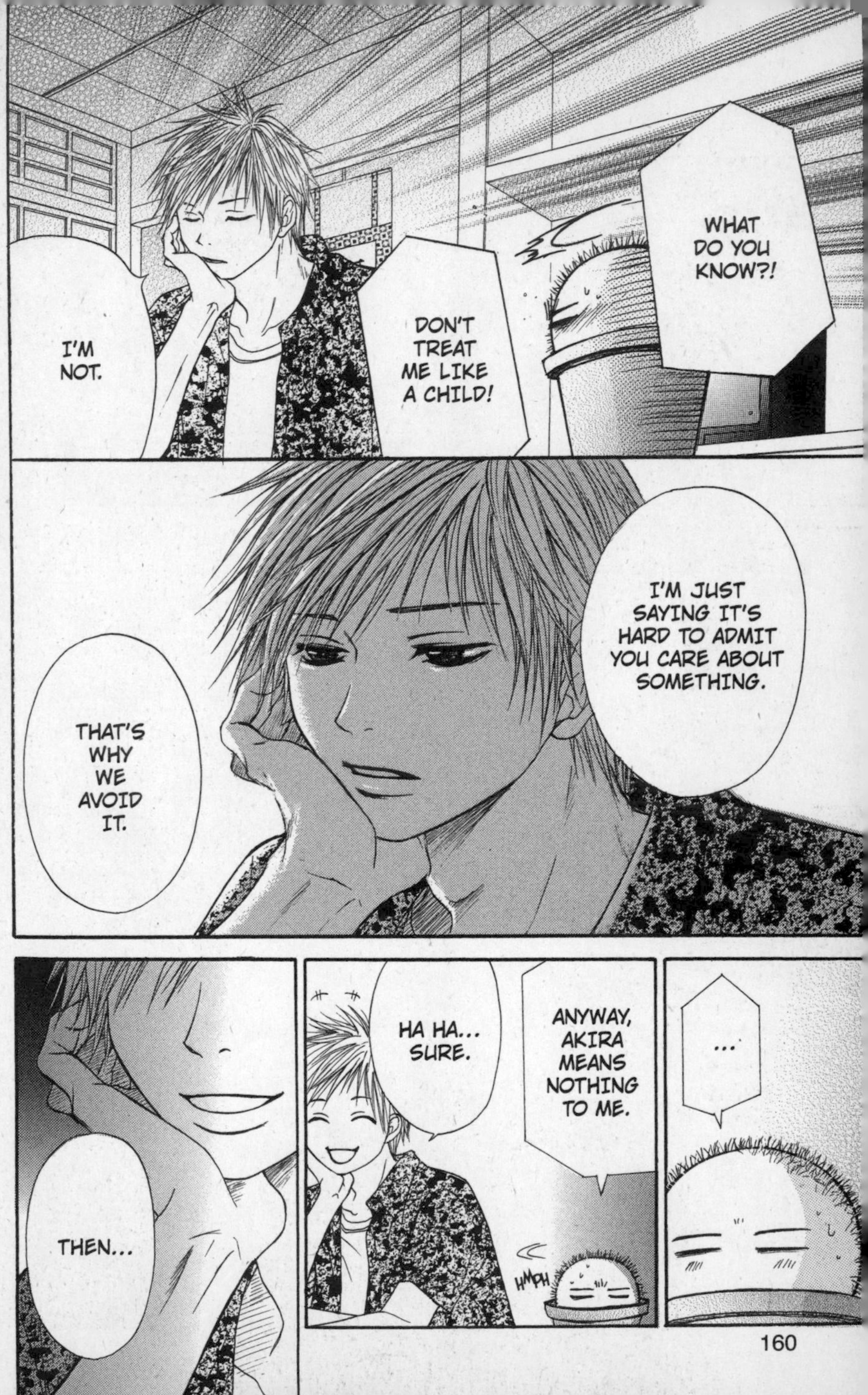
WHAT DO YOU KNOW?!
DON'T TREAT ME LIKE A CHILD!
I'M NOT.
I'M JUST SAYING IT'S HARD TO ADMIT YOU CARE ABOUT SOMETHING.
THAT'S WHY WE AVOID IT.
...
ANYWAY, AKIRA MEANS NOTHING TO ME.
HMPH
HA HA... SURE.
THEN...

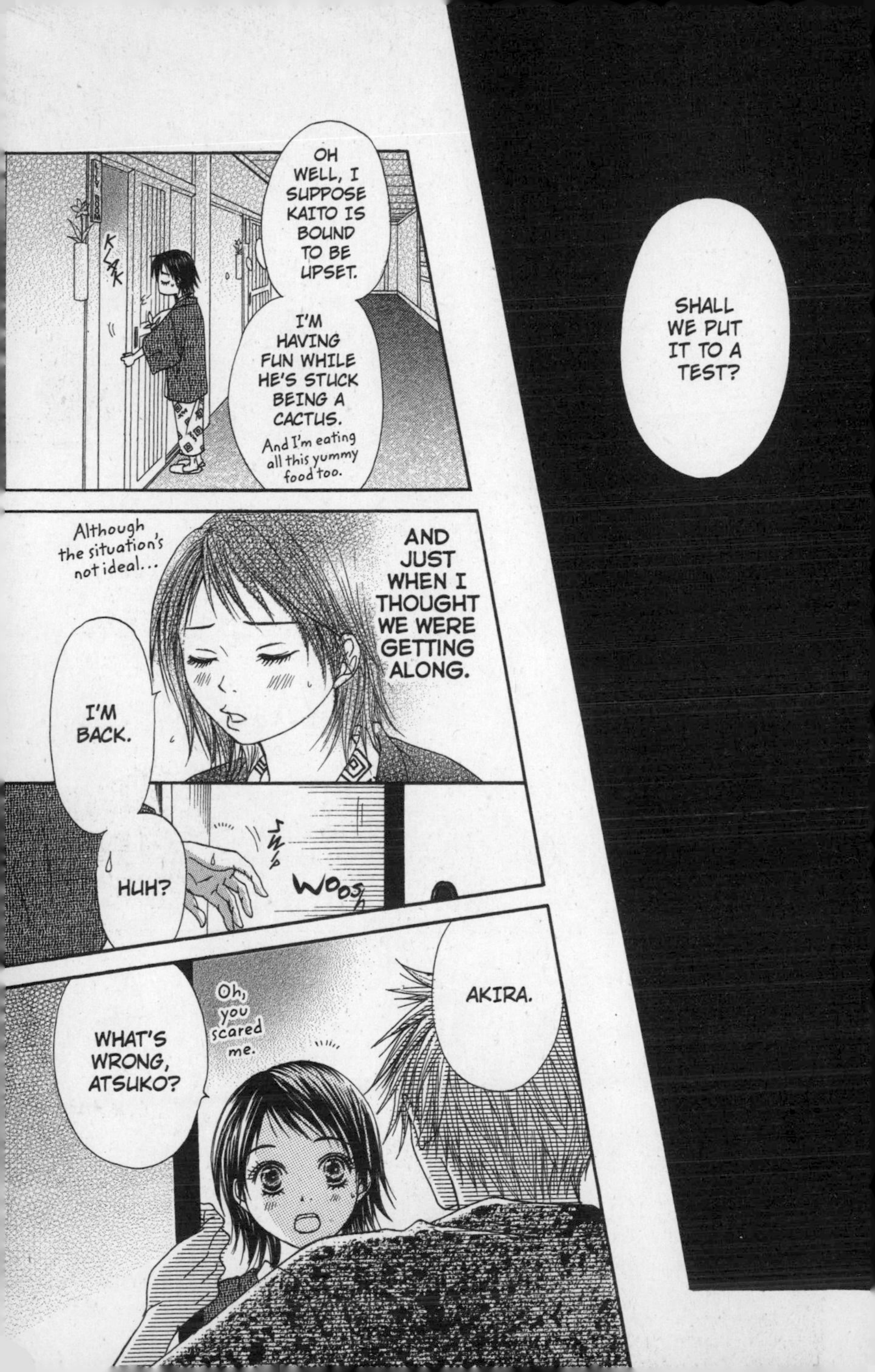
SHALL WE PUT IT TO A TEST?
OH WELL, I SUPPOSE KAITO IS BOUND TO BE UPSET.
KLAK
I'M HAVING FUN WHILE HE'S STUCK BEING A CACTUS.
And I'm eating all this yummy food too.
AND JUST WHEN I THOUGHT WE WERE GETTING ALONG.
Although the situation's not ideal...
I'M BACK.
WOOSH
HUH?
AKIRA.
Oh, you scared me.
WHAT'S WRONG, ATSUKO?

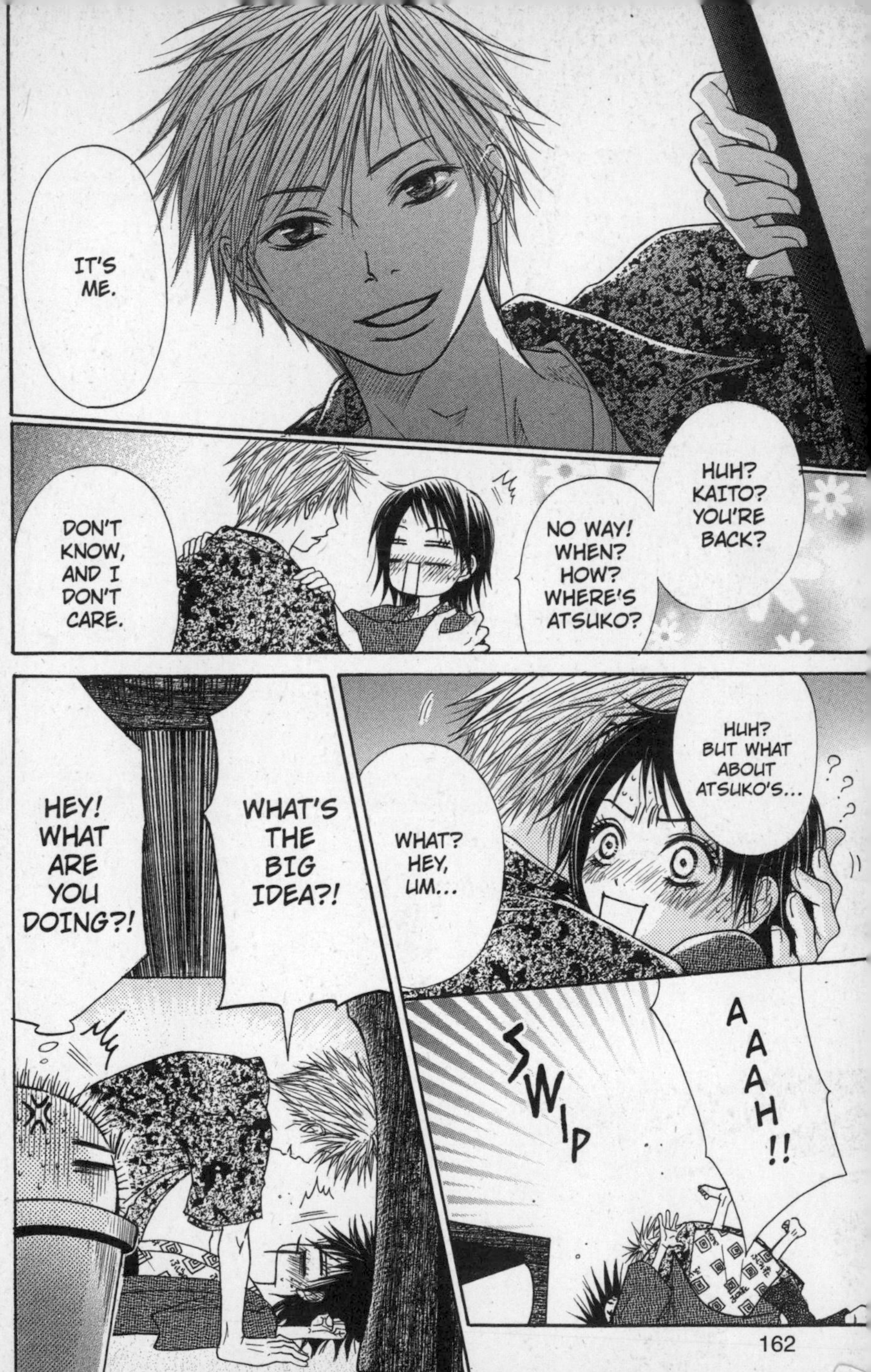
IT'S ME.
HUH? KAITO? YOU'RE BACK?
NO WAY! WHEN? HOW? WHERE'S ATSUKO?
DON'T KNOW, AND I DON'T CARE.
HUH? BUT WHAT ABOUT ATSUKO'S...
WHAT? HEY, UM...
AAAH!!
SWIP
WHAT'S THE BIG IDEA?!
HEY! WHAT ARE YOU DOING?!

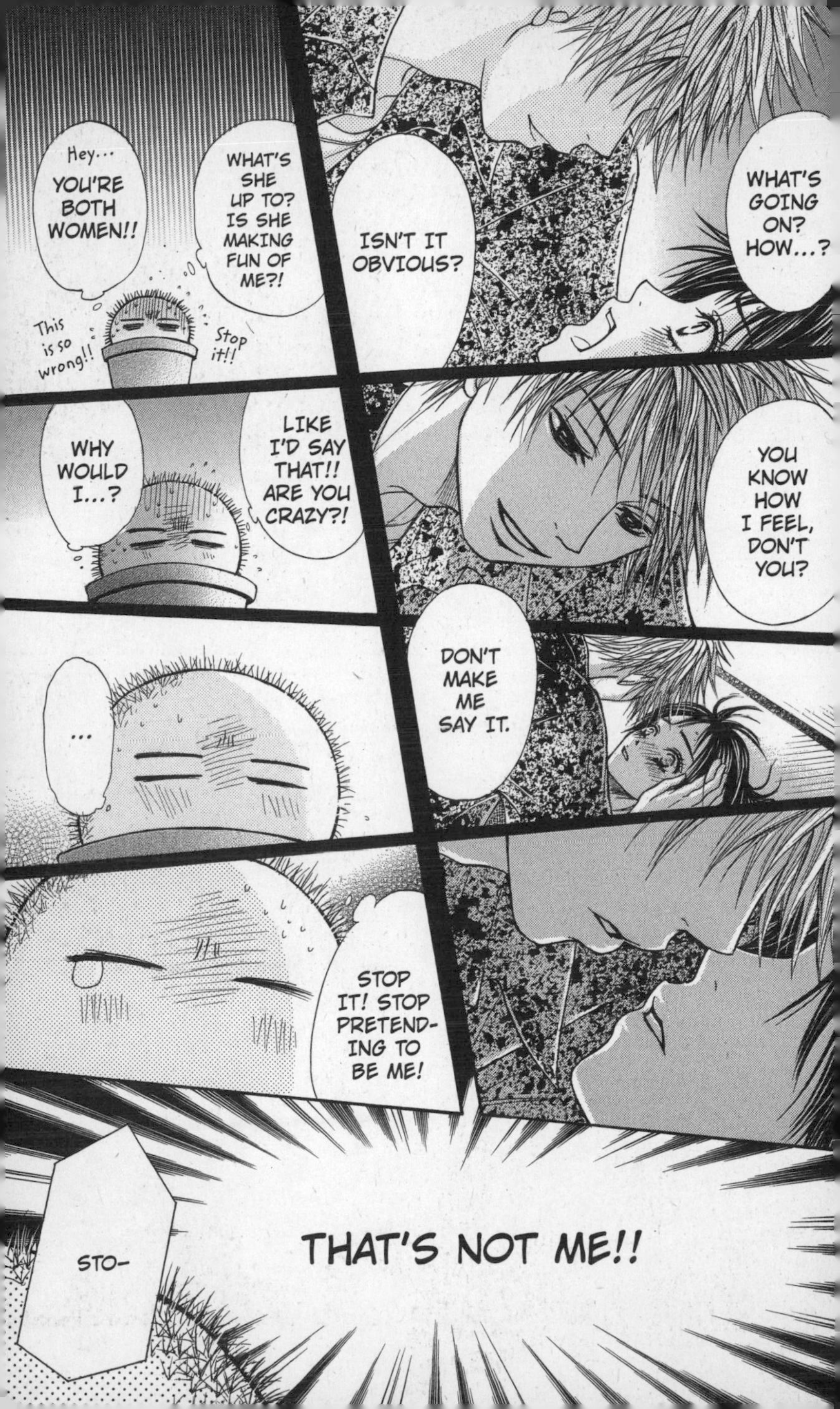
WHAT'S GOING ON? HOW...?
ISN'T IT OBVIOUS?
WHAT'S SHE UP TO? IS SHE MAKING FUN OF ME?!
Hey... YOU'RE BOTH WOMEN!!
Stop it!!
This is so wrong!!
YOU KNOW HOW I FEEL, DON'T YOU?
LIKE I'D SAY THAT!! ARE YOU CRAZY?!
WHY WOULD I...?
DON'T MAKE ME SAY IT.
...
STOP IT! STOP PRETEND-ING TO BE ME!
STO-
THAT'S NOT ME!!

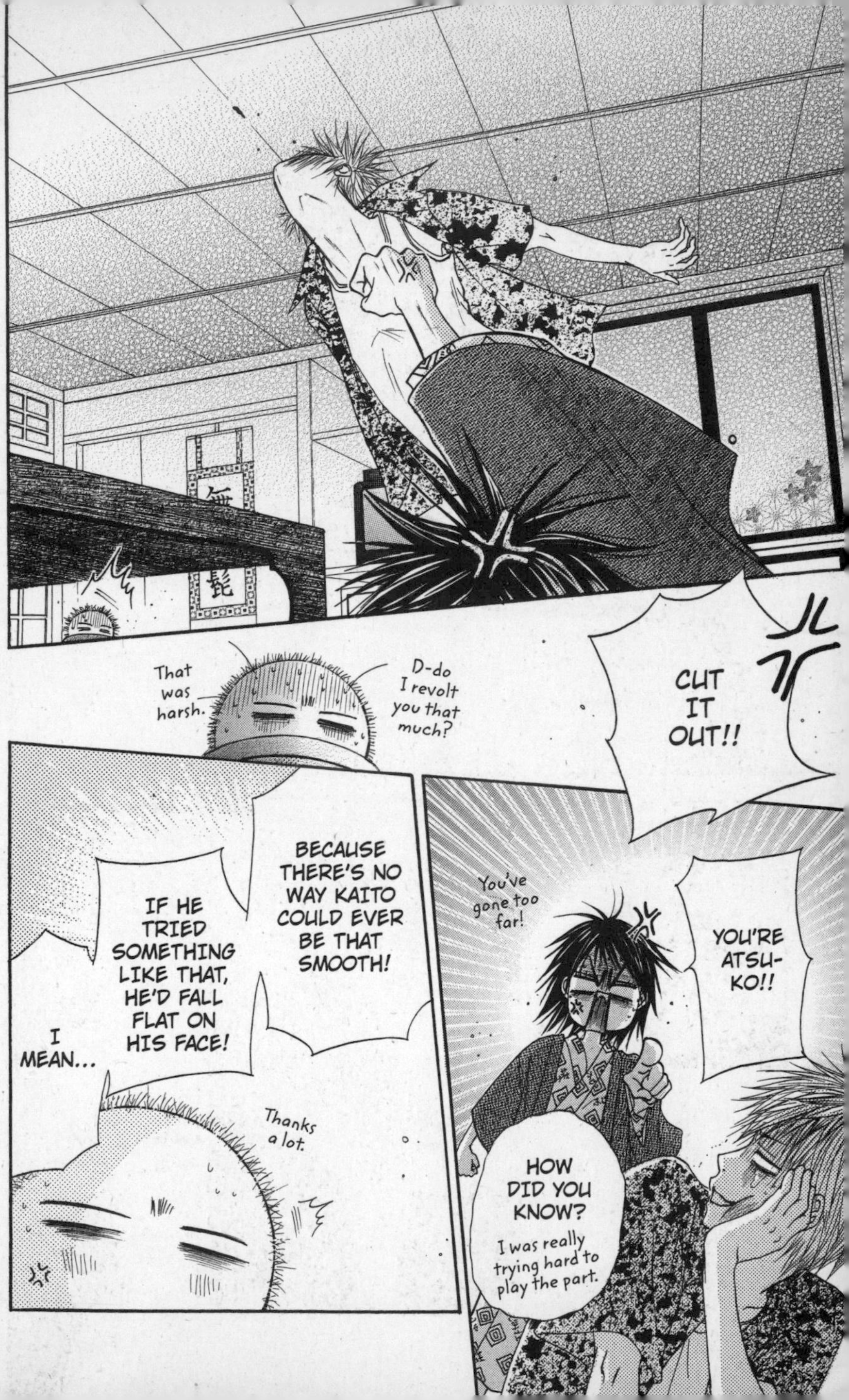
CUT IT OUT!!
D-do I revolt you that much?
That was harsh.
YOU'RE ATSU-KO!!
You've gone too far!
HOW DID YOU KNOW?
I was really trying hard to play the part.
BECAUSE THERE'S NO WAY KAITO COULD EVER BE THAT SMOOTH!
IF HE TRIED SOMETHING LIKE THAT, HE'D FALL FLAT ON HIS FACE!
I MEAN...
Thanks a lot.

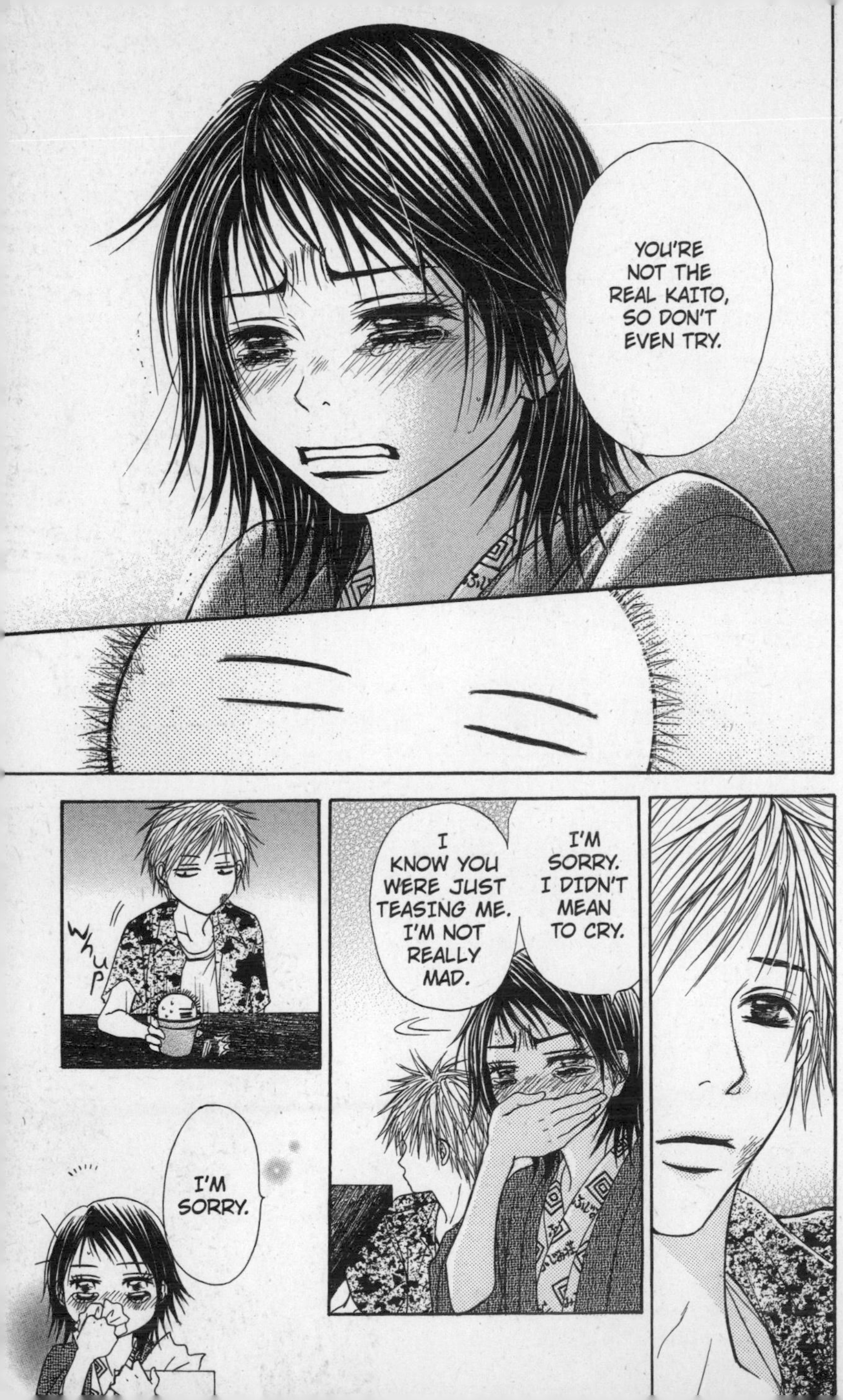
YOU'RE NOT THE REAL KAITO, SO DON'T EVEN TRY.
I'M SORRY. I DIDN'T MEAN TO CRY.
I KNOW YOU WERE JUST TEASING ME. I'M NOT REALLY MAD.
WHUP
I'M SORRY.

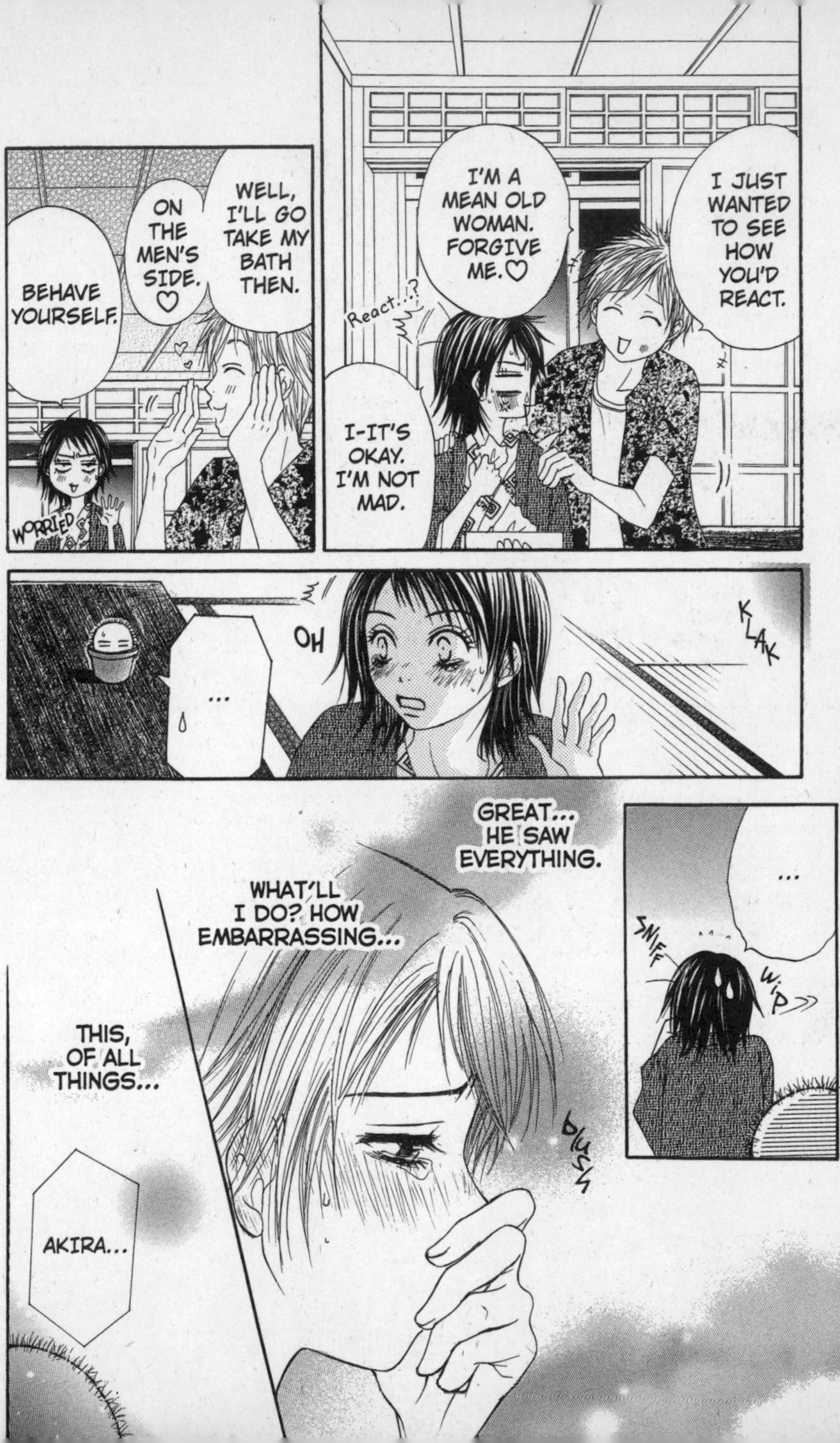
I JUST WANTED TO SEE HOW YOU'D REACT.
I'M A MEAN OLD WOMAN. FORGIVE ME.♡
React...?
I-IT'S OKAY. I'M NOT MAD.
WELL, I'LL GO TAKE MY BATH THEN.
ON THE MEN'S SIDE.♡
BEHAVE YOURSELF.
WORRIED
KLAK
OH
...
...
SNIFF
WIP
GREAT... HE SAW EVERYTHING.
WHAT'LL I DO? HOW EMBARRASSING...
THIS, OF ALL THINGS...
blush
AKIRA...

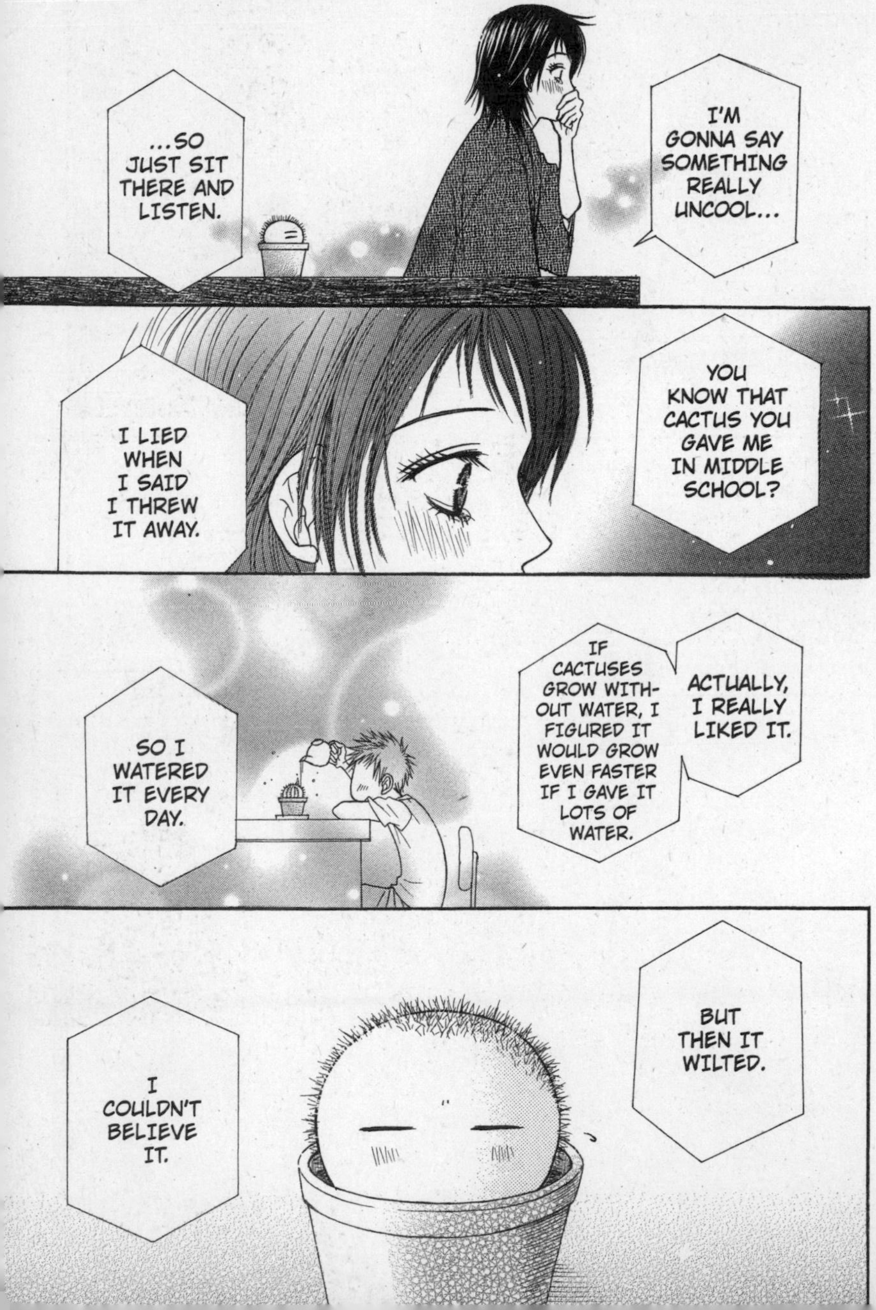
I'M GONNA SAY SOMETHING REALLY UNCOOL...
...SO JUST SIT THERE AND LISTEN.
YOU KNOW THAT CACTUS YOU GAVE ME IN MIDDLE SCHOOL?
I LIED WHEN I SAID I THREW IT AWAY.
ACTUALLY, I REALLY LIKED IT.
IF CACTUSES GROW WITH-OUT WATER, I FIGURED IT WOULD GROW EVEN FASTER IF I GAVE IT LOTS OF WATER.
SO I WATERED IT EVERY DAY.
BUT THEN IT WILTED.
I COULDN'T BELIEVE IT.

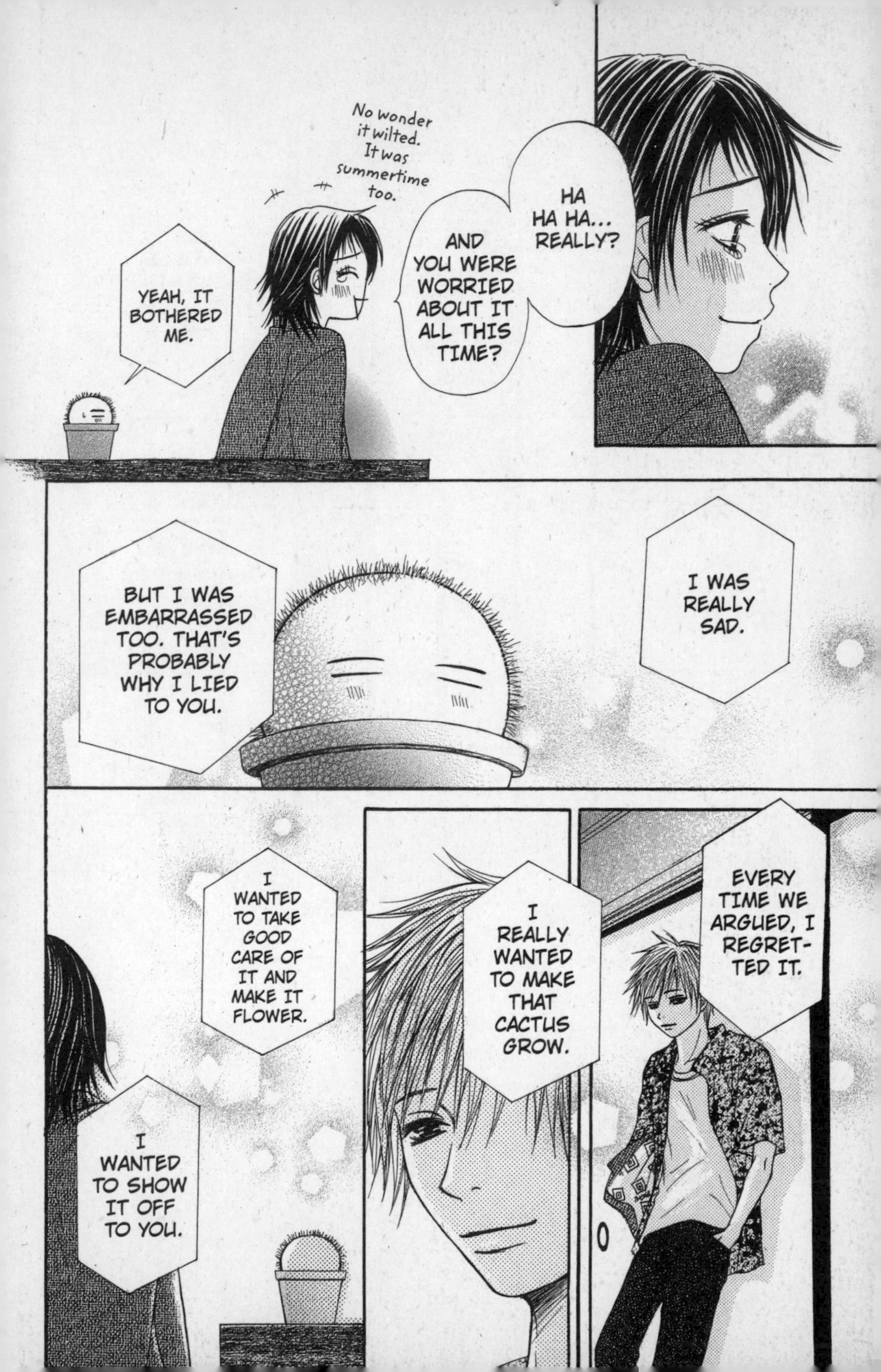
HA HA HA... REALLY?
AND YOU WERE WORRIED ABOUT IT ALL THIS TIME?
No wonder it wilted. It was summertime too.
YEAH, IT BOTHERED ME.
I WAS REALLY SAD.
BUT I WAS EMBARRASSED TOO. THAT'S PROBABLY WHY I LIED TO YOU.
EVERY TIME WE ARGUED, I REGRET-TED IT.
I REALLY WANTED TO MAKE THAT CACTUS GROW.
I WANTED TO TAKE GOOD CARE OF IT AND MAKE IT FLOWER.
I WANTED TO SHOW IT OFF TO YOU.

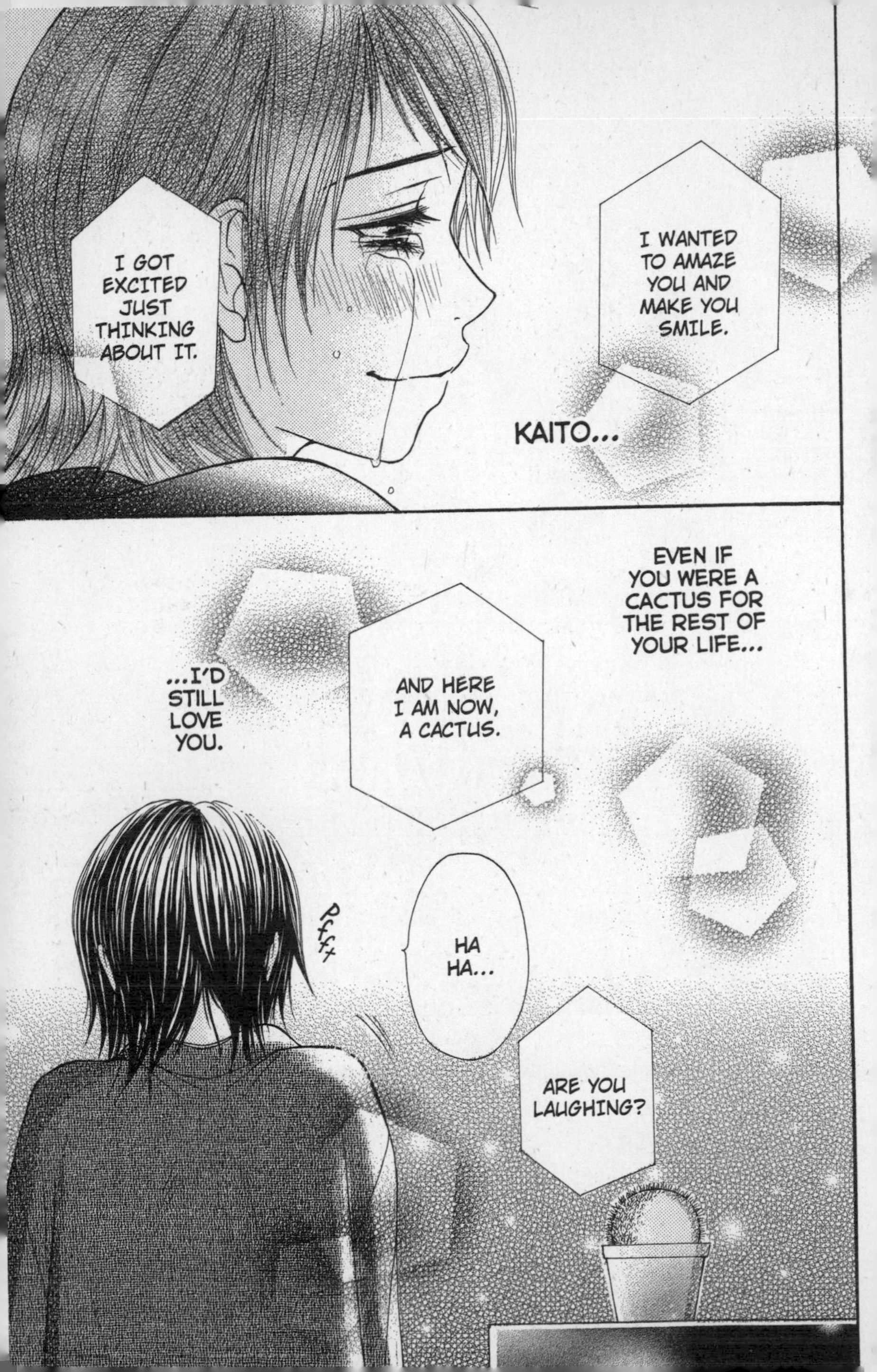
I WANTED TO AMAZE YOU AND MAKE YOU SMILE.
I GOT EXCITED JUST THINKING ABOUT IT.
KAITO...
EVEN IF YOU WERE A CACTUS FOR THE REST OF YOUR LIFE...
AND HERE I AM NOW, A CACTUS.
...I'D STILL LOVE YOU.
HA HA...
Pfft
ARE YOU LAUGHING?

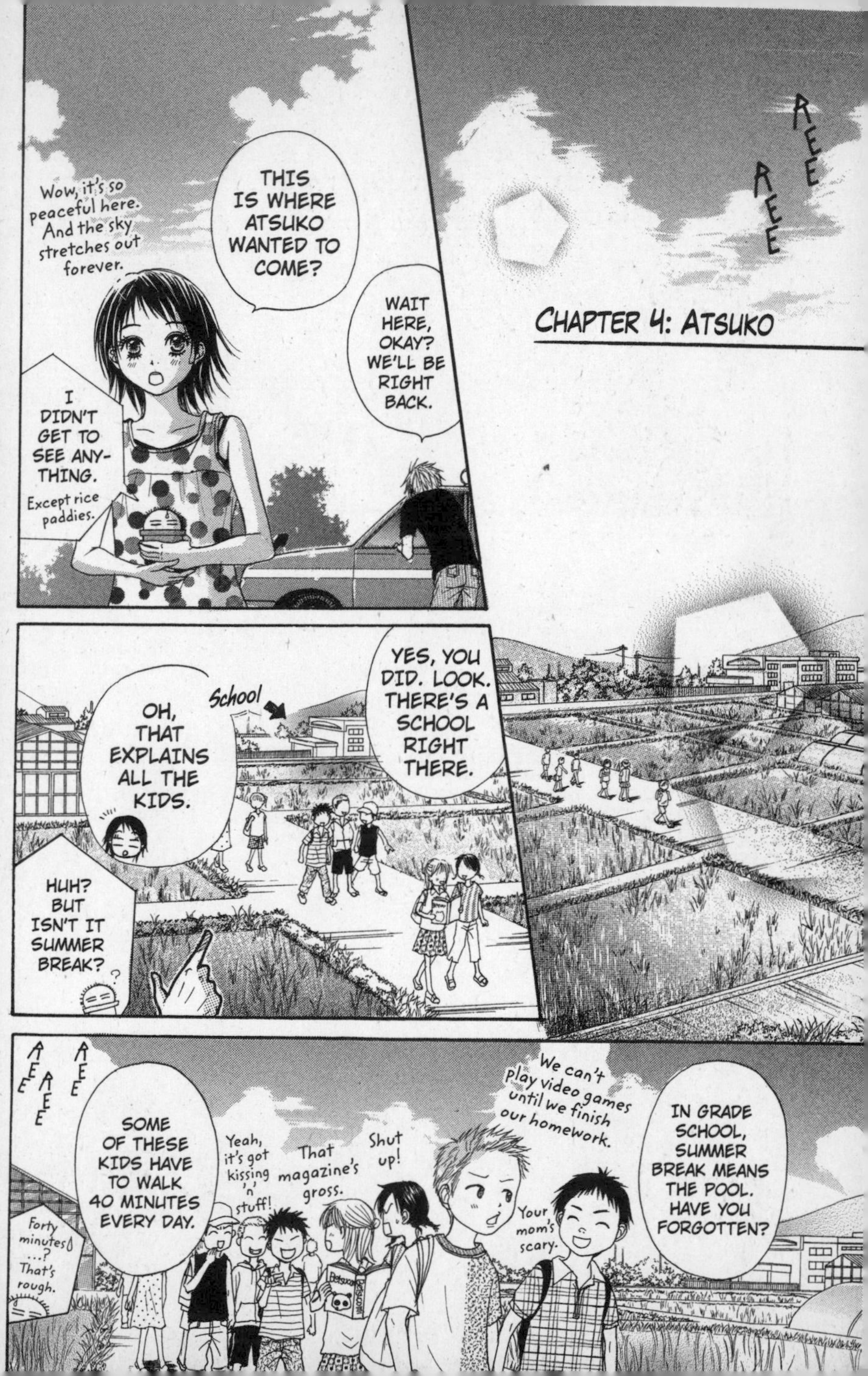
REE REE
Chapter 4: Atsuko
THIS IS WHERE ATSUKO WANTED TO COME?
WAIT HERE, OKAY? WE'LL BE RIGHT BACK.
Wow, it's so peaceful here. And the sky stretches out forever.
I DIDN'T GET TO SEE ANY-THING.
Except rice paddies.
YES, YOU DID. LOOK. THERE'S A SCHOOL RIGHT THERE.
School
OH, THAT EXPLAINS ALL THE KIDS.
HUH? BUT ISN'T IT SUMMER BREAK?
IN GRADE SCHOOL, SUMMER BREAK MEANS THE POOL. HAVE YOU FORGOTTEN?
We can't play video games until we finish our homework.
Your mom's scary.
Shut up!
That magazine's gross.
Yeah, it's got kissing 'n' stuff!
SOME OF THESE KIDS HAVE TO WALK 40 MINUTES EVERY DAY.
Forty minutes...? That's rough.
REE REE REE

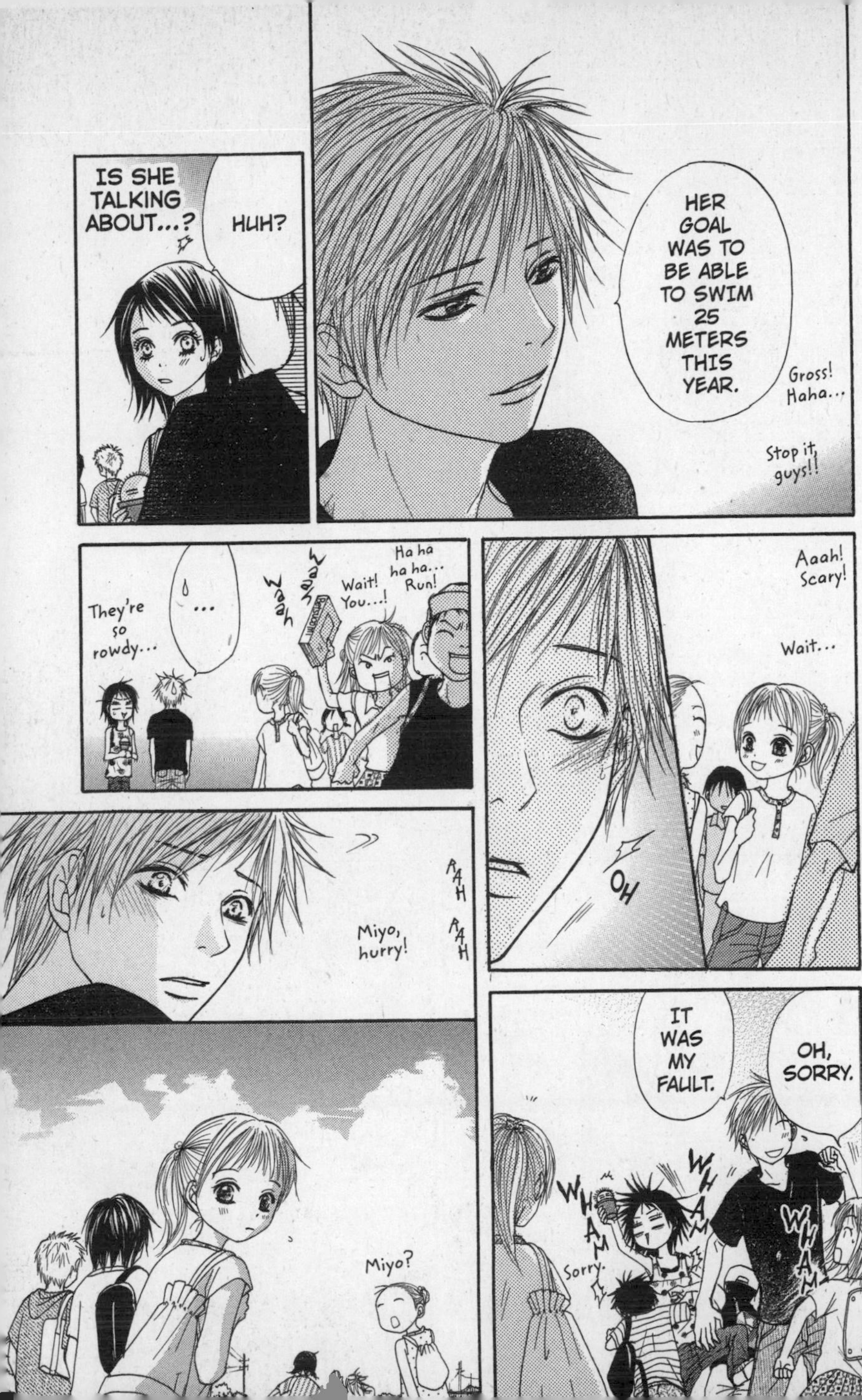
HER GOAL WAS TO BE ABLE TO SWIM 25 METERS THIS YEAR.
Gross! Haha...
Stop it, guys!!
HUH?
IS SHE TALKING ABOUT...?
Aaah! Scary!
Wait...
OH
Ha ha ha ha... Run!
Wait! You...!
Waah Waah
...
They're so rowdy...
RAH RAH
Miyo, hurry!
OH, SORRY.
IT WAS MY FAULT.
WHAM WHAM WHAM WHAM
Sorry.
Miyo?

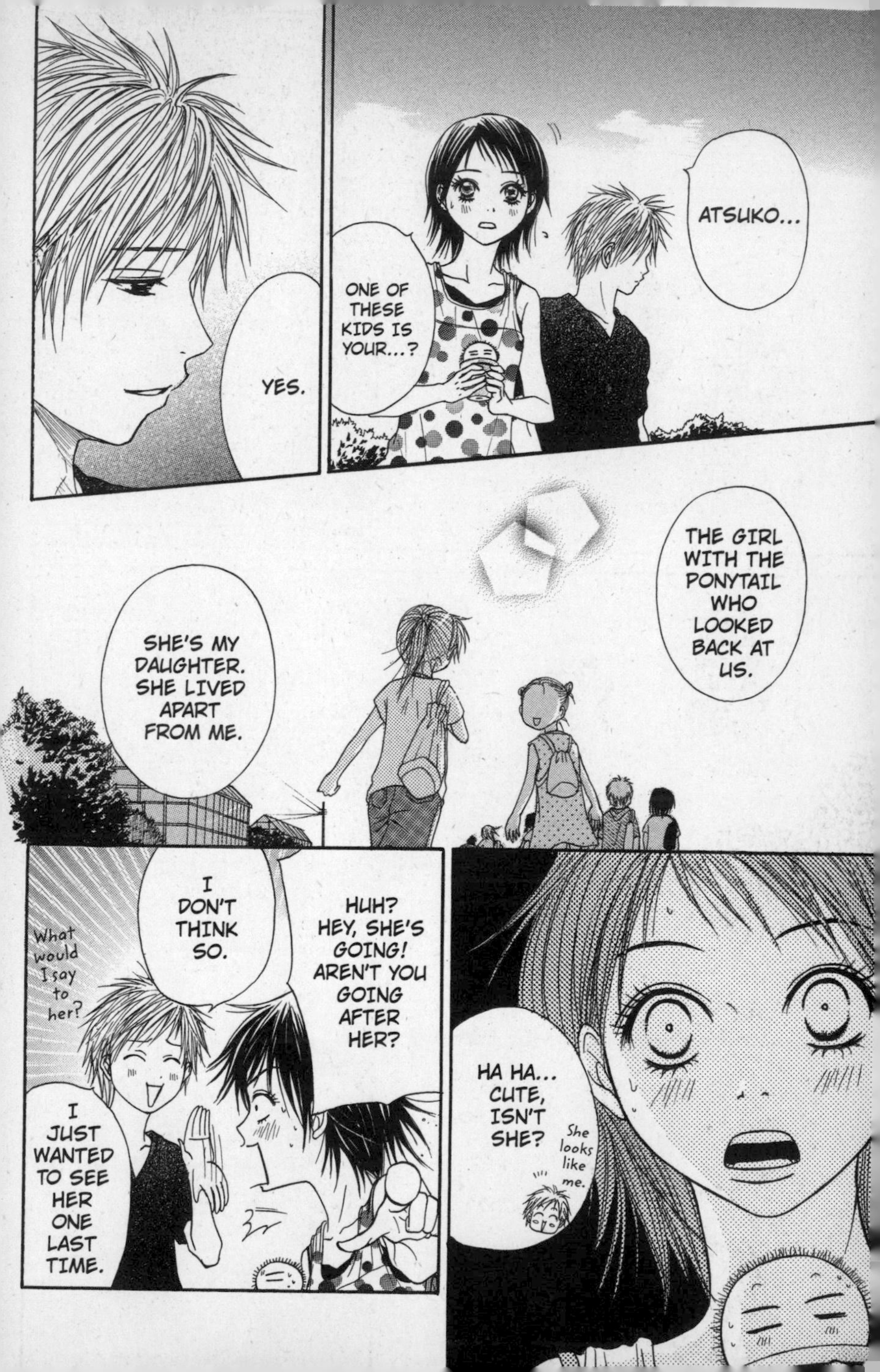
ATSUKO...
ONE OF THESE KIDS IS YOUR...?
YES.
THE GIRL WITH THE PONYTAIL WHO LOOKED BACK AT US.
SHE'S MY DAUGHTER. SHE LIVED APART FROM ME.
HA HA... CUTE, ISN'T SHE?
She looks like me.
HUH? HEY, SHE'S GOING! AREN'T YOU GOING AFTER HER?
I DON'T THINK SO.
What would I say to her?
I JUST WANTED TO SEE HER ONE LAST TIME.

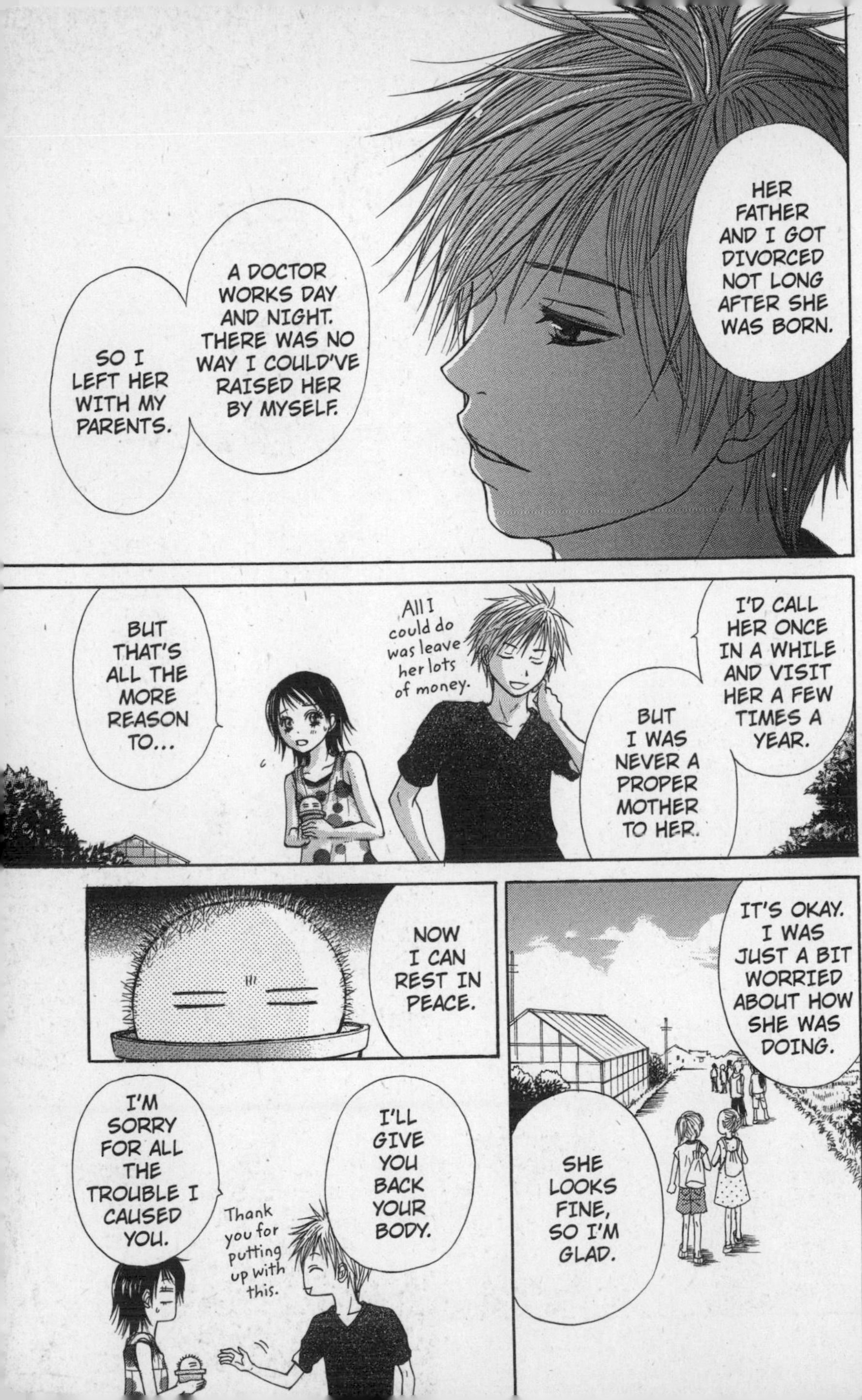
HER FATHER AND I GOT DIVORCED NOT LONG AFTER SHE WAS BORN.
A DOCTOR WORKS DAY AND NIGHT. THERE WAS NO WAY I COULD'VE RAISED HER BY MYSELF.
SO I LEFT HER WITH MY PARENTS.
I'D CALL HER ONCE IN A WHILE AND VISIT HER A FEW TIMES A YEAR.
BUT I WAS NEVER A PROPER MOTHER TO HER.
All I could do was leave her lots of money.
BUT THAT'S ALL THE MORE REASON TO...
IT'S OKAY. I WAS JUST A BIT WORRIED ABOUT HOW SHE WAS DOING.
SHE LOOKS FINE, SO I'M GLAD.
NOW I CAN REST IN PEACE.
I'LL GIVE YOU BACK YOUR BODY.
Thank you for putting up with this.
I'M SORRY FOR ALL THE TROUBLE I CAUSED YOU.

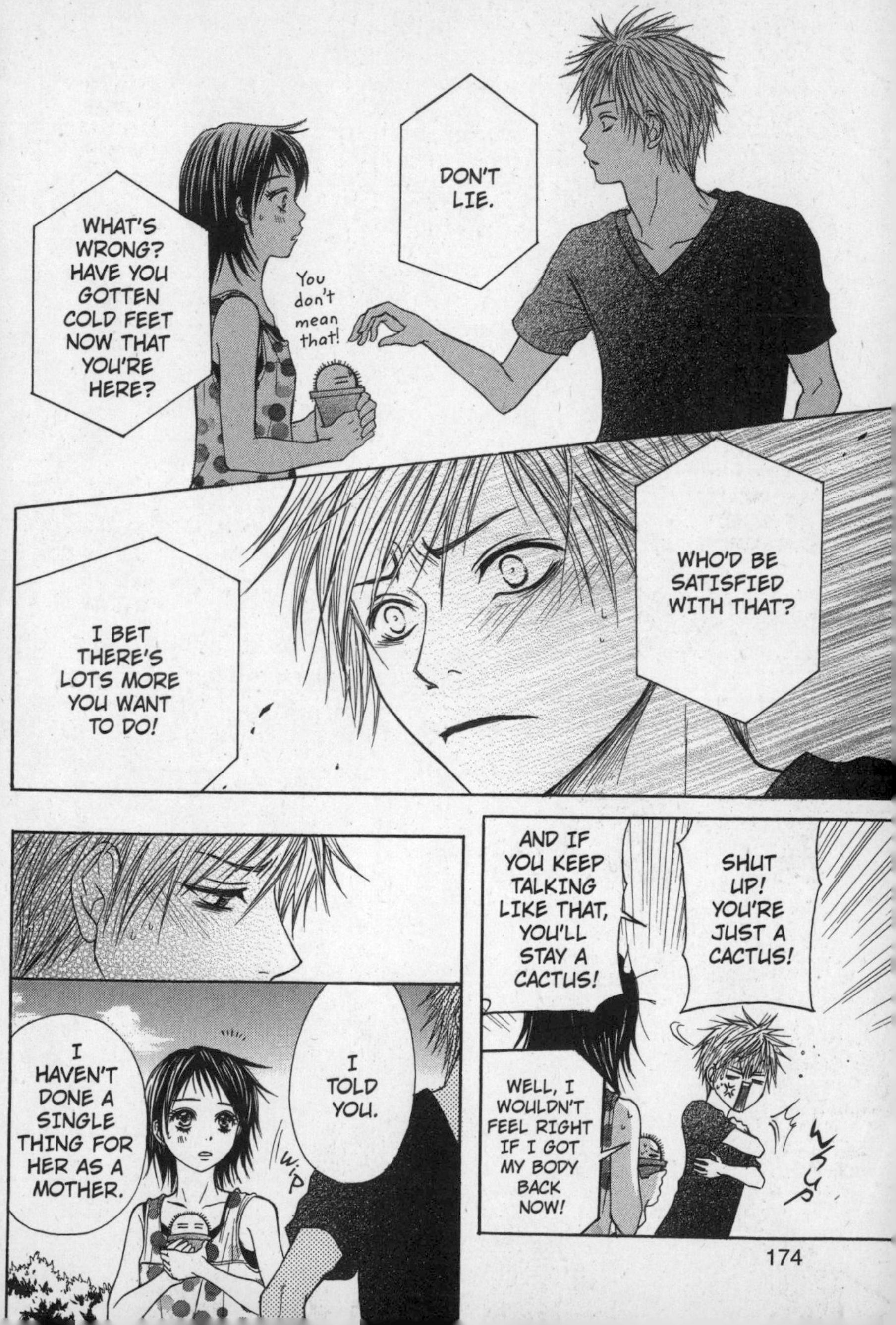
DON'T LIE.
WHAT'S WRONG? HAVE YOU GOTTEN COLD FEET NOW THAT YOU'RE HERE?
You don't mean that!
WHO'D BE SATISFIED WITH THAT?
I BET THERE'S LOTS MORE YOU WANT TO DO!
SHUT UP! YOU'RE JUST A CACTUS!
AND IF YOU KEEP TALKING LIKE THAT, YOU'LL STAY A CACTUS!
WHUP
WELL, I WOULDN'T FEEL RIGHT IF I GOT MY BODY BACK NOW!
I TOLD YOU.
WIP
I HAVEN'T DONE A SINGLE THING FOR HER AS A MOTHER.

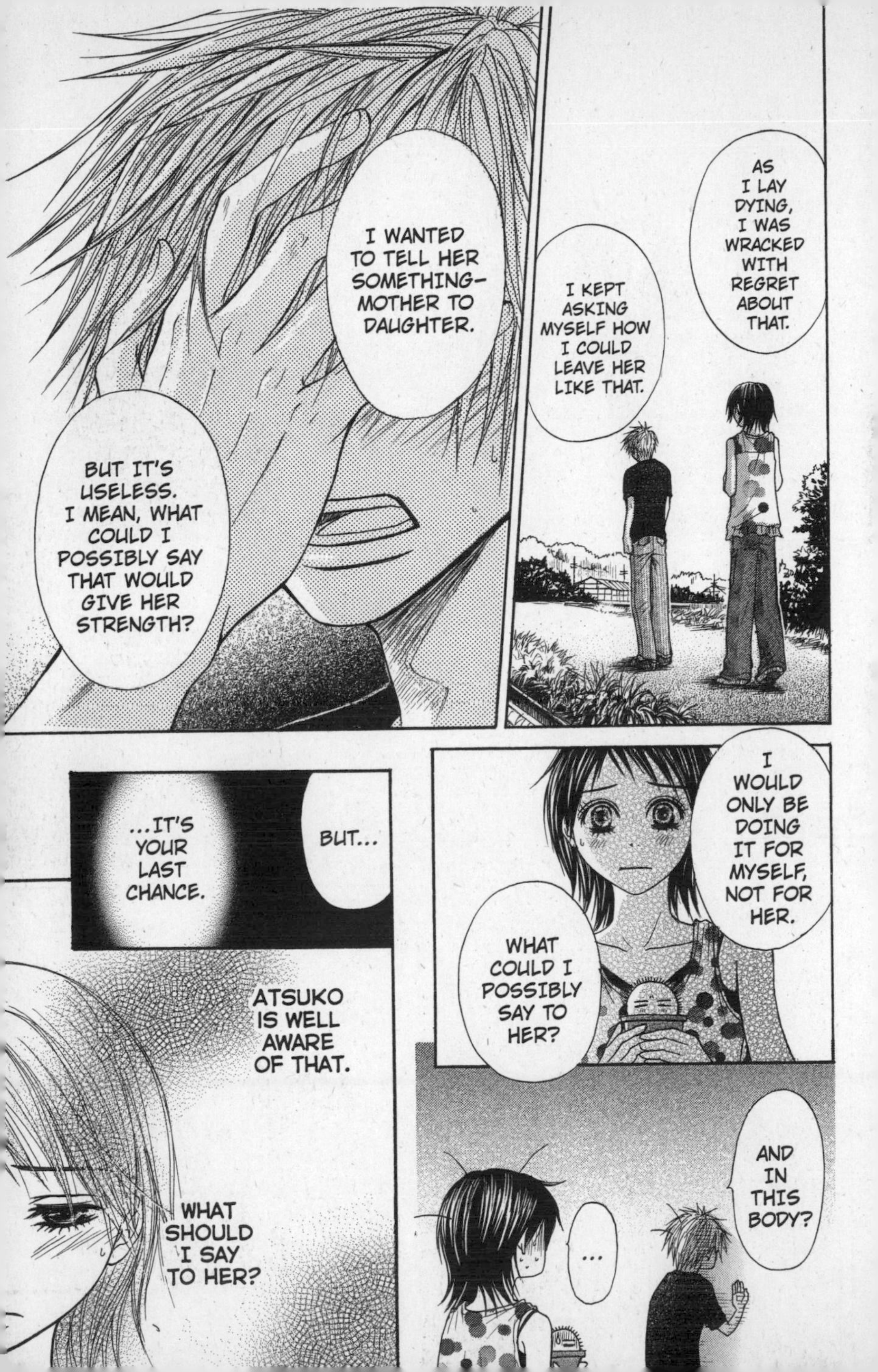
AS I LAY DYING, I WAS WRACKED WITH REGRET ABOUT THAT.
I KEPT ASKING MYSELF HOW I COULD LEAVE HER LIKE THAT.
I WANTED TO TELL HER SOMETHING—MOTHER TO DAUGHTER.
BUT IT'S USELESS. I MEAN, WHAT COULD I POSSIBLY SAY THAT WOULD GIVE HER STRENGTH?
I WOULD ONLY BE DOING IT FOR MYSELF, NOT FOR HER.
WHAT COULD I POSSIBLY SAY TO HER?
AND IN THIS BODY?
...
BUT...
...IT'S YOUR LAST CHANCE.
ATSUKO IS WELL AWARE OF THAT.
WHAT SHOULD I SAY TO HER?

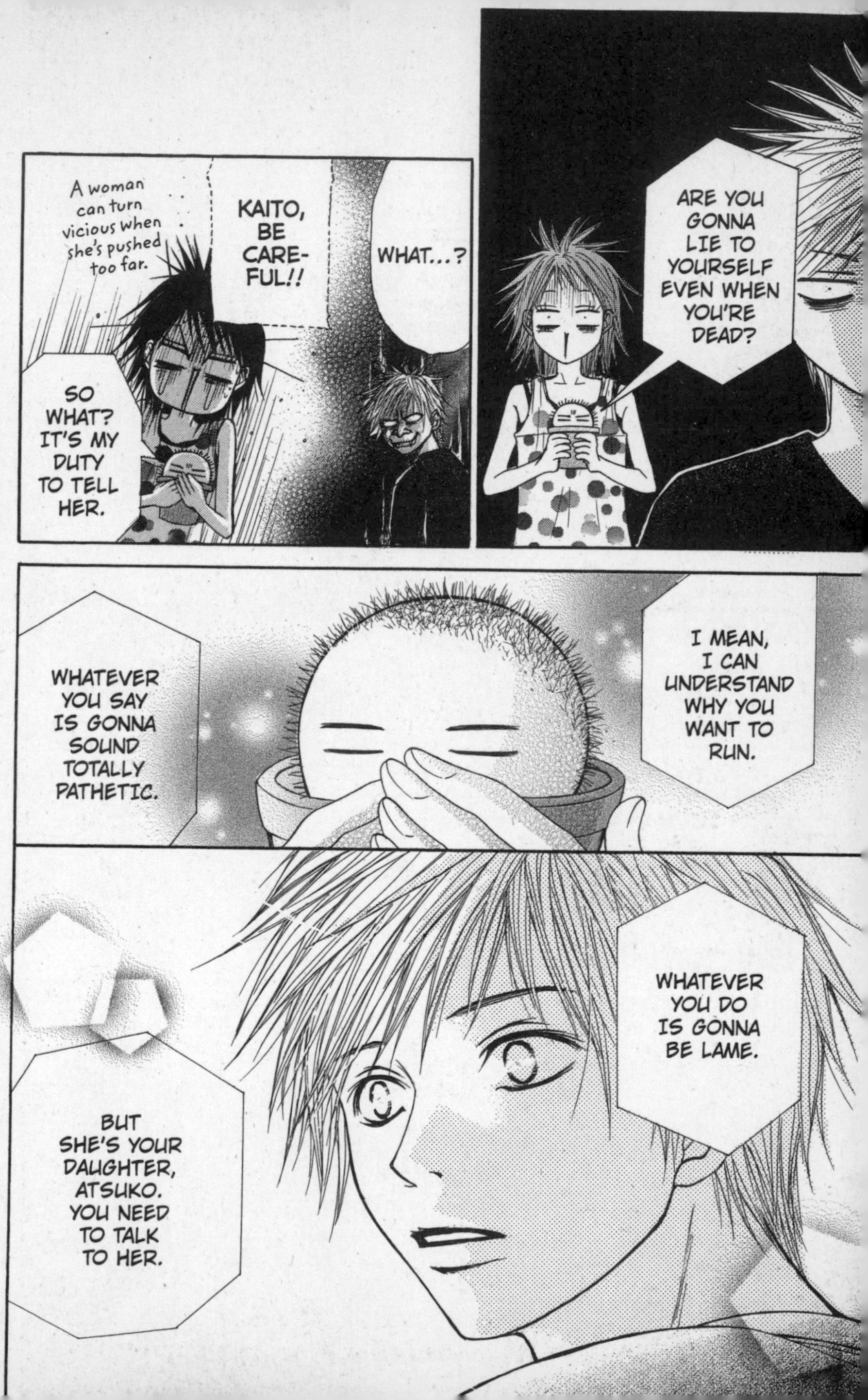
ARE YOU GONNA LIE TO YOURSELF EVEN WHEN YOU'RE DEAD?
WHAT...?
KAITO, BE CARE-FUL!!
A woman can turn vicious when she's pushed too far.
SO WHAT? IT'S MY DUTY TO TELL HER.
I MEAN, I CAN UNDERSTAND WHY YOU WANT TO RUN.
WHATEVER YOU SAY IS GONNA SOUND TOTALLY PATHETIC.
WHATEVER YOU DO IS GONNA BE LAME.
BUT SHE'S YOUR DAUGHTER, ATSUKO. YOU NEED TO TALK TO HER.

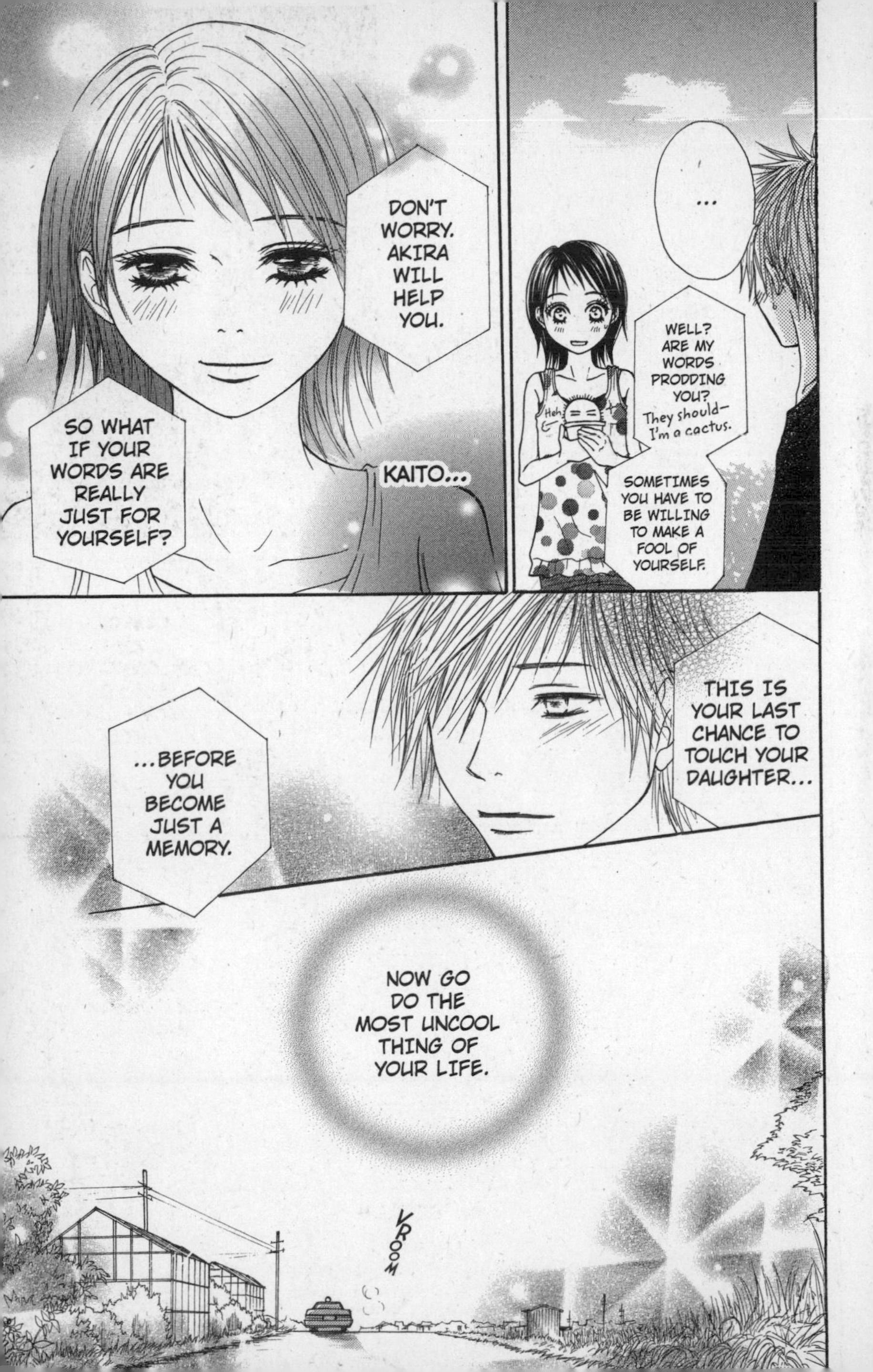
...
WELL? ARE MY WORDS PRODDING YOU?
Heh
They should— I'm a cactus.
SOMETIMES YOU HAVE TO BE WILLING TO MAKE A FOOL OF YOURSELF.
DON'T WORRY. AKIRA WILL HELP YOU.
SO WHAT IF YOUR WORDS ARE REALLY JUST FOR YOURSELF?
KAITO...
THIS IS YOUR LAST CHANCE TO TOUCH YOUR DAUGHTER...
...BEFORE YOU BECOME JUST A MEMORY.
NOW GO DO THE MOST UNCOOL THING OF YOUR LIFE.
VROOM

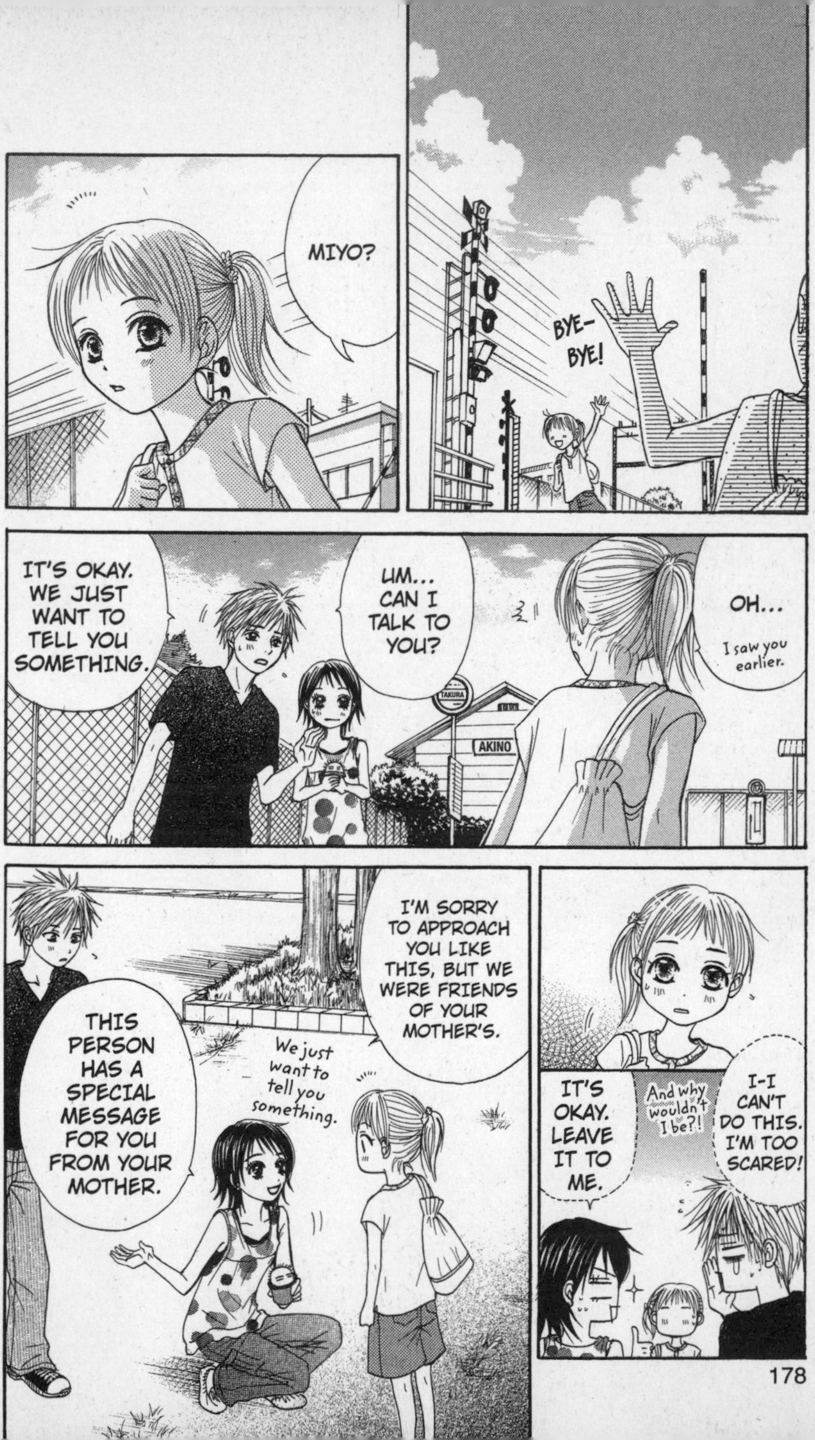
BYE-BYE!
MIYO?
OH...
I saw you earlier.
UM... CAN I TALK TO YOU?
IT'S OKAY. WE JUST WANT TO TELL YOU SOMETHING.
TAKURA
AKINO
I-I CAN'T DO THIS. I'M TOO SCARED!
And why wouldn't I be?!
IT'S OKAY. LEAVE IT TO ME.
I'M SORRY TO APPROACH YOU LIKE THIS, BUT WE WERE FRIENDS OF YOUR MOTHER'S.
We just want to tell you something.
THIS PERSON HAS A SPECIAL MESSAGE FOR YOU FROM YOUR MOTHER.

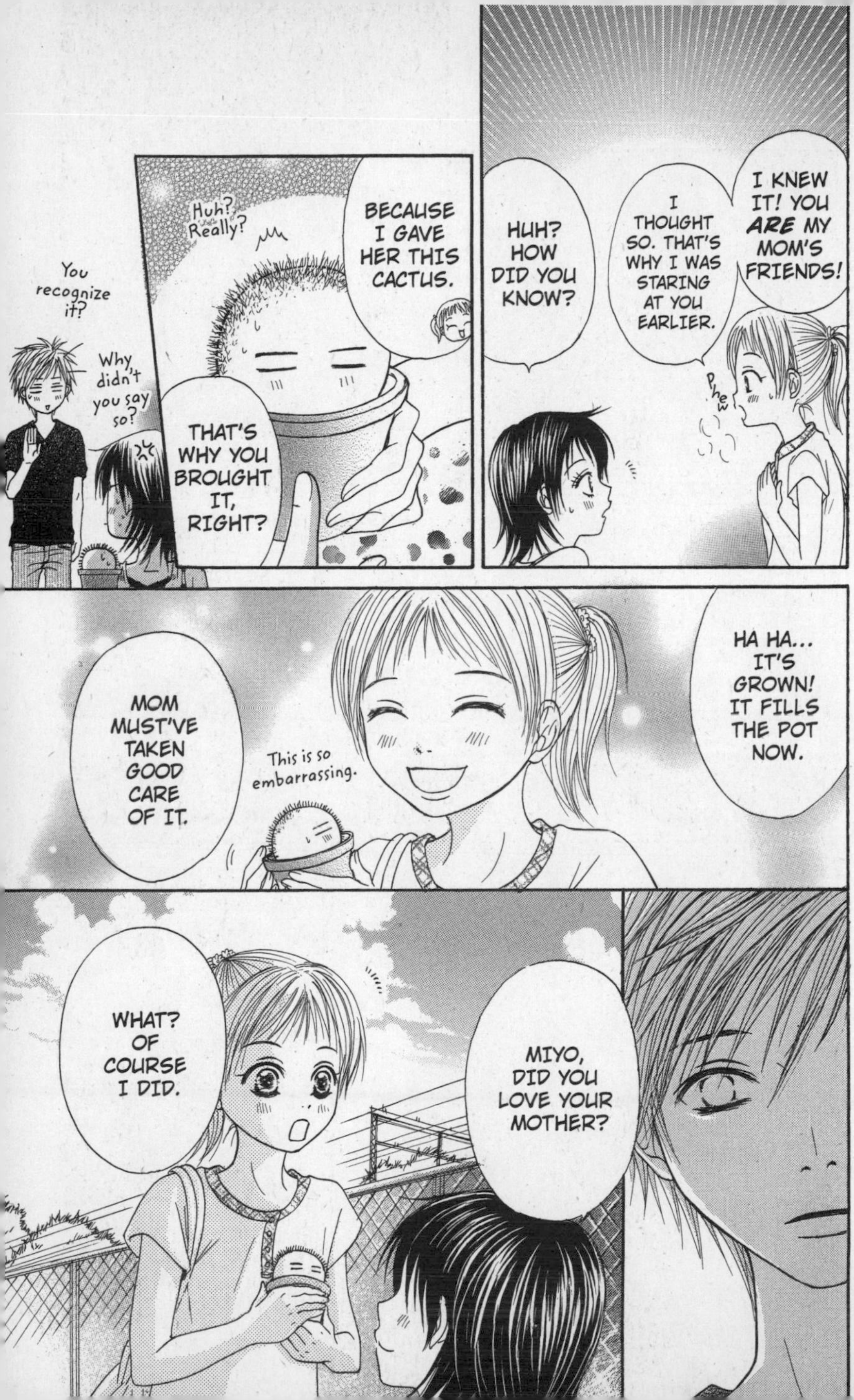
I KNEW IT! YOU ARE MY MOM'S FRIENDS!
I THOUGHT SO. THAT'S WHY I WAS STARING AT YOU EARLIER.
Phew
HUH? HOW DID YOU KNOW?
BECAUSE I GAVE HER THIS CACTUS.
Huh? Really?
THAT'S WHY YOU BROUGHT IT, RIGHT?
You recognize it?
Why didn't you say so?
HA HA... IT'S GROWN! IT FILLS THE POT NOW.
This is so embarrassing.
MOM MUST'VE TAKEN GOOD CARE OF IT.
MIYO, DID YOU LOVE YOUR MOTHER?
WHAT? OF COURSE I DID.

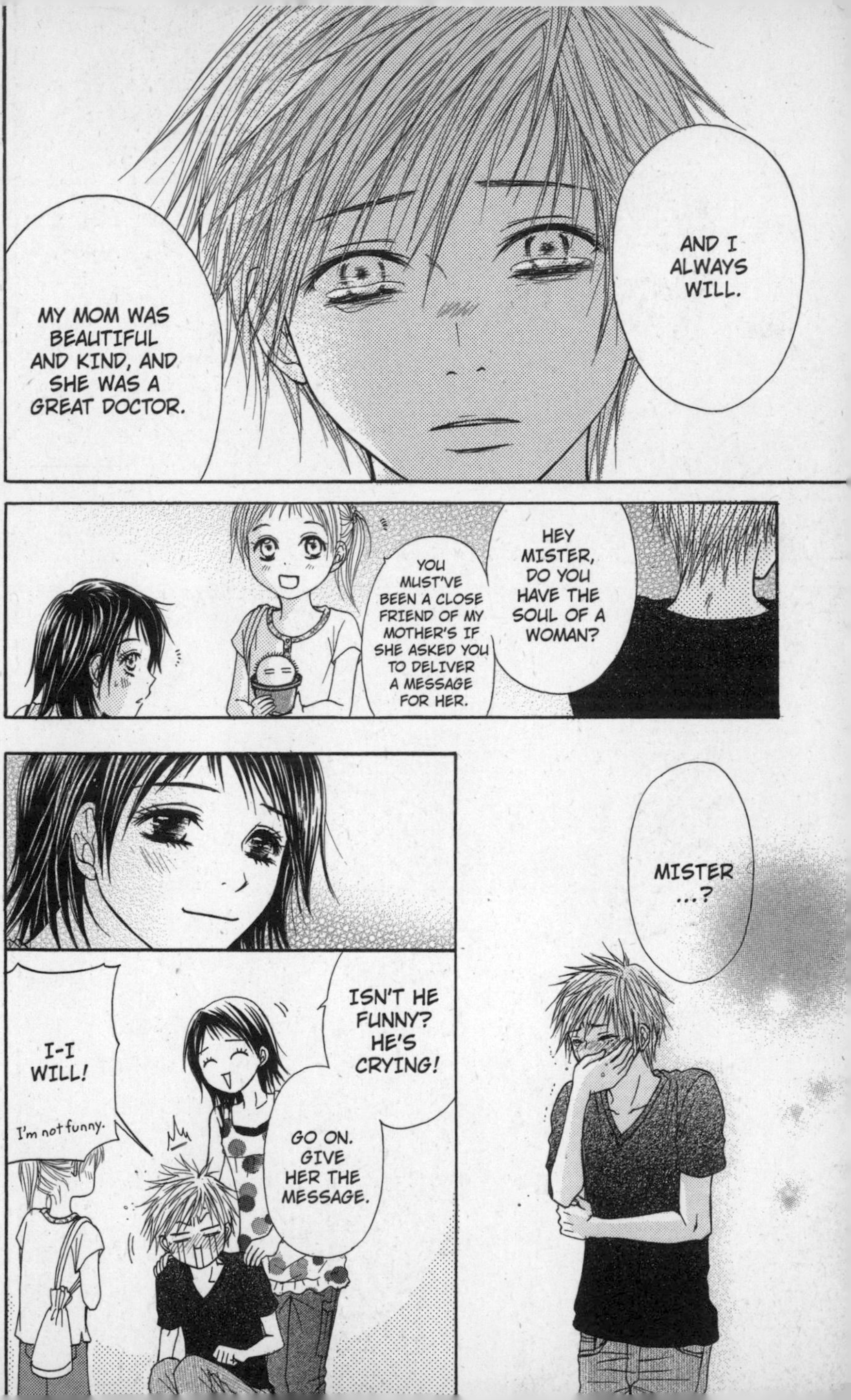
AND I ALWAYS WILL.
MY MOM WAS BEAUTIFUL AND KIND, AND SHE WAS A GREAT DOCTOR.
HEY MISTER, DO YOU HAVE THE SOUL OF A WOMAN?
YOU MUST'VE BEEN A CLOSE FRIEND OF MY MOTHER'S IF SHE ASKED YOU TO DELIVER A MESSAGE FOR HER.
MISTER ...?
ISN'T HE FUNNY? HE'S CRYING!
GO ON. GIVE HER THE MESSAGE.
I-I WILL!
I'm not funny.

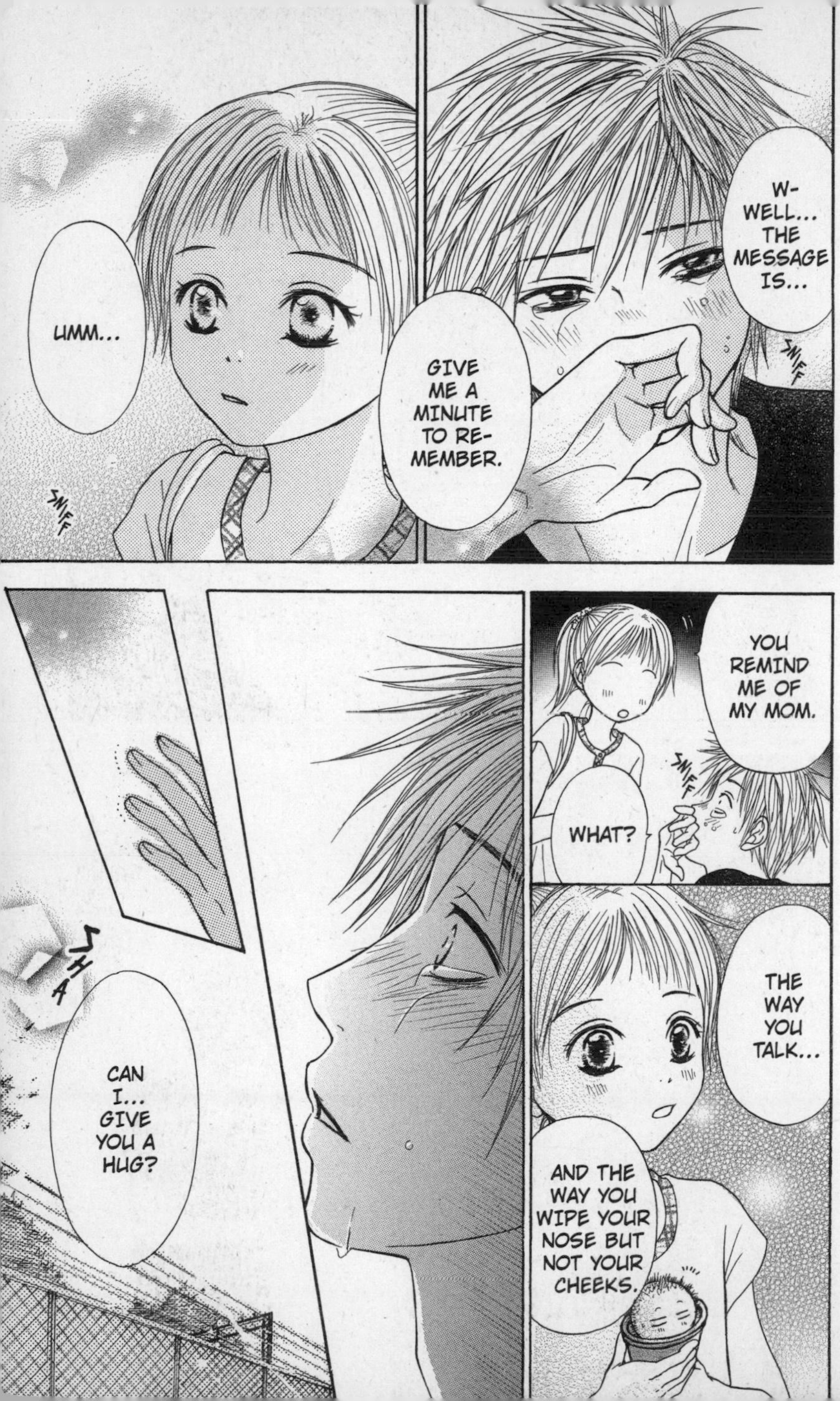
W-WELL... THE MESSAGE IS...
SNIFF
GIVE ME A MINUTE TO RE-MEMBER.
UMM...
SNIFF
YOU REMIND ME OF MY MOM.
SNIFF
WHAT?
THE WAY YOU TALK...
AND THE WAY YOU WIPE YOUR NOSE BUT NOT YOUR CHEEKS.
SHA
CAN I... GIVE YOU A HUG?

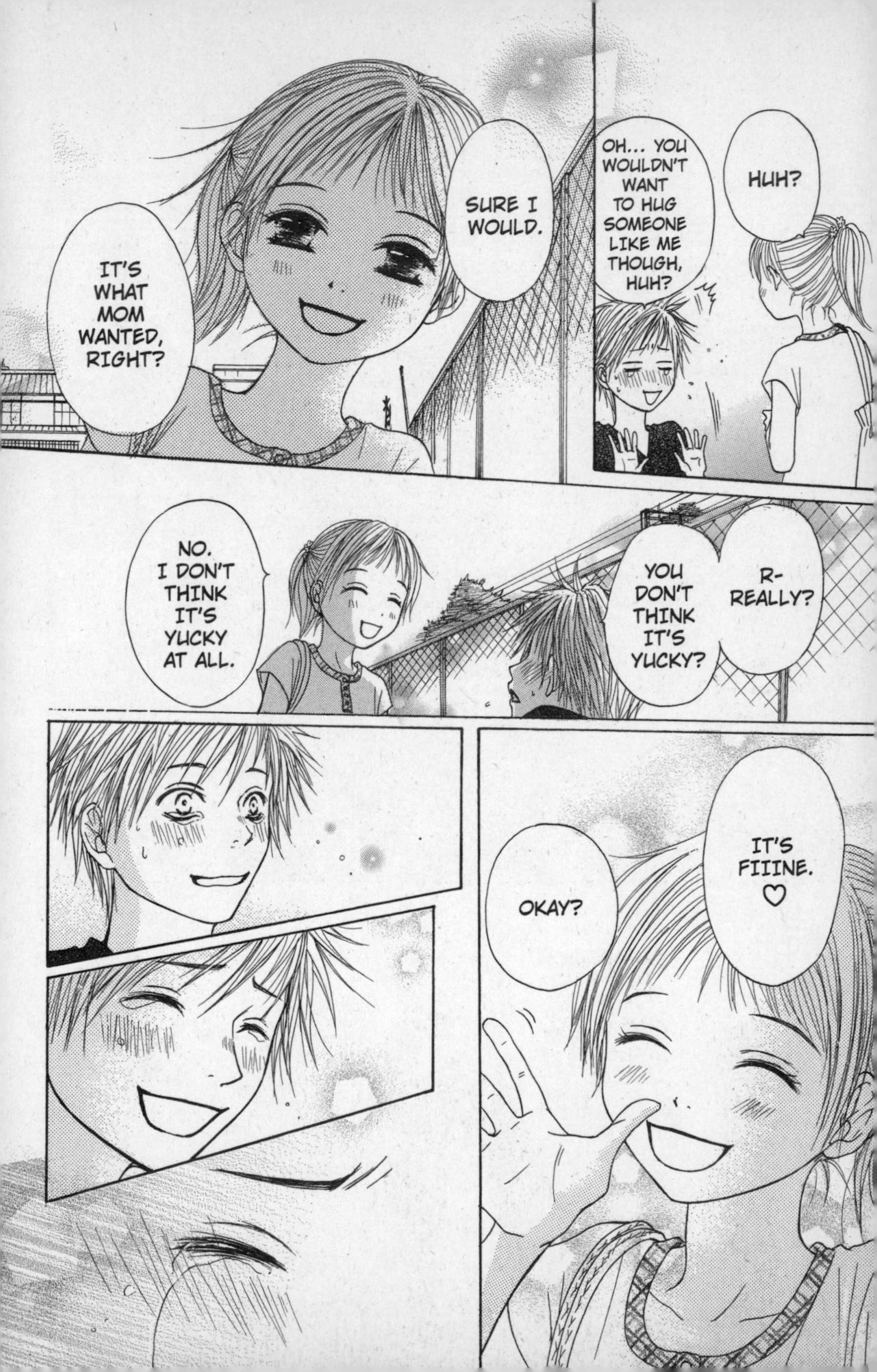
HUH?
OH... YOU WOULDN'T WANT TO HUG SOMEONE LIKE ME THOUGH, HUH?
SURE I WOULD.
IT'S WHAT MOM WANTED, RIGHT?
R-REALLY?
YOU DON'T THINK IT'S YUCKY?
NO. I DON'T THINK IT'S YUCKY AT ALL.
IT'S FIIINE. ♡
OKAY?

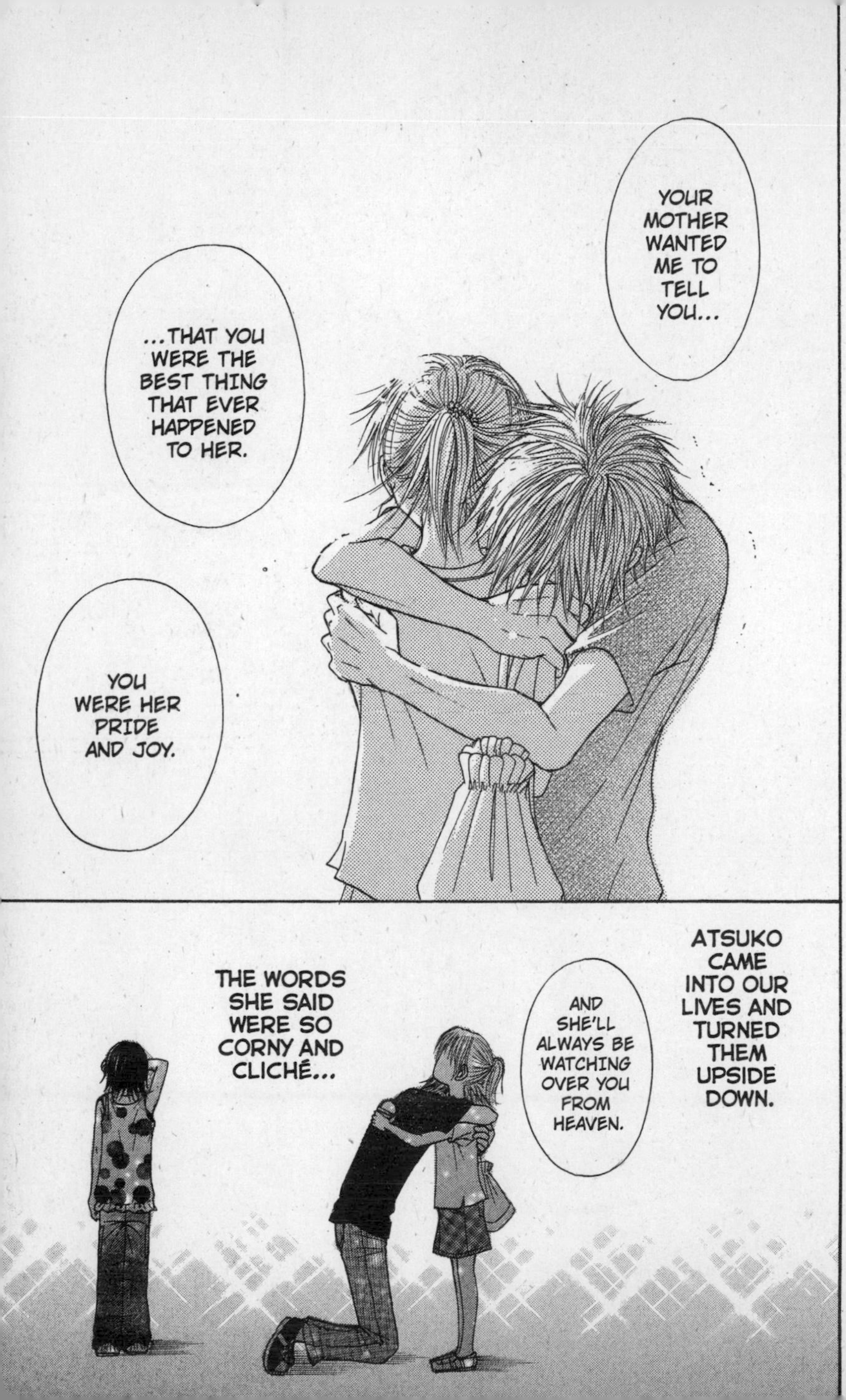
YOUR MOTHER WANTED ME TO TELL YOU...
...THAT YOU WERE THE BEST THING THAT EVER HAPPENED TO HER.
YOU WERE HER PRIDE AND JOY.
ATSUKO CAME INTO OUR LIVES AND TURNED THEM UPSIDE DOWN.
AND SHE'LL ALWAYS BE WATCHING OVER YOU FROM HEAVEN.
THE WORDS SHE SAID WERE SO CORNY AND CLICHÉ...

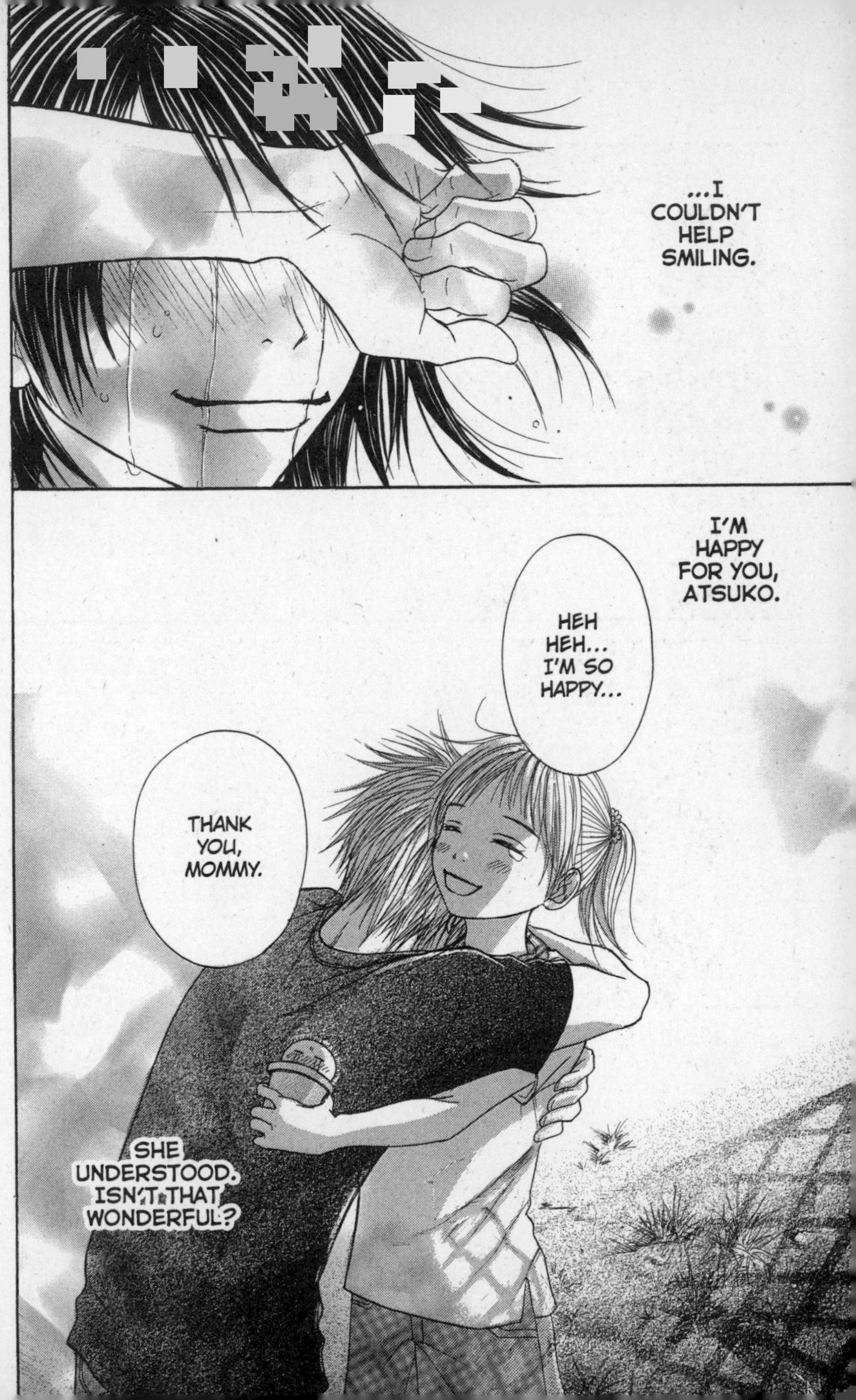
...I COULDN'T HELP SMILING.
I'M HAPPY FOR YOU, ATSUKO.
HEH HEH... I'M SO HAPPY...
THANK YOU, MOMMY.
SHE UNDERSTOOD. ISN'T THAT WONDERFUL?

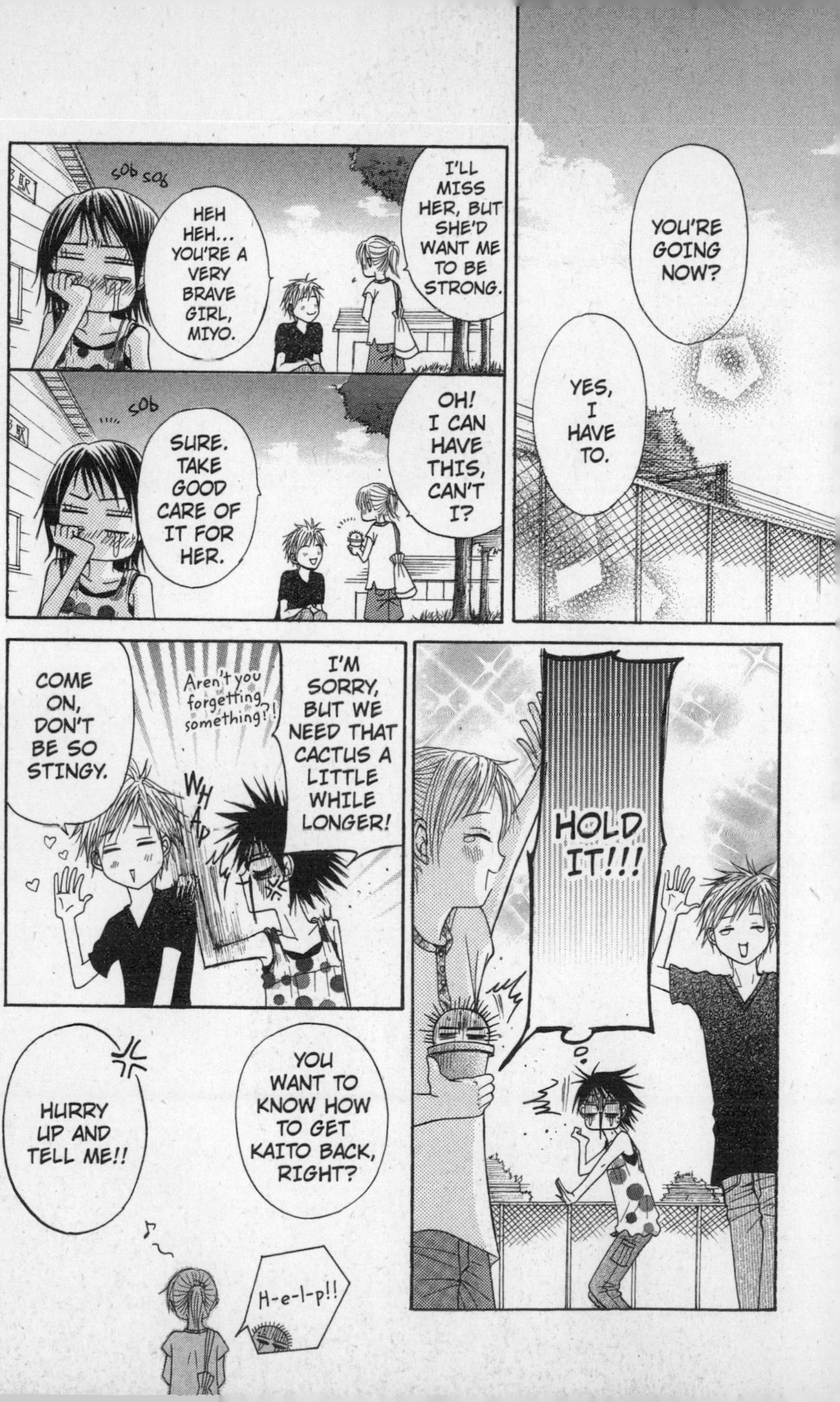
YOU'RE GOING NOW?
YES, I HAVE TO.
I'LL MISS HER, BUT SHE'D WANT ME TO BE STRONG.
sob sob
HEH HEH... YOU'RE A VERY BRAVE GIRL, MIYO.
OH! I CAN HAVE THIS, CAN'T I?
sob
SURE. TAKE GOOD CARE OF IT FOR HER.
HOLD IT!!!
I'M SORRY, BUT WE NEED THAT CACTUS A LITTLE WHILE LONGER!
Aren't you forgetting something?!
WHAP
COME ON, DON'T BE SO STINGY.
YOU WANT TO KNOW HOW TO GET KAITO BACK, RIGHT?
HURRY UP AND TELL ME!!
H-e-l-p!!

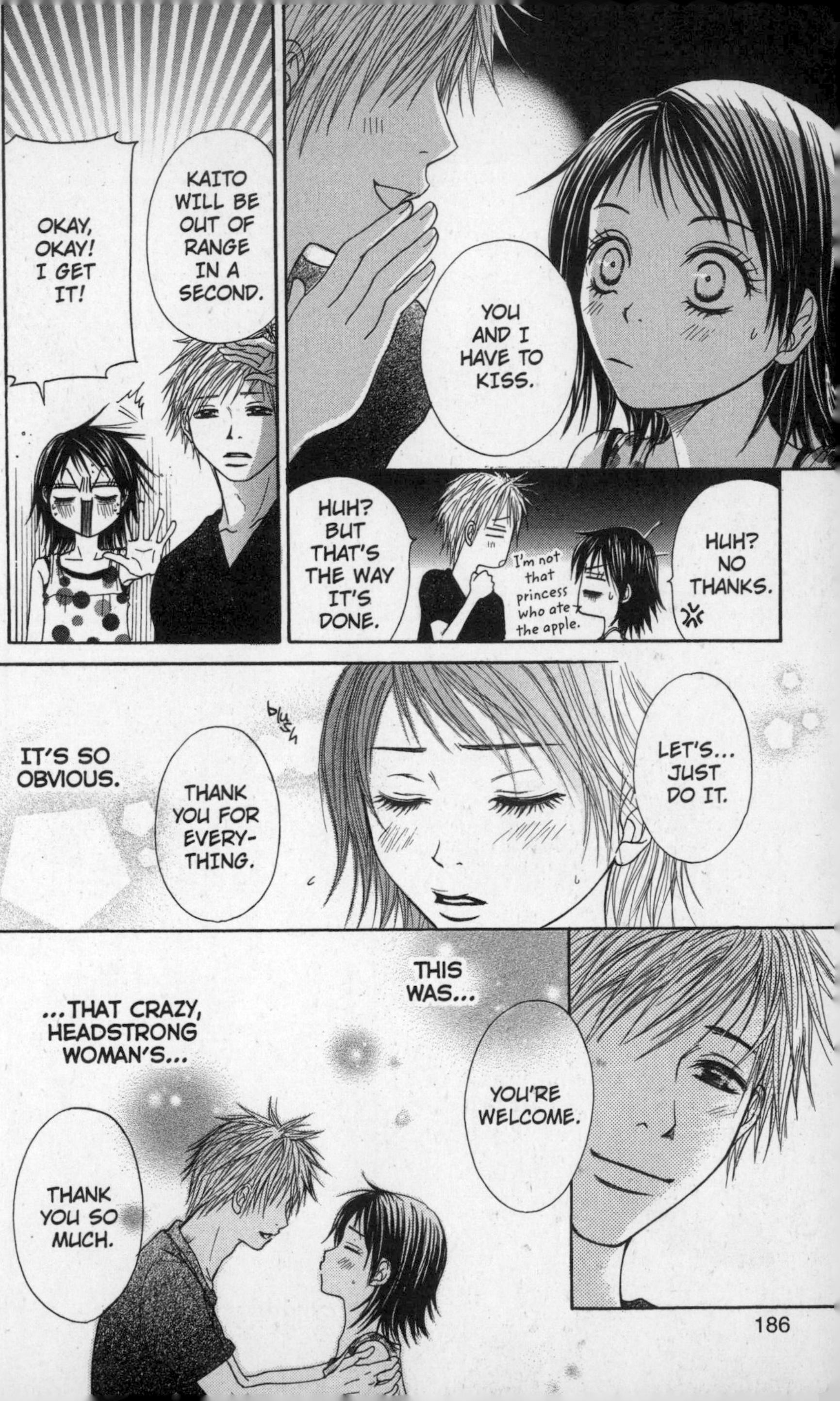
YOU AND I HAVE TO KISS.
HUH? NO THANKS.
I'm not that princess who ate the apple.
HUH? BUT THAT'S THE WAY IT'S DONE.
KAITO WILL BE OUT OF RANGE IN A SECOND.
OKAY, OKAY! I GET IT!
LET'S... JUST DO IT.
blush
THANK YOU FOR EVERYTHING.
IT'S SO OBVIOUS.
YOU'RE WELCOME.
THIS WAS...
...THAT CRAZY, HEADSTRONG WOMAN'S...
THANK YOU SO MUCH.

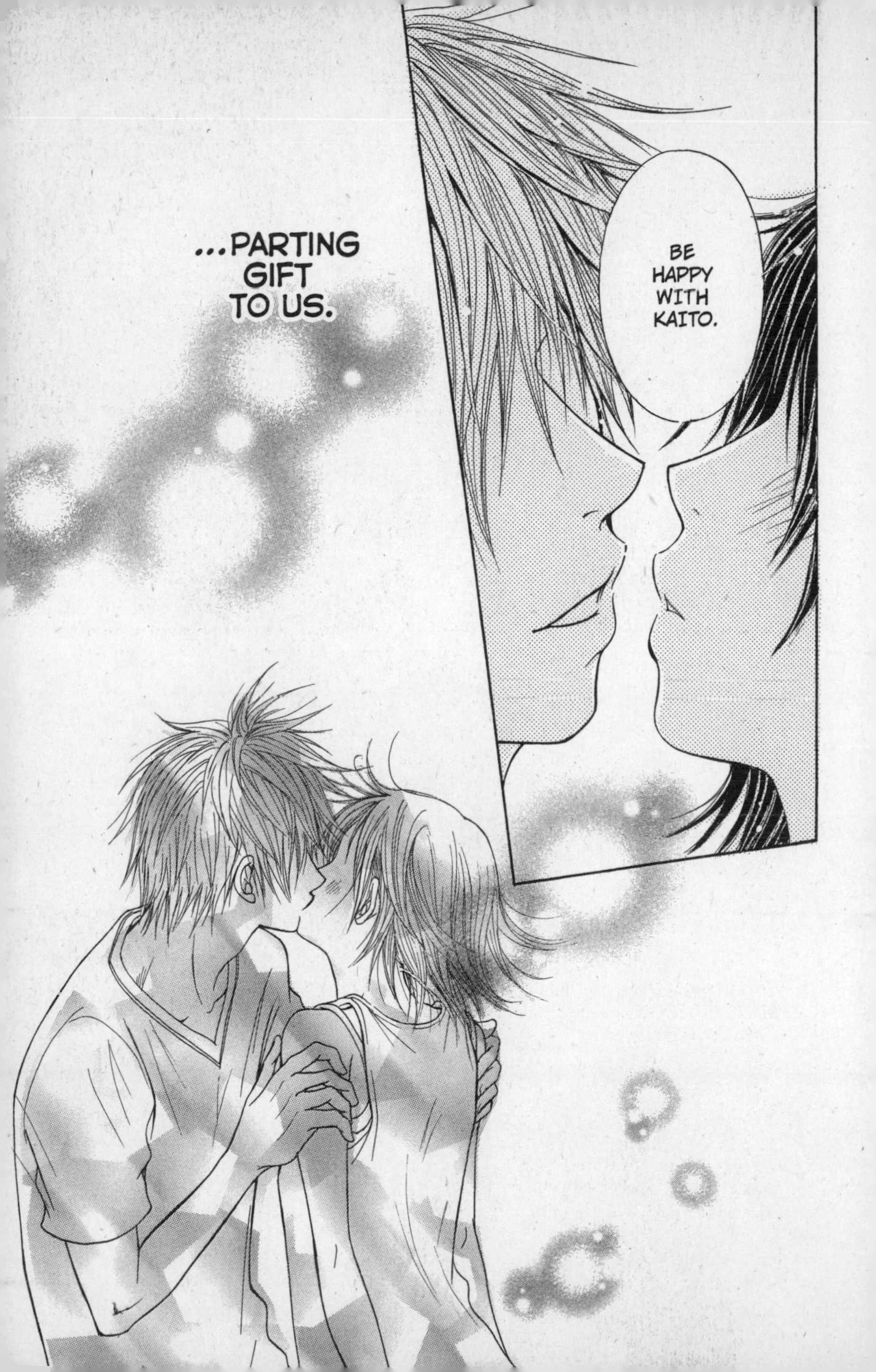
BE HAPPY WITH KAITO.
...PARTING GIFT TO US.

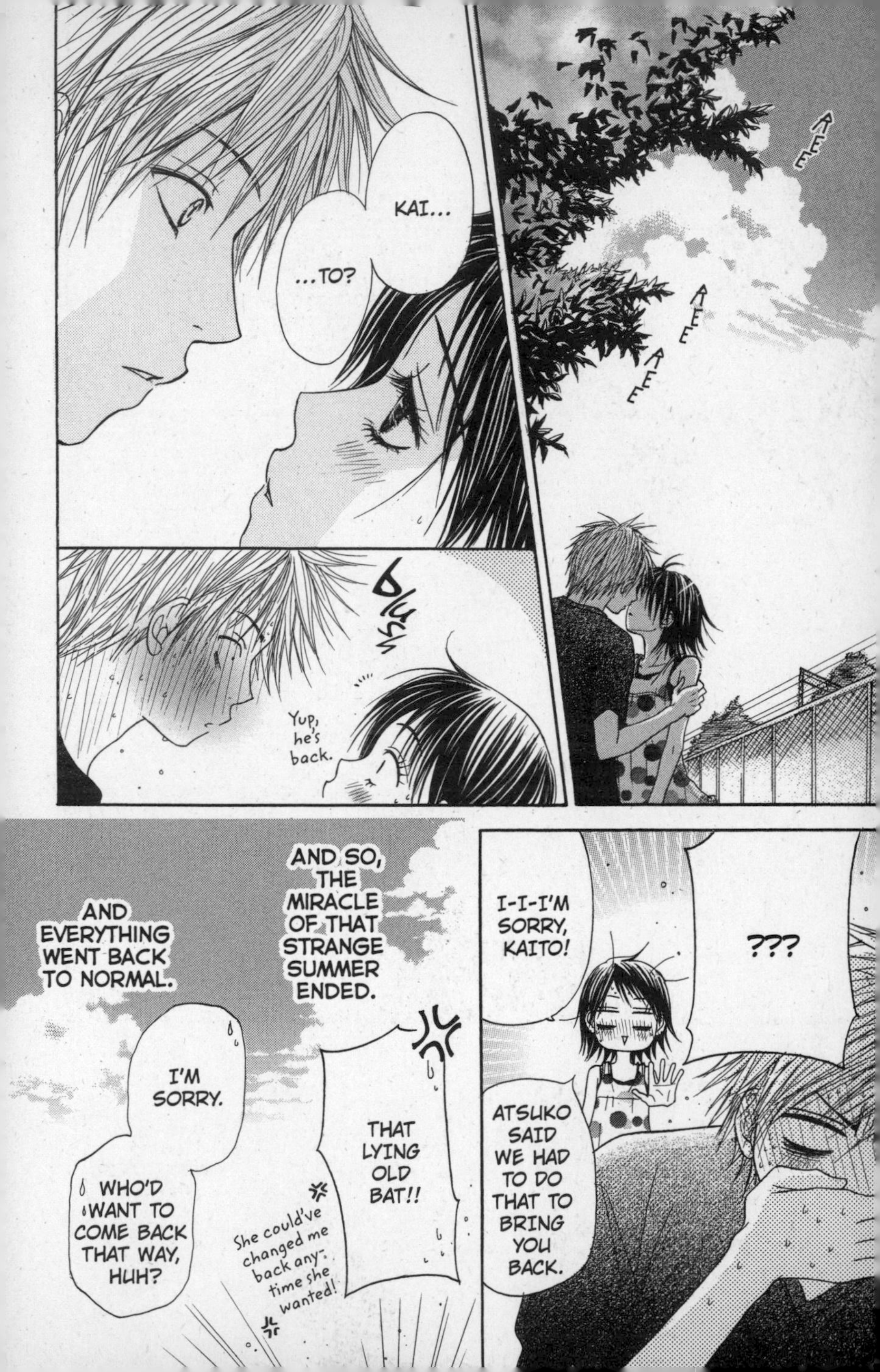

AEE
AEE
AEE
KAI...
...TO?
blush
Yup, he's back.
I-I-I'M SORRY, KAITO!
???
ATSUKO SAID WE HAD TO DO THAT TO BRING YOU BACK.
AND SO, THE MIRACLE OF THAT STRANGE SUMMER ENDED.
AND EVERYTHING WENT BACK TO NORMAL.
THAT LYING OLD BAT!!
She could've changed me back any-time she wanted!
I'M SORRY.
WHO'D WANT TO COME BACK THAT WAY, HUH?

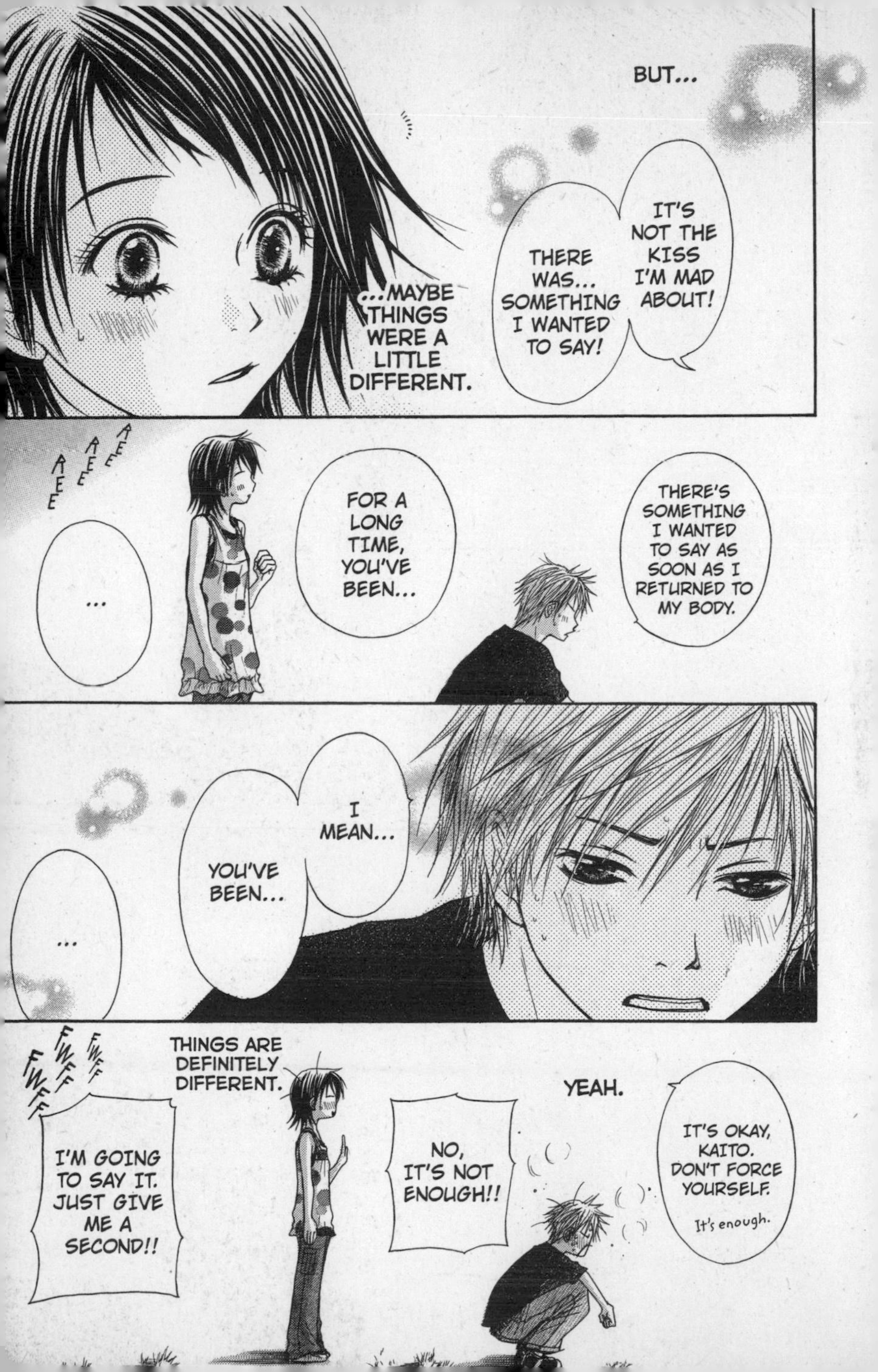
BUT...
IT'S NOT THE KISS I'M MAD ABOUT!
THERE WAS... SOMETHING I WANTED TO SAY!
...MAYBE THINGS WERE A LITTLE DIFFERENT.
THERE'S SOMETHING I WANTED TO SAY AS SOON AS I RETURNED TO MY BODY.
FOR A LONG TIME, YOU'VE BEEN...
REEE
REEE
...
I MEAN...
YOU'VE BEEN...
...
IT'S OKAY, KAITO. DON'T FORCE YOURSELF.
It's enough.
YEAH.
NO, IT'S NOT ENOUGH!!
THINGS ARE DEFINITELY DIFFERENT.
FWFF
FWFF
FWFF
I'M GOING TO SAY IT. JUST GIVE ME A SECOND!!

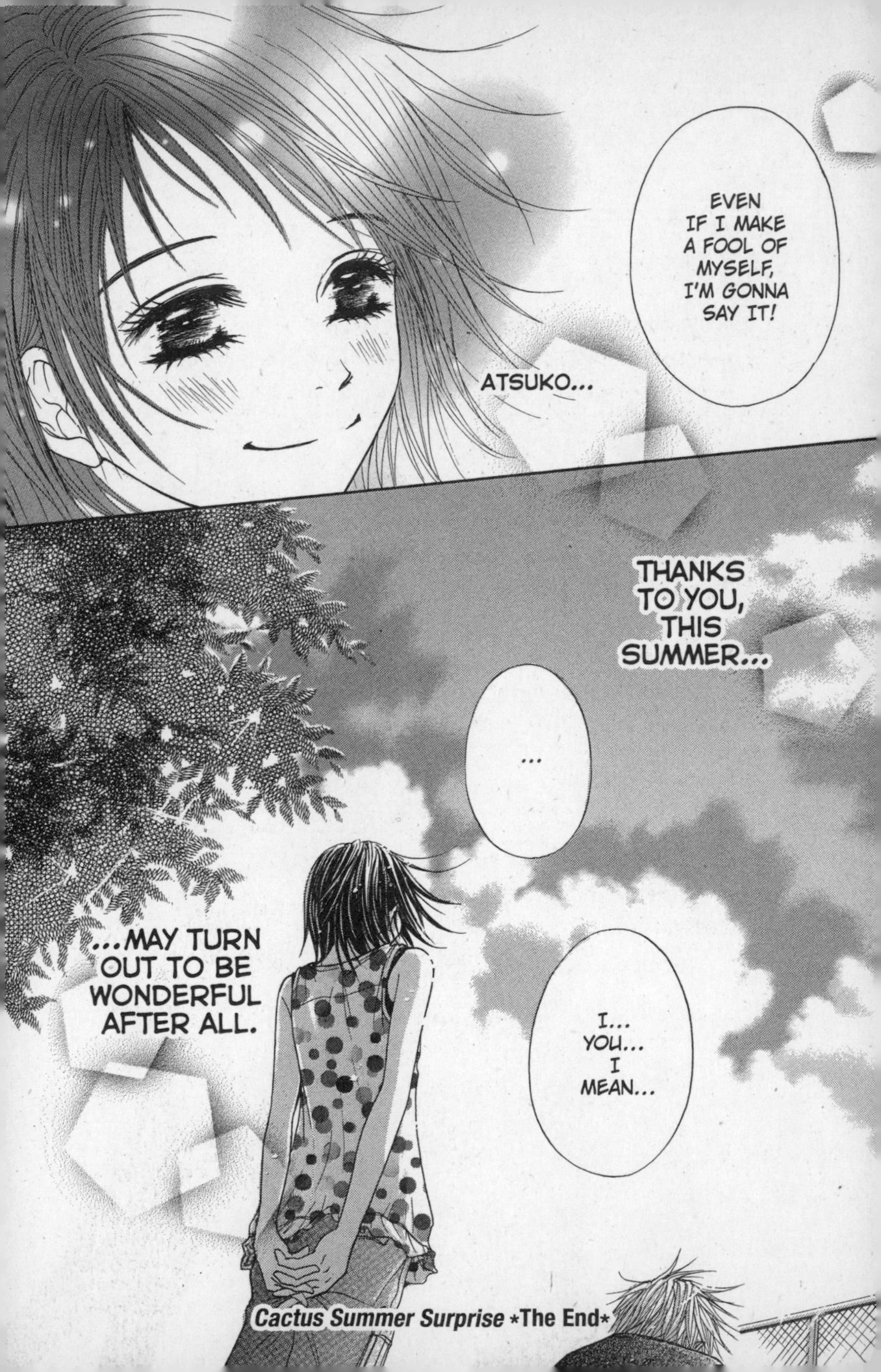
EVEN IF I MAKE A FOOL OF MYSELF, I'M GONNA SAY IT!
ATSUKO...
THANKS TO YOU, THIS SUMMER...
...
I... YOU... I MEAN...
...MAY TURN OUT TO BE WONDERFUL AFTER ALL.
Cactus Summer Surprise *The End*

Well, that's it for *Beast Master* volume 2. This marks the end of the series. I'd like to thank everyone who read it. If you got even a little enjoyment out of it, I'd be really pleased.

I'm currently hard at work on a new manga series that will be published in *Betsucomi* magazine. The characters are totally different from the ones in *Beast Master*. Please check it out!

I know there are a lot of you who prefer manga in graphic novel form, but *Betsucomi* is really, really fun to read! It's full of great manga!

And so, I hope we meet again soon.
I'll continue to do my best.
See you!

This miso expires in nine days.

ShinO MiSo

Sorry. Mr. Miso.

Anyway, this is the leftover miso. [Please see the author's message in volume 1 for details.]

-Kyousuke Motomi

Born on August 1 (a Leo!), Kyousuke Motomi debuted in *Deluxe Betsucomi* with *Hetakuso Kyupiddo* (No Good Cupid) in 2002. She is the creator of *Otokomae! Biizu Kurabu* (Handsome! Beads Club), and her latest work *Dengeki Deiji* (Electric Daisy) is currently being serialized in *Betsucomi*. Motomi enjoys sleeping, tea ceremonies and reading Haruki Murakami.

BEAST MASTER
VOL. 2
Shojo Beat Edition

STORY AND ART BY
KYOUSUKE MOTOMI

English Adaptation/Lance Caselman
Translation/JN Productions
Touch-up Art & Lettering/Monalisa de Asis
Design/Yukiko Whitley
Editor/Amy Yu

VP, Production/Alvin Lu
VP, Sales & Product Marketing/Gonzalo Ferreyra
VP, Creative/Linda Espinosa
Publisher/Hyoe Narita

BEAST MASTER 2 by Kyousuke MOTOMI © 2007 Kyousuke MOTOMI
All rights reserved. Original Japanese edition published in 2007 by
Shogakukan Inc., Tokyo.

The stories, characters and incidents mentioned in this publication are
entirely fictional.

Printed in the U.S.A.

Published by VIZ Media, LLC
P.O. Box 77010
San Francisco, CA 94107

10 9 8 7 6 5 4 3 2 1
First printing, February 2010

www.viz.com   www.shojobeat.com

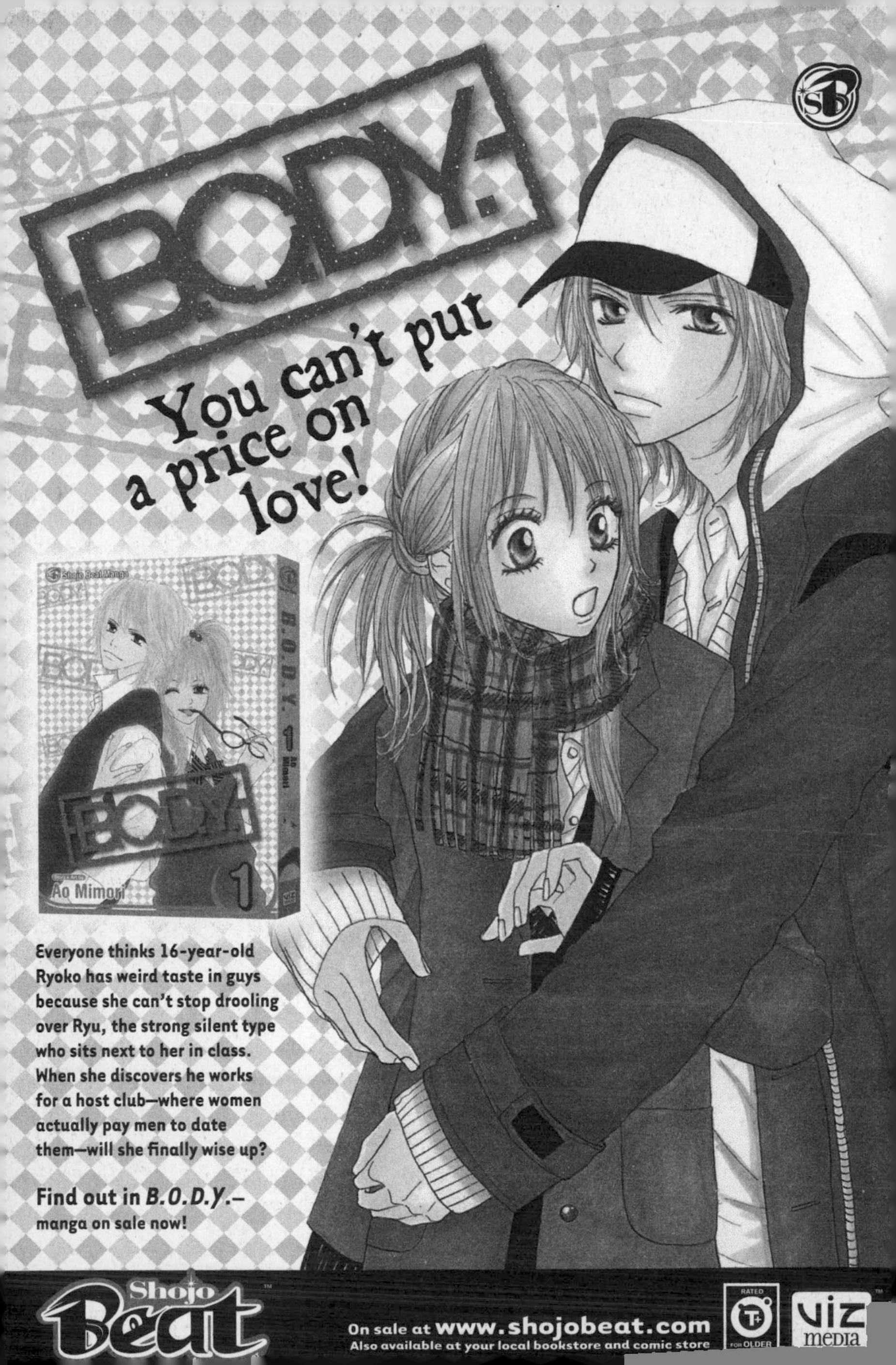
B.O.D.Y.
You can't put a price on love!
Shojo Beat Manga
B.O.D.Y.
1
Ao Mimori
Everyone thinks 16-year-old Ryoko has weird taste in guys because she can't stop drooling over Ryu, the strong silent type who sits next to her in class. When she discovers he works for a host club—where women actually pay men to date them—will she finally wise up?
Find out in B.O.D.Y.—
manga on sale now!
Shojo Beat
On sale at www.shojobeat.com
Also available at your local bookstore and comic store
RATED T+ FOR OLDER TEEN
VIZ media

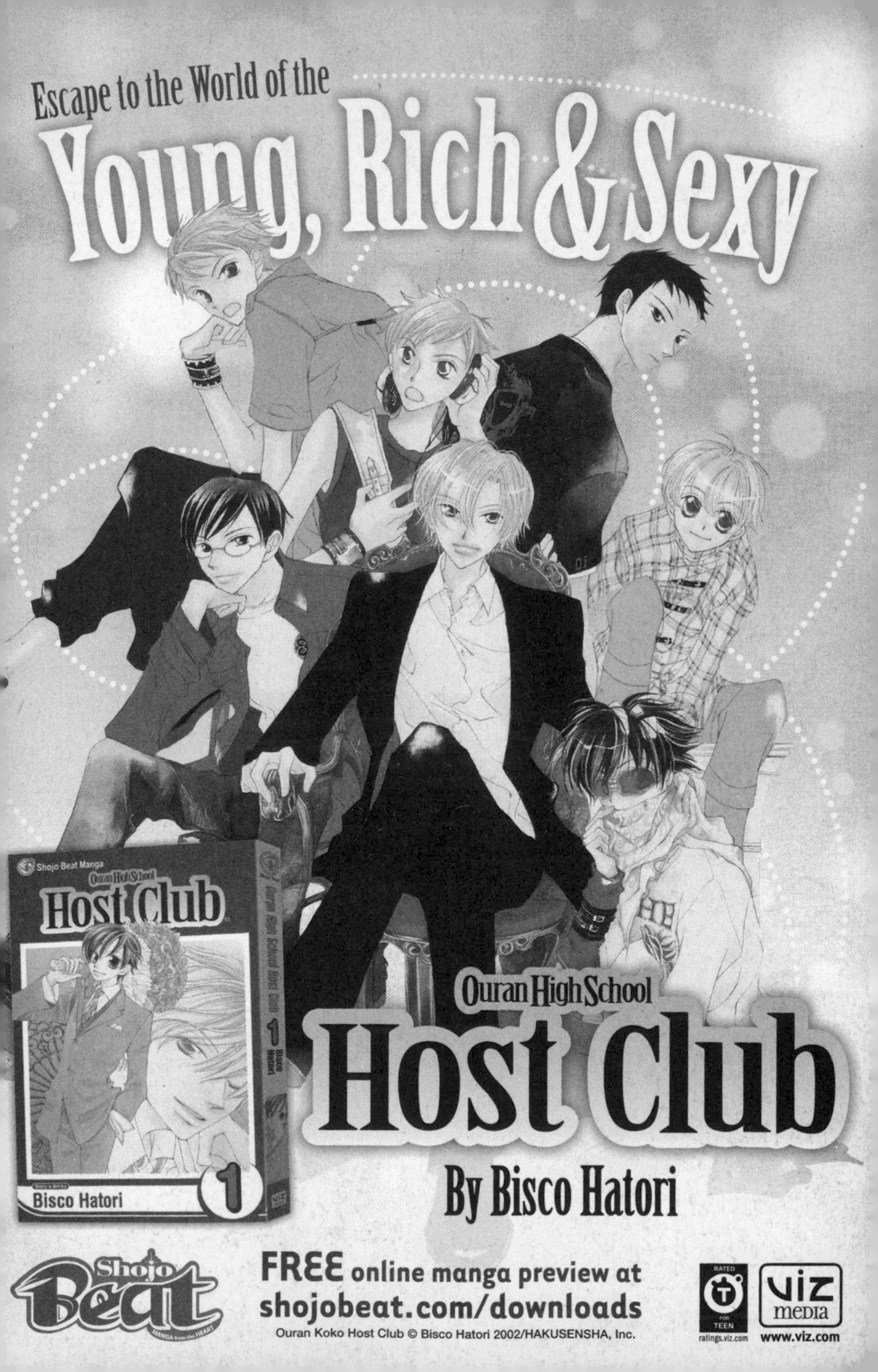

Escape to the World of the
Young, Rich & Sexy
Shojo Beat Manga
Ouran High School
Host Club
Ouran High School Host Club 1 Bisco Hatori
Story & Art by
Bisco Hatori
1
Ouran High School
Host Club
By Bisco Hatori
Shojo Beat
MANGA from the HEART
FREE online manga preview at
shojobeat.com/downloads
Ouran Koko Host Club © Bisco Hatori 2002/HAKUSENSHA, Inc.
RATED T FOR TEEN
ratings.viz.com
VIZ media
www.viz.com

Tell us what you think about Shojo Beat Manga!

Our survey is now available online. Go to:

shojobeat.com/mangasurvey

Help us make our product offerings better!